FREE Study Skills DVD Offer

Dear Customer,

Thank you for your purchase from Mometrix! We consider it an honor and a privilege that you have purchased our product and we want to ensure your satisfaction.

As a way of showing our appreciation and to help us better serve you, we have developed a Study Skills DVD that we would like to give you for FREE. This DVD covers our *best practices* for getting ready for your exam, from how to use our study materials to how to best prepare for the day of the test.

All that we ask is that you email us with feedback that would describe your experience so far with our product. Good, bad, or indifferent, we want to know what you think!

To get your FREE Study Skills DVD, email freedvd@mometrix.com with *FREE STUDY SKILLS DVD* in the subject line and the following information in the body of the email:

- The name of the product you purchased.
- Your product rating on a scale of 1-5, with 5 being the highest rating.
- Your feedback. It can be long, short, or anything in between. We just want to know your impressions and experience so far with our product. (Good feedback might include how our study material met your needs and ways we might be able to make it even better. You could highlight features that you found helpful or features that you think we should add.)
- Your full name and shipping address where you would like us to send your free DVD.

If you have any questions or concerns, please don't hesitate to contact me directly.

Thanks again!

Sincerely,

Jay Willis
Vice President
jay.willis@mometrix.com
1-800-673-8175

LSAT

Prep Books 2020-2021

LSAT Secrets Study Guide

Prep Test Questions

Detailed Answer Explanations

2 Complete Practice Tests

Written and edited by the Mometrix Law School Admissions Test Team

Printed in the United States of America

This paper meets the requirements of ANSI/NISO Z39.48-1992 (Permanence of Paper).

Paperback
ISBN 13: 978-1-5167-1244-1
ISBN 10: 1-5167-1244-7

DEAR FUTURE EXAM SUCCESS STORY

First of all, **THANK YOU** for purchasing Mometrix study materials!

Second, congratulations! You are one of the few determined test-takers who are committed to doing whatever it takes to excel on your exam. **You have come to the right place.** We developed these study materials with one goal in mind: to deliver you the information you need in a format that's concise and easy to use.

In addition to optimizing your guide for the content of the test, we've outlined our recommended steps for breaking down the preparation process into small, attainable goals so you can make sure you stay on track.

We've also analyzed the entire test-taking process, identifying the most common pitfalls and showing how you can overcome them and be ready for any curveball the test throws you.

Standardized testing is one of the biggest obstacles on your road to success, which only increases the importance of doing well in the high-pressure, high-stakes environment of test day. Your results on this test could have a significant impact on your future, and this guide provides the information and practical advice to help you achieve your full potential on test day.

Your success is our success

We would love to hear from you! If you would like to share the story of your exam success or if you have any questions or comments in regard to our products, please contact us at **800-673-8175** or **support@mometrix.com**.

Thanks again for your business and we wish you continued success!

Sincerely,
The Mometrix Test Preparation Team

Need more help? Check out our flashcards at:
https://MometrixFlashcards.com/LSAT

TABLE OF CONTENTS

Introduction

Thank you for purchasing this resource! You have made the choice to prepare yourself for a test that could have a huge impact on your future, and this guide is designed to help you be fully ready for test day. Obviously, it's important to have a solid understanding of the test material, but you also need to be prepared for the unique environment and stressors of the test, so that you can perform to the best of your abilities.

For this purpose, the first section that appears in this guide is the **Secret Keys**. We've devoted countless hours to meticulously researching what works and what doesn't, and we've boiled down our findings to the five most impactful steps you can take to improve your performance on the test. We start at the beginning with study planning and move through the preparation process, all the way to the testing strategies that will help you get the most out of what you know when you're finally sitting in front of the test.

We recommend that you start preparing for your test as far in advance as possible. However, if you've bought this guide as a last-minute study resource and only have a few days before your test, we recommend that you skip over the first two Secret Keys since they address a long-term study plan.

If you struggle with **test anxiety**, we strongly encourage you to check out our recommendations for how you can overcome it. Test anxiety is a formidable foe, but it can be beaten, and we want to make sure you have the tools you need to defeat it.

Secret Key #1 – Plan Big, Study Small

There's a lot riding on your performance. If you want to ace this test, you're going to need to keep your skills sharp and the material fresh in your mind. You need a plan that lets you review everything you need to know while still fitting in your schedule. We'll break this strategy down into three categories.

Information Organization

Start with the information you already have: the official test outline. From this, you can make a complete list of all the concepts you need to cover before the test. Organize these concepts into groups that can be studied together, and create a list of any related vocabulary you need to learn so you can brush up on any difficult terms. You'll want to keep this vocabulary list handy once you actually start studying since you may need to add to it along the way.

Time Management

Once you have your set of study concepts, decide how to spread them out over the time you have left before the test. Break your study plan into small, clear goals so you have a manageable task for each day and know exactly what you're doing. Then just focus on one small step at a time. When you manage your time this way, you don't need to spend hours at a time studying. Studying a small block of content for a short period each day helps you retain information better and avoid stressing over how much you have left to do. You can relax knowing that you have a plan to cover everything in time. In order for this strategy to be effective though, you have to start studying early and stick to your schedule. Avoid the exhaustion and futility that comes from last-minute cramming!

Study Environment

The environment you study in has a big impact on your learning. Studying in a coffee shop, while probably more enjoyable, is not likely to be as fruitful as studying in a quiet room. It's important to keep distractions to a minimum. You're only planning to study for a short block of time, so make the most of it. Don't pause to check your phone or get up to find a snack. It's also important to **avoid multitasking**. Research has consistently shown that multitasking will make your studying dramatically less effective. Your study area should also be comfortable and well-lit so you don't have the distraction of straining your eyes or sitting on an uncomfortable chair.

The time of day you study is also important. You want to be rested and alert. Don't wait until just before bedtime. Study when you'll be most likely to comprehend and remember. Even better, if you know what time of day your test will be, set that time aside for study. That way your brain will be used to working on that subject at that specific time and you'll have a better chance of recalling information.

Finally, it can be helpful to team up with others who are studying for the same test. Your actual studying should be done in as isolated an environment as possible, but the work of organizing the information and setting up the study plan can be divided up. In between study sessions, you can discuss with your teammates the concepts that you're all studying and quiz each other on the details. Just be sure that your teammates are as serious about the test as you are. If you find that your study time is being replaced with social time, you might need to find a new team.

Secret Key #2 – Make Your Studying Count

You're devoting a lot of time and effort to preparing for this test, so you want to be absolutely certain it will pay off. This means doing more than just reading the content and hoping you can remember it on test day. It's important to make every minute of study count. There are two main areas you can focus on to make your studying count:

Retention

It doesn't matter how much time you study if you can't remember the material. You need to make sure you are retaining the concepts. To check your retention of the information you're learning, try recalling it at later times with minimal prompting. Try carrying around flashcards and glance at one or two from time to time or ask a friend who's also studying for the test to quiz you.

To enhance your retention, look for ways to put the information into practice so that you can apply it rather than simply recalling it. If you're using the information in practical ways, it will be much easier to remember. Similarly, it helps to solidify a concept in your mind if you're not only reading it to yourself but also explaining it to someone else. Ask a friend to let you teach them about a concept you're a little shaky on (or speak aloud to an imaginary audience if necessary). As you try to summarize, define, give examples, and answer your friend's questions, you'll understand the concepts better and they will stay with you longer. Finally, step back for a big picture view and ask yourself how each piece of information fits with the whole subject. When you link the different concepts together and see them working together as a whole, it's easier to remember the individual components.

Finally, practice showing your work on any multi-step problems, even if you're just studying. Writing out each step you take to solve a problem will help solidify the process in your mind, and you'll be more likely to remember it during the test.

Modality

Modality simply refers to the means or method by which you study. Choosing a study modality that fits your own individual learning style is crucial. No two people learn best in exactly the same way, so it's important to know your strengths and use them to your advantage.

For example, if you learn best by visualization, focus on visualizing a concept in your mind and draw an image or a diagram. Try color-coding your notes, illustrating them, or creating symbols that will trigger your mind to recall a learned concept. If you learn best by hearing or discussing information, find a study partner who learns the same way or read aloud to yourself. Think about how to put the information in your own words. Imagine that you are giving a lecture on the topic and record yourself so you can listen to it later.

For any learning style, flashcards can be helpful. Organize the information so you can take advantage of spare moments to review. Underline key words or phrases. Use different colors for different categories. Mnemonic devices (such as creating a short list in which every item starts with the same letter) can also help with retention. Find what works best for you and use it to store the information in your mind most effectively and easily.

Secret Key #3 – Practice the Right Way

Your success on test day depends not only on how many hours you put into preparing, but also on whether you prepared the right way. It's good to check along the way to see if your studying is paying off. One of the most effective ways to do this is by taking practice tests to evaluate your progress. Practice tests are useful because they show exactly where you need to improve. Every time you take a practice test, pay special attention to these three groups of questions:

- The questions you got wrong
- The questions you had to guess on, even if you guessed right
- The questions you found difficult or slow to work through

This will show you exactly what your weak areas are, and where you need to devote more study time. Ask yourself why each of these questions gave you trouble. Was it because you didn't understand the material? Was it because you didn't remember the vocabulary? Do you need more repetitions on this type of question to build speed and confidence? Dig into those questions and figure out how you can strengthen your weak areas as you go back to review the material.

Additionally, many practice tests have a section explaining the answer choices. It can be tempting to read the explanation and think that you now have a good understanding of the concept. However, an explanation likely only covers part of the question's broader context. Even if the explanation makes sense, **go back and investigate** every concept related to the question until you're positive you have a thorough understanding.

As you go along, keep in mind that the practice test is just that: practice. Memorizing these questions and answers will not be very helpful on the actual test because it is unlikely to have any of the same exact questions. If you only know the right answers to the sample questions, you won't be prepared for the real thing. **Study the concepts** until you understand them fully, and then you'll be able to answer any question that shows up on the test.

It's important to wait on the practice tests until you're ready. If you take a test on your first day of study, you may be overwhelmed by the amount of material covered and how much you need to learn. Work up to it gradually.

On test day, you'll need to be prepared for answering questions, managing your time, and using the test-taking strategies you've learned. It's a lot to balance, like a mental marathon that will have a big impact on your future. Like training for a marathon, you'll need to start slowly and work your way up. When test day arrives, you'll be ready.

Start with the strategies you've read in the first two Secret Keys—plan your course and study in the way that works best for you. If you have time, consider using multiple study resources to get different approaches to the same concepts. It can be helpful to see difficult concepts from more than one angle. Then find a good source for practice tests. Many times, the test website will suggest potential study resources or provide sample tests.

Practice Test Strategy

If you're able to find at least three practice tests, we recommend this strategy:

Untimed and Open-Book Practice

Take the first test with no time constraints and with your notes and study guide handy. Take your time and focus on applying the strategies you've learned.

Timed and Open-Book Practice

Take the second practice test open-book as well, but set a timer and practice pacing yourself to finish in time.

Timed and Closed-Book Practice

Take any other practice tests as if it were test day. Set a timer and put away your study materials. Sit at a table or desk in a quiet room, imagine yourself at the testing center, and answer questions as quickly and accurately as possible.

Keep repeating timed and closed-book tests on a regular basis until you run out of practice tests or it's time for the actual test. Your mind will be ready for the schedule and stress of test day, and you'll be able to focus on recalling the material you've learned.

Secret Key #4 – Pace Yourself

Once you're fully prepared for the material on the test, your biggest challenge on test day will be managing your time. Just knowing that the clock is ticking can make you panic even if you have plenty of time left. Work on pacing yourself so you can build confidence against the time constraints of the exam. Pacing is a difficult skill to master, especially in a high-pressure environment, so **practice is vital**.

Set time expectations for your pace based on how much time is available. For example, if a section has 60 questions and the time limit is 30 minutes, you know you have to average 30 seconds or less per question in order to answer them all. Although 30 seconds is the hard limit, set 25 seconds per question as your goal, so you reserve extra time to spend on harder questions. When you budget extra time for the harder questions, you no longer have any reason to stress when those questions take longer to answer.

Don't let this time expectation distract you from working through the test at a calm, steady pace, but keep it in mind so you don't spend too much time on any one question. Recognize that taking extra time on one question you don't understand may keep you from answering two that you do understand later in the test. If your time limit for a question is up and you're still not sure of the answer, mark it and move on, and come back to it later if the time and the test format allow. If the testing format doesn't allow you to return to earlier questions, just make an educated guess; then put it out of your mind and move on.

On the easier questions, be careful not to rush. It may seem wise to hurry through them so you have more time for the challenging ones, but it's not worth missing one if you know the concept and just didn't take the time to read the question fully. Work efficiently but make sure you understand the question and have looked at all of the answer choices, since more than one may seem right at first.

Even if you're paying attention to the time, you may find yourself a little behind at some point. You should speed up to get back on track, but do so wisely. Don't panic; just take a few seconds less on each question until you're caught up. Don't guess without thinking, but do look through the answer choices and eliminate any you know are wrong. If you can get down to two choices, it is often worthwhile to guess from those. Once you've chosen an answer, move on and don't dwell on any that you skipped or had to hurry through. If a question was taking too long, chances are it was one of the harder ones, so you weren't as likely to get it right anyway.

On the other hand, if you find yourself getting ahead of schedule, it may be beneficial to slow down a little. The more quickly you work, the more likely you are to make a careless mistake that will affect your score. You've budgeted time for each question, so don't be afraid to spend that time. Practice an efficient but careful pace to get the most out of the time you have.

Secret Key #5 – Have a Plan for Guessing

When you're taking the test, you may find yourself stuck on a question. Some of the answer choices seem better than others, but you don't see the one answer choice that is obviously correct. What do you do?

The scenario described above is very common, yet most test takers have not effectively prepared for it. Developing and practicing a plan for guessing may be one of the single most effective uses of your time as you get ready for the exam.

In developing your plan for guessing, there are three questions to address:

- When should you start the guessing process?
- How should you narrow down the choices?
- Which answer should you choose?

When to Start the Guessing Process

Unless your plan for guessing is to select C every time (which, despite its merits, is not what we recommend), you need to leave yourself enough time to apply your answer elimination strategies. Since you have a limited amount of time for each question, that means that if you're going to give yourself the best shot at guessing correctly, you have to decide quickly whether or not you will guess.

Of course, the best-case scenario is that you don't have to guess at all, so first, see if you can answer the question based on your knowledge of the subject and basic reasoning skills. Focus on the key words in the question and try to jog your memory of related topics. Give yourself a chance to bring the knowledge to mind, but once you realize that you don't have (or you can't access) the knowledge you need to answer the question, it's time to start the guessing process.

It's almost always better to start the guessing process too early than too late. It only takes a few seconds to remember something and answer the question from knowledge. Carefully eliminating wrong answer choices takes longer. Plus, going through the process of eliminating answer choices can actually help jog your memory.

Summary: Start the guessing process as soon as you decide that you can't answer the question based on your knowledge.

How to Narrow Down the Choices

The next chapter in this book (**Test-Taking Strategies**) includes a wide range of strategies for how to approach questions and how to look for answer choices to eliminate. You will definitely want to read those carefully, practice them, and figure out which ones work best for you. Here though, we're going to address a mindset rather than a particular strategy.

Your chances of guessing an answer correctly depend on how many options you are choosing from.

How many choices you have	How likely you are to guess correctly
5	20%
4	25%
3	33%
2	50%
1	100%

You can see from this chart just how valuable it is to be able to eliminate incorrect answers and make an educated guess, but there are two things that many test takers do that cause them to miss out on the benefits of guessing:

- Accidentally eliminating the correct answer
- Selecting an answer based on an impression

We'll look at the first one here, and the second one in the next section.

To avoid accidentally eliminating the correct answer, we recommend a thought exercise called **the $5 challenge**. In this challenge, you only eliminate an answer choice from contention if you are willing to bet $5 on it being wrong. Why $5? Five dollars is a small but not insignificant amount of money. It's an amount you could afford to lose but wouldn't want to throw away. And while losing $5 once might not hurt too much, doing it twenty times will set you back $100. In the same way, each small decision you make—eliminating a choice here, guessing on a question there—won't by itself impact your score very much, but when you put them all together, they can make a big difference. By holding each answer choice elimination decision to a higher standard, you can reduce the risk of accidentally eliminating the correct answer.

The $5 challenge can also be applied in a positive sense: If you are willing to bet $5 that an answer choice *is* correct, go ahead and mark it as correct.

Summary: Only eliminate an answer choice if you are willing to bet $5 that it is wrong.

Which Answer to Choose

You're taking the test. You've run into a hard question and decided you'll have to guess. You've eliminated all the answer choices you're willing to bet $5 on. Now you have to pick an answer. Why do we even need to talk about this? Why can't you just pick whichever one you feel like when the time comes?

The answer to these questions is that if you don't come into the test with a plan, you'll rely on your impression to select an answer choice, and if you do that, you risk falling into a trap. The test writers know that everyone who takes their test will be guessing on some of the questions, so they intentionally write wrong answer choices to seem plausible. You still have to pick an answer though, and if the wrong answer choices are designed to look right, how can you ever be sure that you're not falling for their trap? The best solution we've found to this dilemma is to take the decision out of your hands entirely. Here is the process we recommend:

Once you've eliminated any choices that you are confident (willing to bet $5) are wrong, select the first remaining choice as your answer.

Whether you choose to select the first remaining choice, the second, or the last, the important thing is that you use some preselected standard. Using this approach guarantees that you will not be enticed into selecting an answer choice that looks right, because you are not basing your decision on how the answer choices look.

This is not meant to make you question your knowledge. Instead, it is to help you recognize the difference between your knowledge and your impressions. There's a huge difference between thinking an answer is right because of what you know, and thinking an answer is right because it looks or sounds like it should be right.

Summary: To ensure that your selection is appropriately random, make a predetermined selection from among all answer choices you have not eliminated.

Test-Taking Strategies

This section contains a list of test-taking strategies that you may find helpful as you work through the test. By taking what you know and applying logical thought, you can maximize your chances of answering any question correctly!

It is very important to realize that every question is different and every person is different: no single strategy will work on every question, and no single strategy will work for every person. That's why we've included all of them here, so you can try them out and determine which ones work best for different types of questions and which ones work best for you.

Question Strategies

Read Carefully

Read the question and answer choices carefully. Don't miss the question because you misread the terms. You have plenty of time to read each question thoroughly and make sure you understand what is being asked. Yet a happy medium must be attained, so don't waste too much time. You must read carefully, but efficiently.

Contextual Clues

Look for contextual clues. If the question includes a word you are not familiar with, look at the immediate context for some indication of what the word might mean. Contextual clues can often give you all the information you need to decipher the meaning of an unfamiliar word. Even if you can't determine the meaning, you may be able to narrow down the possibilities enough to make a solid guess at the answer to the question.

Prefixes

If you're having trouble with a word in the question or answer choices, try dissecting it. Take advantage of every clue that the word might include. Prefixes and suffixes can be a huge help. Usually they allow you to determine a basic meaning. Pre- means before, post- means after, pro - is positive, de- is negative. From prefixes and suffixes, you can get an idea of the general meaning of the word and try to put it into context.

Hedge Words

Watch out for critical hedge words, such as *likely, may, can, sometimes, often, almost, mostly, usually, generally, rarely,* and *sometimes.* Question writers insert these hedge phrases to cover every possibility. Often an answer choice will be wrong simply because it leaves no room for exception. Be on guard for answer choices that have definitive words such as *exactly* and *always.*

Switchback Words

Stay alert for *switchbacks.* These are the words and phrases frequently used to alert you to shifts in thought. The most common switchback words are *but, although,* and *however.* Others include *nevertheless, on the other hand, even though, while, in spite of, despite, regardless of.* Switchback words are important to catch because they can change the direction of the question or an answer choice.

FACE VALUE

When in doubt, use common sense. Accept the situation in the problem at face value. Don't read too much into it. These problems will not require you to make wild assumptions. If you have to go beyond creativity and warp time or space in order to have an answer choice fit the question, then you should move on and consider the other answer choices. These are normal problems rooted in reality. The applicable relationship or explanation may not be readily apparent, but it is there for you to figure out. Use your common sense to interpret anything that isn't clear.

Answer Choice Strategies

ANSWER SELECTION

The most thorough way to pick an answer choice is to identify and eliminate wrong answers until only one is left, then confirm it is the correct answer. Sometimes an answer choice may immediately seem right, but be careful. The test writers will usually put more than one reasonable answer choice on each question, so take a second to read all of them and make sure that the other choices are not equally obvious. As long as you have time left, it is better to read every answer choice than to pick the first one that looks right without checking the others.

ANSWER CHOICE FAMILIES

An answer choice family consists of two (in rare cases, three) answer choices that are very similar in construction and cannot all be true at the same time. If you see two answer choices that are direct opposites or parallels, one of them is usually the correct answer. For instance, if one answer choice says that quantity *x* increases and another either says that quantity *x* decreases (opposite) or says that quantity *y* increases (parallel), then those answer choices would fall into the same family. An answer choice that doesn't match the construction of the answer choice family is more likely to be incorrect. Most questions will not have answer choice families, but when they do appear, you should be prepared to recognize them.

ELIMINATE ANSWERS

Eliminate answer choices as soon as you realize they are wrong, but make sure you consider all possibilities. If you are eliminating answer choices and realize that the last one you are left with is also wrong, don't panic. Start over and consider each choice again. There may be something you missed the first time that you will realize on the second pass.

AVOID FACT TRAPS

Don't be distracted by an answer choice that is factually true but doesn't answer the question. You are looking for the choice that answers the question. Stay focused on what the question is asking for so you don't accidentally pick an answer that is true but incorrect. Always go back to the question and make sure the answer choice you've selected actually answers the question and is not merely a true statement.

EXTREME STATEMENTS

In general, you should avoid answers that put forth extreme actions as standard practice or proclaim controversial ideas as established fact. An answer choice that states the "process should be used in certain situations, if..." is much more likely to be correct than one that states the "process should be discontinued completely." The first is a calm rational statement and doesn't even make a definitive, uncompromising stance, using a hedge word *if* to provide wiggle room, whereas the second choice is a radical idea and far more extreme.

Benchmark

As you read through the answer choices and you come across one that seems to answer the question well, mentally select that answer choice. This is not your final answer, but it's the one that will help you evaluate the other answer choices. The one that you selected is your benchmark or standard for judging each of the other answer choices. Every other answer choice must be compared to your benchmark. That choice is correct until proven otherwise by another answer choice beating it. If you find a better answer, then that one becomes your new benchmark. Once you've decided that no other choice answers the question as well as your benchmark, you have your final answer.

Predict the Answer

Before you even start looking at the answer choices, it is often best to try to predict the answer. When you come up with the answer on your own, it is easier to avoid distractions and traps because you will know exactly what to look for. The right answer choice is unlikely to be word-for-word what you came up with, but it should be a close match. Even if you are confident that you have the right answer, you should still take the time to read each option before moving on.

General Strategies

Tough Questions

If you are stumped on a problem or it appears too hard or too difficult, don't waste time. Move on! Remember though, if you can quickly check for obviously incorrect answer choices, your chances of guessing correctly are greatly improved. Before you completely give up, at least try to knock out a couple of possible answers. Eliminate what you can and then guess at the remaining answer choices before moving on.

Check Your Work

Since you will probably not know every term listed and the answer to every question, it is important that you get credit for the ones that you do know. Don't miss any questions through careless mistakes. If at all possible, try to take a second to look back over your answer selection and make sure you've selected the correct answer choice and haven't made a costly careless mistake (such as marking an answer choice that you didn't mean to mark). This quick double check should more than pay for itself in caught mistakes for the time it costs.

Pace Yourself

It's easy to be overwhelmed when you're looking at a page full of questions; your mind is confused and full of random thoughts, and the clock is ticking down faster than you would like. Calm down and maintain the pace that you have set for yourself. Especially as you get down to the last few minutes of the test, don't let the small numbers on the clock make you panic. As long as you are on track by monitoring your pace, you are guaranteed to have time for each question.

Don't Rush

It is very easy to make errors when you are in a hurry. Maintaining a fast pace in answering questions is pointless if it makes you miss questions that you would have gotten right otherwise. Test writers like to include distracting information and wrong answers that seem right. Taking a little extra time to avoid careless mistakes can make all the difference in your test score. Find a pace that allows you to be confident in the answers that you select.

Keep Moving

Panicking will not help you pass the test, so do your best to stay calm and keep moving. Taking deep breaths and going through the answer elimination steps you practiced can help to break through a stress barrier and keep your pace.

Final Notes

The combination of a solid foundation of content knowledge and the confidence that comes from practicing your plan for applying that knowledge is the key to maximizing your performance on test day. As your foundation of content knowledge is built up and strengthened, you'll find that the strategies included in this chapter become more and more effective in helping you quickly sift through the distractions and traps of the test to isolate the correct answer.

Now it's time to move on to the test content chapters of this book, but be sure to keep your goal in mind. As you read, think about how you will be able to apply this information on the test. If you've already seen sample questions for the test and you have an idea of the question format and style, try to come up with questions of your own that you can answer based on what you're reading. This will give you valuable practice applying your knowledge in the same ways you can expect to on test day.

Good luck and good studying!

LSAT Information

The Law School Admission Test, or LSAT, is a requirement for application to all ABA-approved law schools. Test centers throughout the nation offer the LSAT in June, September or October, December, and February, and it is also available at many testing centers worldwide at the same time. And for those farther than one hundred miles from the nearest testing center, it may even be available for a fee at other locations.

Testing must be scheduled in advance, and is usually available only on specified Saturdays. However, students with religious prohibitions against Saturday events can apply to take the examination on the Monday following a regular Saturday test date. Accommodations can also be made for students with disabilities. Left-handed students can request accommodation in seating, although such accommodations may depend on space. Candidates should be aware that the test day can take as long as five hours, with one 15-minute break after section three is administered.

The LSAT is a standardized collegiate examination, similar in construction to the Scholastic Aptitude Test (SAT). It provides a standard measure of the verbal and reasoning skills considered necessary for the legal profession.

While most law schools require an applicant to have taken the LSAT no later than the December prior to anticipated admission, those who test earlier have a greater opportunity to redeem themselves in the event of a low score. In most cases, applicants are allowed to take the LSAT up to three times in any two-year period. Be aware, however, that not all schools go strictly by the highest score—some average all scores together. So, unless your score is many points below your goal, it may not be in your best interests to repeat the test. Check the procedure used at any schools you are applying to prior to repeating the test.

If you are reasonably certain you have bombed the test, you may also cancel your score entirely, provided your written request to do so is received immediately (prior to grading). This voids all record of your having taken the test.

The test itself consists of five topical multiple-choice examinations. The exams contain Logical Reasoning, Reading Comprehension, and Analytical Reasoning questions. An experimental section of one of these types of questions is also included for field-testing future exam questions. The experimental section is not scored, but it is also not distinguishable from the scored sections. A sixth exam, an extemporaneous writing sample, is also on the exam, and is also not scored, but the text of the writing sample is sent along with the LSAT scores. Questions on the LSAT are created and administered by the Law School Admissions Council (LSAC), a nonprofit organization created in 1947 to standardize, facilitate, and improve the admission process for law schools nationwide.

Here are the different multiple-choice sections of the LSAT:

1. Logical Reasoning/Arguments: There are TWO sections of logical reasoning meant to test your ability to either draw reasonable conclusions from a valid argument or detect the fallacies in an invalid argument.
2. Analytical Reasoning: Sometimes called the Games section, this segment tests your ability to follow relationship structures throughout a written passage and properly account for the necessary parts using the conditions set.
3. Reading Comprehension: Precisely what it sounds like—this section tests how well you can read and understand various passages.

4. Variable: This is the ungraded section and can be Logical Reasoning, Analytical Reasoning, or Reading Comprehension. It is basically used to try out new test problems, but since you have no way of knowing which section is live and which is not, you should treat all sections as though they count toward your score.

Timing

It is generally recommended that students take the LSAT by the December before the fall semester the student intends to start. However, there are often benefits to taking the LSAT even earlier in the year; many advisors suggest taking the LSAT in June or October, thus giving students more time to prepare. To that end, students have a wide array of preparation options available, including practice exams, private and online tutoring, and courses designed to refresh and instruct students in the content areas and skills needed to succeed on the LSAT. Because of the nature of the material, and the amount of information that students assimilate, LSAC recommends that all students thoroughly prepare before taking the LSAT, even if they have high confidence in their mastery of the material.

Registering

The easiest and most often recommended method of registration is to create an LSAT student account and register online through the official LSAC Web site. The Web site allows students to select a test time and test center and to pay for the exam fees with a credit card through the secure section of the site. Using online registration is recommended because many of the options that commonly need later modification—test time, test location, college codes, score report locations and so on—can easily be performed online with greater speed and efficiency than through the phone or mail.

For students who are unwilling or unable to sign up online, LSAC also allows for registration through the mail or by telephone. These methods are similar to the online account process, but are more inflexible and they less readily accommodate scheduling changes within the testing period. Students cannot withdraw or cancel registration during the regular registration period and register again for that same test during late period registration. For ease and efficiency of processing, online registration is advantageous and more accessible. Telephone system registration is available only from 8:30 AM to 4:45 PM (7:00 PM in the September–March time frame) and experiences peak traffic on Mondays (LSAC suggests contacting their offices later in the week to avoid the peak traffic experiences at the beginning of the week). Additionally, online registration is substantially faster because it doesn't require an application packet to be mailed and returned by the customer, as the phone registration and paper methods do.

Special Circumstances

The LSAT testing process can accommodate students with disability, economic hardship, and geographic limitations. Here are a few of the options available for students who need accommodation in registering:

Fee waivers – Students who meet certain qualifications as listed on the official LSAC fee waiver form are eligible. The waivers cover the fees for two LSATs (taken within a two-year period), four college reports, and Law School Data Assembly Service (LSDAS) registration. LSAT waiver packets can be obtained through a variety of sources, including the admissions office of most law schools; however, the basic criterion for a fee waiver is the absolute inability to pay. Thus, very few waivers are granted.

Non-Saturday testing – Students who have religious beliefs that prevent them from Saturday testing may apply for scheduled non-Saturday testing.

Geographic limitation – If a student cannot travel to a test center listed in the LSAC registration rolls (through disability or other disadvantage) and must travel more than 100 miles to a registered center listed with LSAC, he or she may apply to take the exam at a non-published test center. Students must contact LSAC at (215) 968-1001 to initiate the documentation process necessary to establish the need for a non-published test center. The student will be required to pay an additional fee for testing at a newly established location.

Disabled students – Students who have disabilities can apply for testing accommodation, including extended time periods and alternate testing formats. To establish eligibility for accommodation, the ACT Policy for Documentation requires that a disability be diagnosed and documented per specific requirements. Students should note that LSAC reserves the right to make final decisions about accommodation; therefore, we recommend that students prepare the necessary documentation and submit it well in advance.

Test Day

Materials Needed

On test day, students need to have several items with them. There are three items that students can't do without: the test center admission ticket, without which the student can't take the test; a current form of government-issued photo identification (a driver's license or current passport is sufficient), without which the student will not be admitted; and three or four soft-lead no. 2 pencils with erasers (no pens or mechanical pencils are allowed). Students must bring their own no. 2 pencils to the test. The test proctor will not provide pencils. It is permissible to bring an analog watch. No digital timepieces, watches, or timepiece displays are allowed.

The following materials may be taken into the testing room with the student, so long as they are stowed in a clear, plastic, sealable bag and placed under the student's seat during the test:

- LSAT Admission Ticket stub
- valid ID
- wallet
- keys
- analog wristwatch
- medical or hygiene products
- #2 or HB wooden pencils
- highlighter
- erasers
- pencil sharpener (no mechanical pencils)
- tissues
- beverage in plastic container or juice box (20 oz./591 ml maximum size) and snack for break only

During the exam, only the following items may be on the student's desktop, in addition to the test:

- tissues
- ID
- wooden pencils

- erasers
- pencil sharpener
- highlighter
- analog wristwatch

There are also specific things that students should **not** bring with them on test day. The following list, while not all-inclusive, covers the majority of items specifically forbidden for students to have with them during the LSAT exams:

- books, including dictionaries
- notes
- scratch paper or other aids
- colored pens or pencils
- correction fluid
- any electronic device (i.e. timer, phone, media player, PDA, camera)
- reading material
- tobacco in any form

Students should leave any items not specifically cited on the allowed materials list at home or in their vehicles during the testing period.

Identification

For the purposes of the LSAT, valid identification is assumed to mean a card, badge, or form that is a) issued by a governmental entity, b) current, meaning the identification was issued within the last two years, and c) bears a recognizable photo of the student, along with the student's first and last name (both names must be shown on the identification document) and the student's signature. Due to recent changes in LSAC policy regarding identification, only identification that meets all three criteria will be accepted as valid ID.

Common forms of acceptable identification include driver's licenses, passports, or other forms of government-issued ID. There are several forms of identification that will not be accepted for the LSAT, and students need to be aware that they will not be admitted to the test center if they attempt to use an invalid form of identification. These invalid forms include out-of-date passports, LSAT admission tickets, learner's permits, birth certificates, Social Security cards, family portraits, Social Insurance cards, credit cards with photos, employee IDs, student IDs, or any other form of identification that does not meet the three criteria outlined above.

Since the LSAT is only offered on certain dates, and since a student's delay in taking the test can adversely impact meeting deadlines for scholarship applications or admission requirements, it is vital that students include proper identification in the materials they bring to the test center. Packing an alternate form of identification in a bag with the materials the student brings to the test series is highly recommended.

Test Day

The test day will begin with the student checking in before the assigned test time. For all exam periods except the June tests, students must report to the test center no later than 8:30 AM; for the June tests, students must report to the test center no later than 12:30 PM. The student will present his or her admission ticket and an acceptable form of identification to test center personnel, who will verify the validity of the information against a list of registered students. Once verified, the test center personnel will show the student to the test room and his or her assigned seat. The proctor will then provide the testing materials. At the assigned test time, the registered students will be allowed to start the exam.

After the third section is completed, the test proctor or center personnel will announce a short break—usually ten to fifteen minutes in length—during which all test materials will be collected. Test materials will remain in the custody of test center personnel during the break; students are permitted to walk around, stretch their legs, or use the restroom. No cell phones or other electronic devices may be used during the break, and students are not allowed to bring any food or drinks back to the test room. Per LSAT regulations, only those items brought to the test location in the previously described clear plastic bag are allowed. After the break, and after all test materials have been returned to the appropriate students, testing will resume. Most students should expect to take approximately five hours to complete the testing cycle, although this may vary from student to student.

Missed Exam Dates

There are several options for students who miss taking the LSAT exam on the scheduled test date. The resolution of problems regarding missed exam dates depends upon the reasons for which the student is unable to attend. If severe weather or natural disaster prevents the student from reaching the center, it is likely the center itself will be closed, in which case the test will be rescheduled. If the test is held on the scheduled date, and the student is unable to arrive at the center at the appointed time, the student should immediately contact LSAC and review the available options. Students who miss their scheduled test date start times for other reasons—accidents, illness, tardiness, not having proper ID—have a different set of options to pursue. A student can request a late test date change, either through their LSAC student account, by faxing LSAC at (215) 968-1277, or by mailing a test change form to LSAC, Box 2000-T, Newtown, PA 18940. However, students should be aware that a $33 fee will be assessed if this option is pursued. When requesting a test date change, the applicant must provide all identifying information: student's name, address, LSAC account number, Social Security or Social Insurance number (or LSAC ID number), the test date, and the first and second choice regarding location. The request must be appropriately signed and dated. An additional option would be to request a refund, thereby canceling the appointment to take the LSAT altogether. Refunds can only be requested through written correspondence or through use of the LSAC Refund Request Form, both of which require the same information as the test date change. Only a partial refund of $45 will be given to students requesting refunds.

Misconduct

Law school applicants should be aware that the LSAC has established very stringent rules regarding possible misconduct during the LSAT. Since lawyers are expected to hold to a set of rigorous ethical standards, the application of those same high ethical standards applies to prospective law school applicants beginning with the application process. The official LSAC statement with regard to the LSAT defines "misconduct" as: "the submission, as part of the law school admission process, including, but not limited to, regular, transfer, and visiting applications, of any information that is false, inconsistent, or misleading, or the omission of information that may result in a false or misleading conclusion, or the violation of any regulation governing the law school admission process, including any violation of LSAT test center regulations."

Because of the stringent standard, the types of behaviors which constitute misconduct under LSAC rules can be applied to a wider variety of offenses than would apply to other standardized tests. Specific actions that are considered misconduct by the LSAC include, but are not limited to, the following:

- submitting an altered or false transcript
- submitting an application with false, inconsistent, or misleading information
- submitting an altered, false, or unauthorized letter of recommendation
- falsifying records
- impersonating another applicant in taking the LSAT
- switching LSAT answer sheets with another applicant
- taking the LSAT for purposes other than applying to law school
- copying from others on the LSAT, or similar forms of cheating
- obtaining advance access to test materials
- stealing test materials
- working, marking, erasing, reading, or turning pages on sections of the LSAT during unauthorized times
- submitting false, inconsistent, or misleading information to the LSDAS
- submitting false, inconsistent, or misleading statements or omissions of information requested on the LSAT & LSDAS Registration Form or on individual law school application forms
- falsifying transcript information, school attendance, honors, awards, or employment
- providing false, inconsistent, or misleading information in the financial aid/scholarship application process

Charges of misconduct on the LSAT are very serious, and can be brought at any time: before a candidate's admission to law school, after admission and/or enrollment at a law school, or even after passing the bar and admission to practice. If misconduct charges are brought against an applicant, the LSAC will immediately notify the school or schools in question. Pending reports and application package information will be halted until a member of the LSAC's Misconduct and Irregularities in the Admission Process Subcommittee has had a chance to investigate the allegations. The LSAC has procedural rules regulating the monitoring of misconduct investigations and guidelines for the methods to be employed. Those procedures begin once a representative has been assigned to investigate the allegation of misconduct.

Once the representative has concluded the investigation and reached a preliminary decision, the LSAC and the affected law schools are notified of the representative's findings, and the decision is appended to the applicant's LSAT and LSDAS reports. Depending on the determination of effect by the investigating representative, other agencies and governmental bodies may be informed as well. The LSAC has no authority to levy punishments or to advise and recommend disciplinary action. Disciplinary decisions are left entirely to the discretion of the affected schools. Since allegations of misconduct can occur at any phase of the law school application process, and extend even beyond the academic period, any violation of the stringent ethical standards of the legal profession can result in a range of penalties, which may include:

- closing of a law school admission file
- revoking an offer of admission
- dismissal from law school via the school's internal channels
- disbarment

Preparation

Tips

Besides the studying and exam prep activities most students undertake before taking the LSAT, there are several basic steps students can take to help maximize their test results:

- Every test booklet has instructions on the front cover; read them carefully. Failure to follow instructions can result in incorrect results or dismissal for not abiding by them.
- Read every question carefully. In many cases the correct answer will depend on a nuanced interpretation of the material, so it is important to be clear on what is being asked.
- Be sure to take the test at a measured pace. There are dozens of questions to go through. Spending too much time on a single question or passage may negatively impact the amount of time left to resolve other questions.
- If the student finishes a test before time is called, it is advisable to go back through and review the answers. The student should use spare time to check the work and make corrections as necessary.
- Score sheets are read by computer, so it is vital that students make mark their answers neatly and with a minimum of smudging. If a mark requires erasure, the student must be sure that the mark is erased completely. Keep in mind that marks and notes made inside the test booklets are not counted toward your score, so make sure that all answers are recorded on the test sheet.
- Once time is called on an exam, students should put down their pencils and make no further marks on the sheet. Failure to do this will result in being dismissed from the exam and the score sheet being discarded.

Writing Prompt Tips

The writing prompt is forwarded to the LSAT test center as a digital image. Though the writing section is not scored, many law school admission offices do evaluate the writing prompt while reviewing the candidate's entire application packet. Therefore, LSAC strongly recommends students do their utmost to complete the writing prompt to the best of their ability in the allotted time. In addition to studying and exam prep activities, there are several basic steps students can take to help maximize their results on the LSAT writing prompt:

Before starting to write the essay, take time to plan how you will present your supporting statements and the rationale for your conclusions as requested in the prompt. Take notes as needed, and follow these guidelines for your planning:

- Carefully consider the prompt. Make sure you understand the issue at stake. Read and think about it again if it seems unclear on the first read.
- Analyze your arguments and consider counter-arguments or flaws in the presentation of your response to questions. Try to address contradictions and weaknesses in your thinking so you can address them in writing the essay.
- Decide how your essay will be structured and organized.
- Outline the issue at the essay's beginning so readers will know you understand it.
- Use clear and logical steps to explain your position.
- Explain the issue's broader implications, or analyze it within a wider context, if possible.
- Present counter-arguments to the opposing views you noted before starting.
- Be specific whenever possible.
- Avoid monotony in your essay by using varied sentence length and structure. Along those lines, be careful to use precision in your word choices.

- Stay on topic, and be sure your transitions from one thought to another and one paragraph to another are clear and reasonable.
- Be sure to present a strong and clear conclusion, reinforcing or summing up your argument in the process.
- If there is time, be sure to review the essay, correcting grammar and syntactical errors, illegible writing, punctuation, and errors in logic. Revisions should be done as neatly as possible.

A Further Look at the LSAT Sections

The LSAT is divided into five individual subject examinations, which cover a total of three skill areas. The material in each exam breaks down into the following categories:

Logical Reasoning – Students are tested on the ability to evaluate, critically analyze, and complete a number of arguments. The questions require the test-taker to read and understand a short passage, and then respond to questions on the passage in a manner that demonstrates logical and critical thought processes. The examination passages require the student to identify the basic assumptions of the argument and other possible conclusions that may be drawn from it. In addition, the student will be asked to identify specific issues presented in the argument, and to formulate parallel arguments that can be made, or to reveal supporting statements that either strengthen or weaken the argument. These skill areas are covered in two separate examinations.

Analytical Reasoning – Students are tested on the ability to examine a table or set of relationships between entities and draw logical conclusions about the relationships. The test, often termed the Games section, is designed to measure the ability to logically analyze complex legal situations. The question format of this section presents a set of initial conditions, followed by a set of rules governing those conditions, and then a prompt for the student to develop reasonable and logical conclusions based on the circumstances, conditions, and rules provided. Follow-up questions may revise or modify the initial set of circumstances, rules, or conditions, requiring students to reorganize and develop new conclusions.

Reading Comprehension – Students are tested on direct reading comprehension and the identification of inferences based on the material presented. The test consists of several prose passages from various academic disciplines, which are then followed by several questions on the passage or selected parts of the passage. The exam calls for the student to draw conclusions based on understanding of the primary argument, and to locate specific information within the passages, or to demonstrate comprehension of the overall structure of the selection. Since reading skills such as determining the main idea and understanding causal relationships are being tested, rote fact checking is not included in the exam.

Unscored section – This section is used to test potential future questions or new test formats. The results of the unscored section are not included in the student's final test score. The section is not identified during the exam, but is generally among the first three sections administered to avoid question fatigue. The unscored section can contain questions covering any of the skill areas addressed in the regular LSAT course.

Writing Prompt

The writing prompt is a short-written exercise that is given at the end of the regular exam. The prompt is not scored; instead, a digital copy is made and sent along with the test scores to the law schools to which the student is applying. The writing exam consists of a decision prompt, which provides a problem for the student to examine and a set of criteria that can be used to analyze the issue and come to a conclusion. The students must write an essay using the criteria and defend his or her decisions in writing. The problem the student must analyze is generally a non-controversial issue that encourages dispassionate critical analysis and logical written argument. For a short time, LSAC included an alternate type of prompt called an argument prompt—wherein a student had to analyze a logical argument similar to those seen in the logical reasoning exams and critique the argument—but that prompt was retired as of June 2007. The decision prompt used currently for the writing exam reflects a formal standard adopted at the LSAT's inception.

Students should be aware that, while the writing prompt is included with the LSAT score, not all law schools place value upon the writing exercise because it does not carry a score. In any case, most law schools require a personal statement as part of the admission packet. However, many law schools do place value on the writing prompt and the writing exam is evaluated as a vital part of the LSAT for the majority of prospective law students.

Number of Questions

Individual test times will depend on several factors—such as the student's reading speed, level of comfort with the material, and preparation time—but the allotted time is the same. Including break time between tests, students can count on the allotted time being approximately five hours. The LSAC recommends students pace themselves accordingly. Students who begin testing on the standard LSAT exam series at 8:30 AM can expect to be finished with the exam no later than 3:30 PM.

Each section of the exam is allotted 35 minutes, including the writing prompt. The number of questions can vary, but in general, each multiple-choice section of the LSAT will have between 15 and 25 questions, depending on the complexity of the passage and the difficulty of questions asked. Thus, the average LSAT test-taker can expect to answer a minimum of 75 and a maximum of 125 questions over the period of the test day. Keep in mind that not only does the number of questions in the total test vary, but so does the number of questions in each section. While there are two sections of logical reasoning, the experimental section (which is not scored, but is also not identified to the student) may draw from any subject in the regular exam series. Consequently, two test-takers on the same day may experience great variation in the number and emphasis of questions being posed during the LSAT series. Since scoring is the same regardless of what questions are asked, students are strongly urged to become familiar with the concepts and practices of each of the subject areas before taking the exam.

Results

Students who create an electronic account with LSAT can generally view their scores online within three to four weeks of the test. While most scores will be made available online at this time, there is no guarantee that scores will be posted within this estimated timeframe. Unless there is an issue that delays the reporting—inconsistent information on the registration forms and test booklet, delay in delivering the test sheets to the scoring center, issues raised by test center personnel and the like—scores will be made available no later than eight weeks from testing. Students should also note that online posting of test scores does not provide a speed advantage in reporting scores to law schools.

In addition to online reporting and mailed reports, students can elect to use TelScore, a telephone reporting service, to obtain their reports if they do not have Internet access. To use TelScore, students must call (215) 968-1200. If students need assistance, they can speak to a representative by calling (215) 968-1001 between 8:30 AM and 4:45 PM (ET) April–August and 8:30 AM to 7:00 PM (ET) September–March.

The scoring process cannot be expedited in any way. Regardless of circumstances, the scores for the LSAT exams cannot be tallied and made available to students sooner than three weeks after the test. Only students with valid student LSAT online accounts can check their scores online; all other students must call TelScore to get their scores or wait for their score reports to arrive in the mail.

If necessary, students can cancel their LSAT scores if they feel their scores are not worthy of reporting. This can be done at the time of the exam itself; instructions for score cancellation are provided on the back of the answer sheet. If the student chooses to cancel score reporting of a test, it is vital that all instructions are precisely followed; otherwise, the score will be reported. Since score cancellations marked on the answer sheets are processed with the regular LSAT test sheets, confirmation of score cancellations will not be issued until approximately four to five weeks after the test date.

If the student decides later (within six days of taking the LSAT) to cancel scoring, the student can petition LSAC to cancel scores via signed fax, overnight letter, or the Score Cancellation Form available directly from LSAC. Requests submitted by these alternative methods must be received by LSAC within six calendar days of taking the test, or the test will be scored per usual procedure. Any request for score cancellation, regardless of the method used, must include the student's signature for it to be considered a valid cancellation request by LSAC.

Score Ranges

Like most admission exams, the LSAT is a standardized test. This means that raw scores are generally adjusted by a formal statistical process to achieve a normal range. In the case of the LSAT, the scores are equated, or adjusted, to minimize differences that result from differing question banks and/or administrations of the exam. The range of adjusted scores falls into a 60-point range. A score of 120 is the lowest possible score; 180 is the highest possible score.

The raw score is computed by tallying the number of correctly answered questions. There is no penalty for guessing, and there is no difference in weighting between individual questions from different sections of the LSAT. On average, the percentile scores generally break down as follows:

Score = **Percentile** (rank relative to other students)
151 = 50th percentile
164 = 90th percentile
173 = 99th percentile
178 = 99.9th percentile

The first year of law school is considered to be the most grueling. While strong performance on the LSAT and other performance factors like undergraduate GPA remain controversial barometers of student success, LSAC maintains that LSAT performance has a fairly strong correlation to success in law school. Consequently, LSAT scores are one of the most critical admissions factors for law school entry, along with undergraduate GPA. The performance scores on the LSAT, combined with undergraduate GPA scores, are also considered a reliable indicator of bar passage, as well as a predictor of overall law school GPA.

Score Computation

Scoring for the LSAT is done in a phased process. The first step is to evaluate the student's answer sheet and tally the correct answers. There is no penalty for incorrect answers; those questions are simply ignored for the purposes of scoring. Once the raw scores have been tallied, the raw scores are then converted into a normalized measure of how well those scores reflect performance yardsticks developed through past score analysis. This process is called equating and yields a statistical breakdown of the scores. The results are considered valid across test dates and test versions, meaning that any given score is equivalent to the same numerical score achieved on a different testing date and a different exam version.

Once the test scores are equated, a model resembling a bell curve is constructed and the final scores are derived. The result is expressed as a score falling between 120 and 180. Because the scores are expressed in statistical models and not pure raw scores, there can be varying degrees of missed responses between different scores. For example, scores of five points' difference in the 95th percentile might differ by three questions, meaning the student who received a 178 may have answered three more questions correctly than a student with a 173 score. On the other hand, scores closer to the median (closer to the center of the bell curve) may differ by more; a student with a 155, for example, may have answered nine more questions correctly than a student scoring 150.

Disputing a Score

If a student feels that a question was scored incorrectly, the student can request that LSAC review the question or questions presented. To generate the review, the student must file a written inquiry with LSAC within 90 days of receiving a score report. This inquiry must specifically state the objection or challenge. The student must be clear in "stating and supporting the reasons why the credited response is not the one and only best answer to the question," as required by LSAC policy. The request for review will then be subject to a three-tiered review process. If the review request is found to have merit regarding the issue raised, corrective action will be initiated.

Moreover, if an event or disruption at the test center—including cancellations, mistimings, deviations from standard procedure, indications of advance knowledge of exam content, or other compromises of the process —LSAC will investigate the matter. If any procedural violations are determined to be the fault of LSAC or the test center, LSAC will consider solutions and offer students an array of possible remedial actions, at the discretion of LSAC.

The student must be aware that LSAC maintains a rigorous ethical standard for both prospective law school applicants and admitted students. Deviations or lapses in these ethical standards are punishable by a variety of disciplinary options, including revocation of admission, closing of an application file, and in some cases, disbarment. Students are strongly advised to familiarize themselves with LSAC ethical standards and guidelines before registering or even beginning to prepare for the LSAT.

Organizations

LSDAS

The Law School Data Assembly Service (LSDAS) is a centralized organization established for providing a standardized format for the evaluation and submission of undergraduate records of law school applicants. It is intended to simplify the overall application process and to ensure fairness by providing a baseline metric for evaluating undergraduate transcripts. Virtually all ABA-approved law schools require applicants to sign up with the Law School Data Assembly Service. Unlike American law schools, Canadian law schools do not participate in or otherwise provide information to the LSDAS, and do not require applicants to use it or register with the service.

The primary function of the Law School Data Assembly Service in the law school application process is the preparation of the performance report sent to each law school to which an applicant submits scores and other data. Each report contains the student's application, personal essay, and as many letters of recommendation as the student provides. In addition to the student-created material, the report also contains an undergraduate academic summary. This summary is made up of all undergraduate, graduate, and other pertinent transcripts. The academic records of other professional or law schools previously attended are also compiled and sent, along with LSAT scores and copies of the writing sample that accompanies the LSAT. Additional supporting information, such as letters of recommendation, is also included in the report. Although Canadian law schools do not participate in the Law School Data Assembly Service, they do receive an LSAT score report and copies of the writing sample.

As with the LSAT, there is no specific timetable for LSDAS registration. That decision is entirely up to the student, and will be contingent upon a variety of factors. LSDAS registration should coincide with the student's chosen exam schedule, the availability of letters of recommendation, and other submission package requirements. However, LSAC advises that law school applicants register a minimum of four to six weeks prior to the application deadlines of the law schools where they intend to apply. In general, it takes roughly two weeks to prepare transcripts from the point where they are received to the point where they are finally processed into an LSDAS report.

It is important for applicants to remember that, although LSDAS is a necessary step for applying to ABA-approved law schools, the LSDAS registration process is separate from the law school application. The fees also are separate. Paying the fee for LSDAS registration does nothing to meet the fee requirements of the law school application. The separate fee structures required for LSDAS registration and for law school application are often misunderstood by law school applicants. When sending in the fee for LSDAS registration, students are strongly advised to adhere to their prospective law school's policies and deadlines regarding the separate application processes and fees. Also, if applying to more than one law school, it is important that students make sure that enough LSDAS reports are ordered. One LSDAS report must accompany each individual law school application.

If a student needs to order additional LSDAS reports, there are three ways to do so. The quickest and most efficient way is to order them through the student's online account, if applicable. If the student does not have an online account, a second method of ordering would be to use the form included in the current LSAT/LSDAS registration packet. That form must be completely and accurately filled out and submitted via mail or fax. If the form is not available for any reason, then applicants can call LSAC at (215) 968-1001 and speak to a representative, who will assist the applicant with the ordering process. Since the lines are not staffed on a 24/7 basis, this is the least flexible and least preferred option.

Applicants do not have to inform LSAC of which schools to send LSDAS reports directly. When an applicant submits the application material to a law school or a group of law schools, those schools contact LSAC and request the relevant reports directly. Again, it is imperative that the student has ordered enough reports to accommodate the number of law schools applied to. If a student has not ordered and paid for the correct number of reports, the transmission of those reports to the appropriate law school admission offices will be delayed. Occasionally, additional information will need to be appended to reports. When this occurs, an updated report will be sent to the law schools identified by the applicant. These updates will be performed at no additional charge to the applicant.

LSAC

The Law School Admissions Council (LSAC) is a nonprofit organization created in 1947 to standardize, facilitate, and improve the admission process for law schools nationwide. In addition, the LSAC provides a number of services and programs related to legal education, such as the creation and administration of the LSAT, operation of the LSDAS, law school forums for educators and students, and operation and maintenance of the Candidate Referral Service (CRS).

The CRS is valuable because it allows applicants to release pertinent biographic, academic, and employment information to schools that are trying to match students with their own recruitment needs. CRS also disseminates information about the student's law school preferences so that schools meeting these preferences may contact the applicant directly. LSAC comprises all law schools approved by the ABA, as well as a number of Canadian law schools recognized by a provincial or territorial law society or government agency (fifteen at the present time), all of which are included in the voting membership of the Council.

While the LSAC is intimately involved in all aspects of the application standardization process, from developing LSAT exams and test prep materials to providing database services to law schools and their admission offices, it is important to note that the LSAC is in no way involved in individual assessments of an applicant's readiness for law school. LSAC provides a fair, level ground for applicants and law schools to evaluate information, but each law school makes its own decisions regarding applicant suitability. Aside from providing general information, LSAC has no input into the law school selection process.

Reading Comprehension Test

The Reading Comprehension section of the LSAT is designed to test your abilities to understand and interpret written materials. Lawyers daily perform interpretation of written information, much of which can be difficult to understand. Reading comprehension skills are critical for success in law school, as students are required to read and understand massive amounts of material. Even though almost all law school applicants are aware that they'll have to do a lot of reading if they're admitted, many law school graduates still report being shocked at finding out just how much reading is required. The Reading Comprehension section of the LSAT is designed to weed out those applicants who don't have the skills to cope with the reading requirements of law school.

On this portion of the LSAT, you will have 35 minutes to answer approximately 27 questions about four reading assignments. Three of these assignments will consist of only one passage, while one will be a comparative reading test, consisting of two passages. The passages are usually between 400 to 500 words in length, and subject matter can be in any field, but most passages are about a topic in law, science, or the liberal arts. You will not need to know any specialized information to understand a passage, even if it includes technical terms you have never encountered before. You are expected to base your answers only on what is stated or implied in the passage or passages.

One aspect of the Reading Comprehension test that makes it so difficult is that you're expected to read and comprehend a large amount of difficult material in a very brief amount of time. Each passage is hundreds of words long, and is often quite ponderous. Passages are almost always densely written, filled with facts and details that may or may not be important for you to remember. The sheer amount of information in a passage can be quite intimidating and unnerving to test takers.

Then, once you've finally navigated your way through the passage, you're confronted with up to eight questions you must answer. Each question will have four possible answers to choose from, and many of them will be obtuse, having been deliberately crafted to be very hard to interpret. Sometimes it will seem as if several answer choices could conceivably be acceptable. For many questions, two answer choices will be so similar that choosing one or the other would seem to be little different than flipping a coin. You will have less than nine minutes to read each passage thoroughly, mark important information, read each question and all four answer choices, compare and contrast the possible answers with each other, and go back to the passage to find the answer. This is a formidable challenge, to put it mildly. There's no denying that the LSAT Reading Comprehension section is a race against the clock; in fact, it's designed to be that way.

However, there's no reason you need to fear the Reading Comprehension test. Yes, it's hard, but in this guide, we'll show you how you can excel on this portion of the LSAT. You'll learn:

- the main question types
- the best plan for tackling the reading material
- powerful reading techniques
- what to focus on in your reading
- what notes to take
- "red flag words" to watch for
- how these "red flag words" can point you to the correct answer
- other factors that can be important signals

- how to choose between answers that are extremely similar
- and much more...

The Passages: What's the Deal?

The passages you'll encounter on the LSAT Reading Comprehension test are unlikely to be similar to any of your regular reading material. In fact, it's very likely you have never run across any of these kinds of passages before. They are usually taken from academic journals, and then adapted for use on the LSAT. They have to be carefully edited and rewritten to suit the 400–500-word format used for Reading Comprehension passages. Any parts requiring technical knowledge on the part of the reader are removed.

That's just the beginning. After any information only understandable by a professional in the field has been excised, the material then must be rewritten to work around the sentences or paragraphs that were removed. Sometimes the results are less than ideal, which explains why LSAT Reading Comprehension passages sometimes seem jarring and disjointed. The reason the passages are so dense is that the editors at the Law School Admissions Council have taken most of the details and facts from an article that was 1500–2000 words and forced them into a passage that is only about a third or fourth as long.

Topics can be all over the map, but most of the time the subject of the reading passage will not be something you are familiar with, but rather an obscure topic. This is done deliberately to keep the Reading Comprehension test fair. By choosing subject matter that virtually all test takers are unfamiliar with, the test creators make the exam a level playing field where no one has the advantage of knowing the subject better than others.

When you add all these factors up—scholarly writing, three or four pages worth of material crammed into a one-page article, and subject matter that isn't even on the average person's radar—it becomes clear that the passages you'll be dealing with on this part of the LSAT are not exactly light reading. Knowing these things before you take the LSAT will help keep you from feeling overwhelmed when you begin this section. You can relax knowing that you're not supposed to be familiar with the material, that it's supposed to be extremely dense, and that everyone else is in the same boat you are.

There's more good news—the LSAT doesn't penalize incorrect answers. In other words, if you choose the wrong answer, it doesn't lower your score. If you're running out of time, and a question completely stumps you, just pick a letter and fill it in. You may get lucky and get it right; if not, there's no harm done, because a wrong answer is scored the same as a blank answer. It won't raise your score, of course, but it won't lower it either, as your score is based only on correct answers.

Another thing to keep in mind is the fact that the LSAT is not scored the same way a typical test is scored. It's a scaled score, and that's very good news if you're the kind of person who tends to worry every time you're not completely sure that an answer is correct. Because of the scaled scoring, a person can get over 40% of the answers wrong and still receive a score that's about average. Of course, an average LSAT score is not going to help your application stand out, but that's missing the point. The important thing is that you shouldn't worry too much about getting an occasional answer wrong. Because if you can miss nearly half the questions and still receive a score that's near the average, just think how high your score can be if you diligently prepare for the exam.

The Big Picture: How to Approach the Reading Comprehension Questions

There are several factors that will contribute to your success on the Reading Comprehension portion of the LSAT, and the first one is having a definite plan for tackling each question from the beginning. Knowing exactly what you're going to do prevents you from wasting time by trying to decide on a plan of attack at the last minute, or even worse, trying out different approaches to each question. These are critical mistakes that many test takers make, resulting in a lower score on the LSAT than they could have achieved had they been better prepared.

One Very Important Tip

There are several different approaches you could take to the material, but they aren't equally effective. In fact, there's one popular approach that is almost guaranteed to waste time and cause confusion if you follow it. We'll look at the various approaches and compare and contrast their strengths and weaknesses in a moment. Before we do, here's one easy rule to help you save time on the Reading Comprehension section:

Do not waste time reading the instructions.

That's right—you should not read the instructions at the beginning of the Reading Comprehension section. You should familiarize yourself with them right now. The instructions have been the same for decades, and there's no reason to think they're going to change any time soon. They aren't complicated at all, so just learn them now and you won't lose any time on test day by taking time to read them two or three times to make sure you're not missing anything. Here are the official instructions that appear at the beginning of the Reading Comprehension section on every LSAT.

Each set of questions in this section is based on a single passage or a pair of passages. The questions are to be answered based on what is <u>stated</u> or <u>implied</u> in the passage or pair of passages. For some of the questions, more than one of the choices could conceivably answer the question. However, you are to choose the best answer; that is, the response that most accurately and completely answers the question, and blacken the corresponding space on your answer sheet.

That's pretty simple and easy to remember. So, learn the directions now and save valuable time on the LSAT.

What Are Your Options?

There are several approaches you can take when you turn to a passage on the Reading Comprehension section. You can start by:

A. jumping right in—reading the passage and then answering the questions
B. skimming the passage, then skimming the questions, answering the easy ones, then reading the passage in full and answering the rest of the questions
C. reading the first and last sentence of each paragraph of the passage, then reading the passage in full and going on to answer the questions
D. reading the questions so that you can look for the answers on your first reading of the passage, then reading the passage and answering the questions

These approaches have their proponents, but there are a lot of reasons to believe that A is the best option. Most people will be more successful if they take a straightforward approach by simply reading the passage and then answering the questions. Now, there's more to "reading" a passage than simply reading it, and we'll get to that. But first, let's look at the different approaches to see how they compare with each other.

We've already told you that *A* is the best, so let's start with *B*. Skimming is often recommended for picking up the gist of material quickly, and in many cases, it works very well. So why don't we recommend it for the LSAT Reading Comprehension exam? There are two reasons: First, because the passages you'll be dealing with on the LSAT, unlike most of the reading material you've encountered before, don't lend themselves to skimming. The second problem amplifies and exacerbates the first one—the correct answers to the questions usually don't involve the kind of information you can pick up by skimming.

Pick up any newspaper and start skimming the main article on the front page, and it's easy to get the gist of it—the President signed a bill requiring better nutritional labeling at fast food restaurants, for example. You may miss the fact that he signed it at an elementary school and not in a Rose Garden ceremony, and you may not notice that the bill only passed by a very slim margin in the Senate, or that three Republican senators broke ranks and voted with the Democrats. But you'll pick up and retain the main information. The same goes for most magazine articles, blog posts, and even many books. In these cases, skimming can be quite effective when you want the big picture and you want it fast.

LSAT Reading Comprehension passages aren't anything like newspaper articles or blog posts, unfortunately. They are so stuffed with information and detail that skimming them is worse than an exercise in futility. Skimming is for articles that use everyday English and contain a few important facts, which are easily picked out and remembered. The passages on the LSAT are dense and difficult to follow, they make complex arguments on different levels, and they almost always rely on technical jargon and/or a highly advanced vocabulary to do so. You won't learn a thing by skimming them, because you *can't.* On the contrary, you'll probably find yourself getting lost and going over the same material several times, which defeats the whole purpose. Second, skimming on tests is best suited for answers to very basic questions. Many exams have questions that simply ask a person to locate information in the text, and don't require any analysis. Questions such as "How old was Beethoven when he wrote his first composition?", "Which continent has the greatest land mass?", and "Who was the last person to arrive at the scene?" are easy to answer by skimming. You won't be seeing any questions of that type on the LSAT Reading Comprehension test.

What's wrong with *C*? There are a couple of drawbacks to this approach. The Reading Comprehension passages are dense precisely because the individual sentences are dense. If you try to decipher one of these sentences you're going to run into the same problem as the person trying to skim—to get anything out of a stand-alone sentence at all, you will most likely have to read it more than one time. Even reading it several times, however, is unlikely to be any more effective. That's because each sentence after the first one interacts with and builds on the foundation laid by all the previous sentences. One sentence simply won't make much sense by itself. Trying to glean some insights into the meaning of the passage by reading the first and last sentences of each paragraph won't yield any meaningful information, because without the details and context from the rest of the paragraph these sentences will be essentially unintelligible.

Just as with skimming, the idea behind the first sentence/last sentence approach is basically sound when it comes to other kinds of reading material. In most kinds of non-fiction writing, the author often puts the main idea of the paragraph in the opening sentence, and often reiterates or stresses it in the closing sentence. However, not only are the LSAT Reading Comprehension passages too dense and complex for this to work, but the LSAT writers are aware of the popularity of this strategy and they take pains to foil it. So, even in the rare cases when a sentence might concisely express the main idea, it's unlikely to be the first or last one of the passage.

Option *D* also looks promising at first glance; in fact, reading the questions before reading the passage might well be the optimum strategy on most reading comprehension tests. When the reading material is not very complex, it makes perfect sense to find out what you need to look for prior to reading the passage. This greatly simplifies your task, and can be a real time saver.

On the LSAT Reading Comprehension, however, reading the questions first and then the passage is a recipe for disaster. On average, each passage will have seven questions, none of which will be easy. Each one will require careful, focused thought just to make sure you've understood the question precisely. In some cases, merely reading the question won't be enough—you'll need to read, consider, and compare and contrast the answer choices with each other to even have an idea of what you should be looking for when you read the passage.

For example, many questions will be some variation of "What is the author's main point?" followed by five answer choices. The five choices will each be lengthy, and a few of them will be remarkably similar. Since you should be able to understand the author's main point by reading the passage, what would you gain by trying to do so while simultaneously attempting to mentally keep several different and highly nuanced answer choices separate as you read? If that doesn't sound difficult enough, imagine trying to do the same thing for up to eight different questions as you read the passage for the first time. For most people, even remembering all the questions while reading the passage would be extremely difficult. Doing so while keeping a couple dozen answer choices in mind at the same time is simply impossible. It's difficult to see how reading the questions before the passage can increase a person's comprehension of a difficult reading selection. On the contrary, using this strategy on the LSAT would almost certainly have a significant negative impact on a person's comprehension and retention of what he or she has read.

The best option, by far, is *A*—start by reading the passage in its entirely, and only then start answering the questions. Once you've finished the passage, you should start with the first question and answer it before moving on to the next one, and then answer each question in turn. Don't bother skimming the questions to see if there are some easy ones you can answer first before concentrating on the harder ones. That won't work, for the same reason skimming the passage itself won't work. There are very few easy questions on the LSAT Reading Comprehension exam. Most questions are either difficult or extremely difficult. If you encounter a question that's particularly difficult, move on to the next one. Never forget that you're in a race against the clock. If you're running out of time and still have some unanswered questions left, just take a guess and fill in a circle. When you stick with this approach, you'll have a much better chance of answering all the questions compared to using any of the other ones, because they simply eat up too much time.

So, when it comes to the LSAT Reading Comprehension a simple, straightforward approach is best. You should read the passage first. Only after that should you even look at the questions. Any other approach will waste valuable time and make answering the questions much more difficult. We think it's pretty clear why the simple approach of reading the passage in its entirety before even looking at the questions is the best one. However, in case you still have any doubts, the Law School Admission Council, the organization that creates the LSAT, also recommends this approach as being the most effective.

There's a Lot More to Reading Than Just Reading

What is the most important skill for achieving a high score on the Reading Comprehension section? That's easy—it's being very good at "active reading." If reading isn't one of your strong suits, now's the time to start working on that. Anyone with average to poor reading skills simply won't have a chance to succeed on this portion of the LSAT without significant improvement between now and test day. However, this doesn't mean that if you possess superior reading skills that you can relax or that the Reading Comprehension exam will be a breeze for you. You may have a leg up on someone with mediocre reading skills, but odds are you're not used to doing the kind of reading that's necessary for success on the LSAT Reading Comprehension test.

The kind of reading needed for success on the LSAT, active reading, is much different than the kind of reading most people are used to, and that includes even those very good readers who have high natural or acquired abilities for comprehension and retention. It's far from being the same kind of activity a person engages in when they curl up with a good book. You may have already used a form of active reading when you underlined important passages in textbooks, but active reading involves a lot more than that. Active reading is work, and to get good at it takes practice.

So, what is active reading all about? Let's start by talking about its opposite. How many times have you been reading a magazine, book, or newspapers and had to stop and start over from the beginning because you realized that you had no idea what you'd just read over the last few minutes? This has happened to virtually everyone, and it happens on a regular basis. In fact, it's not uncommon for people to have to start over several times before the material finally starts registering with their brain. That's because our minds have a natural tendency to wander while we're reading. If what we're reading is emotionally gripping, such as a key passage in a mystery novel, or extremely interesting in other ways, our minds tend to overcome this tendency and we have no trouble staying focused on the material.

Of course, most of the time people fall somewhere between these two extremes when it comes to staying focused while reading. We usually comprehend and retain some of what we read without having to force ourselves. That won't be good enough for the LSAT. The passages you'll be reading in the Reading Comprehension portion of the exam will be neither interesting nor emotionally gripping. They will be exceedingly dry and dull, in addition to being extremely dense, which will make for very tedious reading. It will take a strenuous effort to stay focused on the exam.

That's the beauty of active reading—it forces you to mentally dive into the passage and actively involve yourself in the text. There are both mental and physical aspects of active reading. Both aspects are important, but it's the physical part that plays a bigger role in enabling you to come back and find the information you're looking for after reading the questions. However, in this case, the whole is truly greater than the sum of its parts. It's the combination of keeping both your mind and your hand fully engaged in the text that makes active reading so powerful.

Active Reading: The Mental Aspect

As you read each passage, you'll want to keep several questions in mind:

- What is the author's main point?
- What is the author's point of view?
- What is the author's tone?
- What are some of the author's key arguments?
- What are some other viewpoints the author takes note of?

Keeping these questions in mind isn't difficult, although it might seem that way at first glance. If you think about it, however, most of them are questions that will naturally come to mind any time a person is reading a text he's unfamiliar with. When we read something for the first time we tend to automatically ask ourselves what the author is trying to say and where he's coming from, and we take notice of his tone and the points he's making. Unfortunately, we also tend to brush these things away while we're reading, and that's one of the main reasons we find it so easy to get completely distracted.

You can avoid this problem by choosing to deliberately focus on these questions as you read. If you have this as a clear and definite purpose in your mind as you begin, staying focused and on track for the few minutes it takes to read each passage will not be a problem. This is another reason you should not read the LSAT Reading Comprehension questions before reading the passage. You'll have plenty of questions to be thinking about as you read without adding five to eight more, along with a couple dozen possible answer choices to consider. It will be a challenge to keep the above questions in mind as you read and interpret the passage, but you can do it if you make a serious effort.

There is one more important consideration when it comes to active reading on the exam, and that's how to handle words you're unfamiliar with. These will fall into two categories. The first one is technical jargon relevant to the context of the passage, but unknown to the average person. The second category will consist of advanced vocabulary words of a non-technical nature. Hopefully, most of the unfamiliar words you encounter on the LSAT will fall into the first category. Don't let these worry you, as they will either be explained in the passage, either implicitly or explicitly, or they will be of no importance. As for the non-technical words you run into, if they're not explained explicitly you can often infer their meaning from the context. If you do happen to run into a word and you have absolutely no idea what it means, and the context is no help whatsoever, don't stress about it, as it's unlikely that any questions are going to be based on it.

Active Reading: The Physical Aspect

As you have probably surmised, the physical aspect of active reading involves annotation, or marking up the text. You won't be provided any blank paper during the Reading Comprehension exam for notes, but you will be allowed to makes notes in the text itself, and you'll want to make effective use of the power of annotation. Making the right kinds of notes and markups in the text will enable you to track down the answers to questions much, much faster.

Now, if you've bought a few used textbooks in your academic career, you're no doubt aware that annotation can be taken way too far. Those unfortunate souls who underline nearly every sentence on a page, or even sometimes in a whole chapter, have done themselves no good at all, and only wasted their time. The whole point of marking up a text is to make a word or passage stand out from the whole. If everything on a page has been highlighted, then nothing has been highlighted. That shouldn't be a problem for you with the Reading Comprehension passages, but you should keep in mind that it's easy to make too many notations. Just make sure you don't go overboard and slow yourself down. Also, be as legible as possible. Many of your notations will be a letter or two, or a symbol or numeral, so make sure you can read them with one quick glance. You don't want to be struggling to decipher your own handwriting when seconds count.

What kind of things should you be noting, and how should you mark them? There are several things you'll want to keep an eye out for as you read. Be on the lookout for certain kinds of words or phrases that can be important guideposts when it comes to answering the questions. They show that something is coming that will emphasize an author's point more strongly, or support his argument, or mark a shift of some sort in the writing, such as contrasting or comparing one thing with another. Think of them as "red flags," because they are often important signals that you ignore or skip over at your own peril. Here are some of the main ones to watch for:

Words that signal emphasis: additionally, also, furthermore, in addition
Words that signal support: because, for example, since, regardless
Words that signal a shift in thought: but, after all, in spite of, except, yet, although, admittedly, on the other hand, despite, whereas, still, however, nonetheless, in contrast, even though, nevertheless, unlike

Marking these red flags so they stand out will make it easier to find the correct answer for many of the questions when the answer isn't immediately clear to you. You can circle or underline these words. Using circles might make the words stand out more, but underlining them takes less time.

You also need to highlight the author's main point as soon as you come across it. You could draw a circle around the sentence or sentences that make up the main point, but that would be time consuming. It's best to use some sort of abbreviation such as "MP" off to the side of the key passage.

Sometimes the author will include a number of supporting arguments, points, reasons, etc. You can number these off to the side.

When a passage on the Reading Comprehension exam offers a definition, there's a good chance that the definition will be important. Mark it with a "D" off to the side.

Most passages will feature points or arguments that oppose or conflict with the main point the author is making. Mark these with an "O" off to the side.

Some parts of the passage will likely compare and contrast an argument and a counter-argument, and these sections are usually important. Mark them with a "C" off to the side.

Obviously, in some parts of some passages, you'll encounter more than one thing that needs to be spotlighted, meaning you'll have several notations off to the side in the same part of the passage. This could be quite confusing, which would defeat the purpose of these annotations, so it's best to use an arrow connecting the letter, letters, or number to the appropriate part of the passage. If necessary, use parentheses or brackets to enclose the important sentence or sentences to make it clear exactly what an arrow is pointing to. These enclosures should be used only when necessary, however, because of the time factor.

You may bring a highlighter and a #2 pencil to use during the exam. You can use both of them if you choose, but we recommend using only the pencil. The highlighter is great for one thing, highlighting, but it's not so hot when it comes to making notes, so if you choose to make use of the highlighter, you'll need to use the pencil, too. It's true that highlighting a portion of the text makes it stand out a bit more compared to underlining it or circling it, saving a bit of time when you have to refer back to the passage. However, the small amount of time saved is almost certainly negated by the time lost by switching back and forth between the highlighter and the pencil. It's not a make or break decision, though, so if you feel it would be more efficient to use both the highlighter and the pencil, by all means do so. It's more important that you're relaxed and confident than that you save a few seconds here and there.

The Question Types

The questions you'll have to answer in the Reading Comprehension section will be complex and difficult, just like the passages themselves. Unlike reading comprehension tests you may have taken in the past, there won't be many questions for which only one answer choice will be clearly and inarguably the only possible correct answer. As the official LSAT Reading Comprehension instructions put it:

"more than one answer could conceivably be correct. However, you are to choose the best answer; that is, the response that most accurately and completely answers the question..."

Don't make the mistake of thinking that "more than one" means "two." Sometimes you will encounter questions that have not just two, but several answer choices that could plausibly be correct. It's also a certainty that more than once you will be faced with questions that have two answer choices which seem to be saying almost exactly the same thing, and trying to understand the difference between them in order to choose "the best answer" will seem like an impossible task. Rest assured, however, that in each case only one answer will be acceptable. LSAT test writers spend a lot of time laboring over the precise wording of questions and answers in order to create this level of difficulty. Their purpose is to measure your ability to pick up on nuance and detail, an ability that will be crucial to your success in the legal field.

Fortunately, Reading Comprehension questions fall into a few basic types, which greatly simplifies the challenge you'll face on exam day. Knowing exactly what you'll be up against allows you to be much better prepared to do well on the exam. Here are the main kinds of questions you'll see on the Reading Comprehension test:

- What is the main point the author is making?/What is the author's primary purpose in writing this?
- What is the author implying in this passage?/What can be inferred from this passage?
- Which of the following supports/weakens the author's argument?
- Based on the information in the passage, which of the following must be true?
- What does the author say about X in this passage?

Those are broad generalizations, of course—most questions won't be phrased exactly like any of the above, but approximately 75% of them will be some sort of variation on one of these themes. Here are some examples of the phrasing you'll see in the actual questions on the Reading Comprehension:

- Which one of the following most accurately expresses the main idea of the passage?
- Which one of the following would be the best title for this passage?
- Which of the following inferences is most strongly supported by this passage?
- The author implies which of the following in lines 17–19?
- Which of the following would most weaken the author's argument?
- The author's response to X would most likely be which of the following?
- In writing this, the author primarily seeks to...?
- Which one of the following most accurately and completely expresses the author's main point?

Most of the remaining questions will be about the author's tone, how the passage is structured, and definitions of words (which can be derived from information supplied in the passage).

Breaking Down the Questions

Let's take a deeper look at the main question types.

1) Main Point/Primary Purpose

Nearly every passage on the Reading Comprehension will have a question asking about what the author hopes to accomplish by writing this, or what her overriding point is. There is a lot of overlap between what the author's main point is and what the author's primary purpose is, so you can think of these two kinds of questions as essentially the same question, but expressed in a slightly different way. Basically, both of these questions boil down to this: "What message is the author trying to communicate?"

A) Main Point

Questions about the author's main point are not always phrased exactly alike, but are usually pretty straightforward. By this point in your academic career you should be familiar with this kind of question, as it's not only one of the most common ones on the LSAT Reading Comprehension exam, but it's also standard fare on any test of reading comprehension. By "straightforward," we don't mean to imply that these questions are easy to answer; we're only pointing out that the average test taker will have no trouble ascertaining the point of the question.

Almost all Reading Comprehension passages will contain a sentence that expresses the author's main point. Think of this sentence as the thesis statement of the passage. In a written essay, the thesis statement is almost always found in the last sentence of the first paragraph, but that won't be the case in these passages. You will sometimes find the thesis statement there, but many times you won't. The writers of these passages go out of their way to avoid falling into that kind of pattern, which is why formulaic approaches to the LSAT simply don't work. In fact, in some passages the thesis statement won't appear in the first paragraph at all, but in one of the others.

The biggest difficulty test takers have with Main Point questions is that more than one of the answer choices might be an actual point made by the author, but not her main point. An incorrect answer choice might be a secondary point she made, or it could be one aspect of her main point, without accurately summing up the entire point. In many cases the main difference between a wrong choice and the right answer is that the incorrect one is too narrow, or too broad. Because of the phrasing and sentence construction of the answer choices, it's not always easy to distinguish these plausible sounding answer choices from the one that best encapsulates the main point. It's important to read all the choices carefully and deliberately before choosing an answer.

B) Primary Purpose

Every author has an overriding goal in mind when he writes; this is his primary purpose for writing the piece. His primary purpose can be any number of things. Here are a few possibilities:

- to provide information about a topic
- to demonstrate opposition to a person or thing
- to evaluate or examine a topic
- to challenge an idea, belief or practice
- to demonstrate support for a person or thing
- to convince someone of something
- to convert someone to a viewpoint or cause
- to critique or criticize something or someone
- to satirize or ridicule someone or something
- to clear up confusion about something
- to bring about change in some area

Those are just some of the primary purposes an author might have in mind when he sits down to write; obviously, there are many more. Unlike the main point of a passage, however, the primary purpose will rarely be stated overtly. You must be able to infer the author's primary reason for writing the passage even though it isn't spelled out. As they do with questions about the author's main point, LSAT writers specialize in surrounding the correct answer choice with others that are often remarkably similar to the actual answer. We can't stress enough how necessary it is to read all the answer choices before deciding that one is correct.

2) Implication/Inference

On the Reading Comprehension portion of the LSAT you will encounter many questions about what the author is implying in the passage, or what may be inferred from the passage. Just as in the Main Point/Primary Purpose questions, they will be phrased in a variety of ways:

- With which of the following would the author most likely agree?
- The author implies which of the following?
- With which of the following would the author most likely disagree?
- It can be inferred from the passage that...
- Which of the following inferences is most strongly supported by the author's argument in paragraph two?
- In paragraph three, the author implies that his critics...
- The passage suggests which one of the following about X?
- The passage most strongly implies that the author agrees with which of the following statements?
- The passage provides evidence to suggest that the author would...

No matter how it is phrased, each implication/inference question is asking you about an idea or opinion that the author most likely believes in or subscribes to, even though he has not overtly said so in the passage. Sometimes the question will be about an implication/inference about a narrow sub-topic of the passage. If so, some of the answer choices will be quite similar with only slight differences between them. They can be so similar that a test taker in a hurry could easily fail to see any differences at all between them. Other questions will be broader, with each answer choice representing a clear and discrete alternative to the others. The latter are generally easier to answer than the former.

Review Video: Inference
Visit mometrix.com/academy and enter code: 379203

3) Supports/Weakens

For these questions, you'll be asked which of the answer choices most strengthens or weakens something the author says in the passage. The question could refer to one of the arguments the author makes, one of the conclusions he states, or even the main point. These questions will require you to consider the idea from the passage or the author's statement in light of information not mentioned in the passage, which would most strongly support or detract from the passage or statement. Their phrasing doesn't vary as much as some of the other question types:

- Which one of the following, if true, most supports the author's statement about X in paragraph three?
- Which one of the following, if true, most weakens the author's statement that...?
- Which one of the following, if true, most supports the author's conclusion?
- Which one of the following, if true, most weakens the author's suggestion that X is the best approach to...?

Notice that the correct answer is the one that *most* supports or weakens the statement or idea in question. Rest assured, one or more of the other answer choices will clearly support or detract from the statement or idea, but not quite as forcefully as the correct answer does. Also keep in mind that you will never have to decide if the new information being considered is correct or incorrect. These questions will always qualify the new information with the phrase "if true."

4) Must Be True/Cannot Be True

Must Be True questions are usually phrased along this line:

- Based on the information in the passage, which of the following must be true?
- Which of the following is most consistent with the author's conclusion that...?
- Based on the information in the passage, which of the following cannot be true?
- Which one of the following, if true, is LEAST consistent with the author's claim in paragraph 3?

These questions are the inverse of Supports/Weakens questions. Those questions ask you to assume that some new information is true, and then analyze the author's ideas or conclusions in light of it. On Must Be True questions, you'll be required to go in the other direction. You'll assume that the author's ideas or conclusions are true, and then you'll analyze some new information in light of the passage.

Must Be True questions are closely related to Implication/Inference questions. The main difference is that Implication/Inference questions revolve around the implicit but unwritten thoughts and beliefs of the author of the passage, while Must Be True questions are focused on asking you to use explicit and/or implicit information from the passage to evaluate new information. Again, you'll never need to be concerned about whether or not the information in the passage is actually true. In most cases a layman won't be qualified to make that determination. You'll answer these questions using the assumption that the information in the passage is reliable.

5) Explicit Information

These kinds of questions are the least subjective ones you will come across on the Reading Comprehension portion of the LSAT. Nearly every other Reading Comprehension question will require you to make an inference, interpretation or deduction of one sort or another in order to answer the question correctly. Questions about what the author is implying, what must be true based on the passage, how one thing relates to another, what would most weaken an author's argument, etc., all require you to make some sort of judgment call.

Explicit Information questions are different; there is no conjecture at all required to answer these questions. That is not to say that they're easy; on the contrary, they usually aren't much easier than the more subjective types of questions. Just as with the other question types, answer choices will be written in such a way that at least one of the incorrect choices (and probably more) will be similar enough to the correct one that careful thought will be required to choose the right answer. These questions can take several forms:

- the author lists each of the following drawbacks about the proposed canon revisions EXCEPT?
- the author states which one of the following about computers in the classroom?
- the passage provides information that answers which one of the following questions?
- according to the passage, some X have been mistakenly classified as which one of the following?
- the author states that admissions committees at top tier universities in America have which of the following characteristics?
- which one of the following is mentioned in the passage as an important factor in the development of?
- which one of the following describes a potential pitfall of embracing the new technology mentioned in paragraph four?

The Reading Comprehension portion of the LSAT is quite a challenge, and should not be underestimated. However, armed with the information in this guide, there's no reason to fear it. Study this until you're familiar with these main question types, and how to handle them. Then take the practice tests to ensure you're ready for the challenge on the day of the exam.

Analytical Reasoning Test

The Analytical Reasoning (or Games) section of the LSAT consists of approximately 24 questions, with a 35-minute time limit. Many people refer to this section as Logic Games, but that can be quite confusing, as the other reasoning section of the LSAT is called Logical Reasoning, so in this guide we'll use either Analytical Reasoning or Games. Although the other sections of the LSAT measure skills that are easily connected with doing well in law school, those measured in this section can be harder to pin down. Also, Analytical Reasoning is often considered to be the most time-challenging portion of the test, with only 35 minutes to complete 22 to 24 rather involved questions.

In the following sections, we will break down the question types found within this portion. First, however, it is worthwhile to briefly examine the format these problems will take on the LSAT.

The Analytical Reasoning section will contain four problems. Each problem will be followed by five, six, or seven questions. If you plan to try to answer them all, you will have a little over a minute to answer each of the questions.

Like problems in other sections, the Analytical Reasoning problems will test your ability to wade through a lot of information, think fast under pressure, and keep up the pace. On top of that, this section, more than any other, will require you to identify and keep a running tab on the relationships between different bits of information through various points of convergence. (On the other hand, this is the only part of the LSAT where a test taker can make absolutely sure that his or her answer is correct.)

Many examinees dread this section of the LSAT, with its requirement that you continually track a lot of information and relationships between the various bits of information. And there's no denying that it can be quite confusing. But one thing you will discover by practicing the problems in advance is that one or two of the Analytical Reasoning problem types will be easier for you to grasp and complete, relatively speaking, while others will be more difficult. Particularly since you will be testing under time-sensitive, high-pressure conditions, it is recommended that you first work out the problems that come more easily to you, and then go back around to complete those that take more time.

Also, if your experimental section turns out to be Analytical Reasoning, you will need to tackle both sections as if they were real, since you have no way of knowing which will one be scored and which one won't. But remember – you are not penalized for the number of wrong answers, so when time is short, guessing is a far better strategy than leaving questions blank.

There's no denying that for the vast majority of people the Analytical Reasoning section is by far the most difficult part of the LSAT. The material is itself extremely challenging, and, as if this weren't enough, the test designers intentionally include so many questions that it's nearly impossible to complete them all in a mere 35 minutes. Don't let this discourage you, though, because the Analytical Reasoning part of the LSAT is also the section where thorough preparation can make the biggest difference.

Of course, it's important to prepare for all three sections of the LSAT, but taking the time to learn how to understand and solve Analytical Reasoning games will be the easiest way for most people to significantly improve their score. That's because the other two sections measure skills people already use on a regular basis. It's certainly possible to improve a person's abilities at reading comprehension and/or logical reasoning, but most people taking the LSAT will already be fairly strong in these two areas. There is certainly upside potential there, but it's somewhat limited. The problems in Analytical Reasoning, however, require less commonly used skills, so the upside potential of mastering the skills needed to solve these kinds of problems is huge.

THE *REAL* KEY TO SUCCESS ON THE ANALYTICAL REASONING SECTION

Out of all the powerful information in *LSAT Secrets Study Guide*, if you had to choose only one area to focus on, it should be the information in this section. It's that important.

In the Analytical Reasoning section of the LSAT the problems are in the form of what the LSAC calls *setups*. Each setup contains two main parts. The first is *elements*—these are sets of people (the most common), places, or things. The second is *conditions*—constraints under which the elements operate, which are limits on how they can be manipulated. Many people refer to the conditions as *rules* or *clues*; the three terms are interchangeable in this context. In order to answer the questions after the setup you will need to arrange, classify, group, or otherwise manipulate the elements in accordance with the constraints.

Given that each setup will have several elements and various rules, some of which apply to all of the elements, and others which apply only to some of the elements, it will be virtually impossible to answer all 22–24 questions in the Analytical Reasoning section in the allotted 35 minutes by trying to figure the answers out in your head. In fact, trying to do so is probably the one thing that has the single biggest negative impact on the average person's LSAT score.

Trying to come up with the answers in your head will drag your score down in two ways. First, it's very unlikely that you'll be able to answer all the questions without guessing. You simply won't have time. Odds are high that you'll be forced to either leave a lot of the questions blank, or just take random guesses at them because you're running out of time. While wrong or blank answers won't lower your score in and of themselves, each one represents a question you could have answered correctly if you'd utilized a more effective strategy. In other words, while there's no penalty for an incorrect or missing answer, each one is a missed opportunity for raising your score.

Second, even in those cases where you spent a good bit of time thinking about the question, some of your answers are very likely to be wrong, because solving these problems mentally is extremely difficult. In fact, the key to success on the Analytical Reasoning section of the LSAT lies in understanding that it's not a pure reasoning test by any stretch of the imagination. **In actuality, your success on this section depends not just on your reasoning abilities, but also on your skill at quickly making accurate visual representations of complicated written information. In fact, the latter skill is probably even more important than the former**. In other words, Analytical Reasoning is just as much a diagramming test as it is a reasoning test, if not more so. Of course, LSAC can't come right out and call this section Rapid Diagramming, because that doesn't sound nearly as impressive (or nearly as intimidating) as Analytical Reasoning.

We said earlier that this is the only section where you can be 100% sure your answer is correct. That's because if you draw a diagram properly, you can simply look at your diagram and visually confirm the correct answer. We also said that even though the Analytical Reasoning section of the LSAT is the one that seems the most intimidating, it's also the section that offers the most room for improvement for raising your potential score. If you're like the average person, your skills at diagramming these kinds of problems are starting at what is essentially a baseline of zero. If you get only slightly good at diagramming Analytical Reasoning setups, you can expect a significant improvement in your potential LSAT score. If you take the time and effort to get very good at it, the impact on your score will be huge.

Not everyone who takes the LSAT is capable of achieving a high score. However, many people who actually are capable of ranking in the top percentiles of test-takers fail to do so, and wind up with a mediocre score—one that's nothing to brag about, and isn't good enough to get them into the best schools, let alone win them any scholarship money. For most of these aspiring lawyers, the main reason they didn't achieve the high score they were capable of is a poor performance on the Analytical Reasoning section.

When it comes to getting a high score on the LSAT, the single most important thing you can do between now and test day is to learn how to diagram these Analytical Reasoning setups quickly and effectively.

The Fine Art of Diagramming

We're being facetious, of course—drawing diagrams for the LSAT is about as far away from being a fine art as it can get. So if you're not an artist, you can relax. No artistic ability is necessary in order to be able to draw effective diagrams for the Analytical Reasoning test. If you can draw a stick figure, you've got all the talent you need to create the simple diagrams that can mean the difference between failure and success on this portion of the LSAT. If you do happen to have some artistic ability, just check it at the door of the testing center. You'll want to keep your diagrams as simple and uncomplicated as possible. Doing so will not only reduce the time it takes to draw them, but it will also mean you'll be able to come up with the correct answer more quickly. When it comes to Analytical Reasoning diagrams, less is definitely more.

Essentially, your diagrams will consist of three things: lines (including simple circles, boxes, and tables), symbols, and names of the elements from the setup. Once you've solved a question for a setup, you can keep the basic diagram for the rest of the questions for that setup, but you will sometimes have to erase most of the names and then rearrange them on the diagram for each question.

Now, you may be wondering how you'll be able to write out the names of five or more people, places or things, repeatedly, in the very limited time you'll have available. Well, you won't have to. Most of the time, you will be able to represent each element with only one letter – the initial of the name of the person, place or thing. In the vast majority of cases, the people who write the setups and questions for the LSAT make sure to never have two elements that begin with the same letter. In some cases, when the setups include the names of actual people (such as former Presidents) or days of the week, there may be two elements with the same first letter, but that can easily be dealt with by using the first two letters for those particular elements.

Rule Busters

Each problem provides you with some known information. These are the rules that you have to work with. Rule busters are choices that immediately clash with a rule and can be quickly ruled out.

Example:

John is sitting next to Bob.

> This is a rule. Therefore, any seating combination that does not have John sitting next to Bob is a rule buster, and is wrong. Quickly scan through the list of answer choices and eliminate all of those that have Bob and John sitting apart.

Example:

Mary is not sitting next to Bob.

> Here is another rule. Quickly scan back through the answer choices and eliminate any that have Mary and Bob sitting together. For every rule that is given, quickly check and see if there are any answer choices that immediately bust the rule and eliminate them.

SYMBOLS

Don't try to remember all of the information in your head. Sketch out the problem using the information provided. As much as possible, use symbols to represent the problem. Letters are great for abbreviation. Use *M* as a symbol for a man, and *W* as a symbol for a woman. Use the first letters in names to describe people. Therefore, John becomes *J* and Paul becomes *P*. If the problem involves a seating or standing arrangement, use blanks to represent the possible seats. Then if a rule states that John is in the rightmost seat, put a *J* in the rightmost blank. Fill in as much information as you can using your symbols. Symbols will help you save time from writing the names out and will allow you to make fast and accurate diagrams of the problem.

SCRATCH PAPER

Use your text booklet as scratch paper extensively. It's a great ally! If you finish the Analytical Reasoning section without scribbles throughout, you didn't take advantage of all of your potential resources. A good diagram or drawing of the problem described is a huge aid when it comes to solving the problem.

Be forewarned, though: when creating your drawings, you will need to be efficient. Don't waste time filling in more information than you need. This is why symbols are great tools. They will save time and effort. Don't include useless information on your diagram or spend time making it pretty. Fill in only what is clearly stated, or what you can quickly deduce. Focus on getting the bare essentials down on paper and spend your time more productively trying to solve the problem.

TOUGH QUESTIONS

If you are stumped on a problem or it appears too hard or too difficult, don't waste time. Move on. Remember though, if you can quickly check for obvious rule busters your chances of guessing correctly are greatly improved. Before you completely give up, at least check for the easy rule busters, which should knock out a couple of possible answers. Eliminate what you can and then guess at the remainder before moving on.

FACE VALUE

Always accept the situation in the problem at face value. Don't read too much into it. The LSAT makers aren't trying to throw you off with a cheap trick. If the setup says there are six seats in a row, you can be confident that it is a single file row and one person is seated directly beside the next person and there are two ends to the row. Don't overcomplicate the problem by creating theoretical scenarios that will warp time or space. These are normal problems with solvable answers. It's just that all of the information isn't readily apparent and you have to figure things out.

READ CAREFULLY

Understand what the problem is about. Read the description of the problem carefully. Don't miss the question because you misunderstood the description of the problem. The description is there because it is important for understanding the problem. Don't waste too much time, though. You must read carefully and efficiently.

LOOSE VS TIGHT

Rules are often either loose or tight. Don't confuse the two when you check for rule breakers. A loose rule gives vague details about the problem. A tight rule gives specific details about the problem. Tight rules are much more helpful, because they provide more information, allowing you to make clear determinations about answer choices more easily.

Example:

> Loose: Bob is standing somewhere behind Joe.
> Tight: Bob is standing directly behind Joe.

Don't mistakenly eliminate an answer choice that has Bob standing two spaces back from Joe, if only the loose rule above is given. If the loose rule is given, you can only eliminate answer choices that have Bob in front of Joe.

DOUBLE NEGATIVES

A double negative can be treated as an affirmative. If a rule or answer choice has two negatives, mentally switch it to a single positive.

Example:

> He is not going to not be there. = He is going to be there.

ANSWER SELECTION

Eliminate choices as soon as you realize they are wrong. But be careful. Make sure you consider all of the possible answer choices. Just because one appears right, doesn't mean that the next one won't be even better. Take a second to make sure that the other choices are not equally obvious. Don't make a hasty mistake. There are only two times that you should stop before considering other answer choices. The first is when you are absolutely positive that the answer choice you have selected satisfies all of the rules. The second is when time is almost out and you have to make a quick guess.

Don't worry if you are stuck between two answer choices that seem right. By eliminating the other three your odds of answering correctly are now 50/50. Rather than wasting too much time, play the odds. You are guessing, but guessing wisely, because you've been able to knock out some of the answer choices that you know are wrong. If you are eliminating choices and realize that the answer choice you are left with is also obviously wrong, don't panic. Start over and consider each choice again. There may easily be something that you missed the first time and will catch on the second pass.

COMMON SENSE

When in doubt, use common sense. These problems will not require you to make huge leaps of logic. If you think a leap of logic is necessary, read back through question and the set of conditions in order to gain a better understanding. Don't read too much into the question or set of conditions. Use your common sense to interpret anything that isn't clear. These are normal problems rooted in reality.

FINAL NOTES

Some problems may have complicated reasoning that must be sorted through. Before you pick an answer choice and work it out in great detail, which takes a lot of time, first look briefly through the other answer choices to see if any of them are obviously correct. Always use your time efficiently.

Don't panic, and stay focused. Work systematically. Read the problem carefully. Eliminate the answer choices that are immediately wrong and are rule busters. Keep narrowing the search until you are either left with the answer or must guess at the answer from a more selective group of choices.

Analytical Reasoning Questions: Types

As soon as you look at the Analytical Reasoning section of the LSAT, you will immediately notice a difference in problem style and section structure. Not only are the skills tested a little bit different, but so is the way that testing occurs.

In order to approach the Analytical Reasoning section with confidence, it is important to first become familiar with the types of questions found here. There are four primary types of Analytical Reasoning (Games) questions. While some problems may combine types, the basic question types you will see are as follows:

1. **Ordering:** In this type of problem, the examinee must order the players of the question (and players may be human, animal, objects, or something else altogether) in a specific sequence based on the conditions provided.
2. **Selection:** The examinee must select a smaller group of players from within the larger group, based strictly upon the criteria given.
3. **Assignment:** For these problems, the examinee must assign players into different groups.
4. **Connection:** Given specific criteria or instructions, the examinee is asked to connect some of the players in a particular way.

Not only does the content of the question differ from that of other LSAT sections, but the layout of the problems does as well. Instead of showing you a short text followed by one or more questions, the Analytical Reasoning section will include condition statements as well as a passage. Normally, there will be an introductory statement to familiarize you with the players for the problem. As noted above, these players may belong to any species or type that the test preparers care to incorporate into their creatively worded problems.

The second condition statement will then establish the rules and conditions that you must follow for that problem set. It is rare for a question to change any conditions, but it is not unheard of, so be aware of that possibility. Another detail to keep in mind is that in the Games section, there is only one answer that can conceivably be correct. While other sections may require you to identify the *best* answer, meaning that at least one other answer choice might be partially correct, that's not the case with the Analytical Reasoning section. Answer choices in Games can't be partially correct. They're either right, or they're wrong, with no shades in between. So once you have identified a correct response, you are done with that question and need waste no more time on further analysis, because all other choices are completely wrong.

Analytical Reasoning Questions: Ordering Problems

Analytical Reasoning ordering problems naturally require the examinee to put the players (which could be anything) in a particular order based on the conditions given. The ordered sequence could be any type of configuration—not necessarily a list. With all of the possibilities available, it is certainly a good idea to become very familiar with the specifics of the conditions and instructions as set forth in the problem. Whatever can be definitively known from a careful reading of the conditions will lay the foundation for the questions that come after.

In terms of ordering problems found on the LSAT, you may be asked to do the following types of order-related tasks in Analytical Reasoning problems:

- Identify all of the positions an individual player may or may not occupy within the sequence.
- Decide which players may or may not be across from or next to one another in a given sequence.
- Identify the particular location of an individual player within the sequence.
- Calculate the number of positions separating two particular players within the sequence.
- Determine all players who must come before or after a particular player in a given sequence.

The following example will help illustrate the type of ordering tasks you may be asked to perform. Creating a diagram of the information provided will be helpful in answering these questions quickly and accurately:

Team X has ten players—Joe, Carrie, Miguel, Alice, Walley, Hari, Kris, Damon, Pete, and Helen. During practice, they stand in a circle for passing exercises. The following is a description of the sequence of their drill:

Miguel passes to Helen.
Helen passes to Kris.
Kris passes to Walley.
Walley passes to Carrie.
Carrie passes to Pete.
Pete passes to Hari.
Hari passes to Alice.
Alice passes to Joe.
Joe passes to Damon.
Damon holds the ball.

The first pass is made to the player directly across. Each subsequent pass must be made to a teammate four or five spaces removed from the passing player in an alternating sequence. No player may catch or pass more than once.

The problem is a simple one, but there is a lot of information to sort through and a lot of little pieces to put in order. It is easy to see why working it out in a drawing can be quite helpful in making sense of the problem. Consider, for example, how sketching the description would make the following questions very simple to answer:

1. Where does Damon stand in relation to Miguel?

or

2. Which players stand three removed from Carrie in the circle?

A diagram easily shows you that Miguel is standing right next to Damon; you might figure that one out strictly from a good read of the question. As for Carrie, both Helen and Damon stand three spaces removed from her—a connection that's more difficult to make without a diagram.

Analytical Reasoning Questions: Selection Problems

A universal must-do for the Analytical Reasoning section is careful attention to the conditions set out for the problem; selection problems are no exception. There are a number of facts you will pick up about each player within the conditions, as well as what each may or may not do and how they can and cannot be connected—in other words, strict parameters for how they operate. Selection problems require that you pay special attention to this information because you will be using it to pull smaller groups out of the main one.

Parameters for the problem may look something like this:

Amy must select three employees to go on the junket.

To reach a determination for questions like this, you will need to consider the following aspects:

- Who must be selected according to the conditions delineated
- Who is eligible for selection
- Who is not eligible for selection
- If certain specific players are selected, which other players must or must not be selected
- After considering the information, how many players are actually eligible

The following example will help to illustrate the above concepts:

There are six siblings who attend the same college. They are Naya, Chris, Maggie, Elliott, Joel, and Petra. Five classes are scheduled for the coming semester, which they may attend, subject to the following restrictions:

If Joel signs up for a particular class, then Petra does not sign up for the same class.
If Naya signs up for a particular class, then Chris does not sign up for the same class.
If Petra signs up for a particular class, then either Maggie or Elliott may sign up for the same class, but not both.
If Chris does not sign up for a particular class, then neither Maggie nor Petra may sign up for that class.

As you can see, there is a lot to keep track of, right from the beginning. You can see why drawing a diagram would be necessary to solve these problems. Diagrams make it easier to reference those connections in answering a series of questions for which each creates a slightly different group and can speed response time.

Considering the set of conditions above, try the following question:

If Naya enrolls for a particular class, what is the maximum number of other siblings who may also attend that class?

As you can see, drawing up the connections when you first read through the conditions can prevent you from having to waste precious time in reviewing the conditions for each additional question.

Analytical Reasoning Questions: Assignment Problems

At first glance, Analytical Reasoning assignment questions will look rather similar to selection questions. In both cases, you will be asked to select individuals out of a larger group based on the stated conditions. The primary difference is that in selection problems, you will identify players from the larger group and discard the rest for the purposes of that question. In assignment problems, however, you must select and assign *every* player identified into one group or another—there are no wallflowers in assignment problems.

The following comparison should serve to illustrate the difference:

Selection Problem

> There are six siblings who attend the same college. They are Naya, Chris, Maggie, Elliott, Joel, and Petra. Five classes are scheduled for the coming semester, which they may attend, subject to the following restrictions: . . .
>
> If Naya enrolls for a particular class, what is a complete list of those siblings who may also attend that class?

Assignment Problem

> There are six siblings who attend the same college. They are Naya, Chris, Maggie, Elliott, Joel, and Petra. Two classes, the green class and the yellow class, are scheduled for the same weekdays and times. Each of the siblings must enroll in one of the two classes. All of the siblings mentioned above may attend, subject to the following conditions: . . .
>
> Which of the siblings will enroll in the green class?

It should be immediately obvious that the primary difference between the two problems is that the assignment problem requires that every person be accounted for and assigned a slot in one group or the other. While the same skills used in selection problems can be used in solving assignment problems, many test takers find the assignment problems easier to solve. Because all players must be placed in a group, there are fewer loose ends. This makes it simpler for the examinee to account for everyone and ensure that he or she has not missed something. For this reason, many people prefer assignment problems to selection problems, despite the additional step.

Question types that assignment problems may ask the examinee to address include:

1. Determine which players are required to be in a certain group.
2. Determine which players may be included in a certain group.
3. Determine the number of players to be grouped in a particular category.
4. Determine which players are not eligible for inclusion in a certain group.
5. Determine which players must or must not be paired with other particular players.

Analytical Reasoning Questions: Connection Games

Analytical Reasoning connection games problems are similar to assignment problems in that they require you to place each of the listed players into a group based on specified conditions. With connection games problems, however, you must do this based on connections or characteristics of the different players as delineated in the set conditions: you are *connecting* the players to those characteristics.

There is a lot going on, so it's good to start by breaking the problem down into smaller, more manageable parts. The following systematic progression works well in sorting out the problem prior to tackling the questions:

- Begin by listing the various players. The players are often listed in a consecutive string, which makes this fairly simple.
- Identify and make note of the different characteristics possible for the various players.
- Where possible, match the different characteristics to specific players. Sometimes possible characteristics are listed in the negative (in an attempt to befuddle LSAT examinees). For instance, it could be phrased similarly to this: all players who have Characteristic Y cannot have Characteristic Z.

Consider the following example and practice applying the above steps:

> There are four students: Anna, Brandon, Charles, and Donita. These students dislike the following classes: algebra, biology, and P.E., consistent with the following:
>
> Each student dislikes at least one of the classes;
> No student dislikes all three classes;
> At least two, but not all four, of the students dislike biology;
> If Brandon dislikes a class, then Donita also dislikes that class;
> If a student does not like biology, then that student also dislikes algebra;
> Charles does not like algebra.

From reviewing the above example, it is easy to see how you could get your wires crossed as you go deeper into the questions (which can build on one another).

So, to apply the above steps, we first list out the players: Anna, Brandon, Charles, and Donita. Next, you make note of the various characteristics, which are, in this case, the classes the students do not like. Note the characteristics that are directly attributed to a particular player (Charles does not like algebra), as well as those that are indirectly attributed to a player (if Brandon dislikes a class, then so does Donita).

Once you have done this, you are prepared to face the types of questions that will be attached to the connection games problems, such as:

1. Determine which players must have a particular characteristic.
2. Determine which players could have a particular characteristic.
3. Determine which players definitely could not be connected to a particular characteristic.
4. Separate out which players must, must not, or could possibly be connected to the same characteristics as other players.

Skipping Problems: Some Advice

Because of the difficulty level encountered in Analytical Reasoning, some test takers make a strategic decision to skip some of the problems in this section of the LSAT in order to have more time to concentrate on a lower number of questions, hopefully maximizing the number of questions they answer correctly. This is a common strategy and, given how the LSAT is scored, and the severe time constraints of the Analytical Reasoning section, it can make a lot of sense to follow it. In other words, since you don't have enough time to give all the questions the attention needed to answer them, and since the LSAT score is based only on correct answers, it's quite logical to devote more time to a lower number of questions if it leads to you answering more questions correctly.

If you decide to employ this strategy, it's important for you to know that not all the Analytical Reasoning questions on the LSAT are of equal difficulty. All of them are difficult, of course, but some are less difficult than others, while some are more difficult. So which ones should you skip, and which ones should you focus on? Well, while some people would disagree, most test takers find that assigning setups are the hardest, ordering setups are the least difficult, and grouping setups fall somewhere in between. Also, you should not skip the first setup, as it is never the hardest one on the exam.

Another important consideration is that, generally speaking, setups that have more conditions are usually easier to answer than those with fewer rules. It may seem that the opposite would be true. This is probably due to the fact that reading and grasping more rules takes more time than does reading and grasping fewer rules. They say that appearances are often deceptive, and in this case they're right. It's not reading and grasping the rules that will take up most of your time on the Analytical Reasoning section; it's thinking about how to come up with the correct answer. The more information you have to start with, the fewer things you have to figure out in order to determine the right answer. So when it comes to solving problems quickly, the more conditions, the better.

Logical Reasoning Test

The Logical Reasoning (LR) section of the LSAT consists of two 35-minute exams with approximately 25 questions each. It's the part of the LSAT that most directly tests the skills you will use as a lawyer—comprehending and analyzing an argument and poking holes in it or, if it's valid, following the argument to its logical conclusion. When it comes to your LSAT score, *Logical Reasoning is twice as important as any other portion of the test*, because of the fact that the LSAT includes two LR sections, as opposed to only one 35-minute test for Reading Comprehension or Analytical Reasoning. So, even if you shine on the other sections, it is impossible to get a high score on the LSAT without doing well in Logical Reasoning.

Because of its importance and complexity, we will spend a lot of time discussing study tips for Logical Reasoning. We will break down the basic concepts, question types, underlying suppositions, issues, types of arguments and argumentation patterns, what distinguishes a weak argument from a strong one, and more, showing you how to logically take apart the argument piece-by-piece to determine the correct answer.

Throughout the Logical Reasoning section, keep the following general information in mind:

- There are 24–26 questions in each Logical Reasoning section; on most LSAT versions there are a total of 50–52 Logical Reasoning questions.
- The time factor in Logical Reasoning is not the same as in the Analytical Reasoning section, which is deliberately designed to make it extremely difficult to answer all the questions in the allotted time. The creators of the LSAT believe 35 minutes allows the average test taker enough time to complete the 24–26 questions on each Logical Reasoning exam, so it's best to start with the first question and work your way through.
- Your score depends on the number of correct answers—not the number of wrong ones—so you are not penalized for guessing.
- *You are not trying to determine whether the argument itself is correct, only whether or not it is logical.* That means that sometimes the correct answer to a question will contain a statement or information that is not actually true in the real word. As counterintuitive as it may seem, comprehending the relationship between the different facts and assumptions leading to that answer is more important than the objective accuracy of an argument or answer choice. Answer using only the information provided in the question. The opposite is also true—sometimes an *incorrect* answer choice will contain information that's true in the real world.
- Assuming you have studied the various types of arguments used for the Logical Reasoning section, the best approach is to begin by determining which type of question you are looking at. Accurately identifying the question type will be a big help in sorting correct answers from incorrect ones.

What's in the Logical Reasoning Section?

Just as in the Reading Comprehension portion of the LSAT, you'll be dealing with reading passages in the Logical Reasoning section. Don't worry, though; they aren't nearly as long or complex as the Reading Comprehension passages. Many will be under 10 lines long, virtually all of them will have less than a dozen lines, and you will usually encounter several that consist of no more than four or five lines. The passage itself is known as the **stimulus**, and is followed by a question. You may have seen the term **question stem** used in discussions of the LSAT, particularly in reference to the Logical Reasoning or Analytical Reasoning sections, and wondered what it means. Well, it just means the question itself, not including the answer choices. For simplicity's sake, we'll usually just refer to it as the **question** in this guide.

Sometimes the stimulus will be nothing more than a presentation of some different facts, but in most cases, it will contain an **argument**. Most people think of an argument as a verbal or written conflict between two people, some sort of heated dispute. Two strangers at a bar screaming at each other about politics would be said to be having an argument. However, that is not the meaning of the word in the world of logic and philosophy. On the LSAT, an argument is basically an attempt to persuade by presenting evidence. In an argument on the LSAT, the author states his case.

You will encounter all kinds of arguments on the exam. An argument may be logically flawed, or it may be perfectly logical. It may be weak or strong. Your task on this portion of the LSAT will be to rapidly and accurately comprehend the argument, and then analyze it in some way based on the criteria in the question. In some cases, you won't have much trouble doing so, but for most of the questions you'll have to do some serious reasoning to get to the right answer.

If the stimulus contains an argument, then no matter what kind of argument it is, it will consist of two basic elements – the **premise(s)**, and the **conclusion**. The conclusion is the point the author is trying to convince the reader of, while the premises constitute the evidence he provides to support his conclusion. In other words, an author's conclusion is the *what* of his argument, and the premises are the *why*. Here's an example of a short, concise argument:

Alice has a 4.0 GPA and she scored in the 99th percentile on the Medical College Admission Test, so she is certain to be admitted to an elite medical school.

The conclusion is that Alice should have no worries about being accepted by an elite medical school. The premises are that she has a 4.0 GPA and that her MCAT score is in the 99th percentile. Now, as we said, this is a very basic argument, so let's add some additional information:

Alice has a 4.0 GPA and she scored in the 99th percentile on the Medical College Admission Test, so she is certain to be admitted to an elite medical school. With her work and study habits she will be at the top of her class. When she graduates, she'll have her pick of residencies thanks to her prestigious degree and record. Obviously, Alice is going to have a hugely successful career in medicine.

This changes things quite a bit. The new argument, while not highly complex, is definitely more complex than the one in the first passage. Notice that the point the author was trying to express in the first passage is no longer his conclusion. His new conclusion is that Alice is going to have a very successful medical career. What happened to his previous conclusion? It has now become a **sub-conclusion**, which helps build the case for his actual conclusion. You will run into this kind of argument several times on the LSAT. It's important to be able to distinguish a sub-conclusion from a conclusion, so you must read carefully. Also, there's no rule in logic that says a conclusion must come at the end of the argument. Look at how we can rearrange this argument:

Alice is going to have a hugely successful career in medicine. She has a 4.0 GPA and she scored in the 99th percentile on the Medical College Admission Test, so she is certain to be admitted to an elite medical school. With her work and study habits she will be at the top of her class. When she graduates, she'll have her pick of residencies thanks to her prestigious degree and record.

This is making the very same argument as before, only worded differently. The conclusion is now in the first sentence, appearing before the sub-conclusion. So always keep in mind that the conclusion can appear anywhere in an argument. Furthermore, there can also be more than one sub-conclusion. Careful reading is just as critical on the Logical Reasoning portion of the LSAT as it is on the other sections.

Logical Reasoning Strategies and Tips

Here are some brief tips and guidelines for helping you do your best on this section:

Do NOT Read the Question First

You need to decide on a consistent strategy for attacking each Logical Reasoning problem long before you ever walk into the testing center. In fact, you should do this before you even begin taking practice tests. So, what's the best strategy? *Our strong recommendation is that you should always read the argument before reading the question.* It's important to note that this is the same approach we recommend you employ on the Reading Comprehension section of the LSAT. In fact, we say that one of the worst things you can do on the Reading Comprehension portion is to read the questions first and the passage second, even though this is a popular strategy. The same holds true for the Logical Reasoning section of the LSAT. Reading the question first will often cause you to be distracted or confused while you're reading the argument, and in almost all cases, you'll wind up having to read the question again anyway, wasting a lot of valuable time. Don't try to read the question first, and then the argument. You'll only slow yourself down, making it even harder to complete all of the questions in the very brief thirty-five minutes.

Opposites

Often, when two answer choices are a pair of direct opposites, one of them is correct. The paragraph or passage will often contain established relationships (e.g., when this goes up, that goes down). The question may ask you to draw conclusions from this and will give two similar answer choices that are opposites.

Example:

If other factors are held constant, then increasing the interest rate will lead to a ***decrease*** *in housing starts*

If other factors are held constant, then increasing the interest rate will lead to an ***increase*** *in housing starts*

Once you realize there are two answer choices that are opposites, you should examine them closely. One of the two is likely to be the correct answer. Of course, they often won't be as easy to spot as the two answer choices in this example. In many cases the wording of the two choices won't be nearly as similar to each other as is the case above. However, it's the meanings that are important, not the particular phrasing.

Watch Out for Red Herrings

Are you familiar with the term *red herring*? It's a literary device used by writers to mislead people into drawing a wrong conclusion about something or someone in the story. Novelists and scriptwriters often employ this device. For example, in a murder mystery, the dead man's butler may be subtly portrayed as scheming and greedy, leading many readers to conclude that he committed the murder. In the end, however, the grieving widow is revealed to be the actual culprit, the butler's putative greed and deceit notwithstanding.

Well, novelists and scriptwriters aren't the only people who regularly use red herrings in their line of work; so do the folks at the Law School Admission Council, who are responsible for creating the LSAT. In fact, creating red herrings is a huge part of their job. The designers of the exam deliberately create wrong answer choices that are very close to being correct. One of the most important duties of their job is to go to great lengths to attempt to convince you to choose the wrong answer, and, obviously, they wouldn't be very successful if none of the incorrect answer choices sounded plausible. If that were the case, all you would have to do would be go down the list and eliminate the four choices that are clearly implausible, and the only one left would be the correct answer. That kind of exam wouldn't be much of a challenge, obviously.

However, on most Logical Reasoning questions there will be three answer choices that aren't all that close to being correct, and only one that could really trip you up. That's because there simply aren't very many ways of coming up with an answer choice that sounds *almost* right, but isn't. An answer that's almost right but *not quite* has to strike the test taker as extremely plausible, and that makes it very difficult to create wrong answers that appear to be correct. So, for the most part, you should have no trouble picking out the blatantly incorrect answers. Once you've eliminated the obviously wrong answers, then you only have to choose between two possibilities. That's the good news. The bad news is that while eliminating three answer choices may make it a bit simpler to select the correct answer, it certainly doesn't make it a snap, because you'll now have to decide which of the two remaining answers is correct, and which one is an artfully constructed red herring.

There are several kinds of red herrings. Here are some that LSAT designers employ most often.

1. Taking Things to an Extreme

In many arguments, the LSAT writers will include an answer choice that takes a point made in the passage to an unjustified extreme. Consider this passage:

Many so-called conservatives are eager to have America go to war, while at the same time they condemn President Jones for running up massive federal deficits. This makes no sense. One of the historic foundational principles of conservatism is opposition to deficit spending on the part of the government. Well, President Jones is not to blame for these huge budget deficits; they are actually the fault of his allegedly conservative predecessor, President Smith, who hastily started a long and very expensive war without first exhausting all other options.

Given the statement above, which of the following must be true?
(A) President Jones is not a conservative
(B) The author of the passage is a liberal
(C) President Smith was a Republican
(D) People who are true conservatives should not be eager to go to war, because wars lead to budget deficits.
(E) Many people calling themselves conservative think going to war is more important than having a balanced budget.

As we mentioned earlier, on most arguments you should expect to find three answer choices that you can quickly dismiss. Let's look at each answer, starting with A. If the argument is correct, must it also be true that President Jones is not a conservative? No, not at all. We know that many professing conservatives are condemning Jones for the large deficits, but that doesn't mean that Jones is a liberal or a moderate. Many political partisans are more strident about condemning politicians of their own persuasion who fail to please them than they are about condemning politicians in other camps. Thus, there is absolutely nothing in the passage that means it must be true that President Jones is not a conservative. Therefore, A is out.

How about B, then—is it necessarily true that the author of the passage is a liberal? Again, the answer is no. There is nothing in the passage that requires us to draw the conclusion that the author is a liberal. He might well be, but he could also be a frustrated conservative. For that matter, he could be a moderate, or even an apolitical person, and this argument could be part of a larger "a pox on both their houses" article. So, B is easily dismissed.

Moving on to C, does it logically follow from the passage that the former president was a Republican? No, it does not. Now, of the three answers which are obviously wrong, this is the one that would be most likely to trip a few people up due to careless reading, and mentally bringing in real world facts to solve the problem. We know from the passage that President Smith was allegedly conservative. However, we know nothing of his party affiliation. While in the real world of American politics most people rightfully associate the label conservative with the Republican Party, that doesn't mean that there aren't some Democrats who call themselves conservatives. In fact, in the 1992 election, Bill Clinton and Al Gore won by selling themselves as conservative Democrats, in contrast to liberals such as Michael Dukakis and Walter Mondale. So, conservative does not have to mean Republican. Furthermore, the passage doesn't mention Republicans or Democrats at all. It could be describing a hypothetical future America in which neither party exists any longer. Thus, C is incorrect, too, and obviously so.

So, we have two answers left to choose from. Is D the right choice? Can we conclude from the passage that wars lead to budget deficits? Many people would select this answer. Would you? You should not, as the reasoning is faulty. In fact, it's a great example of how LSAT designers trip people up. Let's look at it more closely.

In this red herring, the test designers take a specific point, but then make far too much of it of it. They start with an inarguable fact from the passage – the author stated that President Jones shouldn't be blamed for the huge federal budget deficits during his tenure; the blame should actually be assigned to the man he succeeded, President Smith, who started an expensive war while he was in the White House. This is a perfectly reasonable argument because wars usually *are* very expensive, and in the recent history of America, they have certainly led to massive deficit spending. Also, for the purposes of the LSAT, we should assume the truth of the facts presented in an argument, unless instructed otherwise.

Furthermore, most conservatives favor fiscal restraint and generally oppose running up deficits. So, a very good case can be made that people who are true conservatives should have opposed President Smith's getting America into an expensive war before all other options had failed.

However, answer choice D goes much further than that. It says that *wars lead to budget deficits.* It doesn't say that wars *tend to* result in budget deficits, or that *most* wars in history have led to deficit spending. It makes a categorical statement that wars result in budget deficits. This is an If/Then statement. Remember, If/Then statements rarely appear on the Logical Reasoning exam in their pure form. They are usually implied. In this sentence, the phrase *because wars lead to budget deficits* contains this implied If/Then statement:

If a country goes to war, then it will experience budget deficits.

However, this does not logically follow from the information we have in the passage. There's nothing in the passage that tells us that all wars in history have caused budget deficits, or that all wars in the future will do so, let alone that war always leads to budget deficits. All we know from the passage is that huge federal deficits under President Jones followed a war started by President Smith. Does this mean that all wars, everywhere, at all times, lead to budget deficits? Is it possible to imagine a scenario where a country goes to war and doesn't experience budget deficits as a result?

Couldn't the government of a country conceivably fund a war without running up deficits by using budget surpluses left over from previous years, or by raising taxes, or a combination of both? Yes, it could. Isn't it also possible that if Nation A goes to war with Nation B, Nation B could surrender almost immediately, resulting in a very short and very inexpensive war, the cost of which could be entirely covered by Nation A's current military budget? Yes, that's certainly a possibility, too.

So, based on the information in the passage, we cannot say categorically that wars lead to budget deficits. The fact that President Smith's wars resulted in budget deficits does not mean that all wars *must* have that same effect. Therefore, D is incorrect, even though it seems to make sense. It's wrong because it goes to an extreme, by taking one occurrence of something and making it into a hard and fast rule.

Notice that this tactic of going to extremes works in the opposite direction, too. Instead of making a leap from something happening *in one case* to a rule about it happening *in every case*, the answer choice could just as easily call for the illogical conclusion that because something *didn't happen* in a specific case it *never happens* in any cases.

Watch carefully for categorical words in arguments and answer choices, such as *always, all, must, never, none, can't, only, absolutely, certainly*, etc. If one of these words shows up in an answer choice, it's usually incorrect, unless the argument also makes a similar categorical claim, either expressed or implied. If one of these kinds of words appears in the argument itself, then look for an answer choice that aligns with it.

Keep in mind, however, that a categorical statement can exist without using any of these tipoff words. In the example above, the word *all* doesn't appear in the critical phrase *because wars lead to budget deficits.* It is clearly implied, however, because there are no modifiers such as *some* or *most* in the phrase that would limit the statement as applying only to a number of wars less than all.

The correct answer is E. Notice that it uses the word *many* as a modifier, just as the author does, and doesn't make a blanket statement about all conservatives. If we assume the argument is true, that means that the first sentence of the argument must be true, which logically leads to the conclusion found in E.

2. IRRELEVANCY | SIMILAR LANGUAGE | PARALLEL REASONING

You'll run across many answer choices that seem to be correct, but which are actually completely irrelevant to the argument.

You'll also find answer choices that attempt to trip you up by using language that is similar to some of the language used in the passage.

You will also come across incorrect answers that seem right because they employ parallel reasoning.

Sometimes you'll encounter answers that combine two or more red herrings. Here's an example combining Irrelevancy, Similar Language, and Parallel Reasoning.

Let's return to the same argument, but change it up a little at the end:

Many so-called conservatives seem eager to have America go to war, while at the same time they condemn President Jones for running up massive federal deficits. This makes no sense. One of the historic foundational principles of conservatism is opposition to deficit spending on the part of the government. Well, President Jones is not to blame for these huge budget deficits; they are actually the fault of his allegedly conservative predecessor, President Smith, who hastily started a long and very expensive war without first exhausting all other options. So-called conservatives who support rushing into war are not real conservatives.

Now, suppose the question was:

Which of the following, if true, would most strengthen the argument?

And suppose this was one of the answer choices:

Historically, conservatives have strongly condemned homosexuality, but today many so-called conservatives actually support the legalization of same-sex marriage.

Would this statement strengthen the argument? At first glance, it might seem to. The fact that people who support same-sex marriage would not have been regarded as conservatives in past generations certainly seems to go along with what the author is saying. Didn't he assert that many self-proclaimed conservatives have moved away from their foundational principles? If conservatives used to strongly oppose homosexuality, but today many conservatives approve of same-sex marriage, isn't that evidence that many of today's self-proclaimed conservatives aren't true conservatives, strengthening the author's argument? Many people would select this answer choice.

However, the author's argument isn't that many self-proclaimed conservatives aren't true conservatives because they have moved away from *some* foundational principles. He only mentions one foundational principle of conservatism—opposition to deficit spending—and that is the only standard he employs for determining if someone is a true conservative. Here is his argument in syllogism form:

The recent war led to budget deficits.

True conservatives oppose budget deficits.

Anyone who is eager to go to war is not a true conservative.

The author's argument is very narrowly focused, and does not address any other aspect of conservatism besides opposition to deficit spending. We have no idea if he believes that self-described conservatives have moved away from any other foundational principles of conservatism, or if he even believes that opposition to homosexuality is a foundational principle of conservatism. So, this answer choice doesn't strengthen the author's argument at all. What conservatives believe now or used to believe about homosexuality or same-sex marriage has absolutely no bearing on the author's argument, which is that anyone who is eager to go to war is not a true conservative. This answer choice not only fails to strengthen the argument, but it is completely irrelevant. Nonetheless, it would fool many test takers.

Why is this answer choice so deceptive? Why is it that many people would think it strengthens the author's argument when, in actuality, it's completely irrelevant? There are several reasons this answer would fool many test takers. First, it's factually true—nearly all conservatives of past generations regarded homosexuality as extremely immoral, but these days many reject that view, and even endorse same-sex marriage. This is enough by itself to trick many examinees into choosing this answer.

We can't stress enough that you must not take real world factual accuracy into consideration at all on this portion of the LSAT; you must think of yourself as being in a self-contained universe while you answer questions on the Logical Reasoning section of the exam. Ignore everything outside of that universe, because the only facts that matter are the ones you're dealing with on the test, and some of them would be wrong in the real world. You must constantly be on guard against this tendency to work factual accuracy into the answer selection process, because it's very easy to fall into it without even realizing it.

Another reason the answer choice is so deceptive is that it uses some of the same language the author uses when it mentions *self-proclaimed conservatives.* This is the exact same phrasing that the author of the passage uses in the first sentence. Many test takers would not even catch this, but their brains would nonetheless make a connection between this answer and the argument without realizing it, simply because it uses the same phrasing.

Furthermore, the phrasing is pejorative, as *so-called* is used only to describe someone we don't regard as authentic, as the real deal. No one would use the phrase "so-called expert" to describe someone they regard as a real expert. Using this phrasing, both the passage and the answer choice convey the idea that there are a lot of phony conservatives running around out there. Because our minds look for reasons to make connections, and because when there's one connection there are often more, it's easy to mistakenly conclude that since the answer choice supports the author's view that many people calling themselves conservatives are no such thing, it also supports his main argument. (Again, this would not necessarily be a conscious thought process.)

Finally, the wrong answer employs parallel reasoning. Both the answer and the passage say that many people calling themselves conservatives aren't actual conservatives, and they both do so based on what the writer sees as a failure or refusal on the part of these people to measure up to a certain standard, by not taking a position that all (or nearly all) conservatives used to take. Because our brains are constantly looking for patterns and connections, and because these two arguments are so similar in their logic, many people will conclude that the answer choice strongly supports the passage, but that's not true. It is a similar argument in its form, but it does nothing to strengthen the author's conclusion.

Benchmark

After you read the first answer choice, decide if it sounds correct or not. If it doesn't, move on to the next answer choice. If it does, make a mental note of it. This doesn't mean that you've definitely selected it as your answer choice; it just means that it's the best you've seen thus far. Go ahead and read the next choice. If the next choice is worse than the one you've already selected, keep going to the next answer choice. If the next choice is better than the choice you've already selected, make it your tentative answer. Repeat this process until you've gone through all five answer choices.

The first answer choice that you select becomes your standard. Every other answer choice must be benchmarked against that standard. That choice is correct until proven otherwise by another answer choice beating it out. Once you've decided that no other answer choice seems as good, do one final check to ensure that it answers the question posed.

New Information

Correct answers will usually contain only information contained in the paragraph and/or question. Rarely will completely new information be inserted into a correct answer choice. Occasionally the new information may be related in a manner that LSAT is asking for you to interpret, but this is rare.

Example:

The argument above is dependent upon which of the following assumptions?

A. Scientists have used Charles's Law to interpret the relationship.

If Charles's Law is not mentioned at all in the referenced paragraph and argument, then it is very unlikely that this choice is correct. All of the information needed to answer the question is provided for you, and so you should not have to make guesses that are unsupported or select answer choices that refer to unknown information that cannot be analyzed.

Logical Reasoning Basic Concept #1: Conditions

Both Logical Reasoning exams on the LSAT contain a variety of problem types, each with its own nuance and ideal solution strategy. Even so, a thorough comprehension of certain foundational concepts will make it much easier to correctly answer the questions regardless of the argument type.

The first foundational concept involves understanding how LSAT test writers make use of two types of conditions: **necessary conditions** and **sufficient conditions**. You'll need an understanding of these two concepts, and the differences between them, in order to do well in Logical Reasoning.

Necessary conditions are those that *must* be present in order for a certain outcome to occur. For instance, in order for a forest to catch fire and burn down, there must be an ignition source. So an ignition source is a necessary condition for a forest fire. A necessary condition is anything that's absolutely required to be present in order for something else to be present. In other words, if *B* can't exist unless *A*, then *A* is a necessary condition for *B*. Here's another example of a necessary condition:

All pregnant people are females.

Since a person cannot be pregnant without being a female, being a female is a necessary condition for being pregnant.

On the other hand, a sufficient condition is enough to bring about an outcome, but is not the only condition that can do so. Returning to the case of forest fires, for example, lightning strikes can cause forest fires. So, a lightning strike is enough, in and of itself, to cause a forest fire. It's not a necessary condition, however, because it's not the only way a forest fire can be started. So, while a lightning strike is not a necessary condition of a forest fire, it is a sufficient condition.

Going back to our second example, is being a female a sufficient condition for being pregnant? No; because other conditions must also be present, such as having undergone puberty, having been inseminated, etc. So, while being a female is a necessary condition for being pregnant, it is not a sufficient condition.

Of course, on the actual Logical Reasoning exam, few conditional statements will be expressed as clearly and succinctly as our example statement about being pregnant. In most cases there won't be a sentence that directly states *all members of A are members of B*, or something similar. In fact, there probably won't be any part of the argument that makes any kind of direct conditional statement. If an argument contains a conditional statement, it will usually be implied, meaning you'll have to reason it out for yourself. The arguments that have conditional statements, whether expressed or implied, will include them as part of a larger passage. You will need to ignore the noise, or the nonessential details of the passage, so you can distill the argument (or the answer choice) down to its essence in order to find the underlying conditional statement.

If/Then Statements

Conditional statements can be easily understood and analyzed when put into If/Then form. Doing so can also help you spot logical fallacies, which is what the Logical Reasoning exam is all about. Here's an example of an If/Then statement.

If it's raining, then Mr. Jones will be indoors.

The first part of the statement (the If part), is called the hypothesis. The second part (the Then part) is called the conclusion.

The statement is straightforward and uncomplicated. It's easy to understand, and hardly anyone would have any trouble with it. Things can get tricky, however, when we change some of the elements up. For example:

If Mr. Jones is indoors, then it's raining.

This is the *converse* of the original statement. But does it logically follow from the original statement? In other words, can we reason logically from the first statement and come up with this statement? No, we cannot. There could be any number of reasons Mr. Jones is indoors. He may be ill. He may be sleeping. He may be surfing the Internet. We cannot say with certainty that, based on the original statement, because Mr. Jones is indoors it must be raining. It does not say that rain is the only condition which causes Mr. Jones to stay indoors. In other words, rain is a sufficient condition for Mr. Jones to be indoors, but it's not a necessary condition. *The converse of a conditional statement may or may not be true.*

Now let's look at the *inverse* of the original statement:

If it's not raining, then Mr. Jones will not be indoors.

Once again, the question we need to answer is this—does this logically follow from the initial conditional statement? No, it does not. Just as with the converse, there are a multitude of reasons Mr. Jones might be indoors. If this inverse conditional statement were true, then Mr. Jones would be required to be outside any time it's not raining, no matter what time it is, or what activity he's engaged in. *The inverse of a conditional statement may or may not be true.*

Now, let's look at one more change to the elements of the statement.

If Mr. Jones is not indoors, then it's not raining.

This is the *contrapositive* of the original conditional statement. Does it logically follow from it? Yes, it does. If Mr. Jones is indoors every time it's raining, then if he is not indoors it cannot be raining. *The contrapositive of a conditional statement is always true.*

Now, when we say that the inverse and converse of a conditional statement may or may not be true, and that the contrapositive of a conditional statement is always true, we're using *true* in the sense that you'll need to understand it for the Logical Reasoning exam. Obviously, it's hard to believe that there could actually be a person alive who has never been caught in the rain, and for the rest of his life will never be outside when it's raining. We're simply taking for granted that the conditional statement itself is true, so when we say that the contrapositive is true, we mean that it logically follows from the conditional statement.

We're not at all concerned with the real-life factual accuracy of a statement, nor should you be when you take the LSAT. *Do not fall into the trap of measuring Logical Reasoning arguments by their factual accuracy.* You must judge them only on their logical consistency. Forget the real world when you sit down for the LSAT. Don't underestimate your tendency to go into fact-based mode. It's easy to think you won't fall into this trap, but we're so used to fact-based exams that it's very difficult for some people to avoid falling back on their experience and knowledge on the Logical Reasoning exam.

Logical Reasoning Basic Concept #2: Reasonableness

Not all arguments on the Logical Reasoning exam will involve If/Then statements. In many cases, you will need to evaluate an argument on the basis of how reasonable it is. That is, you will need to ask yourself if the conclusion makes sense based on the evidence presented. Or is the author making an untenable argument, because he didn't present sufficient evidence to support his conclusion? This represents much of what you'll be doing on the Logical Reasoning portion of the LSAT.

This is what juries in criminal trials do, of course. A prosecutor makes a case against a defendant, and the jury weighs the evidence she presents. If they believe that the evidence is strong enough that there can be no reasonable doubt that the defendant committed the act, they find him guilty. In most *civil* trials, though, the burden of proof is not as heavy—there only needs to be a preponderance of evidence in order to assign liability. In other words, in a civil trial the plaintiff only has to present evidence that indicates that it's more likely than not that the other party committed the act he is accused of.

On the other end of the scale, we all run across people making completely unwarranted leaps of logic on a regular basis, especially while we're surfing the Internet or watching cable news talk shows. In those environments it's common to see people making outlandish claims based on very little evidence, or none at all:

The federal government's response to Hurricane Katrina proves that George Bush is a racist who hates black people.

Anyone who supports raising the minimum wage is a Communist who wants to destroy the American way of life.

Of course, most of the arguments we encounter on a daily basis fall somewhere in the middle of the two extremes of beyond a reasonable doubt, and utterly nonsensical. Consider this:

Jenny said the new Italian café is fantastic. We should go there for lunch tomorrow.

Many people would not consider that to be an argument, but it actually is. Your friend has reached a conclusion (we should eat lunch at the new restaurant tomorrow) and is trying to convince you that his conclusion is correct by presenting the evidence he bases it on (Jenny raved about the place). Is this a reasonable argument? That depends on a lot of different factors. How long have you known

Jenny? Do you trust her judgment when it comes to food and restaurants? How much does she know about Italian food? Does her cousin own the Italian café? Is the speaker telling the truth about what Jenny said?

If you trust the person who told you this, and you think Jenny has a good track record when it comes to restaurant recommendations, then this argument would probably strike you as quite reasonable. The fact that Jenny vouched for the place would be enough evidence for you to agree with your friend's conclusion that you should have lunch there tomorrow.

Now, consider this argument:

Jenny knows good food, and she loves that Mexican restaurant on 23rd street that's for sale. We should buy it and franchise it.

Is this a reasonable argument? In other words, has your friend presented enough evidence to support his conclusion? Even if Jenny is something of a connoisseur, is the fact that she likes the food at a restaurant sufficient evidence for agreeing that putting tens of thousands of dollars (or more) into an extremely risky business venture is a good idea? No, not really. Now, the idea behind the argument is not completely illogical—after all, people generally buy or start a business in hopes of making a lot of money, popular restaurants tend to make a lot of money, good food is one of the main factors in why restaurants become popular, and Jenny, who is a very good judge of food, says the restaurant's food is very good. So, there certainly might be some legitimate reasons to *consider* the idea of buying the restaurant.

However, there are many other factors to consider before making such a decision that your friend hasn't even mentioned. Why is it for sale? What do you and your friend know about running a restaurant? How much is the asking price? Even if you were to decide that buying the restaurant is a good idea, do you really want to be in a business partnership? If so, would your friend make a good business partner? These are just a few of the dozens of questions you would need to answer before agreeing to buy the restaurant with your friend. So, while there might be a good idea at its root, the argument isn't reasonable, because your friend hasn't presented nearly enough evidence to support it.

Logical Reasoning Basic Concept #3: Causality

Examining causality, or what most of us refer to as cause and effect, should help you determine the relative strength or weakness of a particular argument. Given that it is possible that *A* caused *B*, you then have to determine whether it is likely that *A* caused *B* or if there are other causal agents that are more likely to have caused *B*. For example:

The store that burned down didn't seem to be doing well. I'm sure the owner torched it for the insurance money.

Is this a reasonable conclusion as to what caused the fire that burned the store down? No, it really isn't. It is an awfully long logical leap to say that because a store that burned down didn't appear to be doing well the owner probably set fire to it. For one thing, how do we know what kind of financial condition the store was in? Let's say we arrived at the conclusion that the store was struggling because we rarely saw customers going in or out.

Well, there could be a lot of reasons for that. Maybe the only time we passed the store was on our way to and from work every weekday, and the store's peak sales occurred at night and on the weekends. It's also quite possible that, like many brick and mortar businesses these days, the store made far more money from selling merchandise over the Internet than it did from walk-in traffic, but still had enough local customers that it was profitable to keep the doors open.

It's also quite conceivable that the business was only somewhat profitable but, for whatever reason, the owner didn't need the store to make a lot of money and was quite content with the income he was bringing in. There are a great number of reasons why our notion that the store was in bad financial shape might be mistaken. However, even if our opinion about the financial health of the store is actually correct, it's still extremely unreasonable to conclude from that fact that the owner burned the store down to collect the insurance money. Tens of thousands of businesses go under every year in America, but commercial arson is pretty rare.

Now, let's add some more information:

The store that burned down didn't seem to be doing well. I'm sure the owner torched it for the insurance money. After all, he did spend three years in prison during the late 90's for hiring a guy to burn down another store he owned.

Hmm...this information certainly makes our conclusion that the owner torched the place look a lot less unreasonable, as the storeowner has a history involving commercial arson. However, while our conclusion is not nearly as reckless as it was before, it's still not entirely reasonable to definitively conclude that he burned the store down. Many, many people who have been paroled after a conviction for conspiring to commit commercial arson never do such a thing again.

Let's add some more details:

The store that burned down didn't seem to be doing well. I'm sure the owner torched it for the insurance money. After all, he did spend three years in prison during the late 90's for hiring a guy to burn down another store he owned. On top of that, he owes $300,000 in gambling debts to some pretty unsavory characters. Furthermore, several local ex-cons have told the police that the owner offered them money to burn the place down. He also took out commercial insurance policies with three different companies last month. And there's no getting around the fact that surveillance cameras from a nearby business show him carrying what looks like a can of gasoline behind the store just before the fire started.

These new details completely change things. Assuming that the information is all true, is it still possible that the owner had nothing to do with his store burning down? Well, it may be theoretically conceivable, but it's virtually impossible for a rational person to believe. Based on the new information, it's not only reasonable to believe that he torched the place, it would be unreasonable to doubt it. The more evidence we have that supports a conclusion that *A* caused *B*, the more reasonable that conclusion is. At first, we had very little evidence to support the idea that the store's owner burned it down. However, as we were presented with more evidence, the link between *A* and *B* became pretty much indisputable. Of course, the cause and effect relationships you'll encounter on the Logical Reasoning section will be somewhere between these two extremes, but you'll use the same kind of reasoning process to analyze them.

In many instances, the test preparers will link a certain progression of evidence with a conclusion the evidence doesn't entirely support. The information given may be factual and reasonable up to a point, yet somewhere in the argument the examiners have made a leap beyond the bridge they were building with the evidence—or have loaded that bridge with more weight than it can support.

Consider this argument, remembering that you are only meant to determine whether, in this instance, the argument supports the conclusion (regardless of your personal opinion about the topic):

In the United States, over six million middle and high school students read significantly below grade level. American fifteen-year-olds rank twenty-eighth out of forty countries in mathematics and nineteenth in science. Clearly, Americans are not spending enough on public schooling for their children.

For a multitude of reasons, many people would take this argument at face value, accepting the underlying assumption that all systems work better when they are given more financial support. That would be unreasonable, however, because there is very little evidence provided to support the conclusion. How much are we spending per student currently? How does that compare to what higher-ranking nations are spending? How is that money apportioned within the system? If the amount of money being spent isn't the issue, what are other countries doing that we are not? Has our ranking ever been higher and, if so, what were we doing then that we are not currently? In short, is lack of funding ultimately the primary cause of our poor scoring? If you were told the United States is tied for first in terms of spending per student, would you begin looking for other causes? These are all questions which must be considered before deciding that America doesn't spend enough on public schooling, and there are many more.

In the end, there may or may not be a link between the money we're spending on education and the test scores our students are achieving. The point is that accepting the argument requires you to make a huge mental leap in order to justify a conclusion that is not fully supported with the supporting statements. Also note (once again) that the LSAT designers count on the fact that you'll have a certain amount of ingrained bias in favor of a widely-held point of view. They take advantage of this to try to keep you from noticing the logical relationships that have been left out. Many test takers unintentionally supply the missing logical connections as a result of personal bias and lazy reasoning, and thus answer the question incorrectly.

Logical Reasoning Basic Concept #4: Acknowledging the Unknown

In our everyday verbal exchanges with others, it's quite common to pretend to know more than we do. There are several reasons we do this, among them a desire to avoid admitting ignorance of the topic at hand. We're not comfortable admitting that we're unable to connect all the dots someone else is presenting as a complete picture. Sometimes we're afraid we may have missed something, particularly if everyone else is nodding along in agreement, and we feel like we're the only one who doesn't know what is going on. You're eating lunch with a group of friends in the dining hall when another friend walks up and says "Oh, man, have you heard Adele's new song? Isn't it her best one yet?" All your friends are chiming in about how much they love it, and you're nodding your head and making statements to the same effect, despite the fact that you had no idea Adele even had a new single out. For that matter, some of your friends are probably faking it, too. We all do this sort of thing, and we do it constantly.

Well, that skill may work in conversation, at least occasionally, but it will get you nowhere on the LSAT. In fact, part of what the Logical Reasoning section of the LSAT is testing for is the ability to recognize and acknowledge what you do not know—to be fully aware of missing links, disconnected information, and facts that are irrelevant to the key issues.

Take a look at the following example:

Maude hates the city. Last year she moved her family to Montana.

The connection of statements makes it easy to conclude that Maude's reason for moving to a wide-open state like Montana is her hatred of the city. But is that really correct? Do you have enough evidence to conclude that is the case?

Casually linking the ideas in conversation is fine, but it will get you in trouble on the LSAT. Consider instead the universe of facts you don't know in this scenario. Using the analogy of a circle, what we do know fits inside the circle. What we don't know is everything outside that curving line.

First, what we do know: Maude's strong dislike of the city, where she moved, that she has a family of some sort, and very general timing of the move.

What we don't know: that's a much, much longer list. Does she hate all cities or one particular city? Why does she despise them (or it)? Was her move to Montana related to this preference or to some other reason, such as a job change or an urgent family situation? Is she trying to put distance between herself and someone from a failed relationship? Is she happily married, but seeking lots of room for her seven children to run around? Did she feel an urge to hop from state to state alphabetically and she just finished Missouri? What is her family made up of (kids, husband, cats?) and does its relevance in this statement go beyond the incidental? Obviously, we could go on and on.

The point is that there are many, many unknowns between the two statements above. Although some assumptions may be fairly reasonable given the information, and others may be a complete reach, it is still important to comprehend that they are assumptions and are not, in fact, *known*.

Logical Reasoning Basic Concept #5: Spotting Incomplete Arguments

One aspect of LSAT problem solving that we run into over and over is an argument that is somehow incomplete. This can lead to leaps in logic and incorrect assumptions—filling in the blanks. To the test preparers, any specific subject knowledge you may have is substantially less important than the mental skills you will use to identify underlying assumptions and missing pieces. So they will often deliberately pair a statement with a conclusion that doesn't quite match the given evidence, just to see how you deal with it.

First, you should bring to bear skills noted in Basic Concept #4: be aware of what you don't know in a given scenario. Don't assume facts. But here we take that skill one step further. Not only should you recognize what information is missing, you should also be able to identify the underlying assumption attempting to link the two. The following statement is presented to illustrate the point:

Merla's fingernail was chipped, so she stopped at the library.

Huh? In this case, it's obvious that there are missing links between the initial statement and the accompanying conclusion. What do Merla's nails have to do with stopping at the library? If we were provided additional information, like that a nail-care seminar is taking place at the library, this might make more sense, but there is certainly no obvious link between the two thoughts.

However, it is unlikely the LSAT will employ such an obviously unrelated pairing. Try a more subtle example, like the one shown below:

A well-educated citizenry is required to maintain a free society. Robert has perfect attendance at school, so he must be well educated.

As above, it's important to first realize what you do not know. It may be reasonable to assume or it may even be true that Robert is well educated. However, you can't deduce that with any certainty from the above information. We would additionally need to know what is meant by a good education, the steps involved in procuring one (presumably it requires more than merely showing up for school), and how Robert measures up against those standards.

One way the LSAT may test your skills in spotting incomplete arguments is by asking you to identify the assumption in the given passage. In this case, you'd be looking for an answer choice like this:

b. Consistent school attendance results in a good education.

Or you might be asked which statement would most weaken the assumption underlying the author's conclusion. In that case, the correct answer could be something like this:

d. Some of our nation's founders, who were very learned men, never formally attended school.

First, identify what is incomplete in the argument. Dealing with the rest of the problem is easy after that.

The Most Common Question Types

Author's Main Point or Purpose

You should expect to see some questions about the author's main point or purpose on the Logical Reasoning section of the LSAT, as they are quite common. (Sometimes you'll be asked about the main idea; this is the same thing as the main point.) They are also among the easiest questions to answer correctly. In part that's because the passages in Logical Reasoning are so short; there's really no way to express several important ideas in so few words. Some of them might be harder than others, but in general, they're usually the questions that test takers have the least amount of trouble with in this section. It's also because the question itself is so straightforward and easy to understand. Every argument you'll come across on the exam has essentially two parts—a conclusion and one or more premises. Premises are what the author bases his conclusion on. They're the facts or opinions he marshals in support of his conclusion. The conclusion and the main point are always the same thing, so once you've found the author's conclusion you've found the main idea. The *main point* is what the author is trying to say, while the *primary purpose* is what he hopes to accomplish by saying it.

Review Video: Purpose of an Author
Visit mometrix.com/academy and enter code: 497555

Here's an argument that features a Main Point question.

Professional sports associations must make some major changes if they want to stay in business. Drug use, violent crime, and irresponsible behavior are rampant in the NFL, NBA, and MLB and have been for years. It used to be that when people would think of professional athletes, they thought of outstanding people like Willie Mays, Hank Aaron, Roberto Clemente, Oscar Robertson, and Walter Payton. Now they are more likely to think of Mark McGwire, Jose Canseco, Barry Bonds, O. J. Simpson, Ray Lewis, and Rae Carruth. If something isn't done to get people like this out of professional sports, many fans will stop buying tickets.

Which one of the following is the main point of the passage?

(A) There are a lot of people of bad character in professional sports.
(B) People expect professional athletes to be good role models for children.
(C) Pro sports leagues must take drastic action against illegal and immoral conduct of athletes.
(D) Steroid use continues to be out of control in professional sports.
(E) Today's athletes don't possess the same moral caliber of past generations of athletes.

The author clearly believes, and provides some evidence to back up his belief, that *there are a lot of people of bad character in professional sports.* Is that his main point, though? Let's not decide just yet, and keep going.

Does the author say that *people expect professional athletes to be good role models for children*? No, he does not, although that is certainly a reasonable inference of something the author believes. Of course, the author's main point can sometimes be implied as opposed to clearly stated. However, although this does seem like something he would feel strongly about, it certainly isn't his main point.

How about the statement that steroid use has been and continues to be out of control in professional sports, or that today's athletes don't possess the same moral caliber of past generations of athletes? Clearly the author strongly believes the latter, and probably believes the former, but he doesn't mention steroids specifically; only drugs in general. At any rate, neither one is his main point.

His main point is that *pro sports leagues must take drastic action against illegal and immoral conduct of athletes.* This is almost a simple restatement of the first sentence of the passage, but not quite. The first sentence says that professional sports groups need to make major changes if they want to stay in business, while the next section of the article is about illegal and immoral conduct by athletes. It's clear that the major changes he recommends revolve around the bad behavior of athletes. (By the way, on the Logical Reasoning section of the LSAT, the first sentence of the passage is often the author's conclusion, although by no means is this always the case.)

INFERENCE

Inference questions are also common on the Logical Reasoning section of the LSAT. They are more nuanced than Main Point questions, as they require you to read between the lines or put two and two together. They might ask you to determine what the author would agree or disagree with, based on the passage, even though there are no direct statements in the stimulus either for or against the position in an answer choice. Or they might ask you what a reasonable reader could infer from the passage, or what the author implied in the passage. *Imply* and *infer*, of course, are flip sides of the same coin—an author implies something by suggesting it without saying it directly. A reader infers something by forming a conclusion about something the author has not actually stated, by making logical deductions from one or more things he *has* stated. These questions can be phrased in various ways:

The researchers would most likely concur with which one of the following?

The Senator would be least likely to agree with which one of the following?

The argument most strongly supports which one of the following?

Which one of the following can be properly inferred from the passage above?

Review Video: Inference
Visit mometrix.com/academy and enter code: 379203

Here is an argument followed by a typical Inference question:

When you get right down to it, there are only two basic approaches to playing no limit hold 'em poker tournaments—long ball and small ball. Long ball is based on playing very few hands, but making large bets to either drive out opponents when bluffing or to build a huge pot when holding a strong hand. Small ball players take the opposite approach—they get involved in lots of pots by making small bets before the flop, hoping to make a great hand and trap their opponents or to bluff them out of the pot with nothing. Both approaches have their advantages and disadvantages. Choosing which one to use comes down to personal preference.

The author would most likely agree that:

(A) The World Series of Poker tournament has gotten too large and takes too long
(B) All poker players need to be skilled at both approaches to the game
(C) Long ball players tend to win more tournaments
(D) Small ball play is better suited for introverts
(E) Bluffing is an essential skill for poker tournament success

The first answer is obviously wrong because it's completely irrelevant—the author says nothing about the size or length of the World Series of Poker or any other poker tournaments, and there's nothing in the passage to justify this inference.

How about *all poker players need to be skilled at both approaches to the game*? No; nothing like this is either stated or implied, either.

Does the author believe that *long ball players tend to win more tournaments*? No; if he did believe that, why would he say that choosing a style depends on personal preferences? If the long ball approach led to more success in tournaments, surely, he would believe that that should be a major factor in choosing a playing style, and would recommend that approach to the game.

Would the author likely agree that *small ball play is better suited for introverts*? So far, this is the only answer that merits any consideration at all. After all, the author does say that choice of playing styles comes down to personal preference. However, he says absolutely nothing to indicate that he believes that small ball is better suited for introverts. This answer would trip a lot of people up because introverts tend to be shy and quiet, and the long ball style is highly aggressive, so it's natural for our minds to think the long ball style would be a poor match for introverts. However, there's no necessary correlation between personality and playing style and since the author doesn't say that he sees any connection between the two, we can't conclude that he would agree with this statement.

By process of elimination, that leaves *bluffing is an essential skill for poker tournament success*, which is the correct answer. We know that this is the right answer because all the others are wrong, but we can also verify it using logical deduction. The author says that there are only two basic approaches to playing poker tournaments, and then he describes each one, and both include bluffing. In other words, there are no playing styles that don't include bluffing. This means that he would have to agree that bluffing is an essential skill for poker tournament success.

Underlying Assumption

Another common question you'll encounter on the Logical Reasoning exam will ask you to select the answer which contains an assumption the author is relying on to make his argument. It's important to note that an assumption is *not* one of the author's stated premises, or the reasons he gives in support of his conclusion. Assumptions will never actually appear in the passage. Think of them as the unwritten premises standing alongside or behind the author's stated premises, which are the reasons he gives in support of his conclusion.

For example, in the argument, the author may conclude *D*, based on *C* and *B*. However, *B* or *C* actually hinges on *A* being true, even though the author never mentions *A*. So, *A* is an assumption the author is relying on in order to make his case. It's important to keep in mind that assumptions are always unstated, because on most of these kinds of questions at least one of the answer choices will be a slight rewording of one of the author's stated premises. It will be incorrect, because if the author is stating something, he is not assuming it, by definition. Also, while you will only be asked to pick out one, there will always be many, many assumptions underlying an argument. Consider this argument:

O. J. Simpson is a murderer. Murderers don't deserve recognition and honor. Simpson should be removed from the NFL Hall of Fame.

What assumptions is the author relying on? Several, actually, but here are just a few:

Media accounts of Simpson's activities just prior to and immediately after the murders of his ex-wife and her companion can be trusted.

Simpson wasn't framed for murder by racists in the Los Angeles Police Department.

He wasn't framed for murder by a corrupt prosecuting attorney's office.

The 12 jurors who found him not guilty were either incompetent or dishonest.

He (the author) has the capacity, at least in this case, to determine that someone is guilty of murder even though a jury has acquitted him.

Simpson is still in the NFL Hall of Fame.

Being in the NFL Hall of Fame is an honor.

We could go on and on, but that's plenty. These are all assumptions the author is relying on to be true if his argument is to hold water, even if he isn't consciously aware of all of them. If any of the above assumptions are wrong, then his argument falls apart.

That will always be the case if you have chosen the correct answer on an Assumptions question—if the author's argument doesn't fall apart if the assumption *isn't* true, then the answer is incorrect.

Because any time an argument *relies* on an assumption, if the assumption is turned on its head, then the argument *must* fall apart.

Let's return to a previous argument:

Professional sports associations must make some major changes if they want to stay in business. Drug use, violent crime, and irresponsible behavior are rampant in the NFL, NBA, and MLB and have been for years. It used to be that when people would think of professional athletes, they thought of outstanding people like Willie Mays, Hank Aaron, Roberto Clemente, Oscar Robertson, and Walter Payton. These days people are more likely to think of Mark McGwire, Jose Canseco, Barry Bonds, O. J. Simpson, Ray Lewis, and Rae Carruth. If something isn't done to get people like this out of professional sports, many people will stop buying tickets.

Which one of the following is an assumption on which this argument relies?

(A) A large number of professional athletes are criminals or drug users.
(B) Sports commentators are getting increasingly fed up with bad behavior by pro athletes.
(C) In the past, the media helped cover up the immoral behavior of famous athletes.
(D) Many people who buy tickets for sporting events base their decision to do so in part on the good behavior of athletes.
(E) No athletes who use steroids have legal prescriptions for them.

Let's examine each answer choice.

A large number of professional athletes are criminals or drug users. Is this an assumption the author relies on? No. How do we know he's not assuming this? Because he states it expressly in the argument when he says that drug use and violent crime are rampant in the three big professional sports. An assumption, by definition, cannot be something that is stated in the argument.

Is he assuming that *sports commentators are getting increasingly fed up with bad behavior by pro athletes*? Well, if he is, there's really nothing in the argument to indicate that he's doing so. He doesn't mention sports commentators, writers, or analysts, and there's nothing in the passage that implies sports writers in general are getting tired of immorality and criminality on the part of the athletes they cover. While it's certainly possible that the author is himself a professional sports commentator, even if he is, he doesn't claim to be speaking for sports commentators in general, and the passage gives us no basis for inferring that other commentators share his view. Also, when in doubt, you should always run the reversal test of an assumption. So, ask yourself this—if this statement is wrong, would the author's argument fall apart? In other words, if sports commentators *aren't* getting more and more fed up with immoral and criminal athletes, would it ruin his case? No, it would not, because his argument is about the leagues losing revenue due to fed up *fans,* not sports commentators. Reversing the assumption doesn't destroy the argument, so this cannot be the correct answer.

In the past, the media helped cover up the immoral behavior of famous athletes. Does the author assume this in making his argument? No, he does not. If anything, he takes the opposite view, because he seems to believe that athletes of yesteryear really were better behaved than today's athletes, not that they were just as immoral but the media covered it up.

Many people who buy tickets for sporting events base their decision to do so in part on the good behavior of athletes. Does the author's argument rely on this assumption? Well, this answer certainly looks promising. The author argues that the major sports leagues must take serious action concerning the rampant bad behavior among its athletes if they want to stay in business. He says that, unlike in the past, when people today think of athletes, they think of drug users and violent criminals, and then he asks how long they will continue to keep buying tickets to see such players. So, clearly, he must be assuming that a large number of fans will stop buying tickets if something isn't done to crack down on the athletes' bad behavior, because fans don't want to pay to see a bunch of drug abusers and criminals. In other words, many fans buy tickets based in part on the good behavior of athletes. Now, let's reverse the argument: *few people who buy tickets for sporting events base any part of their decision to do so on the good behavior of athletes.* Does this destroy the author's argument? Yes, it does—if few people make decisions about buying tickets based on the good behavior of the athletes, then the presence of a large number of athletes who don't practice good behavior won't necessarily lead to significantly lower ticket sales. So, this must be the correct answer.

Just to be sure, though, let's look at the last choice. *No athletes who use steroids have legal prescriptions for them.* Does any part of the argument rely on this assumption? No. In fact, the author doesn't mention steroids at all, but only drugs in general. It's a reasonable assumption that he's referring, at least in part, to major steroid scandals of the past several years. However, most people upset about steroid use in sports find their use scandalous regardless of whether or not the athlete has a legal prescription for their use. Even if every infamous steroid user in professional sports had acquired the drugs legally, using them is still against the rules of their leagues, as they give athletes a powerful, unfair advantage over their teammates and competitors who don't use them. Thus, even if the author is objecting to steroid use, he hasn't said anything at all to indicate that he's against their use only if they're not legally prescribed. If we run the reversal test, we come up with *all athletes who use steroids have legal prescriptions for them.* Does this destroy the argument? No, because the author is denouncing rampant drug use in general, not simply the use of steroids for which they don't have legal prescriptions. In addition, drug use is only one of three factors he mentions. His argument also involves violent crime and irresponsible behavior.

New Information Questions

Another very common question type on the Logical Reasoning test requires you to analyze or reconsider the argument in light of new information. (This is the exact opposite of Inference questions, which require the test taker to *analyze new information in light of the argument.*) There are a few different types of these new information questions on this section of the LSAT. The two most common are Strengthen questions and Weaken questions. They come in two forms. The first form simply asks which answer choice supports or weakens the argument or conclusion. The second one, however, asks you to select the answer which *most* strengthens or weakens the argument. In other words, you will have two or three answers which support/weaken the argument in some way, and you will need to select the one that does so most powerfully.

This second kind of question is usually phrased along these lines:

Which one of the following, if true, most strengthens the argument?

Which one of the following, if true, offers the most support for the conclusion?

Which one of the following, if true, most weakens the argument?

Which one of the following, if true, most undermines the author's conclusion?

Each of the following, if true, offers support for the argument EXCEPT: (this is actually a Weaken question)

You will see these sorts of questions on arguments where the premises don't strongly support the conclusion. In other words, the evidence is somewhat lacking—the premises make a case for the conclusion, but not one that is airtight and wholly persuasive. You'll be faced with five answer choices that each contain new information; at least one of them will definitely make the argument stronger or weaker, as the case may be.

It's important to note, however, that exactly how much the correct answer strengthens or weakens the argument can vary considerably. With one question, the correct answer might slightly damage the persuasiveness of the argument, while, with another, the new information contained in the right answer would cause the argument to fall apart completely. So, the force of the new information is not an issue, in and of itself. It's only important when you have a *most* question, and new information in one answer is contrasted with the new information in other answer choices. For example, if you're looking for the answer that most strengthens the argument, don't simply choose the first answer that strengthens the argument in some way. It could very well be wrong, as there may be another answer that lends even more strength to the argument. Never forget the *most* in a question.

Also keep in mind that the LSAT designers like to trip test takers up on these kinds of questions by inserting answer choices containing information that seems powerful and relevant, but in reality has nothing to do with the author's actual conclusion, meaning that it's actually completely irrelevant because it doesn't affect the argument at all.

Most Weakens Question

Many people believe that advertising plays a major role in how people choose whom to vote for in presidential elections in America, but our recent study proves that this belief is a myth. We selected 5,000 people, chosen from all 50 states in proportion to each state's percentage of the US population, and divided them into two groups. People in Group A each watched between 10 and 20 hours of television a week, while no one in Group B watched any television at all. Three months before the last election, we asked each person in both groups which presidential candidate they favored. Then, after the election was over, we asked each person whom they had voted for. At the beginning of the experiment, members of Group A favored the Republican candidate by a 51/49 margin, but wound up voting for him by a 56/44 margin. Group B favored the Republican candidate by a 52/48 margin at the start of the experiment, but voted for him by a 57/43 margin. So, in both groups the percentage of actual votes for the Republican candidate was exactly five percentage points higher than the level of support at the beginning of the study, and the level of support for the Democratic candidate was exactly five points lower, proving that advertising does not make a big difference in presidential elections.

Which one of the following, if true, most weakens the argument?

(A) The average number of years of college education in both groups was exactly the same.
(B) The Democrats didn't spend quite as much as the Republicans on television ads.
(C) Members of Group B spent an average of 15 hours a week listening to the radio.
(D) Both candidates had high disapproval ratings.
(E) Two television stations in Alaska refused to run any ads for political candidates.

Does the fact that *the average number of years of college education in both groups was exactly the same* weaken this argument? On the contrary, it would tend to strengthen it, since it reduces the likelihood that a difference in the demographics of the two groups influenced the results.

Let's look at three of the remaining answers together:

The Democrats didn't spend quite as much as the Republicans on television ads.

Both candidates had high disapproval ratings.

Two television stations in Alaska refused to run any ads for political candidates.

Do any of these weaken the argument? Given the results of the study, it's not likely that the fact that *the Democrats didn't spend quite as much as the Republicans on television ads* was much of a factor, but theoretically it could have made a slight difference. If so, that would weaken the argument. Let's hang on to this answer.

Does the fact that *both candidates had high disapproval ratings* weaken the argument in any way? No, it doesn't. In fact, this answer is completely irrelevant. We can reject this answer choice out of hand.

Does the fact that *two television stations in Alaska refused to run any ads for political candidates* weaken the author's case for claiming that advertising doesn't play a major role when it comes to how people choose which presidential candidate to vote for? It's very unlikely, because the people in Group A were proportionally distributed across America. Alaska makes up a tiny percentage of the US population, meaning that very few (if any) members of Group A were affected by the lack of political ads on these two stations. So while it theoretically could have had a miniscule effect, it's very unlikely that it did, and even less likely that it had even the impact that lower spending on the part of the Democrats might have had. So we can discard this answer, too.

Let's examine the remaining answer choice. Would the fact that *members of Group B spent an average of 15 hours a week listening to the radio* weaken the argument? Yes, it would, since it would represent a huge blind spot in the study. The researchers appear to be assuming that the only way Americans can be exposed to ads for presidential candidates is by watching television. However, since the argument doesn't stipulate that fact, we have no reason to assume it's true while analyzing the author's case. Since it's common knowledge that radio stations run a lot of campaign ads during presidential campaigns, and there is nothing in the argument to the contrary, we can use this knowledge in our reasoning. When we do so, it's obvious that it would logically follow that people listening to the radio 15 hours each week would hear a large number of ads for presidential candidates. Since the author based the argument on the assumption that people in Group B weren't exposed to ads for presidential candidates, this information demolishes his case, making it the correct answer.

Most Strengthens Question

Public awareness campaigns have reduced the number of alcohol-related traffic fatalities in the US. One major factor in this reduction is the fact that many states now require persons convicted of driving under the influence of alcohol to install ignition interlock devices (breath analyzers) on their cars. These devices make it impossible for a car to be started when they detect alcohol on a person's breath. However, even after decades of efforts to reduce drunk driving, tens of thousands of Americans are still killed every year by drunk drivers, so more must be done. If Congress passed a law requiring car manufacturers to include ignition interlock devices on every new vehicle sold in America, eventually thousands more lives would be saved every year.

Which one of the following, if true, most strengthens the argument?

(A) The number of alcohol-related traffic deaths dropped sharply in the late 1980s, but has since plateaued.
(B) Rapidly improving technology is making it increasingly difficult for people to evade or defeat ignition interlock devices.
(C) Because of the economies of scale, requiring ignition interlock devices on all vehicles would add less than $100 to the price of a new car.
(D) Seven percent of alcohol-related traffic deaths are caused by people previously convicted of driving under the influence.
(E) In a few years, iris recognition and vein matching technology will be incorporated into most ignition interlock devices, giving prosecutors extremely persuasive evidence in DUI cases.

The correct answer is D. Let's examine the answer choices in order:

The number of alcohol-related traffic deaths dropped sharply in the late 1980s, but has since plateaued. Does this strengthen the argument? No. The focus of the argument is the conclusion, which in this case is that a law requiring breath analyzers on all new cars would save thousands of lives every year. This statement *does* back up the sub-conclusion that more needs to be done about the number of traffic fatalities, but it provides no support for the idea that breath analyzers on every new car would save thousands of people's lives.

Rapidly improving technology is making it increasingly difficult for people to evade or defeat ignition interlock devices. Does this statement strengthen the argument? Yes, it does. If interlock devices are getting more and more effective, then that would make the impact of installing them on all new cars even stronger. However, the statement found in D does much more to strengthen the argument.

Because of the economies of scale, requiring ignition interlock devices on all vehicles would add less than $100 to the price of a new car. Although, if true, this statement would probably make the law more popular with the public and therefore easier to pass, it does nothing to strengthen the notion that installing breath analyzers on all new cars is an effective way to dramatically reduce the number of people killed by drunk drivers.

Seven percent of alcohol-related traffic deaths are caused by people previously convicted of driving under the influence. This is the statement that, by far, does the most to strengthen the author's conclusion. How so? Well, if seven percent of alcohol-related traffic deaths are caused by people who have already been found guilty of driving under the influence that means that 13 out of 14 deaths are caused by drivers who have *not* previously been convicted of DUI, and therefore don't have interlock devices on their vehicles. Since we know from the argument that interlock devices have been a major factor in reducing the number of traffic deaths from DUI, and now we posit that at least 93% of the vehicles involved in DUI fatalities don't have one, it logically follows that installing them on all new vehicles would eventually dramatically reduce the number of drunk driving deaths in America.

In a few years, iris recognition and vein matching technology will be incorporated into most ignition interlock devices, giving prosecutors extremely persuasive evidence in DUI cases. Does this strengthen the argument in any way? No, it doesn't. The argument is about reducing the number of DUI fatalities, not about making it easier for prosecutors to convict people charged with driving under the influence. The statement neither strengthens nor weakens the argument; it is completely irrelevant.

Paradox Questions

For simplicity's sake, we've been referring to the stimuli on the Logical Reasoning exam as arguments, but not all of them actually are. Sometimes a stimulus will merely present a few facts without drawing a conclusion from those facts. If there's no conclusion in the text, there's technically no argument, and the stimulus is merely a reading passage. However, when referring to Logical Reasoning passages in general, it would be very awkward to keep saying "arguments and fact sets" repeatedly, so when we talk about Logical Reasoning arguments in general, we're referring to these passages, too.

Paradox questions take this form. Two or more facts are presented, and some of the facts will seem to be at odds with each other, and the question will ask you to resolve the problem by choosing the answer that resolves the paradox.

PARADOX QUESTION

Medical researchers exploring the obesity epidemic in the US have made an intriguing discovery. With the cooperation of several restaurant owners, they observed and recorded thousands of diners eating lunch over the course of several months. As expected, they found that on average, seriously overweight people consumed far more calories while dining out than did people of average weight. However, when they compared calorie counts only among the seriously overweight diners, they were surprised to find that obese diners who were considered well-dressed consumed significantly fewer calories than did diners of the same weight who were considered casually dressed, even while eating at the same restaurant.

Which of the following statements, if true, would provide the best explanation of the seeming paradox found by the researchers?

(A) Well-dressed diners tend to be more affluent and can more easily afford higher quality, less fattening food.

(B) In all weight categories, casually dressed people tend to eat more food when dining out than well-dressed people.

(C) Casually dressed diners tend to be less educated and therefore less informed about what constitutes healthy eating.

(D) Well-dressed diners tend to be more image conscious, so they eat less in public, but make up for it by eating more at home.

(E) The researchers had unconscious prejudices against people who are overweight and this affected their findings.

Before we examine the answer choices, let's consider the passage. Obesity researchers who studied thousands of lunchtime restaurant patrons over a period of several months discovered what seems to be a paradox. What is the intriguing finding? It's the fact that, on average, well-dressed obese people ate fewer calories than casually dressed obese people who weighed about the same.

What makes this a paradox? It's a (seeming) paradox because one would reasonably assume that in a study involving thousands of people, on average, people who weigh a certain amount would consume about the same number of calories as other people of the same weight. Yet, among obese people of approximately the same weight, there was a significant difference in the caloric intakes of well-dressed people and casually dressed people. Something doesn't add up here. How can casually dressed obese diners take in significantly more calories than well-dressed obese diners while weighing the same? It's your task to decide which one of the answer choices resolves the problem. Let's look at each one.

Well-dressed diners tend to be more affluent and can more easily afford higher quality, less fattening food. As a stand-alone statement, this makes perfect sense. It's common knowledge that when it comes to food, the lower the price, the unhealthier and fattening the food tends to be. Keep in mind, however, that we're not concerned with whether the statement in any of these answer choices makes sense or not, because for the purposes of answering the question, we have to accept it as true.

So, assuming the truth of this statement, does it do anything to resolve the paradox? No, it does not. If well-dressed obese people are eating few calories because they have the means to afford less fattening food, then why do they weigh as much as casually dressed obese people who don't have that option? So, the paradox still stands, and this answer is incorrect.

How about the next answer choice? *In all weight categories, casually dressed people tend to eat more food when dining out than well-dressed people.* Is this the answer we're looking for? No. It simply takes one part of the paradox—casually dressed obese people eat more calories when dining out than well-dressed obese people do—and applies it to everyone in general, irrespective of weight. While this explains that casually dressed obese people eating more calories when dining out than well-dressed obese people do is simply part of a larger pattern that holds true across the board, it does nothing to explain why two groups of obese people with different eating patterns weigh about the same.

Casually dressed diners tend to be less educated and therefore less informed about what constitutes healthy eating. This has a lot in common with A, and it's just as unsatisfactory when it comes to resolving the paradox. Instead of implying that casually dressed people eat poorly because they can't afford to eat healthy food, this answer states that they eat poorly because they're not educated enough to understand the principles of healthy nutrition. While this may very well be true, it does absolutely nothing to resolve the paradox. Because if well-dressed people make healthier food choices because they're better educated, why are they just as heavy as their less educated counterparts?

Well-dressed diners tend to be more image conscious, so they eat less in public, but make up for it by eating more at home. Right off the bat this looks more promising than the first three choices. Why? Because it includes a factor outside of the environment the researchers observed the diners in. That's in its favor, because logically there are very few factors within that environment which could explain how two groups of people can weigh the same despite significantly different calorie consumption patterns. However, that doesn't necessarily make this the correct answer. We have to decide if it resolves the paradox. Yes, it does, and it does so very well. The well-dressed obese diners eat less than their casually dressed counterparts in restaurants because they're self-conscious about their image, but at home, when no one's watching, they eat enough to make up for the caloric gap between themselves and the other group. This explains the paradox of why both groups weigh the same quite nicely. It's the correct answer.

The researchers had unconscious prejudices against people who are overweight and this affected their findings. This answer not only doesn't explain the paradox, it doesn't even make sense. However, since we're required to grant the truth of the statement in order to see if it's correct, let's think about it. Since the paradox involves two groups of overweight people, if the researchers had been biased against the overweight, whether consciously or unconsciously, they would have been equally biased against *both* groups, which, in effect, would mean that they would be treating both groups pretty much the same way. So, this statement does nothing to explain why they found a discrepancy between the groups. Had the researchers been biased against well-dressed people or casually dressed people, that fact certainly could have played a role in the findings, but the notion that they were biased against the overweight explains nothing.

Keep in mind that the correct answer only needs to be the best explanation of the paradox out of the five choices given. It doesn't have to be the best explanation that's theoretically possible. For example, it's certainly possible that the average well-dressed obese person engages in more exercise than his or her casually dressed counterpart. This could explain the paradox, and might even do so better than D above. However, it's not one of the choices. Of the five answer choices we're given, D offers the best explanation of the paradox.

Flawed Reasoning Questions

With most of the questions you'll run into on the Logical Reasoning section of the LSAT, the reasoning in the stimulus will be basically sound. The author won't make any logical errors, and the premises will lead directly to the conclusion. Everything will work nicely together to form a solid argument. However, that won't be the case with every stimulus. In some cases, the reasoning found in the stimulus will be illogical in some way, and your job will be to figure out exactly what's wrong with the author's argument. These are Flawed Reasoning questions.

Sometimes the flaw will be fairly easy to spot, but in a lot of cases it will be much more subtle. In fact, many times it will be so subtle that if it weren't for the question asking you to name the flaw, many people taking the LSAT would never realize that the reasoning was illogical.

(This is one of the main reasons some people recommend reading the question before reading the stimulus, by the way. They say that if you know there's a reasoning flaw in the stimulus before you start reading it you can look for it as you read. They're right about that, but for other types of questions it's better to read the stimulus first, and because the vast majority of questions on the Logical Reasoning section aren't Flawed Reasoning questions, you'll come out way ahead if you read the stimulus first).

There are many different kinds of logical errors an author can make, but they all basically boil down to relying on a false or unjustified assumption: reasoning from only one case to a large number of cases, confusing correlation with causation, assuming that current conditions will continue unchanged, imprecision in numbers or measurement, making poor analogies, etc.

You'll be presented with five answer choices, only one of which will be the actual reasoning flaw in the argument. You must always keep in mind that it's likely that one or more of the answer choices will be red herrings—one of those wrong answers that have been carefully and deliberately designed to trap you into selecting it as your answer. On Flawed Reasoning questions, LSAT designers often trip people up by offering one or two answer choices which mention something the author actually does in the argument, but isn't illogical—it's actually valid reasoning.

Another common technique is to have one or more answer choices which refer to an error of logic that is common and well known, but isn't part of the author's argument. For example, an answer might say the author appeals to authority or the author assumed what he set out to prove, when the author has done no such thing. This second technique isn't as tricky as the first one, but you should definitely be on guard against it, too.

Here is an example of a Flawed Reasoning question:

It has been clearly demonstrated that the average married man earns more income than the average single man. Over two hundred scientifically rigorous studies have been done on this subject, starting nearly fifty years ago and continuing today, by such highly respected institutions as Harvard University, Yale University, and the University of Chicago. All told, these studies have included millions of men, from every level of education, all over the country, in hundreds of different occupations, and every one of them found that the average married man is paid more than the average single man. Obviously, there is widespread blatant discrimination in the employment market against men who aren't married.

Which one of the following best describes the flaw in the reasoning in this passage?

(A) The author appeals to authority to make his case.
(B) The author assumes what he is supposed to be proving.
(C) The author fails to consider other possible causes than discrimination.
(D) The author relies on insufficient or irrelevant data to make his case.
(E) The author fails to use exact figures with respect to average incomes.

Let's look at the argument and consider the answers.

The author points us to over two hundred studies by highly respected organizations that compare the incomes of married men to the incomes of single men, which all found that married men are paid more than single men. He points out that this applies across the board, for pretty much all jobs and education levels, all over the country, and has been going on for a long time. He draws the conclusion that single men are being discriminated against by employers. We know from the question that there is a flaw in his reasoning. We have to determine what the flaw is.

Is it that *the author appeals to authority to make his case*? This sounds promising. A well-known logical fallacy is the appeal to authority and the author relies on studies for his evidence, and points out that some of them have been conducted by elite universities. So he's definitely guilty of committing the appeal to authority logical fallacy, right? Well, not so fast. While this would trip up a substantial number of test takers, it is not the correct answer.

While the author does cite some authorities, he is not committing the appeal to authority fallacy. Some people who have heard that appealing to authority is a logical fallacy seem to think that one can never cite an authority to back up an argument. This is nonsense; these people don't understand the appeal to authority fallacy. Appealing to an authority is only a logical fallacy if the authority has no expertise in the topic under discussion, or in a case where many other equally knowledgeable authorities disagree on the matter.

For example, if we're having an argument over Roman Catholic theology, and you quote a well-known Catholic theologian to back up your point, that is not a logical fallacy, because a Catholic theologian should certainly understand Catholic theology. However, if we're discussing which baseball player was the greatest ever and I say, "It's Babe Ruth because my priest said so," then I've committed the appeal to authority fallacy. Only an appeal to authority outside the subject matter, or a quote from one authority on a topic that is disputed among experts on the subject, are logical fallacies. Citing authorities who know what they're talking about is perfectly logical. So this answer is wrong.

Is *the author assuming what he is supposed to be proving*? This is another logical fallacy, known formally as "begging the question." Here's a simple argument that begs the question: *Cigarettes are unhealthy because they're bad for you.* This argument begs the question because the conclusion is nothing but a restatement of the premise. Like a little boy who says his dad is always right, and his friend asks him how he knows, and the boy replies, "Because Dad said so," this is known as a circular argument. Does the author commit this logical fallacy? No, he does not. His premise, that married men make more money than single men, is not the same as his conclusion, which is that employer discrimination against single men is the cause of the disparity.

How about *the author fails to consider other possible causes than discrimination*? This one sounds like it might have some merit. Because it's the LSAT, we have to assume that the facts in the author's premise are correct, and that hundreds of studies have established that married men make more money than single men as an irrefutable fact. However, does it necessarily follow that discrimination against single men in the marketplace is the cause of this? Are there any other factors that could possibly be causing this phenomenon?

Couldn't experience be one factor that might be involved? Older men are more likely to be married than younger men, and older men are more likely to have more experience than younger men. Since employers usually prefer workers with more experience over those with less, it seems logical that they would pay them more. Another possible factor is motivation—doesn't it make sense that a man with a wife and/or kids might be motivated to work longer hours than a single man, and thereby earn more income? These are just two possible explanations of the pay disparity that don't involve discrimination, and the author didn't consider either one, let alone any others. So this is the correct answer.

What about *the author relies on insufficient or irrelevant data to make his case*? Why is this wrong? Well, if the author had mentioned only one study, he would not have much of a case. Instead, he pointed to over 200 studies by elite universities, involving millions of men from all walks of life, in hundreds of occupations, over a 50-year span, all of which came to the same conclusion. Assuming that the facts that the author cites in a stimulus are true, as we must do on the LSAT, it is clear that there is sufficient, relevant data to establish scientific consensus on this matter.

That *the author fails to use exact figures with respect to average incomes* is true, but completely irrelevant. The 200+ studies have established that there's a pay disparity between single and married men, and he is arguing that the mere existence of the disparity, not its size, is proof that there is widespread discrimination against single men in the workplace. Nothing in the argument requires exact figures to be stated.

Parallel Reasoning Questions

Parallel Reasoning questions are very common on the Logical Reasoning section of the LSAT, and you should expect to see a few of them when you take the exam. They can be more difficult to answer correctly than many of the other question types, so they typically eat up more of the clock you're racing against. That's because with Parallel Reasoning Questions, you're not just analyzing one argument; you're analyzing six—each of the answer choices is an argument, too. Because of this, we're going to spend more time discussing these questions than we spent on the other question types.

On Parallel Reasoning questions, the stimulus will be a very concise argument, comprised of only a few lines. After digesting the argument, you will then be asked to read the five answer choices, and select the one that contains the argument that most closely parallels the reasoning in the stimulus. LSAT designers have several ways of phrasing this, but they are all very similar, so there won't be any doubt that you're dealing with a Parallel Reasoning question. Analyzing and comparing five arguments to the original can take quite a bit of time, and this is another reason some LSAT guides recommend that you read the question before reading the stimulus. They suggest skipping all Parallel Reasoning questions, and only coming back to attempt them after answering all the other questions first.

It's your decision, of course, but we think you'll do better if you stick with our suggestion of reading the stimulus first. For one thing, you won't need to read the question in order to decide that you're looking at a Parallel Reasoning question. That will be obvious since the stimulus will be an argument that's only a sentence or two long. And, for that very reason, reading the stimulus first won't take much time at all, so how much time would you have saved anyway?

This is not to say that you should never skip a question and come back to it later. At times, that might be the wisest approach for you to take. It depends on how hard the question is. Some Parallel Reasoning questions are pretty tough to untangle, but frankly, many are not that hard. If you get bogged down on one of these questions, by all means skip ahead and only come back to it if you've answered all the other questions. (You should always skip ahead if you get seriously stuck on *any* question on the LSAT, no matter what type of question it is.) It's inadvisable, however, to have a blanket policy that you're going to skip all Parallel Reasoning questions until the end, because of the fact that many of them are not particularly difficult. Since other kinds of questions can also be very hard, you could very well be skipping a question you could have easily answered only to run into another question that completely stumps you.

As the name implies, on Parallel Reasoning questions the correct answer must share the very same kind of reasoning found in the original argument. In other words, the two arguments must be similar in logical structure. If the original argument makes an analogy, then the correct answer will contain an analogy. If the stimulus relies on circular reasoning, the correct answer will, too. If the original argument reasons inductively, you'll be looking for an inductive argument in the answer choices.

In some cases, the method of reasoning used in the argument won't be all that obvious or easy to discern, but that usually isn't a problem. The much bigger problem is that some of the answer choices will be so similar, or so opaque, that deciding which one best matches the reasoning in the original argument will seem to be a task whose difficulty falls somewhere between splitting hairs and reading goat entrails. To find the right answer, you'll need to consider and compare several aspects of the two arguments.

The first factor is validity. Sometimes the argument in the stimulus will be valid, in which case the correct answer must also contain a valid argument. Sometimes the stimulus argument will contain a logical flaw. In that case, the argument in the correct answer must also be invalid. You'll be able to know for sure if the argument in the stimulus is valid or invalid because if it's invalid, the question stem will say so. If the question stem doesn't use a word such as flawed, illogical, or questionable to describe the stimulus argument, then the argument is valid.

However, don't put too much weight on validity. It's definitely a requirement, but it's only one factor you must consider when looking for parallel reasoning. Or, to put it in formal logic terms—that the correct answer must match the validity or invalidity of the original argument is a necessary but not sufficient condition. Plus, it's very unlikely that only one answer choice will be valid or invalid, as the case may be.

Next you'll want to compare the conclusions in each argument. Remember, the stimulus and the five answer choices are all arguments, so they all *must* have conclusions (and at least one premise). The conclusion in the correct answer should have a lot in common with the conclusion in the original argument. This doesn't mean that the subject matter will be the same, or even similar. Nor does it mean that the two arguments must have the same placement of the conclusion with respect to the premises. The premises could come before the conclusion in the stimulus, and after the conclusion in the answer (or vice versa), and they could still be a match.

Two of the kinds of similarities you're looking for in conclusions are scope and certainty. These are functions of the language used in the arguments. When the conclusion in the stimulus contains broad, all-encompassing absolutes such as all, always, must, cannot, never, etc., then the conclusion in the correct answer must have the same scope, even if it's not expressed exactly the same way. For example, compare these two conclusions:

People over the age of 50 never win a marathon.

No person over the age of 50 ever wins a marathon.

These are both saying the exact same thing, even though only the first one uses the word *never,* and one sentence refers to *people,* while the other one uses *person.* So, these conclusions are a match.

Now consider these two conclusions:

People over the age of 50 never win a marathon.

People over the age of 50 hardly ever win a marathon.

Are these two conclusions saying the same thing? No, they are not. The first one is making an absolute, categorical statement that a person over the age of 50 winning a marathon never happens. The second one is saying that it's rare for anyone over 50 to win a marathon, but it does not say it never happens. These conclusions do not match up.

So scope, or extent, is a very important clue when determining the correct answer for Parallel Reasoning questions. Certainty is another factor to consider. Consider these two conclusions:

Eating too much might cause you to get diabetes.

Smoking cigarettes will stain your teeth.

In the first one, it is stated that *A* could possibly lead to *B*, while in the second it is asserted that *A* definitely results in *B*. One conclusion is certain, while the other is indefinite, so these conclusions are not a match. Of course, there is quite a bit of overlap between scope and certainty; the main thing to keep in mind is to be on the lookout for any kind of an absolute. If the conclusion in the stimulus has an absolute, then the correct answer must too. If the conclusion of the original argument has an indefinite modifier, then an answer that contains an absolute is wrong. Because conclusions must match in scope/certainty, it's often the case that the argument in the correct answer contains some identical words or phrases as the original. This isn't always the case, and it also shouldn't be treated as a smoking gun level of proof by itself, but it can certainly be an important clue.

So tackle these questions by first seeing if the method of reasoning jumps out at you. If so, then you should generally be able to select the correct answer with no further analysis. If that's not the case, then consider validity, and eliminate all answers that don't match the argument for validity. If you still aren't sure, compare the conclusions for scope and certainty. In most cases, if you need to compare the conclusions in order to determine the right answer, doing so should be enough to enable you to pick the winner. However, if you're still unsure, then compare the premises in the stimulus with the premises in the answer choices, using the same principles just described above. If you're still unsure of the correct answer after that, then it's probably time to move on to another question.

Here is a sample Parallel Reasoning question:

Great college professors love to read. Bob has over a thousand books on his e-reader, so he would make a great college professor.

The flawed reasoning in which one of the following arguments most closely parallels the flawed reasoning in the argument above?

(A) People with analytical minds are good at chess. Everyone in the accounting department has an analytical mind. Zelda works in the accounting department, so she would make a good chess player.

(B) All baseball players can learn to switch-hit if they practice long enough. Jose Ramirez was the American League MVP last year, so he would be able to master switch-hitting in only a couple of weeks.

(C) Everyone who works for an airline loves traveling. Derek has been an airline reservations clerk for seven years, so Derek loves traveling.

(D) When the sky is red in the morning, it usually rains by the end of the day. The sky is red this morning, so it will rain today.

(E) The best restaurant managers like to cook. Zoe throws some terrific dinner parties, so she would be a very good restaurant manager.

Let's look at this in depth.

First, why is this argument flawed? It's illogical because the fact that great college professors love reading doesn't mean we can say that all people who love reading make great college professors. In other words, loving to read is a necessary condition for being a great college professor, but it's not a sufficient condition.

Is *A* the correct answer? In other words, does it have the very same flawed reasoning as the argument in the stimulus?

People with analytical minds are good at chess. Everyone in the accounting department has an analytical mind. Zelda works in the accounting department, so she would make a good chess player.

Let's break it down. It boils down to *all members of A are B, and all members of C are members of A, and D is a member of C, therefore D is B.* Is this reasoning flawed? No, it's not; it's perfectly valid. There's an extra step in there that might conceivably throw some people off, but it's a perfectly logical argument. Therefore, it cannot be correct, as the correct answer must contain flawed reasoning.

Moving on to *B*:

All baseball players can learn to switch-hit if they practice long enough. Jose Ramirez was the American League MVP last year, so he would be able to master switch-hitting in only a couple of weeks.

Is this argument valid or invalid? It's invalid—while the premise says that all baseball players can learn to switch hit, there's nothing that says that the better a player is the faster he'll learn, let alone puts a time limit on the learning curve. This argument takes the premise too far and comes to an unwarranted conclusion. However, that is not the same kind of illogical reasoning the stimulus contains, so this answer is incorrect.

How about *C*?

Everyone who works for an airline loves traveling. Derek has been an airline reservations clerk for seven years, so Derek loves traveling.

This is a valid argument: *All members of A are B. C is a member of A, therefore C is B.* The logic is fine, but we're looking for an illogical argument, so this answer is incorrect.

Next, we have:

When the sky is red in the morning, it usually rains by the end of the day. The sky is red this morning, so it will rain today.

This is pretty obviously flawed – it turns a likely outcome (*usually rains*), into an absolute certainty (*will rain*), but it's not the kind of flawed reasoning we're looking for, so it's out.

By process of elimination we know that *E* must be correct, but let's look at it to find out why.

The best restaurant managers like to cook. Zoe throws some terrific dinner parties, so she would be a very good restaurant manager.

First, notice that the language and structure are very similar, but not identical. This is a good sign. More importantly, though, if we break the logic down, we'll see that it has the very same flawed reasoning. Just because the best restaurant managers like to cook, it doesn't necessarily mean that people who like to cook would make great restaurant managers. Enjoying cooking is a necessary condition for being a great restaurant manager, but it's not a sufficient condition. This is the very same illogical reasoning found in the stimulus, so it's the correct answer.

Less Common Question Types

The majority of the questions you'll encounter on the Logical Reasoning section of the LSAT will fall into one of the question types we've just discussed. That's why we spent so much time dissecting these particular types of questions and explaining how to solve them. However, there are many other kinds of questions used far less frequently by the test designers. You won't see a question from each of these categories on the LSAT when you take it, but you'll definitely run into some of them. It's not necessary to spend nearly as much time prepping for these questions, but you should make sure you're familiar with them before taking the exam. So, here are some other Logical Reasoning question types you can expect to see when you take the LSAT.

Passage Completion Questions

On a Passage Completion question, the last part of the final sentence of the passage is left blank, and the question stem asks you to choose the answer which best completes the passage. On these, the correct answer should not only make logical sense, but it must also fit with the rest of the passage structurally and stylistically. Because of this, it's usually not very difficult to select the right answer. At least two of the choices won't make much sense as an ending for the passage, and the other incorrect choice(s) won't be a good fit when it comes to structure or style.

Must Be True | Deduction Questions

While these are phrased differently, they are essentially asking the same thing as Inference questions. Just follow the principles for solving Inference questions when you run into a question asking you something like, "Based on the passage, which one of the following must be true?" or "Which one of the following statements can be deduced from the passage?"

Point at Issue Questions

Two brief, conflicting statements will be given, each from a different person, and the question stem will ask you to choose the answer that properly conveys the point at issue between the two. The key here is to ignore the noise in the arguments, such as extraneous details, and boil each statement down to its essence. When you do that, the dispute will become clear, and it will reveal the correct answer.

Conclusion Questions

Every now and then you'll see a question asking you to identify the author's conclusion. Don't let the wording on these questions fool you. Remember, the conclusion is the main point the author is making. In other words, these are simply Main Point questions. Follow the principles described in that section and you'll be fine. Always keep in mind that the test designers like to include a premise or two as answer choices, which trips many people up. Don't let that happen to you; make sure you don't choose an answer simply because it contains a reframing of a statement from the argument—the statement that is restated must be the conclusion.

Argument Proceeds By | Method of Reasoning Questions

These questions ask you to choose the answer that best describes the method of reasoning employed by the author, or best shows how the argument proceeds. In other words, the conclusion is not the focus, nor is any inference or deduction that can be made on the basis of the argument. The validity of the argument is also not a factor. The only thing that matters for these questions is how the author makes the argument. Once you identify how the argument is structured, the key to answering these questions correctly is to mentally eliminate the fluff in the answer choices and focus on essentials. Because there aren't very many ways of coming up with incorrect but credible answer choices that can deceive many test takers if written in straightforward language, the LSAT designers tend to employ verbosity and bombast as distractions. That is, they use too many words, or intellectual-sounding language, or both, to gussy up the answer choices to make the wrong answers sound more appealing. When you strip away all the fancy verbal footwork, you'll find that choosing the correct answer is often fairly easy.

Syllogism Questions

A syllogism is a classic argument structure used in formal logic. It contains two premises and a conclusion. Here's a basic syllogism:

When the sun is up it is daytime.

The sun is up.

It is daytime.

You will likely encounter a question or two featuring syllogisms on the Logical Reasoning section of the LSAT. The stimulus will present a syllogism, and then ask which of the answer choices must be true if the syllogism is true. Syllogism questions are probably the most straightforward and easy to understand questions you'll come across in Logical Reasoning. For that reason, they are also some of the easiest to solve. You may find it helpful to draw a diagram illustrating the syllogism, but in most cases that won't be necessary.

Other Question Types

Every now and then the folks at LSAC come up with a new question type, so it's possible you may run into a kind of question that's never before been seen on the LSAT exam. Plus, we have omitted a few question types from this guide because they only rarely appear on the test, and many of them are very close to fitting into one of the categories we've discussed. So, if you encounter a question that doesn't fit into one of the listed categories, there's no need to panic. Logic is logic; if you've used this guide to practice, and you've mastered the skills necessary to tackle the kinds of questions discussed at length in this book, you'll be ready for any curveball the LSAT designers throw your way.

The Writing Sample

How Important Is It?

Reading and writing are a daily part of life for law students and for lawyers. An ability to express your thoughts concisely, clearly, and persuasively in a number of styles from court briefs to personal letters is critical to doing well in the profession. This need for attorneys to possess a mastery of writing skills was ostensibly the primary reason for adding a timed writing section to the LSAT. Another reason often cited is that a writing sample gives the admissions committee a more well-rounded picture of a law school candidate, allowing them to make more holistic decisions about who gets in and who doesn't.

However, there are many people who believe that the Writing Sample is nothing more than window dressing, a sort of diversionary tactic. Law schools have been widely criticized in the past for focusing too much on numbers (i.e., test scores and grade point averages) in making admissions decisions. Critics asserted that this was unfair to many deserving candidates who are perfectly qualified to do well in law school but don't do well on standardized tests, and that law schools' narrow-minded focus on test scores and GPAs resulted in an imbalanced pool of new lawyers, which was stultifying the legal profession.

Law schools dug in their heels for years and resisted changing the test, but they eventually gave in. However, the Writing Sample is unscored and there is little evidence that it has much of an effect on admissions decisions. Some observers insist that it can have a small effect, but almost no one believes that the Writing Sample is really very important when it comes to getting into law school.

Nevertheless, many people who are preparing to take the LSAT have a lot of anxiety about the Writing Sample part of the exam. As you can see, this shouldn't be the case, because the answer to the question of how important the Writing Sample is when it comes to law school admissions falls somewhere between "not very important" and "not important at all." If you've been stressed about the Writing Sample, this should help relieve your anxiety.

Another thing to keep in mind is that if you have what it takes to get good grades in college and a high score on the LSAT, then you almost certainly possess all the skills you need to do well on the Writing Sample. On the other hand, if you lack the skills necessary for success on the other sections of the LSAT, then it won't matter how well you do on the Writing Sample. Also, you will not be expected to produce the kind of writing that appears in magazines or wins literary prizes. Nor will you be trying to craft persuasive arguments for why you'd make a great law school student, as this is not an admissions essay.

You will be given 35 minutes to write a two-page essay taking a position on a question and explaining the reasoning behind your argument. Your writing will demonstrate that you have the ability to think on your feet, look at problems from various angles, organize your thoughts, and express yourself clearly and concisely. These are all skills that will be vital to your success in law school and as a working attorney, and which you should be very good at by this stage in your academic career. So, there is really no reason you should be filled with anxiety about the writing portion of the LSAT. However, you should be prepared to do your best on this part of the exam, if for no other reason than that there is an off chance that your essay might be the tiebreaker in a close admissions decision.

Do not misunderstand—it is not acceptable to leave the Writing Sample blank, to turn in a humorous essay, or to put only a half-hearted effort into writing it. You also should not choose another topic to write about other than the assigned one. Law schools can and do reject applicants for this kind of behavior, and you should strive to do your very best on this section of the exam. We're simply saying that you should not stress yourself by worrying about the Writing Sample, because in the vast majority of cases it simply isn't a decisive factor in the admissions process. If you're prepared and give it your best on test day, you should do just fine. In this section, we'll show you what you need to know in order to be fully prepared for success on the Writing Sample.

The Writing Sample Format

The Writing Sample isn't the typical kind of essay most people have in mind when they think of an essay. Typically, an essay is fairly open ended. There is usually an assigned topic or subject, but the essay writer is allowed a lot of leeway when it comes to choosing how to address the topic. That is not the case with the Writing Sample on the LSAT. It has a very specific format, one that has been deliberately designed to test some of the most important skills a person will need to succeed in law school and a subsequent legal career.

You will be given a brief prompt to read. It will describe a choice that a person or organization is facing. Usually the choice will be along the lines of the following scenarios:

- Choosing one of two non-profit groups to support with corporate giving
- Selecting one of two new international markets to enter
- Selecting one of two new product lines to develop
- Choosing one of two candidates for promotion to regional vice-president
- Choosing one of two locations for the new company headquarters

You will be given a description of two criteria, such as needs or goals, which are important or desirable to the person or organization. These considerations will usually not be complementary; in fact, they will usually be very different, and may even be at odds with each other. Finally, you will be given descriptions of two people or things that are under consideration.

You will be given two sheets of paper, and you will have a 35-minute time limit. You will also have scratch paper to use in this portion of the LSAT. Your task in the Writing Sample will be to argue that one of the candidates or alternatives is a better choice than the other one. Always keep in mind that there is no right or wrong answer; it doesn't matter which choice you make. This aspect of the essay trips many people up, as they see it as yet another test of logic and reasoning. They believe that an important part of doing well is choosing the correct alternative, and that if they give it enough thought one candidate will clearly stand out as a better choice than the other one.

This is not true; in fact, it's the exact opposite of the truth. In the descriptions it will be clear that each option has both strong and weak points and that one will be better suited to meeting one of the two provided criteria, while the other will be a better match for the other criteria. The criteria and candidate descriptions are deliberately written in such a way that each alternative would be a good choice. Your job in the Writing Sample is simply to pick one of the alternatives and make the best case you can for it. Since both alternatives are fine, it's impossible to pick the wrong one.

Another thing to keep in mind is that you won't need any knowledge of the particular aspects of the factors the prompt asks you to consider. If the prompt is about which location an advertising firm should choose for its new offices, for example, you won't be expected to know anything about advertising or commercial real estate in order to write your sample. All the information you need will be provided in the prompt, and you should not spend any of your very limited time thinking about these irrelevant factors.

You should have several goals for your essay:

- It should be completely focused on the prompt. You may include ideas or facts that aren't mentioned in the prompt as long as they have a bearing on the decision-making process. Any information that isn't germane to the decision should be left out.
- It should come across as an organic whole. In other words, even though it is only two pages long, the separate components should work together so that the essay strikes the reader as a well-organized and consistent piece of writing that flows logically. It should have a distinct opening, a main body, and a clear conclusion.
- It must be a strong argument, backed up with facts and sound reasoning. You want to state your case persuasively, and to do so you need to bolster your decision by demonstrating exactly and specifically how your choice is the better one, based on the candidate descriptions and the criteria supplied in the prompt.
- It should incorporate the characteristics of good writing. As we pointed out earlier, your essay doesn't need to be a masterpiece, but it should be well written. That means it should hold the reader's interest. You should use proper grammar and spelling, of course. You should also try to demonstrate a great command of vocabulary, while making sure not to misuse any words in an effort to impress. It's also important to use a variety of sentence structures. An essay with mostly long sentences is boring and hard to follow, while one with mostly short sentences is jarring and unpleasant. You need to write as legibly as possible. If necessary, use block print instead of cursive.

Writing Sample: Your Action Plan

Planning

Carpenters have a saying that can help you craft a great Writing Sample—measure twice, cut once. The meaning is that measuring only once often leads to having to make two cuts, wasting time and possibly material. In other words, it's better to play it safe by measuring twice, even though doing so takes longer than doing the bare minimum. This adage is a pithy expression of the critical importance of taking enough time to properly prepare for a task. Of course, unlike carpenters who can start over with another piece of wood if they make a mistake, you won't get a second chance, so it's even more imperative to take some time to plan your essay before you start writing it.

Start by reading the prompt all the way through, taking your time and not rushing. Then do it again. Use the scratch paper provided to make a note of things that will be important for you to incorporate into the essay. You should really concentrate on the candidate descriptions and the criteria given to guide you in your choice, as these will be the key points you need to cover in your essay.

While it's important not to rush the planning of your essay, you should decide as quickly as possible if you're going to argue for choice A or choice B. It may be that you're able to decide which choice to support immediately after your first reading of the prompt. If that turns out to be the case for you, you're off to a great start. If you're still having trouble making a choice even after your second reading, there's no need to panic, because there is an easy way to make your decision, which we'll get to in a moment.

Whether or not you've made a clear choice as to which option to argue for, it's time to make a couple lists. On your scratch paper, make a separate heading for each choice. Under each heading, quickly list all the pro and cons you can think of with regard to that option, based on the criteria in the prompt. Don't spend too much time thinking about this step. It isn't complicated; most of the pros and cons should be pretty clear from your reading of the prompt. If you've already made your choice, once you have your lists of pros and cons for each candidate, you can begin the writing process. If you haven't yet been able to make your decision, now is the time to choose *A* or *B*.

How? It's very simple—when you have finished making both lists, one is likely to have more pros than cons. If so, make that the one you argue in favor of. If both options are close to being equal, just flip a coin and pick one and stick with it. The point is to write about the one you think it would be easier to make a case for. If they're relatively equal, then that becomes a moot point, because you should be able to make a good case for either of them. We can't stress enough that there is no right answer, and it's important to keep that in mind. It will be very easy to get distracted and make the all too common mistake of trying to decide which choice is better. Don't let it happen to you—either choice is fine. It's how you make your case that counts.

Ideally you should spend no more than about 5 minutes planning your essay.

Writing

Once you have made your lists of the pros and cons for each alternative, and you've chosen which one to argue for, it is time to begin writing. The clock will be ticking, and you will need to create two pages worth of solid reasoning and writing in a very short time. This will be a real challenge, but there's no reason you can't accomplish it, especially if you've built a solid foundation by going through the planning steps outlined above. Depending on your handwriting, it will take between 400 and 600 words to fill two pages. This is not a lot of words; it adds up to four to six short paragraphs. The challenge for most people will be the quality of their writing, not the quantity.

Some Common Mistakes to Avoid

Don't use an artificially large script in an effort to fill the pages more easily. It will be obvious that you did so, and such a blatant attempt to game the Writing Sample will leave a very negative impression on any readers.

While writing your essay, you should assume that you're writing for a person who is familiar with the prompt you're writing about. There's no need to begin by rehashing the scenario, or outlining the main facts or questions. Doing so would not only be redundant, but might also be viewed as attempting to pad your essay with nonessential material. There's absolutely no need to restate the problem, and doing so can only weaken your Writing Sample. (Of course, when you're giving your reasons for preferring *A* or *B*, feel free to refer back to the decision criteria and the candidate descriptions in order to demonstrate why your choice is the better option. That isn't padding your essay with fluff; it's giving proof to back up your argument.)

Another thing to avoid is the generic open, which is a commonly used method of padding a written piece. Don't begin your essay by stating obvious facts that have only a tenuous connection to the prompt and do nothing to advance your argument. Here are some examples of a generic open:

- "In today's economy, it's critical that companies promote the best candidate...etc."
- "Taking care of the elderly is expensive, and the aging of the Baby Boomers means...etc."
- "Choosing which college to attend is one of the most important decisions a person...etc."

Along these same lines, do not write about how difficult it is to make the decision because each alternative would make a good choice, and both have strengths and weaknesses, etc. As the prompts are written precisely to create a situation in which a person or organization is faced with a difficult decision, this would only be stating an obvious fact which does nothing to help persuade the reader that your choice is the correct one.

Do not be informal. The tone of your writing should be semi-formal. It does not need to be as formal as a doctoral dissertation, but neither should it read like something you wrote to a friend. Also, write your essay in the third person. "I" and "you" are two words that should never appear in an LSAT Writing Sample.

Do not use superlatives such as "best" or "most qualified" when comparing the two alternatives to each other. Superlatives should only be used when discussing three or more people or things. Use the comparative forms such as "better" or "more qualified" when comparing the choices in your Writing Sample, because only two are involved.

The Opening

For many people taking the LSAT, coming up with the opening is the most difficult part of writing a good essay. It's easy to waste a lot of time trying to think of a good opening and time is precious on the LSAT. Each minute you spend thinking about this is one less minute you will have for the actual writing, so you need to be ready to put pencil to paper as soon as you've finished your planning.

The format of the prompt makes this easy to do, fortunately. Your essay should essentially be a piece that simply compares and contrasts the two possible choices in light of the criteria in the prompt. Because you are so constrained in the way you should handle the subject matter, there is much less room for error when it comes to stylistic choices. There is no need to attempt to be creative or open with some elegant rhetoric. Instead, you should simply get right to the point and state that *A* or *B* is the better choice.

At first glance this suggestion that there is one ideal way to begin your Writing Sample may sound limiting. It *is* limiting; deliberately so. However, limitations are not always negative and they can prevent a lot of bad things from happening. Many of the law school hopefuls sitting for the LSAT will turn in a poor Writing Sample because they spent far too much time trying to decide how to get started. Indecision is a luxury a person cannot afford on the LSAT. That's why it's best to decide right now that you're going to begin your Writing Sample by declaring which option is better. The fact that it's also the opening style that is best suited to the format of the Writing Sample makes the decision even easier.

There are several effective ways of phrasing your opening, but it will always be some version of *"A is the better choice, and here is the broad reason why."* (The body of your essay will flesh out the why.) Here are a couple of examples:

- Acme should choose Jenkins for the promotion, because his years of experience in the field will be more valuable to the company than Smith's advanced degree.
- Smith's possession of a Ph.D. will give Acme much needed credibility in the market, and this makes him the superior choice to Jenkins.

The Body: Contrasting the Choices

(For the rest of this section, A will denote the option you chose to argue in favor of, and B will denote the one you rejected.)

After a brief opening in which you declare that *A* is better, you will move into the heart of your essay, which will consist of arguments as to why that is the case. In other words, you'll be backing up the claim you made in your opening with actual evidence. You will do this by contrasting *A* with *B*, demonstrating how *A*'s strengths outweigh *B*'s strengths, and showing how *B*'s weaknesses outweigh *A*'s weaknesses. This will be somewhat subjective, of course, because the two choices will usually be pretty evenly matched, as we pointed out earlier.

You should not worry about that. The fact that either choice would be fine is immaterial; the only thing that matters is your ability to write and reason well on the topic. The scenarios are created in such a way that you should easily be able to think of a few areas in which *A* is stronger than *B*, and vice versa. You should be careful to avoid the glaring mistake of discussing only the strengths of *A* and the weaknesses of *B*. An essay that mentions only those factors in *A*'s favor will come across as having been written with blinders on. Your Writing Sample should strike the reader as balanced and evenhanded, not as lopsided and tendentious.

You will have more leeway in writing the body of your essay than you did in writing the opening. There are several ways you can effectively structure your argument in favor of *A*, and none of them is necessarily better than the others. No matter which structure you choose, you will be ready to start writing immediately because you made a list of the pros and cons for each candidate in your planning stage. Now you will take them and expand on them. You may introduce elements that aren't mentioned in the prompt, as long as they are common knowledge. You could use the fact that gas prices are of growing concern, for example, if that were germane. However, extraneous information should always take a back seat to the given criteria.

One good way to write the body is to start with the decision-making criteria given, and examine each candidate in light of them. For example, assume that you're being asked to choose which new product a company should introduce, and the two criteria given are to 1) gain market share, and 2) raise profit margins. In this approach, you would examine both choice *A* and choice *B* for effectiveness in meeting the first goal. Then you would compare and contrast them in light of the second goal.

Another good approach is to thoroughly cover all the strengths and weaknesses of *B*, followed by an examination of the strengths and weaknesses of *A*. If you decide to use this structure, it's best to start with the choice you're rejecting and end with your preferred choice, as this makes for a stronger essay.

A third variation is to begin by comparing the weaknesses of *A* and *B*, and then going on to compare their strengths. You should end with the strengths for the same reason you should end with your choice of candidates in the previous structure—it makes for a stronger essay.

Any of these structures will work well. There are other ways of organizing your argument, but you should choose between one of these three, as other approaches tend to come off as disorganized and ineffectual. Finally, you should decide which writing structure you are going to use before test day. It will be one less thing you have to think about during the LSAT. You cannot afford to waste any time trying to decide how to format your argument, so make sure you know which one you will use before you walk into the testing center, and stick with it.

The Conclusion

Your writing sample will only be 400–600 words long, which doesn't leave a lot to work with when it comes to writing a conclusion. This is not really much of a problem, though, because the format of the Writing Sample doesn't require a strong conclusion. Unlike a thesis or a research paper, the Writing Sample is essentially nothing but one long conclusion. You begin by saying *"A is the best choice, and here is the broad reason why."* You then go on to flesh out the why in the body of your essay. After that, having a powerful conclusion set off from the rest of the essay would be difficult to pull off. Even if you could make it work, it would be redundant. All you really need is an effective way to end the essay. Something along the lines of *"These are the reasons Jenkins is the superior choice"* will be just fine. The last thing you want to do is simply repeat what you've just said in the body of your essay.

Your Writing Sample should consist of four to six paragraphs, and you should spend no more than 25 minutes writing it.

Review Video: Drafting Conclusions
Visit mometrix.com/academy and enter code: 209408

Reviewing and Editing

Once you've finished writing your essay, you should have at least five minutes left. You should use that time to proofread it and correct any errors that you find. Misspelled words are common, but they are hardly the only thing to be concerned about. Other errors to look for are vague or mismatched pronouns, dangling modifiers, lack of subject/verb agreement, wrong verb tense, etc. Do your best to find and correct all errors, while keeping an eye on the clock. You do not want to be in the middle of making a correction when the time limit is reached.

Review Video: Revising and Editing
Visit mometrix.com/academy and enter code: 674181

EXAMPLE PROMPT AND WRITING SAMPLE

Acme Kitchen Appliances is entering the Latin American market and is trying to choose which candidate to hire to lead the effort. Write a brief essay making your best case for choosing one or the other candidate. Keep these two criteria in mind when making your choice and writing your essay:

1) The company wants to establish a reputation as a provider of kitchen appliances of the highest quality that are worth paying more for.

2) Acme seeks to establish a presence in each Latin American country as soon as possible in order to build cash flow and make the division self-sustaining.

Raul Gonzales heads up the Latin American sales department for a top US-based soft drink company. Before that, he was a regional vice-president for one of Mexico's largest snack companies. Gonzales has 25 years of business experience in Latin America, and he has traveled extensively in the region.

James Anderson is the vice-president for marketing for the US division of a large Asian automobile manufacturer. In his 20-year career at the firm, the company has gone from being perceived as a maker of low-priced cars of shoddy quality to a company that makes sleek, reliable vehicles geared toward an upper-middle-class clientele.

Acme Kitchen Appliances should choose Raul Gonzales to lead their entry into the Latin American market, as he is a better choice than James Anderson. His 25 years of experience all over Latin America will be an important asset as the company seeks to build its business south of the border.

At first glance, Anderson might seem to be the better choice in light of Acme's goal of establishing a reputation as a provider of expensive but high-quality kitchen appliances. Upon further analysis, however, that first impression does not hold up. While it's true that Anderson has helped improve the image of his company over the past two decades, the automaker's products are geared toward a specific demographic, and Acme plans to market its products to a wide range of customers.

Anderson's achievement is impressive, but there is no indication that he has what it takes to persuade Latin American consumers that Acme's kitchen appliances are the highest quality products available and they should pay a lot of money for them. Furthermore, this kind of brand imaging can take years, if not decades, to create in the minds of the public.

Acme's second consideration of establishing a market in every country in the region should take priority in choosing whom to hire, as this is likely to be much more easily achieved than creating a brand identity as a high-end product right out of the gate. Once they have a foothold and a self-sustaining Latin American base, they can then work on creating an image of a top of the line manufacturer.

This is why Raul Gonzales is a much better candidate for the position than James Anderson. While it's true that his marketing experience has been with companies selling low-priced food and drinks, he has decades of extensive experience in the entire region. He has thousands of business contacts, in every Latin American country; James Anderson has spent his entire career in the US. Gonzales grew up speaking Spanish; Anderson would need a full-time interpreter if he took the job.

Gonzales doesn't just have the contacts and the language skills necessary for the task; he also has 25 years' worth of intimate knowledge of the culture and business practices of the Latin American market. His career success is a clear indicator that Gonzales is a man who can open doors and sell products in Latin America. Establishing a foothold in the market should be Acme's first priority, and in that regard, James Anderson simply can't compete with Raul Gonzalez, who is clearly the better candidate for this position.

Practice Test #1

Section I

Time – 35 minutes

25 Questions

Directions: The questions in this section are based on the reasoning given in brief statements or passages. It is possible that for some questions there is more than one answer. However, you are to choose the best answer; that is, the response that most accurately and completely answers the question. You should not make assumptions that are by commonsense standards implausible, superfluous, or incompatible with the passage. After you have chosen the best answer, blacken the corresponding space on your answer sheet.

1. **Nutritionist: Obesity is becoming a very serious problem in this country, and we must actively pursue a means of combating it. I have recently conducted a 12-week weight loss study to see which is the best method for obese adults to lose weight. My study shows that the consumption of a healthy, balanced diet and the incorporation of exercise were highly successful. All patients who participated in my study lost weight by eating the recommended diet and by adding a little exercise each day.**

   Which of the following statements, if true, most seriously undermines the statement above?

   (A) The nutritionist's income is subsidized by a government agency committed to encouraging people to lose weight by adding daily exercise.
   (B) All of the patients had a very similar physical makeup and metabolic rate, two significant factors that affect the ability to lose weight.
   (C) The nutritionist has been unable to come to an agreement with a colleague on what constitutes a healthy diet.
   (D) All of the nutritionist's patients incorporated exactly the same form of exercise to their daily routine.
   (E) There were only eighty patients who participated in the nutritionist's weight loss study.

2. **A company specializing in the sales of industrial flooring has been hit hard by the recent economic downturn. Mike has worked for this company for fifteen years and now holds a senior sales position. In recent years, his sales record has been stellar, but over the last few months, his sales have been low due to the slowdown. His boss has asked to meet with him next week. Mike is convinced that the company will not fire him: "I've been working with the company for well over a decade, and I have an excellent sales record. If anyone can find a way to boost sales and benefit the company, I'm the person. Therefore, I have no doubt that my job is safe."**

   The flaw in Mike's reasoning is that he

   (A) believes that his loyalty to the company will guarantee that he keeps his job
   (B) does not realize that the company is already bankrupt and has to lay off many employees
   (C) equates his past success with future opportunity regardless of the economic conditions
   (D) is a close friend of his boss and knows that his boss would not risk firing a friend
   (E) assumes that the company has as much confidence in his ability to improve his sales record as he does

Questions 3 and 4

The vast majority of extant music from the medieval period is recorded on manuscripts. The production of medieval manuscripts was very costly, because all manuscripts were painstakingly copied by hand onto an expensive form of parchment. As a result, few people were able to produce or own them, and the Catholic Church, which had literate scribes as well as considerable wealth, produced and maintained most manuscripts during the Middle Ages. Any medieval music not recorded on manuscripts has now been lost to history. Most of the medieval music still in existence is sacred music.

3. **The claims made in the above passage, if true, best support which of the following statements?**

   (A) The greatest music of the medieval period was sacred music, and for this reason it was recorded on manuscripts.
   (B) Because the Church did not value popular music, the scribes were not allowed to copy it onto manuscripts.
   (C) As the Catholic Church was the center of medieval life, popular music paralleled sacred music very closely.
   (D) In addition to the Church, many wealthy aristocratic households held large numbers of music manuscripts.
   (E) Because the Church primarily recorded sacred music on manuscripts, historians are unable to confidently describe medieval popular music.

4. **The passage above implies all of the following EXCEPT:**

   (A) The parchment on which medieval music was copied was difficult to produce.
   (B) Few were qualified for the time-consuming task of copying manuscripts.
   (C) The Church was selective about what music was copied down.
   (D) The copying of manuscripts was limited to people who knew how to read.
   (E) Most of the non-sacred music from the medieval period has been lost to history.

5. **Lito: The island of Kauai features a number of one-lane bridges that are potentially very dangerous. Kauai has recently seen a rise in the number of tourists visiting the island, and most tourists are not familiar with navigating the one-lane bridges. Over the last year, the number of car accidents has increased, and most of these accidents have occurred at the one-lane bridges. These bridges need to be widened to accommodate tourists and prevent future accidents.**

   Miteki: Kauai has a traditional commitment to environmental integrity. The one-lane bridges were installed to minimize the impact on the island environment. To widen the one-lane bridges could have a dangerous effect on the native plant and animal life.

   As a response to Lito's argument, Miteki's comment is flawed because she

   (A) relies on faulty information to support her argument
   (B) uses circular reasoning to make her main points
   (C) focuses on a minor issue instead of a more important one
   (D) responds to a supporting point instead of a main point
   (E) fails to address the substance of Lito's claim by making a secondary argument

6. **Art scholar Herbert Read has noted of Impressionist artist Pierre-Auguste Renoir that he was the final painter representing the artistic tradition that started at Rubens and ended at Watteau. Peter Paul Rubens, the Flemish artist who flourished in the seventeenth century, is renowned for his creative choice of subject matter, from landscapes to allegory. Antoine Watteau, the French-born painter who died early in the eighteenth century, is generally remembered for his ability to interweave themes from Italian theatre into his paintings. During the late nineteenth century in which he thrived, the French artist Renoir was particularly renowned for his application of light and shading, his use of vibrant color, and his ability to create an intimate scene.**

   Which of the following best summarizes the main conclusion of the passage above?

   (A) Like Rubens and Watteau, Renoir selected subject matter that was creative and theatrical.
   (B) Read believes that Rubens, Watteau, and Renoir are among the greatest painters in Western history.
   (C) Read believes that apart from Renoir, no great artist of note has arisen since the early eighteenth century.
   (D) Relative to other painters of Renoir's era and later ones, Renoir best carried on the tradition of individual style that defined earlier artists.
   (E) The painters who had the greatest impact between the seventeenth and late nineteenth centuries were either Flemish or French.

7. **School Principal: Recent testing indicates that students in our school are struggling in math. At this time, the students are spending only forty-five minutes each day on math lessons. The testing also indicates that students are excelling in reading, however. The students currently spend one and a half hours each day on reading. Therefore, we need to increase the amount of time spent on math in order to improve the math skills of students in our school.**

   The weakness in the school principal's argument is similar to the weakness in which of the following arguments?

   (A) Family psychologists have found that the children with the best speech development are those whose parents read to them at an early age. Therefore, all parents should read to their young children in order to enhance their speech development skills.
   (B) Travel agents routinely see that families who have the most comfortable and relaxing vacations are those who stay in three- or four-star resorts. Therefore, any family hoping to have a comfortable and relaxing vacation should restrict accommodation choices to three- and four-star resorts.
   (C) Research has shown that traders who put their money in options tend to be more likely to suffer from losing trades. Research also suggests that traders who put their money in stocks, which require a larger investment up front, tend to be more successful. Therefore, traders should put their money into stocks if they hope to have winning trades.
   (D) Studies suggest that students who are most successful in college have attended advanced placement classes in high school. Therefore, those students who hope to be most successful in college should strive to be accepted into advanced placement classes.
   (E) Caitlyn and Moira discovered that Caitlyn was spending a little more than Moira at the grocery story each month. But Moira usually stopped at the grocery store several times each week, while Caitlyn never shopped more than once a week. Therefore, Caitlyn and Moira are actually spending the same amount, because Moira must pay the extra cost of gas for several trips to the store.

8. **The CEO of a major fast-food chain just released a statement indicating that the chain has revamped its ingredient list and revised its menu options so that all selections on the menu are now healthier than any of the menus from competing fast-food chains. Among the changes that will be made, the fast-food chain will be eliminating unsaturated fats and downsizing portions. He claims, "We've heard the request of our customers for healthier meals, and with the changes we're making we'll be offering our customers better choices. Our customers will now have healthy fast-food options that put all other fast-food chains to shame."**

   Which of the following, if true, most seriously undermines the CEO's claim of offering healthier selections to customers?

   (A) While the fast-food chain is improving certain ingredients, they are still including additives that tend to make customers addicted to the fast food.
   (B) The CEO is receiving a large bonus for the potential boost in sales that the new menu options are expected to bring.
   (C) A focus group unanimously complained that the food was bland and not as tasty as items on the previous menu.
   (D) The fast-food chain has begun marketing heavily to children, encouraging children to ask for the healthier options when ordering in a restaurant.
   (E) The fast-food chain has not removed many of its previous menu items but has instead simply replaced the unhealthy ingredients with healthier options and reduced the portion sizes.

9. Head of a regional psychiatric association: As an organization, we have found that patients over the last two decades are increasingly likely to suffer from depression that in some cases can lead to an early death. At the same time, we have found that those patients who already practice some form of spirituality tend to be less likely to suffer from depression and thus to live longer and healthier lives. A recent study in a major psychological journal confirms this experience. As a result, we suggest that our members begin encouraging their patients to explore spirituality in the hopes that it will provide them with longer and healthier lives.

The primary argument made by the head of the regional psychological association depends on which of the following assumptions?

(A) All of the patients being treated by psychiatrists in the regional psychiatric association are suffering from depression.
(B) All patients noted for their longer and healthier lives were practicing the same form of spirituality.
(C) All members of the psychiatric association must also pursue spirituality in order to make educated recommendations to their patients.
(D) When untreated, depression is a serious condition that leads to death.
(E) All forms of spirituality are equally healthy, and any form of spirituality will provide patients with longer and healthier lives.

10. Economists have noted in recent weeks that the price per barrel of crude oil has decreased sharply over the last few months, dropping as much as seventy percent. They have also found, however, that the price of gasoline at the pump has not seen a similarly sharp reduction, and gasoline prices have dropped only about fifty percent.

Given the statements above, which of the following most helps to explain the difference between the drop in the price of crude oil per barrel and the drop in the price of gasoline at the pump?

(A) The demand for crude oil worldwide has suddenly decreased; this has led to a drop in the price of crude oil.
(B) While crude oil prices were high, refineries that processed crude oil into gasoline absorbed a large part of the cost; these refineries are now recovering some profit by not yet passing the decreased price in crude oil to customers at the pump.
(C) Oil companies have recently discovered a large and previously untapped oil reserve; this discovery immediately sent crude oil prices plummeting.
(D) A major wind energy company unexpectedly announced plans to provide a large-scale alternative energy option to citizens in several nations; this created a competition for crude oil that negatively affected its price.
(E) Due to the increasingly low cost of crude oil, the cost of production now exceeds the return in value; this has forced some oil production companies to go out of business.

11. It is generally assumed that although some restrictions exist on the freedom of speech or expression—restrictions that usually forbid any speech or expression that might be described as hateful or dangerous—no restrictions do or can exist on freedom of thought or conscience. In fact, the Universal Declaration of Human Rights guarantees that all people have the right to the freedom of thought, the freedom of conscience, and the freedom of religion. But although thought cannot successfully be controlled through legal means, it can be controlled through propaganda, or even through an educational system: if children are taught from an early age to think or believe a certain way, it might not be possible for them to have real freedom of thought or conscience as adults, if they have no real ability to think for themselves.

Which of the following best summarizes the argument implied within the passage?

(A) Freedom of thought or conscience cannot really exist, despite international laws that guarantee it.
(B) Freedom of thought or conscience is controlled in the same way as freedom of speech or expression.
(C) In some cases, thought might be controlled to such an extent that genuine freedom of thought does not exist.
(D) The Universal Declaration of Human Rights is necessary for the guarantee of freedom of thought or conscience.
(E) Restrictions on freedom of speech or expression should be eliminated in order to guarantee real freedom of thought.

12. Conrad: The town of Ecoville is a leader in the green movement and is establishing excellent standards for all citizens, standards that will make the town one of the greenest in the country. By the year 2020, all residents in the town of Ecoville will be required to drive vehicles that adhere to certain environmental standards, such as standards regarding reduced emissions and better gas mileage. These new standards will improve the air quality and environmental health of Ecoville.

Eloise: The new environmental standards for vehicles in Ecoville are good, but they should be delayed or revised until funding for the standards can be established. As currently planned, the standards will place undue burden on lower-income families, many of whom do not have the extra income to meet the requirements. Even the greenest town will have lower-income residents, and these residents might not have the means to buy new vehicles or convert current vehicles to adhere to the standards.

Eloise counters Conrad's argument by doing which of the following?

(A) She acknowledges the reasonableness of his argument but presents a counter-argument that shows the difficulty of implementing the new requirements.
(B) She agrees with the substance of his conclusion but suggests alternative reasons for that conclusion.
(C) She points out a flaw in his reasoning and offers a different perspective that is more logical.
(D) She disagrees with his argument entirely by proving that the established standards will accomplish very little.
(E) She overlooks the substance of his argument and redirects the attention to a secondary point.

13. The largest public health organization in the country has raised concerns about the herbal sweetener stevia, claiming that it has conducted extensive testing and that in its opinion the dangers of stevia outweigh its potential benefits. The organization claims that people who consume stevia are at risk for cancer or other life-threatening health problems. As a result, the public health organization has recommended that the FDA recognize the dangers of stevia and ban it for human consumption.

Which of the following, if true, most seriously undermines the public health organization's claim that stevia is dangerous?

(A) The head of the largest artificial sweetener manufacturer in the country has financed the studies exploring the health dangers of stevia.
(B) It is common knowledge that stevia is widely used in Japan, and no negative side effects have been reported.
(C) The head of the public health organization is currently on the short list for a senior position in the FDA.
(D) A large national diabetes association has publicly supported stevia as a safe sugar alternative for diabetics.
(E) No tests conducted by the public health organization indicate that stevia has ever caused cancer or any other health problems in human beings.

14. The primary hospital in the town of Riverton has been criticized for declining to accept patients who do not have insurance or who have insufficient insurance to cover their medical care at the hospital. Responding to the criticism, the mayor of Riverton has denounced the hospital for discrimination and demanded that the policy be revised. The mayor has also encouraged the city council to pass an ordinance requiring hospitals to accept all patients, regardless of insurance coverage. The city council has declined, however, arguing that as a private business the hospital has the right to refuse customers who are unable to pay for hospital services.

Which of the following assumptions can be inferred from the city council's argument that the hospital has a right to decline treatment to patients?

(A) The majority of residents in the town of Riverton have sufficient insurance coverage, so there will be very few patients who are refused service.
(B) The city council believes that anti-discrimination laws do not cover a hospital refusing service to patients who are unable to pay for their medical services.
(C) The uninsured and insufficiently insured patients will be covered by state and federal funding, so the hospital will ultimately not need to turn patients away.
(D) There is a large hospital in a town very near to Riverton that accepts all patients regardless of their insurance coverage.
(E) The mayor is a member of a different political party than most members of the city council, so they tend to oppose him on every recommendation he makes.

15. Scientific journal: Recent testing was conducted to examine the health benefits of drinking milk and what effect it has on calcium levels in women over the age of forty. The test was conducted on 200 women in similar states of health over the course of three months. The women were asked to drink two eight-ounce glasses of milk each day. All participants followed this stipulation closely. Results show that 75% of the women showed a mild increase in calcium levels, whereas 25% of the women showed a sharp improvement in calcium levels.

Which of the following, if true, most explains the inconsistency among study participants in their testing results?

(A) Twenty-five percent of the women drank whole milk each day, whereas the other 75% chose to drink low-fat milk.
(B) Seventy-five percent of the women were suffering from osteoporosis and thus did not absorb as much of the calcium from the milk.
(C) Seventy-five percent of the women were over the age of fifty, whereas the other 25% were under the age of fifty.
(D) Twenty-five percent of the women were taking a multi-vitamin with added calcium in addition to drinking two eight-ounce glasses of milk each day.
(E) Seventy-five percent of the women had given birth, while the other 25% had never had children.

16. Traditional regional performing arts groups across the country provide an important service to small communities. Most of these groups focus on the performance of time-honored material and offer people within the communities an opportunity to experience excellent traditional performances without having to travel far. Unfortunately, federal funding tends to support avant-garde groups whose focus is largely on progressive material. Although these groups are unquestionably an essential facet of the performing arts, they do not generally draw as wide of audiences and thus are receiving an undue amount of federal funding for the service that they provide to a community and the return on the federal investment. Those responsible for providing federal grants to performing arts groups should reconsider the allotment of funding in order to favor traditional performing arts groups with respect to their service to a community.

The argument in the passage above proceeds by

(A) presenting a general statement, developing it with details, and suggesting an action to be taken
(B) demanding attention for a cause, citing potential dangers for ignoring it, and insisting upon change
(C) undermining the opposition, calling previous activity into question, and drawing a conclusion
(D) beginning with a call to action, pointing out problems with those who oppose it, and concluding with a general remark
(E) publicizing a concern, discussing possible alternatives to address it, and encouraging action

17. Editorial within local Williamsburg newspaper: Here in Williamsburg, we have an amazing educational opportunity in the form of the extraordinary colonial project that takes visitors back in time to the early days of American history. It has come to my attention that very few local schools take students on field trips there, and I believe that students are missing out on this opportunity. All local schools should be required to take the students to the colonial center, and funding should be provided to make this recommendation a reality. A visit to this wonderful place will benefit all school children and will offer them an experience they will cherish for years.

Which of the following, if true, most seriously undermines the argument made in the editorial?

(A) Williamsburg schools focus heavily on field trips with hands-on activity, and the colonial center in Williamsburg provides such opportunities for students.
(B) The writer of the editorial is the head of the marketing department at the colonial center and has been charged with increasing student traffic there.
(C) Local schools have polled the families of students, and it has been found that 99% of students have already visited the colonial center with their families.
(D) The colonial center at Williamsburg already offers significant discounts to school groups, and the city has little money to provide additional funding.
(E) Gasoline prices have risen sharply in the last few months, causing schools to cut back on field trips and focus on projects that can be completed in the classroom.

18. A large airport in a major city has proposed certain changes intended to improve the ease of flying for domestic passengers but that will also have the negative effect of creating burdens for travelers flying internationally. A number of travelers who frequent the airport for international flights have signed a petition requesting that the airport alter the proposed plans. The airport considered the petition carefully but has decided to proceed with the original plans, despite the fact that many of the travelers who use the airport for international travel have announced that they will begin booking their flights through a different airport.

Which of the following can be inferred from the decision made by the airport to continue with the changes?

(A) There nearest airport that offers international flights is too far for many of the travelers to switch.
(B) Other airports offering international flights are just as burdensome for travelers.
(C) The airport has already spent a large sum on the proposed plans and it is not cost-effective to give them up.
(D) The benefits from the changes for domestic travelers will bring in enough new domestic passengers to outweigh the loss of the international travelers.
(E) Although the changes will negatively affect international travelers in the short term, the airport has a long-term plan to improve international travel.

19. Conservative voter: Universal healthcare is a very controversial issue in our country that conservative voters have traditionally opposed, because of the cost to the taxpayer. Conservative voters should support universal healthcare, however, because under such a healthcare system the government would actually spend fewer tax dollars than at present. In other countries with universal healthcare, the governments spend less tax money per patient than our government currently spends for a healthcare system that is not universal.

A weakness in this argument lies in the fact that the voter

(A) gives an inconsistent definition of universal healthcare
(B) assumes that universalizing is the only way to reduce the cost per person
(C) making unfounded claims in order to establish a conclusion
(D) deviates from a partisan position to make a policy recommendation
(E) couches an ad hominem (or personal) insult in constructive criticism

20. Language development specialists have discovered that most children learn languages best before puberty. During the years leading up to puberty, children's brains are capable of absorbing new languages with less effort than the brains of children who are post-pubescent. As a result, pre-pubescent children are able to think in a new language far more quickly than their post-pubescent counterparts, and children prior to puberty are also able to retain those languages more easily than if they learn the languages after puberty. Funding is limited for second language programs, so schools in this country tend to delay the study of modern languages until high school, but young children would benefit from second language programs in the elementary years.

Which of the following best summarizes the main point of the passage?

(A) Children learn languages best before puberty because their brains absorb new languages more easily than the brains of those who are post-pubescent.
(B) There is currently not enough government funding to provide for second language programs at the elementary level.
(C) Because of a difference in brain development, children before puberty can learn to think in a new language more quickly than children after puberty.
(D) It is a mistake to delay the teaching of second languages until high school, as there is little chance that students will be able to retain a second language.
(E) Because children learn languages more easily before puberty, schools should adopt second language programs at the elementary level.

QUESTIONS 21 AND 22

The village of Eyam in central England is often referred to as "plague village." In the summer of 1665, an outbreak of the plague was discovered in the village, and the people of the village cut off all outside contacts and let the disease run its course. For almost a year and a half, the plague touched families throughout Eyam, and when villagers finally reopened their village to outsiders, over 75% of the population had died. More interesting, however, was the fact that nearly 25% of the population was still living. In some cases, the plague carried off all but one member of a family: Elizabeth Hancock is remembered for having lost her husband and six children, but she never contracted the plague, even while nursing them. Hancock's story is not unique; most of the survivors proved to be immune to the infection altogether. Some researchers have found that a large proportion of the descendents of plague survivors from Eyam carry a mutation of a gene known as delta 32.

21. Which of the following conclusions can best be inferred from the information in the passage?

(A) The delta 32 mutation was limited to residents of the village of Eyam and now appears only in their descendents.
(B) The people of the village of Eyam indicate a disproportionately high rate of the delta 32 mutation.
(C) Since the descendents of many of the plague survivors carry the delta 32 mutation, some researchers believe this gene helped people resist contracting the plague.
(D) The plague survivors from the village of Eyam developed the delta 32 mutation in response to the outbreak of plague and are thus immune to future outbreaks.
(E) The people of the village of Eyam were wrong to isolate themselves during the outbreak of the plague, because it guaranteed death for so many residents.

22. Which of the following, if true, most undermines the implications made within the passage?

(A) In laboratory studies with rats, other researchers have discovered that the delta 32 mutation does not contribute to resisting contraction of the plague.
(B) The delta 32 gene has been found in people throughout Europe, as well as in America in people of European ancestry.
(C) Some researchers believe that the delta 32 gene also protects individuals against the contraction of HIV.
(D) During the seventeenth century, it was believed that vinegar stopped the spread of plague by killing off the disease.
(E) The plague that struck Eyam (in Derbyshire) also struck London around the same time.

23. When first presented on the market, the now-ubiquitous microwave oven was anything but a hit with consumers. Percy Spencer, an employee with Raytheon who discovered the potential for cooking with microwaves, first presented the Radarange in 1947, a massive oven that weighed over 700 pounds and was around six feet tall. Over the next few years, Raytheon made some minor improvements to the microwave oven but was unable to elicit a positive reception from the public. It was not until Raytheon's competitor Litton began developing microwave ovens of its own in the 1960s that the public embraced the new technology on a wide scale. Litton's new oven jumpstarted the craze for microwaves and by 1975 about a million of them were in American homes.

Which of the following, if true, best provides an explanation for why Litton was more successful at selling microwave ovens in the United States than Raytheon?

(A) Litton marketed the microwave oven at a large trade show in Chicago, thereby gaining more consumers through publicity.
(B) Litton expanded its marketing to Japan, where the microwave ovens proved to be very popular.
(C) Litton made the microwave so popular that more than 90% of families in the U.S. now have a microwave.
(D) Litton's model redesigned the microwave oven to its now-familiar compact size, so that it was affordable and fit easily into a kitchen.
(E) Litton had long been developing the technology for microwave ovens and had surpassed the technology used by Raytheon.

24. The English scientist Edward Jenner (1749–1823) is usually credited with the discovery of vaccines in the late eighteenth century, when he began vaccinating against cowpox (hence the term "vaccine," which derives from vacca, meaning cow). But at least one hundred years before Jenner's discovery, the Ottoman Turks were already using methods of inoculation to prevent disease. Lady Montagu, wife of the British ambassador to Turkey during the early eighteenth century, records that she had her son vaccinated in Istanbul using a method that the Turkish had been employing for decades. The Ottoman Turks, however, were not the first to use vaccines. It is believed that the Chinese had discovered the value of inoculation as far back as 200 BC, and one scholar has suggested that vaccination as a common means of disease prevention might have been widespread in India as early as the eleventh century.

Which of the following best summarizes the main point of the passage?

(A) Edward Jenner is mistakenly credited with the discovery of vaccines, because Lady Montagu inoculated her son in Istanbul in the early eighteenth century.
(B) Although Edward Jenner is usually credited with the discovery of vaccines in the late eighteenth century, research indicates that vaccines were used in the East long before Jenner began using them.
(C) Historians believe that doctors in China and India were using vaccines as early as the eleventh century and maybe even as far back as 200 BC.
(D) The Ottoman Turks are wrongly credited for the discovery of vaccines in the early eighteenth century, because vaccines were used in China and India long before this.
(E) Edward Jenner took credit in the late eighteenth century for the discovery of a vaccine that Lady Montagu used prior to this to inoculate her son in Turkey.

25. Economist: In a weak economy when the stock market is struggling, the U.S. dollar traditionally falls, and the price of gold rises in response to the declining dollar. Recent economic data indicates that the markets are currently struggling: the key stock indexes are lower than they have been in at least two years, and various market sectors are in decline. At the same time, the value of the dollar is still high, and the price of gold remains low. Therefore, the price of gold suggests that we are due for a market turnaround soon.

Given the information above, the economist's argument is flawed because:

(A) He relies entirely on traditional data without adequately considering anomalies in the market's movement.
(B) He bases his commentary on stock indexes, which are traditionally unreliable for determining market direction.
(C) The price of gold is currently fixed at the government level, so it is impossible to rely on that as an indicator of market direction.
(D) He should be focusing more closely on the movement of certain market sectors instead of the price of gold.
(E) He fails to take other significant market indicators into effect and thus comes to a conclusion too quickly about the market's movement.

Section II

Time – 35 minutes

24 Questions

Cluster 1:

There are five people—Sarah, Bill, Eric, Molly, Nick—scheduled for appointments at a doctor's office on a specific morning, plus a walk-in, Katie. There are five appointment slots: 9:30, 10:00, 10:30, 11:00, and 11:30. The following conditions apply:

Katie will only get a slot if one of the five people with an appointment does not show up.

Sarah is not scheduled for 10:00 or 11:00.

Eric is scheduled for 11:30.

Molly's appointment is immediately before Nick's.

1. **Nick's appointment CANNOT be in which appointment slots?**
   (A) 9:30 or 10:30
   (B) 9:30 or 10:00
   (C) 10:00 or 11:00
   (D) 10:00 or 11:30
   (E) 9:30 or 11:30

2. **Which one of the following is a possible ordering of the 5 people's appointments?**
   (A) Sarah, Molly, Nick, Eric, Bill
   (B) Bill, Sarah, Molly, Nick, Eric
   (C) Sarah, Molly, Bill, Nick, Eric
   (D) Sarah, Molly, Nick, Bill, Eric
   (E) Molly, Nick, Bill, Sarah, Eric

3. **If Sarah's appointment is at 10:30, which one of the following must be false?**
   (A) Bill's appointment is at 11:00
   (B) Sarah's appointment is before Nick's
   (C) Nick's appointment is before Sarah's
   (D) Bill's appointment is after Sarah's
   (E) Molly's appointment is at 9:30

4. **If Bill does not show up for his appointment, which possible appointment slot has opened up for Katie to take?**
   (A) 9:30 or 11:00
   (B) 10:00 or 10:30
   (C) 10:00 or 11:00
   (D) 10:30 or 11:00
   (E) 10:00 or 11:30

5. **If Molly's appointment is at 10:00, then Bill's appointment must be at:**
   (A) 9:30
   (B) 10:00
   (C) 10:30
   (D) 11:00
   (E) 11:30

6. **If Eric switches appointment times so that his appointment is now at 11:00, if none of the other conditions change, who now has the 11:30 appointment slot?**
   (A) Bill or Molly
   (B) Katie or Sarah
   (C) Molly or Nick
   (D) Nick or Bill
   (E) Sarah or Bill

Cluster 2:

A group of six friends—Jack, Kimberly, Lee, Melissa, Nick, Olivia—go out to eat at a restaurant. They are seated evenly around a circular table based on the following conditions:

Melissa does not sit next to Jack.

Jack sits next to Olivia or Nick, but not both of them.

Kimberly sits next to Nick.

If Olivia sits next to Jack, then she doesn't sit next to Lee.

7. **Of the following, which one is a possible seating arrangement of the six friends?**
   (A) Kimberly, Nick, Jack, Olivia, Melissa, Lee
   (B) Lee, Melissa, Kimberly, Jack, Olivia, Nick
   (C) Melissa, Lee, Jack, Nick, Kimberly, Olivia
   (D) Lee, Melissa, Jack, Nick, Kimberly, Olivia
   (E) Lee, Olivia, Jack, Kimberly, Nick, Melissa

8. **If Jack sits next to Kimberly, then which one of the following pairs of people must be seated next to each other?**
   (A) Lee and Nick
   (B) Melissa and Nick
   (C) Jack and Nick
   (D) Melissa and Kimberly
   (E) Olivia and Kimberly

9. **If Jack and Olivia sit next to each other, then Lee CANNOT sit next to both:**
   (A) Jack and Nick
   (B) Jack and Kimberly
   (C) Nick and Melissa
   (D) Jack and Melissa
   (E) Kimberly and Nick

10. If Jack sits next to Olivia, then which of the following is a complete and accurate list of the people who could also sit next to Jack?

(A) Lee
(B) Nick, Melissa
(C) Lee, Melissa
(D) Lee, Kimberly
(E) Lee, Nick, Kimberly

11. Which of the following must be false if Jack sits next to Nick?

I. Kimberly sits next to Lee.
II. Nick sits directly opposite Melissa.
III. Lee sits next to Jack and Olivia.

(A) I only
(B) III only
(C) I and II only
(D) II and III only
(E) I, II, and III

12. If Olivia sits next to Nick, then which of the following must be true:

(A) Melissa sits next to Nick and Lee.
(B) Nick sits next to Kimberly and Lee.
(C) Olivia sits next to Nick and Jack.
(D) Lee sits next to Olivia and Jack.
(E) Melissa sits next to Jack and Lee.

Cluster 3:

A new security code for a bank's vault is generated at the beginning of each day using only the letters V, W, X, Y, and Z. The code is generated using the following rules:

Rule 1: V W X Y Z is the basic code
Rule 2: If V W is immediately followed by X, then V W can be moved to the end of the code.
Rule 3: If the Y Z occurs at the end of a code, then they can switch places.
Rule 4: A copy of the last three letters in the code can be placed at the front of the code

13. Which one of the following is NOT a possible vault code?

(A) V W X Y Z
(B) V W Y Z X
(C) V W X Z Y
(D) X Y Z V W
(E) X Y Z V W X Y Z

14. Which of the following letters can end a code?

I. V
II. Y
III. W

(A) I only
(B) II only
(C) III only
(D) I and II only
(E) II and III only

15. The code X Y Z X Z Y V W can be formed from the base code by applying the rules in which one of the following orders?

(A) 2 3 4
(B) 3 4 2
(C) 4 3 2
(D) 4 3 3 2
(E) 4 2 3

16. If a fifth rule is added to the other four which states that whenever a V or X begins a code, it can be dropped and the result is still a valid code, then which of the following is NOT a code?

(A) W X Z Y
(B) Y Z V W
(C) Z Y V W X Z Y
(D) V W X Y Z V W
(E) Y Z W X Y Z

17. If the fourth rule was changed from copying the last three letters to the front of the code to moving the last two letters to the front of the code, which one of the following is a valid code?

(A) Z V W X Y
(B) Y Z X V W
(C) X Z V W Y
(D) W V X Z Y
(E) Z Y X W V

Cluster 4:

A lunch line at a school has a number of different options as the students progress from station to station:

Station 1—Buns:
Multigrain, White

Station 2—Meat:
Turkey, Beef, Chicken

Station 3—Toppings:
Lettuce, Tomatoes, Onions, Cheese, Pickles

The following rules must be followed by every child going through the lunch line:
One bun, one meat, and three toppings must be chosen.
If Lettuce is chosen, then Pickles will also be chosen.
Pickles will not be chosen as a topping on a White bun.
If Beef is chosen as a meat, then Onions may not be chosen as a topping.
Every burger must include 3 of the five healthy options - Multigrain, Turkey, Lettuce, Tomatoes, and Onions.

18. If a white bun is chosen, which of the following must also be chosen?

(A) Turkey and Onions
(B) Chicken and Cheese
(C) Chicken and Tomatoes
(D) Chicken and Lettuce
(E) Lettuce and Cheese

19. Which of the following cannot be on the same burger?

(A) White, Turkey, Cheese
(B) White, Beef, Lettuce
(C) Multigrain, Turkey, Onions
(D) Multigrain, Beef, Pickles
(E) Multigrain, Chicken, Tomatoes

20. How many valid topping combinations can go on a Multigrain and Chicken burger?

(A) 1
(B) 2
(C) 3
(D) 4
(E) 5

21. If Beef is chosen as the meat, what is a complete list of toppings that could be chosen?

(A) Tomatoes, Onions, Cheese
(B) Lettuce, Tomatoes, Cheese
(C) Lettuce, Tomatoes, Pickles
(D) Lettuce, Onions, Pickles
(E) Tomatoes, Pickles, Cheese

22. If a burger has Pickles, Cheese, and Turkey which of the following can be the two remaining options?

(A) Tomatoes and White
(B) Tomatoes and Onions
(C) Lettuce and White
(D) Lettuce and Beef
(E) Lettuce and Multigrain

Cluster 5:

A security company employs six guards—A, B, C, D, E, F—to guard a chemical plant. Each guard can either be on duty or off duty, but at least one guard must be on duty at any given time.
If A is on duty, then neither B nor C is on duty.
D and E cannot be on duty at the same time.
F can only be on duty if A is also on duty.
If C is on duty, then D is also on duty.

23. What is the maximum number of guards who can be on duty at the same time?

(A) 1
(B) 2
(C) 3
(D) 4
(E) 5

24. If A and D are both off duty, which one of the following is a complete and accurate list of the other guards who could be on duty?

(A) B
(B) B and E
(C) B and C
(D) B, C, and F
(E) B, C, E, and F

Section III

Time – 35 minutes

27 Questions

Directions: Each passage in this section is followed by a group of questions to be answered on the basis of what is stated or implied in the passage. Some questions may have more than one possible answer. However, you are to choose the best answer, that is, the response that most accurately and completely answers the questions, and blacken the corresponding space on your answer sheet.

Passage 1

Until the early part of the twentieth century, Federalist No. 10, James Madison's essay on the issue of dealing with factions in a society that seeks to be unified, received very little attention. First published in November of 1787, No. 10 has generally been overshadowed by the more famous No. 51, No. 78, and No. 84, all of which are considered to be highly influential statements about the requirements for establishing a republic that survives and operates successfully. Within the last few decades, however, scholars have given No. 10 more consideration as they apply Madison's arguments to a society now clearly divided by political parties and various individual interests. That being said, No. 10 was just as relevant in its own time, as there was no shortage of partisanship and individual interests. The difference seems to lie in the fact that the partisanship of late eighteenth-century American politics has long since disappeared and is no longer relevant for the modern reader.

Written in a joint effort by James Madison, Alexander Hamilton, and John Jay (later first chief justice of the Supreme Court), the eighty-five Federalist Papers were composed as a rebuttal to the Anti-Federalists. This group, which included such statesmen as Patrick Henry and George Clinton, opposed the ratification of the Constitution out of fear that a strong central government would strip the states of their rights and that a President would ultimately become a monarch. One of the primary arguments of the Anti-Federalists was that a nation formed by states as large and diverse as the American states could never truly be united. Arguing under the pseudonym "Cato," the Anti-Federalists claimed that a nation of states as diverse as the American states could never unite fully without requiring that the states compromise sovereign rights for the benefit of the central government; they argued that the "unkindred legislature" recommended by the Constitution would lead to the biblical example of the house collapsing because it has been divided against itself. In essence, the Anti-Federalists believed that factions would always exist and that it would be impossible to forge a union without forcing uninterested factions together in an uncomfortable state of existence. To some extent, the fears of the Anti-Federalists were proven justified: in 1789, the Constitution was ratified (with the inclusion of the Bill of Rights, which Madison suggested as a means of compromise between Federalists and Anti-Federalists), and the Anti-Federalists more or less ceased to exist, its members left with little choice but to accept the system that had been adopted.

With the silencing of the Anti-Federalist faction and the enthusiasm of unity surrounding the ratification of the Constitution, Madison's arguments in Federalist No. 10 seemed to lose their relevance in the latter days of the eighteenth century. According to historian Douglass Adair, it was his fellow historian Charles Beard who turned scholarly attention on No. 10 by his interpretation of the Constitution as a tool used to exploit the lower classes, an interpretation given at a time when Marxist theories were increasingly in vogue and such interpretations were gaining credibility in academia. For his part, Adair chose to see No. 10 as a document that was exclusive in application and in relevance to the time of its composition. But other historians have recognized the significance of Madison's thesis in Federalist No. 10 for the modern age, especially with regard to his arguments about the need to quell factions for the good of societal unification, and it is now considered to be far more relevant to this era than to its own. What historians have failed to appreciate is that No. 10 has a continuing relevance by speaking to an issue that has always been, and will probably always be, a part of any functioning political system. In this, perhaps, the Anti-Federalists have the last word.

1. **The passage can be described as doing which of the following?**

(A) Contrasting two viewpoints and then arguing in favor of one of them
(B) Defending a traditional argument by supporting it with scholarly sources
(C) Offering a new perspective on an ongoing scholarly argument
(D) Defining a term and presenting a thesis in defense of it
(E) Considering a popular academic position and challenging it with new evidence

2. **Which of the following best expresses the author's main point?**

(A) Federalist No. 10 discusses a political reality that the Anti-Federalists understood and that is not limited by era.
(B) Federalist No. 10 has been ignored for too long and deserves more attention by scholars.
(C) Federalist No. 10 had virtually no relevance when it was written and has acquired relevance in recent decades only.
(D) The Federalists did not appreciate the reality that factions are and always have been inevitable.
(E) The Anti-Federalists were ultimately correct in their understanding of human nature within a political system.

3. **Which of the following can be inferred from the statement by Douglass Adair that Federalist No. 10 was a "document that was exclusive in application and in relevance to the time of its composition"?**

(A) Adair believed that all of the Federalist Papers applied only to the eighteenth century and the problems of that age.
(B) Adair disagreed with Charles Beard about the Federalist Papers as instruments of class exploitation.
(C) Adair agreed with the Anti-Federalists about the inevitability of factions within eighteenth-century politics.
(D) Adair believed that Federalist No. 10 might have contemporary relevance if the current political situation developed problems similar to those in the eighteenth century.
(E) Adair did not believe that Federalist No. 10 could be applied directly to the current political conditions.

4. **The passage above suggests which of the following?**

(A) The Federalist Papers were an essential contribution to America's understanding of the Constitution and its purpose.
(B) Although the Federalists won the primary argument for the Constitution, the Anti-Federalists were ultimately correct in their belief that the country could not be fully united.
(C) More eighteenth-century Americans should have paid attention to the Anti-Federalists, because silencing them after the ratification of the Constitution had long-term consequences for free speech.
(D) It is a great irony of eighteenth-century America that the ratification of the Constitution, a document committed to establishing freedoms, actually succeeded by quelling the opposition.
(E) Contemporary historians are correct in their belief that Federalist No. 10 is a significant contribution to the Federalist Papers, though not as important as some of the others.

5. **The passage implies that the author would agree with which of the following?**

(A) Federalist No. 51, No. 78, and No. 84 remain the three most important essays of the Federalist Papers.
(B) The Marxist theories touted by Charles Beard failed to interpret the Federalist Papers accurately or effectively.
(C) The Anti-Federalists were forced to remain quiet about some of their ideas after the ratification of the Constitution.
(D) Douglass Adair's argument that Federalist No. 10 is primarily of eighteenth-century relevance is intentionally misleading.
(E) The Anti-Federalists had a more realistic appreciation of social and political challenges than the Federalists did.

6. **Which of the following best expresses the meaning of the word "unkindred," as used by "Cato" in line 22 of the passage?**

(A) Diverse
(B) Disorganized
(C) Disparate
(D) Unique
(E) Antagonistic

7. **Which of the following best describes the organization of the passage?**

(A) The author presents several theories, narrows the focus to one, and then defends a primary argument.
(B) The author suggests a main point, diverts to discuss historical context, and then returns to the main point to summarize.
(C) The author begins with a wide historical focus and ultimately narrows to a contemporary focus.
(D) The author states a thesis, defends it with historical research and quotes from leading scholarly authorities, and then restates the thesis.
(E) The author presents an idea, offers historical context, and then argues a main point.

Passage 2

English language scholars generally agree that the modern English language developed from several sources: the Anglo-Saxon language, or Old English, spoken by the Germanic peoples who migrated to the island of Britain in the fifth century; the Old Norse influences of the Vikings and the Danish kings of England in the ninth and tenth centuries; the French influence of the Norman invaders in the eleventh century; and the Latin influences of the earlier Roman inhabitants and the Catholic Church. However, one mystery remains. When the Anglo-Saxons arrived in Britain, there were numerous Celtic inhabitants dwelling alongside what remained of the Roman population. Why, then, did the Anglo-Saxons, and thus the English, not absorb *more* of the Celtic languages? The English language ultimately adopted very few Celtic words, so few in fact that scholars are at a loss to explain the reason with any certainty. One thing is certain: the Celtic languages are in no way related to Anglo-Saxon, indeed developing from an entirely different family of languages, so there is no question that the Anglo-Saxons did not adopt Celtic words simply because they already had very similar words of their own. So, what happened? Some scholars have suggested that the Anglo-Saxons already had enough words of their own and thus did not need to borrow from the Celts, even upon arriving in a new place. For instance, if the day-to-day elements of life in Britain were similar enough to those in the Anglo-Saxon homeland, the Anglo-Saxons would not feel the need to make use of foreign words to describe their new life. This theory, however, is inconsistent with evidence that the Anglo-Saxons borrowed everyday words from other languages such as Old Norse and French. Other scholars have suggested the theory that the Anglo-Saxons chose to avoid the Celtic words because the Celts were essentially a conquered people—an explanation that is strongly supported by the rapid disappearance of Celts from south and central England and their subsequent movement north and west into what would become Cornwall, Wales, and Scotland.

Leading linguistic scholar David Crystal disagrees with this latter hypothesis, however. He points out that among the Anglo-Saxons it was not uncommon to find children with Welsh names. The great Christian poet Cædmon and Cædwalla, the king of Wessex in the seventh century, were both noteworthy and highly respected Anglo-Saxons who bore Welsh names. From a purely practical perspective, it is unlikely that Anglo-Saxon parents would bestow Celtic names on their children if those names were closely associated with a despised language or a group of people deemed inferior. As a modern example, during World War I people in England began changing their names to avoid sounding too Germanic. Even the royal family, up to that point bearing the name Saxe-Coburg-Gotha, changed the family name to Windsor due to the long connection of that name with a specifically English history. Additionally, the respected Battenburg family in England, closely connected to the monarchy, felt the need to change their name to Mountbatten, as it had a less decidedly German connotation.

Perhaps more significantly, David Crystal raises the possibility that the word *cross*, steeped in important religious meaning for many English speakers, came from a Celtic background. In Latin, the word is *crux*, and the Scandinavians rendered it *kross*. But there is, on the whole, very little linguistic influence on early English religious terminology from the Germanic languages or the Germanic peoples, who were decidedly pagan upon their arrival to England. On the other hand, the Irish Celts were enthusiastic and thorough in their missionary efforts to England and other parts of Europe, and they rendered the Latin *crux* as *cros* in Old Irish and as *croes* in Welsh. It is highly possible that the English word *cross* and the Old Norse word *kross* were influenced by the Irish missionary work. It is unlikely that the mystery of the missing Celtic words will ever be solved satisfactorily, but what little evidence remains suggests that the mystery can no longer be written off as a case of a conquered people becoming linguistically obsolete.

8. Which of the following best states the main idea of the passage?

(A) Although linguistic scholars do not know why the English language has so few Celtic words, it can no longer be assumed that the Anglo-Saxons avoided Celtic words in the belief that the Celts were inferior.
(B) The possible Celtic derivation of the word *cross* suggests that the Anglo-Saxons interacted more closely with the Celts than was previously thought.
(C) New evidence suggests that the traditional belief about the Anglo-Saxon, Old Norse, French, and Latin influences on the English language is erroneous and misleading.
(D) The actions taken by the English during World War I indicate strongly that their forebears eradicated Celtic words for similar reasons.
(E) The appearance of Welsh names among significant Anglo-Saxon figures indicates that of all the Celtic peoples, the Welsh had the greatest linguistic impact on Anglo-Saxon daily life.

9. The use of the word *connotation* in line 37 most closely suggests which of the following?

(A) Clear relationship
(B) Linguistic origin
(C) Theoretical definition
(D) Potential association
(E) Emotional correlation

10. The discussion of the word *cross* in the passage is intended to show which of the following?

(A) Although they were previously ignored by scholars, it is clear that many important Celtic words were indeed absorbed into the English language.
(B) Scholars now realize that many Celtic words influenced Old Norse words and not the other way around.
(C) It is incorrect to assume that there was a very great influence on the English language from Celtic words.
(D) Linguistic scholar David Crystal believes that Celtic words make up an important part of the English language.
(E) The significance of the few Celtic words within the English language suggests a more important influence than was previously thought.

11. The author provides examples of English behavior toward German last names during World War I in order to do which of the following?

(A) Prove definitely that human nature does not change
(B) Undermine the theory of the Welsh influence on English names
(C) Use a fairly recent event to provide context for a hypothesis
(D) Show that the English changed names because they considered Germans inferior
(E) Suggest that many of the so-called "English" names are really German

12. Which of the following best describes the author's attitude toward the theory that there are few Celtic words in the English language because they viewed the Celts as inferior?

(A) Self-righteous insistence
(B) Scholarly disagreement
(C) Patronizing disapproval
(D) Justifiable concern
(E) Vitriolic dissent

13. The primary purpose of the passage is to do which of the following?

(A) Caution against making an historical judgment without considering further linguistic evidence
(B) Introduce a new theory and support it with linguistic evidence
(C) Defend a scholarly position by citing leading authorities in the field
(D) Dispute a long-held scholarly position by disproving the linguistic evidence in support of it
(E) Compare several theories and argue in support of one of them

14. The passage suggests that the author would probably agree with which one of the following?

(A) There is less Latin and Old Norse influence on the English language that there is Celtic influence.
(B) Although there seem to be few Celtic words within the English language, these words suggest a significant linguistic role.
(C) The possible Celtic derivation of the English word *cross* alone suggests that the English viewed the Celts favorably.
(D) The Anglo-Saxons did not adopt many Celtic words because they had enough everyday words in their own language.
(E) Because some of the Anglo-Saxons gave their children Welsh names, the Anglo-Saxon people unquestionably had a high opinion of the Celts.

Passage 3

The question of beauty has captivated and frustrated artists, writers, and scholars for centuries. What defines beauty, and who can justifiably be described as beautiful? Is there a universal "look" that is beautiful in contrast to one that is not? History and literature are replete with descriptions of women who are said to be the "most beautiful." Greek myth claimed that Helen of Troy was the most beautiful woman in the world, with a "face that launched a thousand ships," as well as a ten-year war between Greeks and Trojans. But there is no clear account of Helen's appearance, and even Hollywood has been unable to agree on this issue, rendering Helen a variety of ways in different movie productions about the Trojan War. Today, scientists are beginning to consider the question of beauty and to devise tests that attempt to quantify attractiveness. The goal is to see whether beauty is simply a subjective perception or if people in general tend to agree on who is beautiful and who is not. In some tests, participants from a variety of cultural backgrounds are asked to compare different faces and to decide who is beautiful and who is not. In the majority of these tests, the participants agree in large percentages that the faces most likely to be considered beautiful are in fact beautiful. Some scientists have even tested infants, showing them pictures of different faces. The tests indicate that the gaze of the infants tends to linger more on the beautiful faces rather than on the faces not traditionally considered beautiful.

Other scientists have found that this potential for a universal appreciation of beauty leads to interesting consequences. As psychologist Nancy Etcoff notes, beauty can affect belief in one's character. That is, beautiful people are often assumed to be better than unattractive people in terms of character or other traits. There is evidence that in classroom situations beautiful children are often scored higher than unattractive or less beautiful children, apparently under the assumption that the beautiful children *must* be doing well. Scientists are quick to note that this is not a conscious decision on the instructor's part but is an unconscious response to the child's appearance. Even adults are not immune to this bias. In applying for jobs, attractive applicants often receive the desired employment, whether or not they are more qualified than a less attractive applicant. Political analysts also claim that the attractive candidate wins the election, regardless of his or her political platform. Historians have found that during the Nixon and Kennedy debates of 1960, viewers tended to favor Kennedy in the video debates and Nixon in the radio debates, and it has been suggested that Kennedy's attractive and youthful appearance gave him the leading edge.

Scientists claim that a certain combination of features is universally considered beautiful, but one element that has not been tested to any great extent is the effect of personality on beauty. In the immediate sense, beauty might be associated with character, with beautiful people assumed to be morally or ethically better than others. But perhaps there is a reverse relation to consider. That is, character might affect beauty, and not the other way around. Etcoff hints at the effect of character or personality in determining beauty: she records that upon meeting the writer George Eliot, a woman who was generally considered to be very unattractive, her fellow writer Henry James was immediately struck by her ugly appearance; but in the course of talking with her for only a few minutes he discovered an inner beauty that completely altered his opinion of her outward appearance. It may be that although physical features are indeed important in determining beauty, beauty itself is not simply "skin deep" and can be defined by more than an arrangement of eyes, nose, and lips. Scientists studying the phenomenon of beauty would do well to turn their attention to the more intangible qualities that define beauty and to consider what lies beneath the skin in addition to what lies on it.

15. Which of the following best summarizes the central idea of the passage?

(A) Despite society's claim that all are beautiful in their own way, scientific studies show that beauty is quantifiable and some faces are always considered beautiful.
(B) Scientists testing for beauty need to consider more than mere outward appearances to determine what makes a person beautiful.
(C) Beauty is related far more to personality and character than it is to outward appearances.
(D) Beauty is inevitable, and the beautiful will always find more success than those who are less attractive.
(E) Because beauty is subjective, scientists will never succeed in quantifying beauty, despite developing complex tests in an effort to do so.

16. It may be inferred from the passage that the author believes which of the following?

(A) After long ignoring beauty, scientists have finally recognized its importance and have begun to quantify beauty in objective tests.
(B) There is a specific combination of features that is considered beautiful across cultural boundaries.
(C) Beauty should never be associated with a person's character or personality, because personality cannot determine outward appearance.
(D) Beauty is determined entirely by cultural standards, and what one culture perceives as beautiful another might dismiss as unattractive.
(E) Personality might play a significant role in determining whether or not a person will be perceived as beautiful.

17. Which of the following best expresses the reasoning behind the author's main argument?

(A) Beauty is so subjective that much more testing is required to obtain any definitive results about what constitutes beauty.
(B) Infants can identify beauty because they recognize the qualities of a person's character, as well as the features on a person's face.
(C) Given the mystery that sometimes surrounds perceptions of beauty, it is likely that beauty is determined by more than an arrangement of facial features.
(D) Beautiful people have received inappropriate privileges that have created long-term consequences in society.
(E) Because scientists have been able to quantify beauty, it is indeed possible to determine that certain physical features are beautiful.

18. The information that in classroom situations teachers respond differently to attractive students than to unattractive students is intended to do which of the following?

(A) Indicate that beauty sometimes plays a role in the perception of a person's character or qualities.
(B) Illustrate that society gives unnecessary privileges to the beautiful
(C) Show that the personality or character of the schoolchildren affected their outward appearance
(D) Suggest that youth is inevitably associated with beauty
(E) Indicate that this is a phenomenon that appears around the world

19. The example of Henry James's meeting with George Eliot is intended to indicate which of the following points?

(A) There might be intangible qualities that contribute to the perception of beauty.
(B) George Eliot would be considered beautiful today by scientific standards.
(C) It was possible to understand George Eliot's beauty only by interacting with her.
(D) Henry James abandoned his unnecessarily high standard of beauty after meeting George Eliot and coming to know her better.
(E) Standards of beauty are universal, so if George Eliot were considered unattractive then, she would be considered unattractive now.

20. Which of the following phrases best replaces the use of the word *phenomenon*, in describing beauty, in line 45?

(A) Unexpected reality
(B) Intriguing occurrence
(C) Strange quality
(D) Abstract experience
(E) Subjective analysis

21. The author's tone toward the claim that beautiful people are often assumed to be of good character and receive privileges for their appearance can best be described as which of the following?

(A) Combative skepticism
(B) Mocking amusement
(C) Quiet resignation
(D) Informative interest
(E) Righteous anger

Passage 4A

Adam Smith's comments in *The Wealth of Nations* have stood the test of time. Smith claimed that a country should consider its available resources and manufacture those products that are cheapest for it to make at home. If that country finds that another nation can provide products more cheaply than it can make for itself, the country should engage in trade and purchase the products from the other country, while applying its workforce to domestic manufacturing.

Today roughly 90% of Americans support unrestricted free trade and do not oppose the idea of outsourcing by American businesses. Harvard economics professor Gregory Mankiw argues that the majority of economists also recognize the importance of free trade, believing that it improves economic growth, as well as the standard of living around the world. In other words, free trade provides comparatively inexpensive products for Americans, thus freeing them to put more of their money into the economy, while also providing jobs for people in countries with smaller and potentially weaker economies and giving the workers better payment for their work than they might be able to earn with opportunities in their countries. Although some argue that the jobs provided for these workers are hardly up to the wage standards that most Americans would accept, it is important to note that the cost of living is considerably lower in many of these countries; so, the workers are better off with the jobs, even if their wages do not compare to those of workers in the United States. Mankiw also cautions against faulting the free movement of imports into the U.S. during a time of economic weakness, because imports are not necessarily to blame for economic weakness. It is not a question of the U.S. importing too much but rather a question of the U.S. exporting too little. The U.S. has traditionally manufactured enough goods to balance its roster of imports, but in recent years has focused more on consumption than on production. Adam Smith argued that free trade allows a nation to import items that it could not manufacture cheaply, but as Mankiw suggests, this does not mean an importing nation should fail to manufacture altogether. A balance of imports and exports is required to maintain a stable economy, and an increase in manufacturing for exports during economic weakness can actually bolster a struggling economy.

Passage 4B

As most economists agree, free trade is a sound economic practice and necessary for the U.S. to function effectively in a global economy, but unrestricted free trade is fraught with potential dangers that few economists seem willing to acknowledge or address. Leading economist Ha-Joon Chang expresses concerns about the disadvantages of free trade on less developed nations. In a global economic system that is constantly changing and evolving, many small businesses will be successful one day and gone the next. In large nations such as the U.S., there are welfare systems in place and a variety of loans available to support these business owners until they can reestablish their businesses or develop new ones; in smaller nations with weak or less developed economies, the governments cannot support welfare systems, and the workers who lose businesses have little recourse to help them get back on their feet. As a result, the old statement about the poor just getting poorer is often true when workers in smaller and weaker economies fail to withstand a decreased demand for the goods they produce. It is historically significant that the U.S. was heavily protectionist until it became a world leader in the economy. In Sweden, economics professor Peter Soderbaum adds that the issue of free trade is usually discussed only at the level of commodity cost, but that this fails to consider other important issues for economies—issues that include environmental concerns, cultural upheaval, the loss of traditional ways of life, and so forth. These issues incur significant costs on nations and their economies, and to ignore them is to disregard the factors that may contribute to an economy's ability to sustain free trade for long periods of time, as well as the ability of workers to exist within that economy in a gradually improving way of life. As some economists now indicate, what is needed is a new approach to free trade, along with the resources to quantify the cost/value ratio of free trade. This new approach would be an attempt to view free trade from a variety of angles, including angles not traditionally viewed through economic lenses, thereby providing a "big picture" and thus a more accurate perspective.

22. The authors of the two passages would likely agree on which of the following statements?

(A) A global economy ensures the economic survival of smaller nations, because it improves the quality of life among the workers.
(B) Free trade must contribute to the creation of stable jobs for an economy to survive during an economic downturn.
(C) Although free trade can create controversy at times, most economists agree that free trade is an important part of any economic system.
(D) Free trade runs the risk of damaging one economy while improving another and thus has as many negative qualities as positive qualities.
(E) Export rates in the U.S. must increase if the U.S. economy is to overcome its economic weakness and heavy dependence on imports.

23. Which of the following best summarizes the main point of Passage A?

(A) Adam Smith's economic theories about free trade, as described in *The Wealth of Nations*, were sound and remain applicable to contemporary economics.
(B) Free trade can cause economic weakness if a nation fails to generate enough exports in comparison to its imports.
(C) Economic weakness in the U.S. is related to domestic concerns and does not relate to unrestricted free trade.
(D) Free trade is valuable to an economy and does not necessarily need to be restricted, but an economy needs to balance imports and exports.
(E) The outsourcing of U.S. businesses has positive effects on economic growth in the U.S. and is thus strongly supported by Americans.

24. Which of the following best expresses the main point of Passage B?

(A) Free trade is essential for any society that hopes to grow in a global economy.
(B) Economists fail to address the real problems with unrestricted free trade by focusing only on the price of commodities.
(C) Unrestricted free trade has the potential for causing serious problems for weaker economies when small businesses fail and they have no governmental support.
(D) A welfare system provides a fallback opportunity for business owners in weaker and smaller economies by offering support until the business can be reestablished.
(E) Unrestricted free trade has too much potential for causing problems in some economies, so a new approach is needed to address peripheral effects of free trade.

25. Which of the following best describes how Passage B responds to Passage A?

(A) Passage B points out a logical flaw in the argument of Passage A.
(B) Passage B acknowledges a part of the argument in Passage A but then offers an alternate thesis.
(C) If the author's claims in Passage A are true, they negate the claims made in Passage B.
(D) The details about secondary problems detailed in Passage B undermine the definition of free trade as described in Passage A.
(E) The argument in Passage A proceeds under the assumption that the argument in Passage B is true.

26. The use of the word "protectionist" in line 13 of Passage B is intended to indicate which of the following?

(A) Protecting a domestic economy from unrestricted free trade
(B) Protecting free trade without any restrictions on imports or exports
(C) Protecting a domestic economy from encroaching globalism
(D) Protecting a domestic economy through government intervention
(E) Protecting small businesses through welfare programs and federal loans

27. Passage B differs from Passage A in that the author's tone concerning the issue of free trade is more

(A) Sophisticated
(B) Speculative
(C) Cautious
(D) Debating
(E) Pragmatic

Section IV

Time – 35 minutes

25 Questions

Directions: The questions in this section are based on the reasoning given in brief statements or passages. It is possible that for some questions there is more than one answer. However, you are to choose the *best* answer; that is, the response that most accurately and completely answers the question. You should not make assumptions that are by commonsense standards implausible, superfluous, or incompatible with the passage. After you have chosen the best answer, blacken the corresponding space on your answer sheet.

1. **It is important to distinguish between criticism and opinion. The purpose of criticism is to direct a commentary on someone or something with the particular goal of change. A person who criticizes the behavior of another is specifically hoping to affect a modification. The purpose of opinion, on the other hand, is simply to offer a viewpoint that does not require a change. A person who shares an opinion is generally providing a perspective that is intended to help another in making a decision. As a result, *criticism* usually has a negative connotation, whereas *opinion* does not. More importantly, not everyone is necessarily entitled to *criticism*, but everyone should be entitled to *opinion*.**

   Considering the statements made in the passage above very carefully, which of the following may be inferred?

   (A) Criticism that is worded as opinion can be both appropriate and effective, because it provides the pretense of opinion while still effecting a change.
   (B) Criticism and opinion are often confused with one another, because some mistake a negative opinion for criticism.
   (C) Opinion is simply the phase of thought before one reaches criticism, so there is often not a clear distinction between the two.
   (D) Positive, or constructive, criticism is equivalent to opinion, so all are entitled to share constructive criticism.
   (E) The freedom of speech and of thought guarantees that all are allowed opinions, so government cannot and should not restrict the sharing of opinions.

2. **A large department store was looking for a new "face" to represent its brand, with certain clear requirements in mind, based on the popularity of the previous representative: the new representative needed to be friendly and articulate, and she must possess a clean image. Several applicants were interested in the position, and one in particular campaigned heavily for the job, expressing to the company her view that she fit the requirements well. The company believed that this woman would be perfect for the job and hired her quickly, deciding that no market research was then required since she had all of the necessary qualifications. Within a few months, however, the company began pushing her aside in favor of the previous representative, who was rehired for her old job.**

   Based on the information in the passage, which of the following best provides a reason for why the department store decided to push its new representative aside in favor of the old one?

   (A) The department store performed market research after hiring the new representative and found that she was unpopular among customers.
   (B) A tabloid hinted that the new representative had an unsavory past inconsistent with the clean image she presented to the company.
   (C) A competitor department store hired a new representative who was far more popular than the first department store's new representative.
   (D) Department store staff believed they had made a mistake with the new representative and decided to look for another one to replace her.
   (E) The new representative did not enjoy the position, so she began ignoring her responsibilities.

3. **A snowstorm during the night in the city of Denver is expected to cause considerable delays for people going to work. All news outlets in the city warn that traffic will be very slow, and employers should expect their employees to be late. Therefore, all the employees at First Community Bank of Denver will be late to work.**

   The flawed reasoning in the passage above is similar to the flawed reasoning in which of the following statements?

   (A) Testing shows that food with MSG, or monosodium glutamate, is known to cause migraines in many people; therefore, everyone who eats food with MSG should expect to develop a migraine.
   (B) Theodore is two years old than Ferdinand; therefore, Theodore is taller than Ferdinand.
   (C) A major power outage in Chicago occurred in an area with 300,000 customers; therefore, the majority of these customers were without power.
   (D) Edward accidentally broke an antique vase that belonged to Nina's great-grandmother; therefore, Nina will likely be angry with Edward for breaking her great-grandmother's vase.
   (E) Lunchtime is served to students at Adams Elementary at noon every day; therefore, some students are hungry at noon.

4. **A major automobile manufacturer is planning to increase its production of vehicles due to an unexpected period of strength in the economy. The company CEO believes that now is the best time to add to the company's supply of vehicles, when the strength in the markets makes this decision economically feasible. At this time, many of the primary supplies needed to build the cars have artificially low prices, and the auto manufacturer hopes to produce the cars while the cost-value ratio is still low.**

   Based on the information contained within the passage, which of the following, if true, most supports the decision by the auto manufacturer?

   (A) The automobile manufacturer's stock is expected to rise within the next few months due to the economic strength.
   (B) A major producer of car batteries is expected to go out of business within six months, leaving few car battery suppliers for auto manufacturers.
   (C) A recent study indicates that the steel used by the auto manufacturer is expected to increase considerably in price over the next few months.
   (D) The auto manufacturer is planning to merge with another auto manufacturer that has a considerable number of surplus vehicles.
   (E) The cost of oil is expected to rise, a factor that will make consumers less likely to buy new cars.

5. **An IT company is planning to open a new office in the large industrial city of Nizhny Novgorod, Russia. The IT industry has, in recent years, become one of the most important industries in Nizhny Novgorod and provides the majority of high-paying jobs for residents. At the same time, the city is currently undergoing a minor economic downturn, and a number of its residents are out of work. Additionally, the IT industry has been struggling to remain strong in Nizhny Novgorod, and many of the original IT businesses, which have traditionally been the city's most successful businesses, are failing. The IT company that plans to open a new office, however, is confident it will be highly successful.**

   Given the passage above, which of the following best explains the discrepancy between the current economic situation in Nizhny Novgorod and the IT company's confidence in its likely success?

   (A) The IT company, unlike most of the original IT companies, is at the cutting edge of the IT industry and can keep its costs low.
   (B) The IT company is acquiring the building of a failed IT company, so it will not have to spend funds to build a new office.
   (C) The IT company is expected to bring much-needed jobs to Nizhny Novgorod, and many residents are excited about the new office.
   (D) The IT company is not opening the new office within Nizhny Novgorod, instead locating the office where there is less industrial scenery.
   (E) The IT company has had to take out considerable loans for the construction and maintenance of the office building.

6. **Member of a local school board: All classrooms in our school district need computers. A recent poll indicates that our city is one of the few in the state that has not acquired computers for every classroom, and as a result our schools are suffering. Our school district has actually seen a loss in student body due to parents relocating to other school districts. Adding up-to-date technology to classrooms would encourage parents to remain in our school district. More importantly, though, my research indicates that schools with computers in every classroom have the highest graduation rates and go on to receive higher-paying jobs than students who were not educated with computers. Therefore, we need to put computers in all of our classrooms.**

   The school board member's reasoning is flawed because it fails to establish which of the following?

   (A) Proof that the local school district currently has the funds required to place computers in every classroom in the school district
   (B) Support for the claim that a school district with a decrease in student body should be investing in new technology
   (C) Evidence that the lack of computers alone contributes to the decision by parents to relocate to new school districts
   (D) Information that students who are educated with computers are more likely to graduate and receive higher-paying jobs
   (E) That computers offer better classroom management opportunities because they keep students occupied and reduce the risk of classroom disorder

Questions 7 and 8

In recent years the fashion industry has become increasingly unable to ignore the reality of eating disorders among models. Although models are, as a group, thin beyond the "normal" standards of society, many have succumbed to nutritionally deficient eating habits in order to sustain unnatural weights, even for their super-physiques. The fashion industry has, in recent years, begun addressing the issue more openly. Some countries have gone so far as to establish rules that require models to maintain a certain BMI if they expect to walk the runways. Additionally, the industry recently held an international conference on the issue of eating disorders. But the overall mood there was one of resistance, among models as well as designers. Most of the models claim that they are just naturally very thin and are modeling for that very reason. They admit that some do develop eating disorders, but claim these disorders are often based on individual problems and not on the industry. Among the designers, the resistance was equally palpable. Most resented the interference and claimed that the fashion world has always relied on thin models and that it is unfair to single out a single industry for eating disorders, because eating disorders are connected to personal issues. Overall, the hope within the industry is that there will be awareness about eating disorders but not extra rules: models should know that help is available should they need it and that the industry will support them as they seek treatment.

7. **Which of the following best expresses the main point of the passage above?**

(A) The fashion industry believes that eating disorders are inevitable and thus cannot be entirely eliminated among models.
(B) The fashion industry does not feel responsible for eating disorders among models, claiming that eating disorders arise from personal situations and should be treated individually.
(C) The fashion industry believes that models need to be thin, and many of the models are naturally and not unhealthily thin.
(D) The fashion industry resents the intrusion because it ultimately hopes that the models will recognize when they have a problem and seek help.
(E) The fashion industry knows that any rules established to combat eating disorders by requiring a healthy BMI will ultimately be ignored.

8. **Given the passage above, the reasoning within the fashion industry is vulnerable to criticism because it fails to consider which of the following?**

(A) The public is tired of the excessively thin image propounded by the fashion industry and would prefer to see models of average weight.
(B) Fashion trends are constantly changing, and the trend for very thin models will ultimately give way to a trend for models of different sizes.
(C) Eating disorders affect people for many reasons, and there are as many people struggling with eating disorders in the fashion industry as there are elsewhere.
(D) The women chosen to model are selected entirely for their height and build and are perhaps naturally thin, rather than suffering from eating disorders.
(E) Models suffering from eating disorders might not have the means or the ability to acknowledge their problem and pursue help.

9. **All of the employees at the Marshalltown Packing Warehouse receive a 3% bonus each Christmas. The company owner instituted the Christmas bonus at the company's inception ten years earlier, and the company handbook includes a guarantee to new employees that they will receive the bonus annually. The company has recently hired a new financial officer whose review of the books indicates that the company's budget might not allow for the Christmas bonus this year due to a decline in advertising revenues for the company. The financial officer sends out a memo to all employees, informing them that the company will be unable to provide the Christmas bonuses this year unless all employees contribute to an improvement in advertising revenues.**

Consider the passage above carefully. If the information contained within it is true, which of the following must also be true?

(A) If advertising revenues are down, the company is not responsible for providing Christmas bonuses to its employees unless the employees are willing to help improve advertising revenues.
(B) By asking the employees to contribute to an improvement in advertising revenues, the company is essentially asking employees to contribute to their own bonuses.
(C) If the company has always been able to provide the Christmas bonus in the past, there is no reason it should be unable to do so in the present, so the financial officer must be falsifying the numbers.
(D) Unless employees contribute to the advertising revenues, the only other choice for the company will be to downsize and lay off employees.
(E) Because the company has guaranteed the Christmas bonuses in the employee handbook, the employees will likely go on strike if they do not receive the bonuses.

10. Philatelist: The Swedish Treskilling Yellow is the rarest stamp in the world. It was issued in 1855, when Sweden first began issuing postage stamps. The Treskilling, or three-skilling, stamp was originally intended to be printed in blue, but was accidentally printed in yellow, the color reserved for the eight-skilling stamp. A number of Treskilling Yellow stamps were printed before the mistake was noticed in 1858. A stamp collector located the first Treskilling Yellow and sold it to another collector. Soon, it became apparent that this particular stamp might be the only remaining variety of the mistaken coloration, and the Treskilling Yellow became a desired item among stamp collectors. In 1996, it was sold for $2.06 million, making it the costliest stamp in the world. Therefore, the Treskilling Yellow is also the most valuable stamp in the world.

Which of the following statements represents the assumption on which the philatelist's conclusion depends?

(A) If another Treskilling Yellow stamp happens to be found, it will bring in a price as high as that of the current Treskilling Yellow stamp.
(B) It is the unique quality of having been printed in error that makes the Treskilling Yellow stamp as rare and valuable as it is.
(C) Because the Treskilling Yellow stamp is the only one of its kind, it would be worthless if another such stamp were located.
(D) Because the Treskilling Yellow is the only one of its kind and has currently sold for the highest price among stamp collectors, it must have the most intrinsic value.
(E) Most of the finest and costliest stamps in the world have originated from printing errors in Sweden.

11. When first published in 1867, Karl Marx's massive thesis on capitalism, *Das Kapital*, was anything but a bestseller. In fact, the book hardly made a dent on the public consciousness at first. So little was it noticed that Marx's friend and colleague Friedrich Engels began to write glowing reviews of *Das Kapital* under assumed names. The book received little attention during Marx's lifetime, much to his personal disappointment as he believed that he was offering hope for the future of politics through economic revolution. After his death in 1883, however, there were growing changes in the international political climate, and *Das Kapital* grew in popularity, ultimately becoming one of the most influential political treatises of the twentieth century.

Considering the above statements, which of the following can be inferred from the passage to explain the reason for the eventual popularity of Das Kapital?

(A) *Das Kapital* became popular after people began questioning traditional capitalist values during the late nineteenth and early twentieth centuries.
(B) *Das Kapital* was censored in several European countries and thus was unavailable to the general reading public until the mid-twentieth century.
(C) *Das Kapital* is about three thousand pages in full and thus is limited in readership to those willing to undertake such a lengthy book.
(D) Karl Marx was not known as an authority in the field of political philosophy, so the book was poorly received among academics.
(E) *Das Kapital* was originally published in German and was unavailable in translation form until early in the twentieth century.

12. Although most scholars agree that the Black Plague was a massive blight that killed as much as 60% of the European population, some scholars now argue that the plague might have contributed to Europe's social system in unexpectedly positive ways. These scholars point out that the plague saw no social boundaries and affected noblemen as well as serfs; when the noblemen began to die, their serfs were left free and able to work for themselves. The argument claims that the Black Plague, by wiping out large portions of the land-owning aristocracy across Europe, contributed to the development of the middle class: the now-freed serfs began developing trades and grew wealthy and powerful over time.

Which of the following, if true, most undermines the claims made by scholars about the positive impact of the Black Plague?

(A) The Black Plague actually struck very few members of the European peasantry, because they had already developed immunity to the infection.
(B) Historians have calculated that more men than women were killed from plague infection between 1340 and 1400.
(C) Some scholars have noticed an increase in pre-industrial productivity immediately after the Black Plague, suggesting a rise in new trades.
(D) The Black Plague weakened the aristocracy to the point of irrelevance in society, in addition to reducing the value of lands by as much as 70%.
(E) Historians have found that a thriving middle class was already in development when the Black Plague first struck Europe in the 1340s.

13. Politician: Although our country has traditionally benefited greatly from trade with our chief trading partner, we need to cease any and all trade with this trading partner immediately, due to its clear and egregious human rights violations. Reports indicate that our long-time trading partner has been engaging in practices that our country considers utterly insupportable and that the United Nations has frequently condemned. As a nation, we have always stood for clear human rights standards, and we cannot risk practicing a double standard. We must instead set the standard and encourage respect for human rights around the world.

The argument made by the politician depends on which of the following assumptions?

(A) Ending trade with the chief trading partner will help put a stop to the trading partner's current human rights violations.
(B) The human rights violations are closely connected to the specific products traded between the countries.
(C) The need to stand by a standard of human rights is of greater value than the trading loss that will occur by ending trade.
(D) The politician is currently head of a committee that is responsible for keeping track of human rights violations among trading partners.
(E) This country will end trade with the chief trading partner in order to encourage other nations to do the same.

14. Letter to the editor of a Dublin newspaper: The traditional Gaeilge language is currently being taught in some Irish schools with funding from the Irish government. This should be stopped at once. Gaeilge is the language of revolution among the Irish and has done more throughout history to contribute to unrest and even open conflict in Ireland than it has done to bring about peace. The teaching of this language will ultimately bring about division in Ireland. The Irish government should rethink its funding and remove it as soon as possible.

Considering the statements above, the reasoning in the letter to the editor is flawed because of which of the following?

(A) The author fails to note that language is an important part of any culture, and the loss of that language will deprive a people of an essential link to their past.
(B) The author assumes that events occurring in history when the Irish spoke Gaeilge will occur once again simply by teaching students the language.
(C) The author relies on obsolete sociological data to derive a conclusion about current events.
(D) The author focuses on an isolated historical event and assumes that it establishes a trend for the modern day.
(E) The author ignores other traditional languages in Ireland, and fails to explain why they should not be taught as well.

15. A local farmer is hoping to establish a certified organic farm but is concerned about the cost of setting it up. A certified organic farm requires far fewer supplies than a non-organic farm, and most of the supplies are less costly in comparison. Also, because an organic farm does not use expensive pesticides or tools, the cost of maintenance is also fairly low in comparison to the maintenance cost of a non-organic farm. But the set-up of the certified organic farm remains expensive, and the farmer is unsure if the return on his investment will justify the cost.

Which of the following statements best explains the farmer's concern about the high cost of setting up a certified organic farm?

(A) There is little demand in the community for more certified organic food.
(B) More resources are required for establishing a certified organic farm than a non-organic farm.
(C) There are three other certified organic farms in the community that are much larger than the farm the farmer is planning to establish.
(D) The licensing fees for the farmer to acquire certification add considerably to the cost of set-up.
(E) The supplies needed to set up the certified organic farm are unique and must be special ordered.

16. Commercial: Men who struggle with hair loss need worry no longer—they can now purchase Extra-Strength Spray-On Hair Growth! This amazing product will stimulate hair to re-grow and offer you a full head of hair once again. But if you don't try our Extra-Strength Spray-On Hair Growth, your chances of having a full head of hair again will vanish, along with your hairline. So, try Extra-Strength Spray-On Hair Growth today!

The reasoning in the commercial is flawed similar to the reasoning in which of the following?

(A) Students who attend universities tend to be more successful in life; therefore, all students should attend a university in order to be successful and not fail in life.
(B) If you walk in the rain with your head uncovered, you will develop a cold; therefore, you should carry an umbrella.
(C) Over time, ovens develop a buildup of food residue that gets burned into the bottom of the oven; therefore, ovens should be cleaned annually.
(D) "Green" products lessen the toxic impact on the environment; therefore, people should purchase green products as one way to help the environment.
(E) Stan is unpopular among the members of his team because of his temper; therefore, Stan will be removed from the team.

Questions 17 and 18

The state of Hawaii plans to build a nuclear power plant in a town along the leeward coast of Oahu. The nuclear power plant is expected to provide new jobs for people in Oahu. The town in which the power plant will be located, however, is unhappy with the plan. A spokesperson for the town reveals to the local news station that the residents are concerned about the dangers of nuclear power, as well as the potential for another accident of the magnitude of the Chernobyl disaster. As the spokesperson notes, Chernobyl was the nuclear power plant in Ukraine where a reactor exploded in 1986, creating extremely unsafe levels of radiation for residents throughout Ukraine and parts of Eastern Europe. The long-term effects of the Chernobyl explosion included permanent health damage for many residents and a variety of birth defects among children. These possible consequences are what the Hawaiian town residents most fear, in the event that a nuclear facility in Hawaii suffers a similar accident.

17. Which of the following most undermines the spokesperson's primary argument?

(A) The nuclear fallout that occurred at Chernobyl was a one-time historical event, and it cannot be assumed a similar event would occur in Hawaii.
(B) The spokesperson is a paid member of an anti-nuclear power organization that frequently lobbies against the building of new nuclear power plants in the U.S.
(C) The advances made in nuclear power plants since the days of Chernobyl ensure that the chance of a similar nuclear explosion is almost nonexistent.
(D) The nuclear power plant will bring high-paying jobs to the community and ensure excellent benefits for all employees.
(E) The voters of the state of Hawaii have voted overwhelmingly in support of the building of the nuclear power plant.

18. Which of the following statements would, if true, most seriously undermine the state's attempt to build the nuclear power plant?

(A) The community is unsure whether the new nuclear power plant can be built within the required budget.
(B) Many of the jobs that the nuclear power plant would bring are not higher-paying than the jobs that are currently available.
(C) The state and federal governments are offering large tax incentives for communities that begin using nuclear power.
(D) A local builder is planning a neighborhood near the expected site of the nuclear power plant and has already sold 75% of the lots.
(E) Ocean water surrounding Hawaii is too warm to cool a nuclear reactor, so the plant would have to use extra energy to keep a nuclear reactor cool.

19. The female earless seal has a gestation period that usually spans nine to eleven months, depending on the classification. Each female carries and gives birth to and nurses only one pup at a time. The mother fasts while she is nursing the pup, due to the distance between the breeding ground and the area where the seals feed. As a result, the earless seal mother burns a considerable amount of energy during lactation. During a bad season, as many as three earless seal mothers in a colony will die around three months after giving birth. It is not uncommon, however, for all of the seal pups to survive.

Which of the following, if true, most explains the discrepancy between the number of deaths among the earless seal mothers and lack of deaths among the pups during a bad season?

(A) Female earless seals can nurse two pups at a time, thus ensuring that at least two pups will live.
(B) During a good season, no female earless seals die, and marine biologists note that there have been more good seasons than bad in recent years.
(C) Some of the female earless seals do not give birth during breeding season.
(D) The earless seal pups nurse only for a brief period of time, with the longest nursing period being one month.
(E) Some of the female earless seals will live as long as six months after giving birth, thus guaranteeing that their pups have a better chance of survival.

20. William Paley was an eighteenth-century Christian apologist credited with developing what is now known as the watchmaker analogy. This analogy has often come under attack for a logical flaw. Paley's argument followed this reasoning: Suppose a person found a watch lying on the ground and did not know it was a watch. Would the person assume that it simply came into being without some sort of intelligent design? Most likely not. This is because a watch contains a carefully crafted and highly complex series of mechanisms in order to make it work correctly; due to the complexity of its design, it cannot have come into being *ex nihilo*, or out of nothing, and thus it indicates intelligence and a designer. In the same way, the universe exhibits a carefully crafted and highly complex system. As with the watch, the universe cannot have come into being without intelligence and a designer.

Which of the following logical flaws best expresses the flaw in Paley's reasoning?

(A) A red herring, or a strategy used to create a distraction
(B) A bad comparison that fails to create a clear similarity between two items
(C) An *ad hominem*, or personal attack
(D) An appeal to sympathy that uses an emotional quality to make the argument
(E) An appeal to authority that uses the claimed authority of an outside source

21. The climate extremes of the North Atlantic nation of Iceland ensure that little plant growth will be able to survive there. The majority of the island is covered in low grasses, with only one tree species known to exist. Deforestation in previous centuries depopulated the entire island of its trees. Because of both the severe cold and the severe heat, plants require a long period of time to grow in Iceland, and modern residents have only just begun replanting the trees. Plant life in Iceland is also notoriously delicate, and off-road vehicles are allowed only in certain areas; in some cases, hikers are required to walk around certain plants to ensure that the plants will survive even during the extreme weather that constantly surrounds Iceland.

Considering the claims below within the context of the passage above, which claim is most likely to be true?

(A) More developed plant growth exists closer to the island's center, where volcanic warmth allows the plants to survive.
(B) The plants that manage to survive in Iceland are extremely hardy.
(C) The only type of tree capable of growing successfully in Iceland is the northern birch.
(D) Global warming in recent decades has encouraged plant growth, with a corresponding improvement in the development of Icelandic plant life.
(E) Off-road vehicles can cause permanent or long-term damage to the re-growth of some plants.

22. The short and shaggy Highland Cattle are an iconic feature of Scotland and closely connected to that nation's history. This sturdy, resilient breed is highly familiar with the cold rainfall and bitter winds of the mountainous Scottish Highlands, and it has existed in that landscape for unknown centuries. The Highland Cattle are most common in the remote areas of the Highlands where they live and breed wild. They are known for their hardy ability to withstand the elements; in fact, many of them live upwards of eighteen to twenty years, giving birth as many as fifteen times.

Which of the following assumptions can be drawn from the information in the passage above?

(A) Due to their stature and tough hides, the Highland Cattle cannot be used for human consumption and are good only for grazing.
(B) As it is native to the Scottish Highlands, the Highland Cattle is the only breed that can survive in Scotland.
(C) Having lived in the Scottish Highlands for centuries, the Highland Cattle have adapted to the climate and developed the ability to survive there.
(D) The shaggy coats of the Highland Cattle have long been used by the Highlanders for a variety of household purposes.
(E) Scotland's Highland climate severely limits the plant life that can grow and survive there, leaving the Highland Cattle with limited food to eat.

23. Colorblindness is a vision deficiency that limits the ability of the sufferer to see certain colors clearly. The condition may affect a person in varying degrees, ranging from mild colorblindness with a red or green color deficiency to complete colorblindness with no ability to distinguish any colors beside dim shades of brown. The primary cause of colorblindness is believed to be a mutation on the X chromosome. Men carry a single X chromosome, possessing an XY-chromosome makeup, while women carry two X chromosomes, thus having the potential to combat colorblindness with an extra X chromosome.

If the passage above is true, which of the following can be inferred from it?

(A) Colorblindness is a rare condition that affects very few members of the population.
(B) Despite the handicap, those who are colorblind might have certain advantages, particularly in seeing camouflage.
(C) Women alone are capable of passing on a gene for colorblindness.
(D) Because of the way colorblindness affects the X chromosome, men are more likely to be colorblind than women.
(E) Colorblindness is entirely inherited and can be tested and identified at birth.

24. Set on the wild and rugged Bodmin Moor of Cornwall, Jamaica Inn is most remembered for playing the starring role in a story by Cornish-born writer Daphne du Maurier. In du Maurier's book, a young woman moves in with a family member at Jamaica Inn, only to discover that the inn is playing a sinister role in the crime of wrecking, that is, setting up lights along the coastline to draw ships in and wreck them on the rocky coast. Du Maurier's book is hardly an historic textbook; anecdote suggests that du Maurier derived much of the source for her tale from the ghost stories she heard while staying briefly at Jamaica Inn. This being said, wrecking was a real activity in Cornwall during the eighteenth and nineteenth centuries, and Jamaica Inn's remote locale made it an excellent place to hide from the law.

Which of the following best expresses the main point of the passage above?

(A) Daphne du Maurier's story *Jamaica Inn* has been overlooked by literary historians for its contribution to the history of Cornwall.
(B) Daphne du Maurier's story *Jamaica Inn* takes inevitable creative license but reflects with some accuracy the reality of deliberate ship wrecking in Cornwall.
(C) Lights were lit along the coastline in order to lure ships in and force them to wreck along the coast, giving the residents freedom to plunder the ship's goods.
(D) Daphne du Maurier frequently used Cornwall, and the Cornish coastline in particular, as a setting for her books.
(E) The story of *Jamaica Inn* falsely represents the historic details of shipwrecking.

25. Psychologists have found that there are fascinating differences between children and adults when it comes to learning a new musical instrument. In particular, the piano is an instrument that knows no one age for learning and presents multiple opportunities for the successful attainment of musical skills. It does, however, offer a variety of challenges both to children and to adults—due to the differences in mind development—with children developing certain skills more quickly and more effectively than adults. How quickly children learn is often limited by their motor skills, but they are more likely to remember in detail the pieces they learn and to retain that knowledge over long periods of time. At the same time, adults are more likely to retain the muscle memory of the pieces that they learn and reproduce them blindly, just by allowing their fingers to recall the correct notes.

If the passage above is true, all of the following may be concluded EXCEPT:

(A) Adult minds learn the skills required to play the piano differently than children's minds.
(B) Adults might not recall the exact details of the piece they learned, but the muscle memory in their fingers makes them very likely to remember the notes.
(C) The piano is the only instrument that both children and adults can learn to play well.
(D) Learning the piano is not limited to children, because adults can learn to play well.
(E) Adults are more likely to learn hand and finger movements on the piano faster than children do.

Writing Sample Topic

(35 Minutes)

Isobel McGavin has been serving in the U.S. Army Corps of Engineers for the past ten years but is looking to transition out of the military and into a civilian position. She has used a placement company to help her find a job in the oil and gas industry, and two different oil and gas companies have offered her a senior position. Write an argument for her taking one job over the other based on the following criteria:

- Isobel wants to be able to use the knowledge she has gained as an Army engineer by applying it to cutting-edge technology in the oil and gas industry.
- Isobel wants a position that allows her to set her own goals for success and challenge herself on a daily basis.

The first company is an established leader in the oil and gas industry. The company has a history of hiring former military personnel due to the education and experience such people receive. The company is also known for using time-honored techniques with an additional concentration on innovative technology. It is currently the largest oil and gas company in the country. Isobel would replace a long-time employee who is retiring and who is known for having broadened the company's focus and contributed to considerable growth in several sectors of the oil and gas industry.

The second job offer is for a start-up company composed of experts in the oil and gas industry. These experts are hoping to incorporate innovative ideas in industry techniques. The company's stock has risen considerably since its inception two years ago, and the oil and gas industry has responded well to the company's progressive approach to drilling and production. In fact, the company is considered to be one of the most dynamic participants in the industry. Isobel would be pioneering a position for the company, one that is expected to contribute extensively to growth and development and retain the company's progressive focus.

LSAT Answer Key

SECTION I

Question	Question	Question	Question
1. B	8. A	15. D	22. A
2. C	9. E	16. A	23. D
3. E	10. B	17. C	24. B
4. A	11. C	18. D	25. A
5. E	12. A	19. B	
6. D	13. E	20. E	
7. C	14. B	21. C	

SECTION II

Question	Question	Question	Question
1. E	7. C	13. B	19. B
2. D	8. A	14. E	20. D
3. B	9. E	15. C	21. C
4. C	10. D	16. D	22. E
5. D	11. A	17. B	23. C
6. E	12. C	18. A	24. B

SECTION III

Question	Question	Question	Question
1. C	8. A	15. B	22. C
2. A	9. D	16. E	23. D
3. E	10. E	17. C	24. E
4. B	11. C	18. A	25. B
5. C	12. B	19. A	26. A
6. C	13. A	20. B	27. C
7. E	14. B	21. D	

SECTION IV

Question	Question	Question	Question
1. B	8. E	15. D	22. C
2. A	9. B	16. A	23. D
3. A	10. D	17. C	24. B
4. C	11. A	18. E	25. C
5. A	12. E	19. D	
6. C	13. C	20. B	
7. D	14. B	21. E	

LSAT Answers and Explanations

Logical Reasoning, Section I

QUESTION 1

Overview: This question asks students to select the statement that *most seriously* undermines the nutritionist's claims that his method of applying diet and exercise alone helped patients struggling with obesity to lose weight and that this method of losing weight is the *best* method. The student must consider each answer choice in the context of what the nutritionist says in order to determine which answer is most correct.

THE CORRECT ANSWER:

B The nutritionist's statement that a healthy, balanced diet and the incorporation of daily exercise is strongly undermined by the information that significant factors in weight loss include physical makeup and metabolism, and that the nutritionist worked only with adults with very similar physical makeups and metabolisms. This information throws into question whether the nutritionist's methods would work for adults with different physical makeups and metabolism, thereby undermining the claim the nutritionist's method for weight loss is the best method. Therefore, **answer choice (B)** is the correct answer.

THE INCORRECT ANSWERS:

A Answer choice (A), although tempting, is ultimately irrelevant to the nutritionist's direct claims about the best method for weight loss; answer A is considered an *ad hominem* claim, that is, a claim directed about a person making an argument rather than about the merits of the argument itself. Simply because the nutritionist receives funding from the government does not mean that the nutritionist's study is biased. Nothing in the passage suggests that it is. Answer choice (A) is not correct.

C Like answer choice (A), answer choice (C) is interesting but does nothing to undermine the nutritionist's claims. It is not surprising to learn that another nutritionist disagrees with him, but disagreement with a colleague does not necessarily undermine his test results. Answer choice (C), therefore, is incorrect.

D Far from undermining the test results and the nutritionist's claims, answer choice (D) actually supports them. This is because different methods of exercise might have different results regarding weight loss. Thus, answer choice (D) can be eliminated at once.

E The statement about the number of patients provides further information about how the nutritionist carried out his test. However, it does not necessarily undermine the results. Eighty patients could conceivably provide the nutritionist with a large enough study group to derive useful results, so this choice does not necessarily undermine his claims. Answer choice (E) is incorrect.

QUESTION 2

Overview: Question 2 presents a scenario in which someone (Mike) is attempting to predict future events on the basis of his past experience. Three important factors must be considered: (1) the company for which Mike works is suffering due to the economic downturn, (2) the detail that Mike has had a strong sales record in the past but has struggled to maintain it in recent months because of the weak economy, and (3) the fact that Mike's boss has asked to see him. Mike concludes that his boss will *not* fire him because of his time with the company, his excellent record, and his potential to succeed in spite of the crisis. The student is asked to consider how Mike's reasoning is flawed.

The Correct Answer:

C **Answer choice (C)** is the only selection that takes all of the elements into account and summarizes the substance of the problem with Mike's argument: he believes his success in the past will translate automatically to future success, despite his failure over the last few months to keep his sales high. He also believes that the company will look only at his past success and will not consider current factors, including his recent struggles and the economic situation as a whole. Thus, answer choice (C) is correct.

The Incorrect Answers:

A, E Although answer choices (A) and (E) do address separate parts of the problem with Mike's reasoning, neither addresses all of it. Mike's belief in his loyalty to the company ("I've been working with the company for well over a decade") and in the company's confidence in his ability to overcome the tough economy ("If anyone can find a way to boost sales and benefit the company, I'm the person") both contribute to the flaw in his argument, but neither encompasses it fully. Both answer choices (A) and (E), therefore, are incorrect.

B Answer choice (B) provides an interesting piece of information, but in terms of Mike's argument it is largely irrelevant and does not address the flaw in Mike's reasoning in any way. It contributes a piece of information that might support the theory that the company will indeed fire Mike, but it fails to explain how Mike's own argument is problematic.

D Answer (D), again, is interesting but irrelevant to Mike's argument and does not address the flaw in his reasoning. That Mike is a close friend of his boss might make it more difficult for his boss to fire him, but since Mike does not mention this in his statement in any way, it cannot be assumed that this contributes to his reasoning. Answer choice (D) is incorrect.

Questions 3 and 4

Overview: Questions 3 and 4 regard a passage about the manuscript history of medieval music, noting specifically four important facts: (1) manuscripts were expensive to produce, (2) the Catholic Church was one of the few institutions able to take on this expense, because it had both the wealth and the human resources as represented by scribes, (3) most extant music from the medieval period has been recorded on manuscripts, and (4) the majority of this music is sacred music. The passage includes the added suggestion that most popular music from that era is unknown today because very little was recorded on manuscripts.

Question 3

The Correct Answer:

E In question 3, the student is asked to select a statement that is supported by the claims made in the passage. To do this, the student must infer from what is stated directly. Based on these claims, **answer choice (E)** is the only one that fulfills this requirement. The passage states quite clearly, "Any medieval music not recorded on manuscripts has now been lost to history. Most of the medieval music still in existence is sacred music." If most extant medieval music is sacred music, and any music not recorded on manuscripts has been lost to history, then it follows that most popular music was not recorded on manuscripts and thus has been lost to history. It can safely be inferred from this fact that historians do not know much about popular medieval music because they have almost nothing to study. Answer choice (E) is correct.

The Incorrect Answers:

A Answer choice (A) is incorrect because the passage does not offer an evaluative judgment on the music that is still extant, nor does it suggest anywhere that sacred music was recorded because it was the "greatest music" of the period. Historians might rightly debate this issue, but the passage does not discuss it or imply anything about it.

B As with answer choice (A), the passage does not imply answer choice (B). The passage describes facts about the way medieval music was recorded and about what medieval music still exists, but it does not provide an answer to *why* most of the extant music from the Middle Ages is sacred music. Therefore, in no place in the passage does the author suggest that the Church recorded only medieval music because it did not value popular music. Answer (B) should be eliminated immediately.

C While answer choice (C) might very well be true, the substance of this statement is not discussed at all in the passage and cannot be inferred from any statement made within it. Answer (C) is thus irrelevant and should be eliminated immediately.

D The passage does indicate that the Church was not necessarily the *only* institution to have the means of affording manuscripts: "As a result, **few** were able to produce or own them, and the Catholic Church, which had literate scribes as well as considerable wealth, produced and maintained **most** manuscripts during the Middle Ages." This suggests logically that other institutions such as the aristocracy might very well have been able to produce and maintain some of the manuscripts. But nowhere does the passage discuss the contents of aristocratic households or that aristocrats might have held *large numbers* of manuscripts, so this statement cannot be inferred from the passage.

Question 4

The Correct Answer:

A In question 4, the student is asked to consider which statement *cannot* be inferred from the passage. The passage makes a number of claims about manuscripts in the medieval period, but the only comment on the parchment from which the manuscripts were made is that it was expensive. It might seem logical to argue that if the parchment was expensive, it must also have been difficult to produce, but there is no statement in the passage that supports this claim in any way, so the conclusion cannot be drawn safely. Therefore, **answer choice (A)** is correct.

The Incorrect Answers:

B The passage notes that the manuscripts were "painstakingly copied by hand" and that the only people qualified to do this work were the scribes (who were literate), suggesting that the work required a great deal of time and effort and that few people were able to copy manuscripts. From this, answer choice (B) may be inferred from the passage and is thus incorrect.

C The passage claims that the Church produced most of the manuscripts. The passage also indicates that the majority of extant medieval music is sacred (i.e., deriving from the Church), so it may be inferred that the Church was selective about what music was copied down. Therefore, the passage does imply the statement in answer choice (C). (Note that this does not necessarily suggest that the Church did not value popular music—see answer choice (B) from question 3—but that it was selective. The two qualities must be distinguished from one another.)

D The passage notes that the manuscripts were "copied by hand" and that the Church had "literate scribes" to do this job, suggesting that within the Church they alone were qualified to copy down manuscripts. As a result, the passage does imply that only the literate (those who know how to read) were allowed to copy down manuscripts. Note that the question does not say that of all members of society, the scribes alone were allowed to copy down manuscripts. It is entirely possible that literate members of the aristocracy copied down manuscripts. What is significant with regard to this question is that scribes were *literate*, not that they were members of a certain class within society.

E The passage comments, "Any medieval music not recorded on manuscripts has now been lost to history. Most of the medieval music still in existence is sacred music." From this it may rightly be inferred that most non-sacred music from the medieval period has been lost to history, so the passage implies answer choice (E), and answer choice (E) is incorrect.

Question 5

Overview: Question 5 records a conversation between Lito and Miteki, with Lito making an argument about an action he believes needs to be taken and Miteki responding to that argument. Specifically, Lito notes that the one-lane bridges on the island of Kauai have become dangerous due to the increase of tourist traffic and argues that the bridges should be widened. Miteki rebuts with a comment that Kauai is committed to protecting the plant and animal life on the island and that widening the bridges could endanger these plants and animals. The question asks the reader to identify the flaw in Miteki's response.

The Correct Answer:

E In her response, Miteki ignores the substance of Lito's argument—the potential danger from the one-lane bridges and the need to widen them—and instead tries to redirect the conversation toward a related but different topic, specifically the environmental impact of widening the bridges. Thus, **answer choice (E)** correctly evaluates the flaw in Miteki's response: she fails to address the core of Lito's comments and instead develops a secondary argument.

The Incorrect Answers:

A The conversation does not discuss the accuracy of the information in either Lito's argument or Miteki's, so there is no way to know whether Miteki is relying on faulty information. Answer choice (A) may be eliminated immediately.

B Although Miteki's response does indeed fail to address the substance of Lito's argument, her mistake is not that of circular reasoning, so answer choice (B) may also be eliminated immediately.

C There is no suggestion in the conversation that either topic is more important than the other, so the judgment that the substance of Miteki's response is less important than Lito's cannot be inferred from the conversation. Moreover, such a judgment does not address the flaw in Miteki's reasoning, so answer choice (C) cannot be correct.

D Miteki responds to Lito by picking up on one element of his argument—the one-lane bridges—and then developing an unrelated argument of her own. She does not, however, develop any of Lito's supporting claims (i.e., that the number of accidents has increased, that there are more tourists in Kauai), so answer choice (D) is incorrect.

Question 6

Overview: Question 6 offers a quotation from an art scholar about the Impressionist artist Renoir, in which Renoir is discussed within the context of two earlier artists. The passage offers details about these earlier artists, as well as information about Renoir's personal artistic style. The question asks for a statement that best summarizes the conclusion of the passage. Because the passage does not state its main point directly, the student must infer that statement of summary from the information within the passage.

The Correct Answer:

D In describing each of the three artists named—Rubens, Watteau, and Renoir—the passage offers very different details about each one. Rubens is remembered for "creative choice of subject matter," Watteau for his "ability to interweave themes from Italian theatre into his paintings," and Renoir for "his application of light and shading, his use of vibrant color, and his ability to create an intimate scene." None of these qualities is closely related, so the only answer that explains the purpose of each description is **answer choice (D)**, in which Renoir is noted for following a tradition of individual style. What is more, read notes Renoir as the "final representative," so it is safe to say that Read believes there is no painter after Renoir who has this quality. Answer choice (D) is thus correct.

The Incorrect Answers:

A The only artist noted specifically for his subject matter is Rubens, and the passage does not indicate that this quality may be attributed either to Watteau or Renoir, so answer choice (A) is incorrect.

B Herbert Read comments on Renoir carrying on the "artistic tradition that started at Rubens and ended at Watteau," but this statement does not indicate Read's personal opinion about whether or not all three men may be considered the greatest artists in Western history, so answer choice (B) cannot be correct.

C Read notes that Renoir is the "final painter" of a certain artistic quality, but he makes no comment about artists after Renoir, nor does he suggest that no great artists have arisen since Renoir. It is, of course, possible that he makes this claim elsewhere in his analysis, but the claim is not recorded in this particular passage, so answer choice (C) cannot be inferred and is thus incorrect.

E Again, Read makes no comment on whether or not Rubens (Flemish), Watteau, and Renoir (both French) were the greatest painters of the seventeenth and eighteenth centuries. What is more, Read notes that Renoir carries on a tradition that "runs directly from Rubens to Watteau," so it is very possible that the unnamed painters who fell between Rubens and Watteau were not Flemish or French.

Question 7

Overview: This question presents a statement by a school principal regarding how well students are doing in certain subject areas. The students recently completed some testing, and the principal notes that the students scored badly in the math tests compared to their performance on reading tests. The principal then notes that students spend more class time on reading than on math and concludes that students need to spend as much time on math as on reading in order to improve the math scores. The question asks the student to compare the flaw in the principal's reasoning to the flaw in the reasoning of the answer choices.

In order to find an answer choice with a comparable flaw, it is first necessary to identify how the principal's argument proceeds and then decide where the flaw develops. The principal first looks at the test results of two different subjects and sees that the students did badly on one and well on the other. Looking for a quality that distinguishes these two, the principal realizes that the students spend less time on math than on reading. Thus, the conclusion follows that students should spend as much time on math as on reading. The problem with this is that the argument assumes quantity = quality, with no regard for other considerations, such as the skills of the math teachers at the school, the usefulness of the curriculum, and so forth. The correct answer choice will follow this pattern of quantity = quality, with a specific outcome desired based on the investment of a certain quantity and a disregard for other significant considerations.

The Correct Answer:

C The reasoning in **answer choice (C)** is similarly flawed to the principal's reasoning in that two items are compared (options trading and stock trading), and the outcome is assumed to be based on the invested quantity (money in options vs. money in stocks). The argument indicates that traders invest more money in stocks than they do in options and that they also tend to make more money. No other considerations are mentioned in this comparison, such as the skill of the trader, the history of the stock's movement, and so forth. The conclusion about outcome is reached solely upon the basis of the quantity invested, so the reasoning in answer choice (C) most closely parallels the principal's reasoning.

The Incorrect Answers:

A, D Answer choices (A) and (D) are incorrect, because the conclusions reached in both arguments do not parallel the principal's conclusion in any way. The argument in choice (A) is that parents should read in order to help improve their children's speech development skills. The argument in choice (D) is that students should take certain kinds of high school classes to be successful in college. Both answer choices suggest that a specific action should be taken to achieve results of certain quality, but the formula quantity = quality is not present in any form in either answer choice.

B This answer choice seems promising at first, with the conclusion that the number of stars identifying a resort (quantity) translates automatically to the comfort of a stay there (quality). But unlike the principal's conclusion, this conclusion does not require a specific change in the quantity of action or investment to reach it, so it is not close enough to parallel it. Had answer choice (B) indicated that the resorts with the most stars tend to be the most successful, with the conclusion that a specific resort should improve its business plan and seek to obtain more stars, it would be comparable. As it is, though, answer choice (B) may be eliminated.

E Answer choice (E) has no relevance to the principal's conclusion and can be eliminated immediately. The conclusion in (E) relates only to quantity; the question of quality does not arise at any point in this particular example.

Question 8

<u>Overview:</u> Question 8 presents a scenario in which the CEO of a fast-food chain makes an announcement about upcoming revisions to the chain's menu. The company is completely overhauling its menu items so that all items offered will now be healthier. Specifically, the

announcement notes that the company will be removing unhealthy fats and offering smaller portions. The question asks the student to consider which of the answer choices most undermines the effect of the CEO's announcement. To find the correct answer, it is necessary to focus on the details in the CEO's comments and on what, in particular, would call into question the validity of the CEO's remarks.

The Correct Answer:

A **Answer choice (A)** states that although the fast-food chain is indeed making the announced changes in its menu, it is also retaining certain addictive additives that have, by implication, long been in its food. As a result, the continued inclusion of these additives calls into question the company's actual commitment to offering healthy foods and raises questions about the claim that the company's food will be a healthier option than that offered by other fast-food chains. Therefore, choice (A) most seriously undermines the CEO's statements.

The Incorrect Answers:

B That the CEO is receiving a large bonus is potentially suspicious, but it does not by itself undermine the CEO's claim about providing healthier food options. In other words, nothing about the bonus suggests that the menu will not in fact offer healthier items than before; answer choice (B) does not address evidence for or against the CEO's claim. There is no reason to be surprised that the company is rewarding the CEO in advance for a plan that will benefit the company. Thus, answer choice (B) is incorrect.

C The response of the focus group calls into question the way that customers will respond to the food, but it does not call into question the CEO's comments about the healthy qualities of the food. Thus, answer choice (C) may be eliminated immediately.

D While the merits of advertising to young children might be arguable, the ads themselves seem to support the company's claim that it is offering healthier choices by encouraging children to request the better menu items when they visit the fast-food chains. As a result, this answer choice seems to bring some validity to the CEO's claims of a commitment to better health, and it is incorrect.

E The CEO makes no claim to having removed all items from the old menu. Instead, he claims that the ingredients have been improved and the menu revised. Answer choice (E) does more to support the CEO's claims than it does to undermine it, so it is incorrect.

Question 9

Overview: In question 9, the head of a regional psychiatric association makes a statement about a study that suggests the importance of spirituality in helping patients live longer, healthier lives. The head of the association also comments that depression has been noted, in some cases, to shorten the lives of patients. The speaker concludes that members of the psychiatric association should encourage patients to pursue spirituality in the expectation that it will provide them with longer and healthier lives. The question asks the student to consider on which assumption the speaker's conclusion is based.

The Correct Answer:

E In reaching his conclusion, the head of the psychiatric association does not distinguish between different forms of spirituality. As a result, the conclusion he reaches suggests that all forms of spirituality are equally healthy and that all will be equally beneficial to the patients. **Answer choice (E)** therefore, is, the most correct answer.

The Incorrect Answers:

A While the head of the psychiatric association indicates that some of the patients being treated by members of the association have suffered from depression, he does not indicate that all of them have. Therefore, answer choice (A) may be eliminated, because the conclusion in the passage is clearly not based on this assumption.

B As the head of the psychiatric association only mentions the practice of spirituality as being healthy, it cannot be assumed from the passage that he bases his conclusions on the practice of a specific kind of spirituality or that the patients who experienced positive results from the practice of spirituality were practicing the same form. Answer (B) cannot be correct.

C The head of the psychiatric association indicates that the positive aspects of spirituality were observed among the patients, but he does not comment anywhere on whether members of the psychiatric association practice spirituality or whether they should. Rather, his conclusions relate directly to the patients practicing spirituality, and it cannot be assumed that his conclusion is based on the importance of spirituality to the association members. (It might be true that he also recommends the practice of spirituality to members, but this is an inference from his comments, not an assumption on which they are based.)

D The head of the psychiatric association does say specifically that depression "in some cases can lead to an early death." He does not suggest, however, that the result of depression is inevitably death. Further, his conclusion that the members of the psychiatric association should encourage patients to practice spirituality is not based on the assumption that depression will always lead to death, but rather that it can shorten the lives of some patients. Answer choice (D) is incorrect.

Question 10

Overview: In question 10, the student is asked to consider which of the answer choices most explains the disparity in price drop between the cost of crude oil per barrel and the cost of gasoline at the pump. In order to determine the difference, it is necessary to think about the specific statements made within the passage. This question asks for inferences only inasmuch as those inferences can be made directly from the information in the passage. Several of the answer choices provide distant possibilities, but only one sufficiently explains the discrepancy in price without deviating from the details of the passage. Question 10 presents a scenario involving cause-and-effect, and cause and effect are what students need to consider: what cause directly explains the effect of a drop in the price of crude oil that is not reflected in prices at the gasoline pump?

The Correct Answer:

B **Answer choice (B)** is the correct answer because it provides a logical explanation for the disparity in price while not deviating from the details in the passage. The cause suggested is that refineries have had to absorb the higher price of crude oil in recent months; this has had the effect of those refineries delaying passing on the lower price of crude oil to customers at the gas pump.

The Incorrect Answers:

A, C Although answer choices (A) and (C) provide some explanation for the drop in the price of crude oil per barrel, they provide absolutely no explanation for the higher price at the gasoline pump, leaving open the question regarding the disparity in price. As a result, both may be eliminated immediately.

D Answer choice (D) also offers some indication about what might affect the price of crude oil per barrel, but it fails to address the discrepancy in price, that is, why the cost of crude oil has decreased without a corresponding drop in prices at the gasoline pump. If anything, answer choice (D) raises further questions, since if there are alternative energy options, the price of gasoline should naturally decrease according to the laws of supply and demand.

E Answer choice (E), although it reflects a potential result of continued low crude oil prices, does not address the question of why gasoline prices are still high in comparison to crude oil prices. While it might be inferred that the loss of oil production companies entails less competition (and therefore higher prices), there is not enough information in the passage to imply such a conclusion or to select (E) as the best answer.

Question 11

Overview: Question 11 presents a passage that considers how possible restrictions on freedom of thought or freedom of conscience could render these otherwise guaranteed freedoms impossible. The passage quotes from the Universal Declaration of Human Rights, a document that establishes the need for all to have the freedom of thought, the freedom of conscience, and the freedom of religion; the passage points out that these freedoms might ultimately be nonexistent in the face of thought-controlling techniques. More specifically, the passage notes the potential for propaganda, or even educational manipulation, that would train children to think a certain way from childhood, thus removing from them any real freedom of thought or conscience, while still allowing them to believe that they have such freedoms. The question asks the student to summarize the argument implied in the passage. An implied argument is one that is not overtly stated, so the student must read between the lines, so to speak, to arrive at a conclusion about the point of the passage. That being said, the passage contains all information necessary for deriving such a conclusion, so the student does not require extraneous information.

The Correct Answer:

C The passage states quite clearly, "if children are taught from an early age to think or believe a certain way, it might not be possible for them to have real freedom of thought or conscience as adults if they have no real ability to think for themselves." This suggests that the purpose of the passage is to explain the subtle restrictions that might exist on freedom of thought or conscience. Such restrictions are not explicit or codified in law but (according to the passage) could be used to control these freedoms while allowing the perception that they still exist. Thus **choice (C)** is the correct answer.

The Incorrect Answers:

A Answer choice (A) seems very likely, but it is important to realize that although the passage suggests that freedom of thought or conscience *might not* be able to exist, it does not state anywhere that they absolutely *do not* or *cannot*. Instead, the passage makes a hypothetical suggestion about what might occur in some cases, but not in every case. Therefore, answer choice (A) cannot be correct because it assumes too much about the point of the passage.

B Nowhere does the passage state that freedom of thought or conscience is controlled in the same way as freedom of speech or expression. In fact, the passage states that there are laws restricting freedom of speech or expression but that there are no laws restricting freedom of thought or conscience. Answer choice (B) may be eliminated immediately.

D The passage cites the Universal Declaration of Human Rights to make a point about the perceived guarantee of freedom of thought or conscience, but it then goes on to undermine this Declaration with the information that these freedoms can still be restricted. There is no indication that the passage makes a statement on the need for the Declaration, so answer choice (D) is incorrect.

E At no point does the passage suggest that the restrictions on freedom of speech or expression should be lifted, so answer choice (E) is clearly incorrect and can be eliminated immediately.

QUESTION 12

Overview: Question 12 records a conversation between Conrad and Eloise, during which the two discuss an upcoming change in environmental standards for vehicles in the town of Ecoville. Conrad states that the town is making "excellent," beneficial changes, but Eloise points out that immediately implementing the new standards would place a financial burden on those in a lower-income bracket. Since it is impossible to expect any town not to have some lower-income residents, Eloise suggests that Ecoville delay or revise the standards until the requirements can be better funded. The question asks the student to consider the method Eloise uses to counter Conrad's argument.

THE CORRECT ANSWER:

A **Answer choice (A)** offers the best summary of Eloise's argument: she does acknowledge the reasonableness of Conrad's argument about the importance of new environmental standards, but she also offer evidence that indicates a potential problem in the implementation of these standards. If lower-income families cannot afford to purchase new vehicles or convert them according to the new standards, then the town will be unable to bring the standards into effect. Therefore, answer choice (A) is correct.

THE INCORRECT ANSWERS:

B Eloise does agree with the substance of Conrad's argument (regarding the value of new environmental standards), but she does not offer any alternative reasons for that argument. She merely points out that the plans need to be delayed or revised, and the details she provides explain her reason for this claim; they do not constitute alternative reasons for Conrad's argument itself. Therefore, answer choice (B) is incorrect.

C At no point does Eloise point out a flaw in Conrad's reasoning: instead she points out a weakness in the implementation of the new environmental standards. She does not provide a more logical perspective but offers evidence that undermines the claim that the standards should be implemented immediately. Therefore, answer choice (C) cannot be correct.

D Eloise begins by agreeing with Conrad about the importance of the new environmental standards, so it is obvious from her first sentence that she does not disagree with him entirely. Therefore, answer choice (D) can be eliminated immediately.

E Eloise addresses Conrad's argument directly by agreeing with him in theory if not in every detail, and she goes on to address very specific problems with the potential implementation of the standards for which he is arguing. So, she clearly does not redirect the argument to a secondary point. Answer choice (E) is incorrect.

QUESTION 13

Overview: In Question 13, a large public health organization has recommended the banning of the herbal sweetener stevia on the grounds that stevia poses cancer risks, among other health concerns. The public health organization specifically requests that the FDA acknowledge the dangers and ban the sweetener for human consumption. The student is asked to select the answer choice that most undermines the public health organization's claim about the dangers of stevia.

The Correct Answer:

E **Answer choice (E)** claims that the public health organization has no tests to back up its claims about the dangers of the sweetener. If studies have shown no correlation between consumption of stevia and incidence of cancer or other health problems, this suggests that the public health organization has no evidence to support its claim that stevia is dangerous. Therefore, answer choice (E) most undermines the organization's argument.

The Incorrect Answers:

A Although the fact that the studies were funded by the head of the largest manufacturer of artificial sweetener raises questions about a conflict of interests, this in itself does not directly undermine the claims of the public health organization. That is, an apparent conflict of interest does not necessarily mean that the public health organization offers biased or unreliable results. Therefore, answer choice (A) cannot be the best answer.

B The use of stevia in Japan without reported negative side effects is interesting, but it does not prove that stevia is not dangerous. This answer choice does not suggest that formal studies, for example, indicate that there is no correlation between consumption of stevia and incidence of cancer or other health problems. Mere common knowledge that stevia is used commonly in Japan does not imply that stevia is safe. Answer choice (B) is incorrect.

C Once more, this answer choice raises a question about a conflict of interests—is the head of the public health organization trying to get a job in the FDA by providing an important health warning and thus indicating his usefulness to the FDA? Perhaps. But the passage does not indicate this in any way, nor would this motivation necessarily mean that the organization's claims are incorrect or unreliable. Answer choice (C) does not clearly undermine the organization's claims and is therefore incorrect.

D The endorsement of a large diabetic association indicates that some believe in the health value of stevia, but this does not undermine the claims of the public health organization. As there is no indication that the diabetes association has conducted studies illustrating that stevia is safe, for example, the endorsement of stevia by the diabetes association is irrelevant to the public health organization's argument. Answer choice (D) can be eliminated at once.

Question 14

Overview: Question 14 presents a scenario in which a large hospital in the town of Riverton has an established policy of turning away patients with no insurance or with insurance that is insufficient to cover their medical needs. The mayor of Riverton has taken a stand against this practice and has asked the city council to pass an ordinance that requires hospitals to accept all patients, regardless of their insurance coverage. The city council has refused on the grounds that the hospital is a private business and should not have to serve those who cannot pay. The student is asked to consider which assumption among the answer choices can be inferred from the city council's argument.

The Correct Answer:

B Although the passage does not directly mention anti-discrimination laws, it does mention that the mayor perceives the hospital's policy to fall under these laws and thus explains his reason for taking the matter before the city council. The city council's decision, then, indicates that they do not believe any laws forbidding discrimination apply to a hospital that is refusing service to uninsured or underinsured patients.

The Incorrect Answers:

A There is nothing in the city council's decision or in the passage to indicate that the majority of residents in Riverton already have sufficient coverage. In fact, the outcry raised against the hospital suggests otherwise, so answer choice (A) cannot be correct.

C, D There is no information in the passage to suggest that the city council bases its decision on the possibility of government funding or on another hospital accepting patients. The passage does mention that the hospital under discussion is the "primary" one, indicating that there might be others, but there is no suggestion regarding a hospital in a nearby town or about its policies concerning uninsured patients. Therefore, answer choices (C) and (D) cannot be correct.

E Although the city council might very well be composed mostly of members who support a different political party than that of the mayor, it is impossible to deduce from the passage that the council is so composed or that this contributes to the city council's decision regarding the hospital. Answer choice (E) is clearly incorrect.

Question 15

Overview: Question 15 recounts information about a test regarding the effects of drinking milk on calcium levels in women over the age of forty. The passage details what the participating women were asked to do, mentioning specifically that all followed the requirements closely. But the passage also notes that the test results indicated a disparity between the rise in calcium levels in some women over others. The question asks the student to choose a statement that best explains the discrepancy in results. To select the correct answer, the student must give close attention to the details in the passage and be careful not to assume details that are inconsistent with the information the passage presents.

The Correct Answer:

D The passage indicates that all of the women were required to drink the required two eight-ounce glasses of milk each day, and that all did this faithfully. There is nothing, however, to indicate that the women were not allowed to take a multi-vitamin with calcium, so **answer choice (D)** provides the best explanation about why some women had higher levels of calcium than others, when all were following the stipulations of the test carefully.

The Incorrect Answers:

A Although the difference between whole milk and low-fat milk might result in different calcium levels, it is impossible to deduce this from the passage; contrast this with correct answer choice (D), which specifically indicates that the vitamins some women took included calcium. Because one cannot infer from the passage that the fat content of milk affects its calcium levels, it also cannot be inferred with any certainty that the fat content of the milk contributed to the disparity in the test results. Answer choice (A) is incorrect.

B The passage states quite clearly that all of the participants in the test were "in similar states of health." Answer choice (B) contradicts this and can therefore be eliminated immediately.

C As with answer choice (A), it is possible that an age difference affected the results, but there is no indication in the passage or in the statement itself that this explains the difference in calcium levels among the women. Had answer choice (C) made the additional claim that women over the age of fifty have more difficulty in absorbing calcium, this choice might be reasonable. As it is, though, it must be eliminated.

E Answer choice (E) provides no explanation for why giving birth would affect calcium levels in women, so it cannot be correct within the context of the passage.

Question 16

Overview: In question 16, the passage presents an argument about the need for better standards to determine federal funding for the performing arts, and the student is asked to identify the way in which the argument proceeds. In order to do so, the student should consider the argument step by step: (1) a general claim about the importance of performing arts groups who offer traditional repertoire, (2) a claim about the value to small communities of such groups, including their close proximity to small communities, (3) the comment that federal funding favors groups with progressive material, even though these groups draw smaller audiences than traditional groups, and (4) the claim that federal funding should allot more money to traditional groups. With these steps of the argument in mind, the student can consider the answer choices.

The Correct Answer:

A Based on the outline presented above, it is clear that **answer choice (A)** is the one that best describes the pattern of reasoning in the passage. The author of the passage begins by presenting a general statement about the importance of traditional groups, develops this view with supporting details, and then concludes with a suggestion for future action. Therefore, answer choice (A) is the correct answer.

The Incorrect Answers:

B Although the author of the passage raises awareness about a problem, there is no indication that the author is demanding attention at any time, and based on the opening of the passage it is clear that the author does not *begin* the argument with a demand; rather, the author begins by presenting a general claim. Answer choice (B) is incorrect.

C Far from undermining the opposition, the author points out that avant-garde groups contribute something very important to the performing arts. And although the author does raise questions about the way federal funding is allotted to the performing arts, the author does not draw a conclusion from this but rather offers a suggestion for an alternative action. Therefore, answer choice (C) may be eliminated.

D The author does not begin the passage with a call to action. Instead, the author opens with a general remark about the importance of traditional performing arts groups. What is more, the author does not at any point discuss problems with those who oppose the argument in the passage, so answer choice (D) is clearly incorrect.

E The author does publicize a concern within the passage and encourage action to be taken, but the author does not discuss alternatives for addressing the concern. Nor does this answer choice reflect the progression of the author's argument within the passage. Answer choice (E) is incorrect.

Question 17

Overview: In question 17, the student must consider an editorial in the Williamsburg newspaper, in which the writer claims that all students in local schools should be required to attend the colonial center at Williamsburg because of its exceptional historical value. The question asks the student to consider which of the answer selections most undermines the writer's argument. To do this, the student must consider the substance of the argument—that "students are missing out on this opportunity," that "very few local schools take students on field trips" to Williamsburg and thus that "All local schools should be required to take the students to the colonial center, and funding should be provided to make this recommendation a reality"—and then consider what would most undermine the reasonableness of this argument.

The Correct Answer:

C **Answer choice (C)** claims that local schools have already polled families and have found that almost all the students in the local schools have already visited Williamsburg with their families. Although this does not call into question the editorial writer's claim that the schools are not taking students to the colonial center, it does offer a reason for why schools do not do so, and it strongly undermines the claim that students are missing out on the opportunity to visit the center. Therefore, answer choice (C) undermines the argument that schools should be required to take students to the center and that extra funding should be made available. Therefore, answer choice (C) is most correct.

The Incorrect Answers:

A If anything, answer choice (A) only validates the editorial writer's argument by indicating that the local schools in the Williamsburg area focus on the kind of field trips that the colonial center would offer. Answer choice (A) can be eliminated at once.

B Although answer choice (B) suggests that the editorial writer is motivated by the writer's job (as head of marketing for the colonial center, responsible for bringing more students there), that the writer has this job does not necessarily undermine his argument itself. If the writer's claim that very few children from local schools have been to the colonial center is true, for example, then perhaps the argument is still strong. Answer choice (B) is incorrect.

D Like answer choice (A), answer choice (D) provides support to the writer's argument by indicating that the school would receive a discount, so the funding itself would not create too much of a burden. Answer choice (D) can be eliminated immediately.

E Answer choice (E) provides a reason for why the schools might have refrained from pursuing too many field trips in recent months, but the editorial indicates that the lack of field trips to the colonial center is not a new concern but an ongoing one. Additionally, since the writer of the editorial is arguing for funding, the price of gasoline should not be as much of a concern, as that would be budgeted into the funding. Answer choice (E) does not sufficiently undermine the editorial and is thus incorrect.

Question 18

Overview: Question 18 presents a scenario in which a large airport is planning to make changes that will benefit domestic passengers but create hassles for international passengers. The hassles are such that many international travelers who frequent the airport have signed a petition and have promised to take their business elsewhere if the airport proceeds with the proposed changes. Nevertheless, the airport has made the decision to go forward with the changes. The question asks the student to select the answer choice that can be inferred as having contributed to the airport's decision to continue with the new plans.

THE CORRECT ANSWER:

D The correct answer choice must indicate some kind of alternative benefit that would explain the airport's willingness to risk the loss of international travelers. Because the proposed changes to the airport will benefit the domestic passengers ("changes that are intended to improve the ease of flying for domestic passengers"), the airport must have decided that the changes will bring in more domestic passengers who will more than offset any loss of international passengers. Therefore, **answer choice (D)** is most correct.

THE INCORRECT ANSWERS:

A, B Although the airport might very well be counting on the reasons given in answer choices (A) and (B), nothing in the passage suggests that the airport made a decision based on those reasons. Answer choices (A) and (B) must be eliminated because they are not supported by the passage.

C Although answer choice (C) could be a valid reason, nothing in the passage leads the reader to assume that the airport has already spent a large amount of money on the proposed changes. Instead, it suggests that the airport expects to benefit monetarily by drawing new domestic travelers. Answer choice (C) is incorrect.

E Answer choice (E) describes a plan the airport might very well use, but there is nothing in the passage to suggest it, so it cannot be inferred that the airport made its decision based on distant plans for improvements in international travel. Answer (E) is incorrect.

QUESTION 19

Overview: In question 19, a conservative voter comments on a policy traditionally opposed by conservative voters in an attempt to prove to fellow conservatives that the policy is worth supporting. Specifically, the conservative voter argues that universal healthcare is not as costly to taxpayers as other conservative voters usually believe and that the government should universalize health care because it would thereby actually spend less money per person than it currently spends. The student is asked to locate a weakness in the voter's argument.

THE CORRECT ANSWER:

B The weakness in the voter's argument rests on the fact that the voter seems to assume that the only way to reduce the cost of health care per person is to universalize health care (the voter argues for universal health care strictly on the grounds that it would save money relative to the current health care system). But there might be other options for reducing the cost of health care per person without universalizing health care. **Answer choice (B)** is most correct because it accurately states this problem.

THE INCORRECT ANSWERS:

A Answer choice (A) is incorrect because the voter does not explicitly define what he means by universal healthcare. Because he does not define what it would mean for healthcare to be universal in the first place, he does not offer an inconsistent definition of universal healthcare. Therefore, answer choice (A) cannot be correct.

C There is no evidence that the voter's claims are unfounded. We cannot know from the passage alone whether his claims of government spending are based on fact or are inflated. Answer choice (C) cannot be correct.

D The conservative voter does reject his usual partisan position in order to encourage other conservatives to support something that is not traditionally a part of the conservative platform. However, doing so does not necessarily weaken his argument. Rather, it shows that the voter has considered the position carefully before deciding to go against his party's usual stand. Therefore, answer choice (D) is incorrect.

E An *ad hominem* attack is a personal attack, and there is no indication of any personal insults in the conservative voter's argument. Therefore, answer choice (E) can be eliminated immediately.

QUESTION 20

Overview: Question 20 asks the student to consider an argument about language development in children before puberty and to summarize the main point of the passage. Specifically, the passage begins by pointing out that specialists in language development know that pre-pubescent children learn languages better than post-pubescent children, as the brains of pre-pubescent children are more adapted to absorbing languages. The passage then points out that funding is generally limited for incorporating second language lessons to elementary children, so schools tend to delay the learning of second languages until high school, or after puberty. In order to discern the main point, the student must consider the purpose of these details, sorting out primary details and secondary details, and consider them in the context of the argument in the passage. It is important to remember that the student is not necessarily being asked to restate the argument itself (that schools should teach second languages to pre-pubescent children), but to summarize the entire point of the passage in the context of the argument.

THE CORRECT ANSWER:

E **Answer choice (E)** best combines all of the primary elements within the context of the argument to arrive at a main point: that because of children's ability to absorb new languages before puberty, schools should adopt second language lessons for elementary-age children. Therefore, answer choice (E) is most correct.

THE INCORRECT ANSWERS:

A Answer choice (A) summarizes the point of the details in the passage but does not place these details in the context of the argument being presented. The fact that children learn languages best before puberty is significant, but it needs to be placed alongside the argument about the importance of schools teaching second languages to pre-pubescent children. Answer choice (A) is incorrect, because it leaves out important elements of the passage.

B The author of the passage does point out that there is not enough government funding for teaching second languages, but this point seems to be made within the context of *why* schools delay language classes until the high school years; it is not a primary detail. Therefore, answer choice (B) is not correct.

C Answer choice (C) offers a secondary detail but does not place this detail within the bigger picture offered by the passage. It does not summarize the main point of the passage and can be eliminated at once.

D Although the author of the passage does indicate clearly that children would greatly benefit from learning second languages in the elementary years, he does not pass judgment on schools that do not offer these programs. Instead, the author provides an explanation for why these programs do not exist, suggesting that such hindrances should be overcome. Answer choice (D) fails to summarize the main point of the paragraph, so it is incorrect.

Questions 21 and 22

Overview: Questions 21 and 22 are based on information contained within a passage about the English village of Eyam, widely known as "plague village" because of the village's decision in 1665 to isolate itself during an outbreak of plague, rather than risk infecting others. Over a year later, more than 75% of the people in the village had died from the plague. But almost 25% had *not* died, and most of these survivors never caught the plague at all. The passage concludes by noting that researchers have discovered that descendants of plague survivors from Eyam carry a specific gene mutation known as delta 32. Question 21 asks the student to consider the purpose of the paragraph and infer a conclusion from it. Question 22 then asks the student to consider which answer choice would most undermine the conclusion implied in the passage.

Question 21

The Correct Answer:

C The final sentence in the paragraph is not immediately linked to the previous sentences, but there is an implied connection: that some researchers believe the delta 32 mutation found in descendants of the plague survivors helped them resist infection. Since most of the survivors did not contract the disease at all ("Hancock's story is not unique; most of the survivors proved to be immune to the infection altogether"), the statement regarding the researchers' discovery suggests that they believe the gene contributed to survival. Therefore, **answer choice (C)** is most correct.

The Incorrect Answers:

A Although answer choice (A)—that the delta 32 mutation is limited to the village of Eyam—might very well be accurate, the passage does not claim this anywhere. It claims only that descendants of survivors carry this gene, with the implication that their ancestors who survived the plague carried it as well. But the passage does not rule out the possibility that the gene appears in people in other parts of the world who also survived the plague. As a result, answer choice (A) is incorrect.

B Again, answer choice (B) might be true, but the passage does not claim or suggest this anywhere. The passage is focused instead on the possibility that the gene contributed to the survival of certain residents. Answer choice (B) is incorrect.

D The passage makes no suggestion that the delta 32 mutation developed in response to the plague. If anything, it seems to suggest that the gene might already have been carried by certain residents in Eyam and was thus responsible for the survivors' ability to resist the plague infection. Answer choice (D) is clearly incorrect.

E The passage makes no evaluative statement regarding the decision by the residents of Eyam to isolate themselves: it merely presents the information as fact. Therefore, answer choice (E) can be eliminated immediately.

Question 22

The Correct Answer:

A **Answer choice (A)** presents a situation in which other researchers have discovered that the delta 32 mutation does *not* actually resist plague infection in lab rats, with the suggestion that the conclusion drawn by earlier researchers (about the gene's resistance to the plague) is false. If true, answer choice (A) would most clearly undermine the conclusion of the passage and is thus the correct answer.

The Incorrect Answers:

B As the passage does not imply that the delta 32 mutation was exclusive to the village of Eyam, answer choice (B) does not undermine the conclusion of the passage in any way. In fact, the presence of the delta 32 mutation in others suggests that the gene did contribute to plague resistance and might go toward supporting the conclusions of the passage. Answer choice (B), therefore, is incorrect.

C Answer choice (C) provides an interesting piece of information, but this information does not undermine the conclusions of the passage. That the delta 32 mutation might also appear to resist HIV infection merely suggests a possible connection between plague infection and HIV. This is, however, irrelevant to the conclusions made in the passage, so it can be eliminated as an answer choice.

D, E Neither answer choice (D) nor answer choice (E) offers any information that undermines the conclusions implied in the passage. Both present potentially apocryphal details that add context to the passage but have no clear connection to its purpose or conclusion. Therefore, both answer choices (D) and (E) are incorrect.

Question 23

Overview: Question 23 provides information about the origins of the microwave oven, explaining Percy Spencer's role in its invention and its subsequent development by Raytheon. The passage gives details about Raytheon's original model, and notes that the company was never able to attract a wide consumer audience to its Radarange microwave oven. However, in the 1960s, the Litton company began developing and marketing microwave ovens, with immediate success. The question asks students to consider which of the answer choices best explains the reason for Litton's commercial success, in contrast to Raytheon's lack of success.

The Correct Answer:

D In the middle of the passage, the author notes that Raytheon's Radarange model of the microwave oven was a large, heavy appliance for which general consumers had little interest. **Answer choice (D)** indicates that the Litton company developed a far more compact oven that is still familiar today. Given the size of the Radarange and the negative public response, it is reasonable that consumers were far more interested in a small oven that could fit easily into a kitchen. Therefore, answer choice (D) is the best answer.

The Incorrect Answers:

A The fact that Litton marketed its new oven at a trade show in Chicago might very well have contributed to the public awareness of the oven, but there is nothing within the passage to suggest that Raytheon did not do something similar. The best answer choice, therefore, indicates a reason for why consumers would clearly choose one over the other *within the context of the passage*, so answer choice (A) cannot be correct.

B The question specifically asks why Litton was more successful at selling microwave ovens *in the U.S.*, so information about the response in Japan is irrelevant. Answer choice (B) can be eliminated at once.

C That Litton's model made the microwave oven a popular appliance with American families, and the claim that more than 90% of American families own microwaves today merely adds to the information in the paragraph and proves that Litton was very successful. It does not, however, explain why Litton was more successful than Raytheon. So, answer choice (C) cannot be correct.

E Answer choice (E) is tempting, because it indicates that Litton might have had better technology than Raytheon, and that the public responded by purchasing Litton's oven instead of Raytheon's. There is nothing in the passage to suggest, however, that Raytheon's technology was flawed or inferior—only that Raytheon's model was large and cumbersome. Thus, answer choice (E) requires inferences that cannot reasonably be drawn from the passage, and it cannot be correct.

Question 24

Overview: In question 24, a passage provides information about the origin of vaccines, describing conflicting details: the English scientist Edward Jenner usually receives credit for being the first to develop vaccinations in the late eighteenth century, but historical evidence suggests that the Ottoman Turks were inoculating people before that. Additional details indicate that the peoples of China and India have been using various forms of vaccination for centuries. The student is asked to select an answer choice that best summarizes the main point of the passage.

The Correct Answer:

B All the details in the passage lead to one central suggestion: although the Englishman (and hence Westerner) Edward Jenner is usually credited with the discovery of vaccines in the late eighteenth century, historical evidence suggests that peoples in the East were using vaccines long before Jenner began using them. This most clearly summarizes the passage, so **answer choice (B)** is the best answer.

The Incorrect Answers:

A The information regarding Lady Montagu's experience with vaccines in Turkey is useful in establishing that inoculations were already familiar to some societies before Jenner's discovery, but it is not the main point of the passage. Therefore, answer choice (A) can be eliminated for having insufficient information.

C Answer choice (C) summarizes important details in the paragraph, but it fails to summarize the larger point—that *because* there is evidence of vaccination during earlier centuries in China and India, Jenner cannot necessarily be credited with the discovery of vaccines. Answer choice (C) leaves important information out of the summary, so it is incorrect.

D The information about inoculation use in China and India well before Jenner's work strongly suggests that the Ottoman Turks cannot claim the discovery of vaccines, but the passage makes no claim that the Ottoman Turks discovered vaccines (or that they are said to have discovered vaccines). Rather, the passage claims only that they were using them before Jenner. Answer choice (D) is incorrect.

E The passage makes no claim that Jenner himself took credit for the discovery of vaccines, claiming only that Jenner is generally credited with this discovery. What is more, there is no indication in the passage that Lady Montagu's son was vaccinated for cowpox, the illness that Jenner treated with his vaccines. Therefore, answer choice (E) is clearly incorrect.

Question 25

Overview: Question 25 is one of the more difficult questions in this section of the test because it requires the student to pay very careful attention both to the information in the passage and to the question itself in order to deduce the flaw in the economist's reasoning. The economist makes a claim about traditional indicators during a weak economy: the value of the dollar falls, and the price of gold rises. The economist then notes that all economic indicators point to a weak economy, but the expected low dollar/high gold movement is absent. The economist then concludes that the market can be expected to turn around. From a purely economic perspective, there are a number of problems with the economist's reasoning; however, the student does not need to know specific details about economics beyond the information contained in the passage. The most important consideration is that the economist notes a specific precedent: when there is a weak economy, the dollar should fall and gold should rise. Because gold is not rising, the economist concludes that the precedent still holds firm and that the market will be strong again. This conclusion raises the central question of whether the market precedent is still relevant, and this is an issue the economist fails to account for.

The Correct Answer:

A In deriving his conclusion, the economist discusses only the precedents that determine market movement. His information, however, suggests that the movements in the market might be anomalous and thus that precedent alone cannot determine the conclusion that he reaches. Therefore, the economist's conclusion does not adequately consider the anomalies he indicates, as he draws an incorrect interpretation from them. **Answer choice (A)** most clearly states this and is the correct answer.

The Incorrect Answers:

B, C Answer choices (B) and (C) require knowledge about economics in general (and the market in particular) that is not contained within the passage. Although both answer choices might very well be true, this cannot be determined from the information provided within the passage. Thus, answer choices (B) and (C) cannot be correct.

D Answer choice (D) suggests that the economist should focus on the movement of market sectors over stock market indicators and the prices of the dollar and gold. But the passage does not suggest anywhere that an economist should focus on one element of market movement over another, so this answer choice makes assumptions that cannot be inferred from the passage. Answer choice (D) is incorrect.

E Answer choice (E) is tempting because it suggests that the economist is overlooking key data in reaching his conclusion, but the passage offers no indication that certain data is required to reach a conclusion—only that certain precedents are traditional in reaching a conclusion. Therefore, answer choice (E) makes assumptions that cannot be inferred and is incorrect.

Analytical Reasoning, Section II

Cluster 1:

There are five time slots for the appointments at 9:30, 10:00, 10:30, 11:00, and 11:30.

9:30	10:00	10:30	11:00	11:30

First, the conditions should be diagramed. Start with the most restrictive condition and build from there. This is condition #3; Eric must have the 11:30 appointment slot.

9:30	10:00	10:30	11:00	11:30
				Eric

The second most restrictive is condition #2; Sarah cannot have the 10:00 or 11:00 appointment slot. Since Eric is already in the 11:30 slot, this leaves two possible slots for Sarah.

9:30	10:00	10:30	11:00	11:30
Sarah				Eric

9:30	10:00	10:30	11:00	11:30
		Sarah		Eric

Next we add condition #4; Molly's appointment slot is immediately before Nick's. If Sarah has the 10:30 appointment, then there is only one place Molly and Nick's appointments can be.

9:30	10:00	10:30	11:00	11:30
Molly	Nick	Sarah		Eric

However, if Sarah has the 9:30 then there are two possible places for Molly and Nick's appointments.

9:30	10:00	10:30	11:00	11:30
Sarah	Molly	Nick		Eric

9:30	10:00	10:30	11:00	11:30
Sarah		Molly	Nick	Eric

Condition #1 does not figure into any of the diagrams since Katie is only included if one of the other patients cancels, so the only thing left is to fill in the blanks with Bill's appointment into the three final diagrams.

Diagram #1

9:30	10:00	10:30	11:00	11:30
Molly	Nick	Sarah	Bill	Eric

Diagram #2

9:30	10:00	10:30	11:00	11:30
Sarah	Molly	Nick	Bill	Eric

Diagram #3

9:30	10:00	10:30	11:00	11:30
Sarah	Bill	Molly	Nick	Eric

1. **E.** Looking at the three diagrams, Nick can have an appointment at 10:00, 10:30, or 11:00. So 9:30 and 11:30 or E is the correct answer.

2. **D.** This is solved by simply comparing each choice to the diagrams until one matches. A is incorrect since Eric isn't in the 11:30 slot, B and E are incorrect since Sarah can't be in the 10:00 or 11:00 slots, and C is incorrect since Nick must come immediately after Molly. D is the correct answer as it matches the second diagram.

3. **B.** Since the question specifies that Sarah's appointment is at 10:30, the first diagram is the one to use. While each answer could be compared the diagram until one that doesn't match is found, the quickest way is to notice that B and C are exact opposites and so one of them must be the correct answer. Looking at the first diagram, Nick's appointment comes before Sarah's, making B false and thus the correct answer.

4. **C.** Condition #1 states that Katie only gets an appointment if one of the others cancels, so since Bill has canceled this means that his slot is open. Looking at the diagrams for where Bill's appointment is, this means that either 10:00 or 11:00 has opened up and that C is the correct answer.

5. **D.** Look at each of the three diagrams and find the one where Molly's appointment is at 10:00, which is the second diagram. In the second diagram Bill's appointment is at 11:00 making D the correct answer.

6. **E.** This one actually changes one of the conditions and requires a new diagram. Eric's appointment is moved from 11:30 to 11:00.

9:30	10:00	10:30	11:00	11:30
			Eric	

The question asks who is now in the 11:30 slot. Condition #4, requiring Molly and Nick's appointments to be back-to-back, mean that neither of them can fill that time slot. This leaves Sarah and Bill as possibilities and E is the correct answer.

Cluster 2:

To diagram this problem, translate the conditions into symbols. Condition #1, Melissa does not sit next to Jack, translates into **~(MJ)**. Condition #2, Jack sits next to Olivia or Nick, but not both of them, translates into **JO e/or JN**. Condition #3, Kimberly sits next to Nick, translates into **KN**. And Condition #4, If Olivia sits next to Jack, then she doesn't sit next to Lee, translates into **OJ -> ~(OL)**. So, the symbol translations of the conditions for this problem are:

~(MJ)

JO e/or JN

KN

OJ -> ~(OL)

Next, draw a visual representation of the table, recalling that the question states that they are sitting evenly around a circular table:

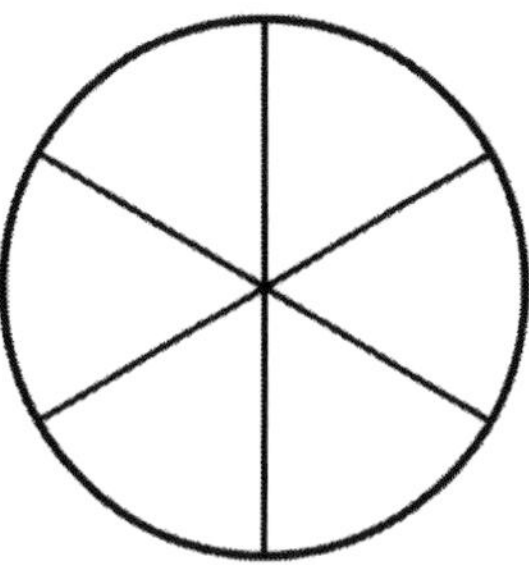

Or simply:

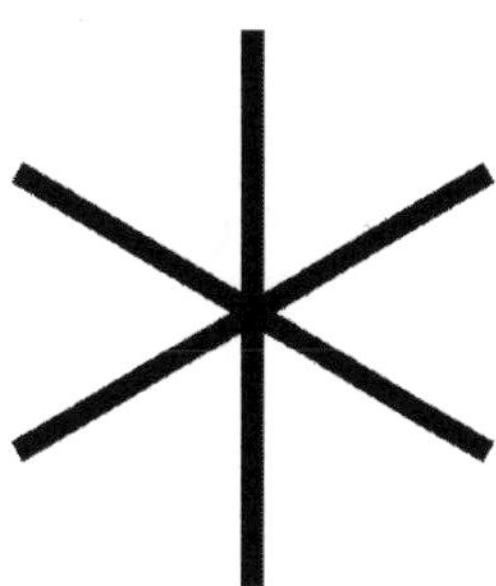

7. **C.** Simply compare each answer choice to the conditions. A breaks JO e/or JN, B breaks KN, D breaks ~(MJ), and E breaks OJ -> ~(OL). Only C doesn't break any of the conditions, making this the correct answer.

8. **A.** Start off by placing Jack and Kimberly into their spots at the table, the specific spots don't matter as long as they are next to each other. Next place Nick next to Kimberly to satisfy condition #3, KN. Since condition #2, JO e/or JN, requires that either Olivia or Nick sits next to Jack and Nick is already placed at the table two seats away from Jack, place Olivia next to Jack. Condition #4, OJ -> ~(OL), prevents Lee from sitting next to Olivia since she is already sitting next to Jack, so place Lee next to Nick to leave a space between Olivia and Lee. And finally place Melissa in the only remaining empty space.

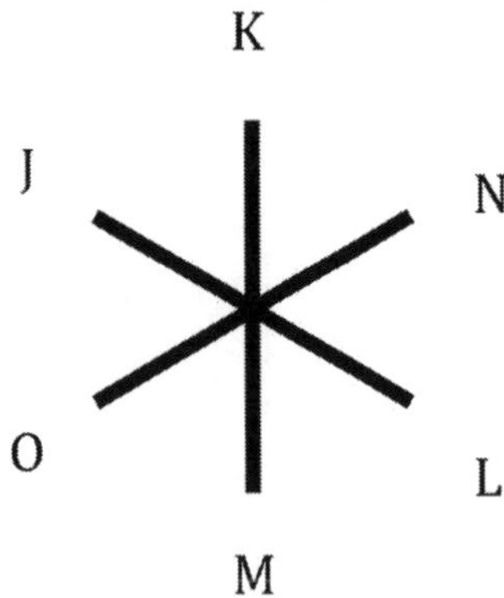

Now it's an easy matter of comparing each answer choice to the diagram and seeing that only the pair in choice A are seated next to each other.

9. **E.** There is no need to diagram this problem. Looking at the answer choices, it's immediately clear that E breaks condition #3, KN, and is thus the answer.

10. **D.** Condition #1, ~(MJ), eliminates B and C, and condition #2, JO e/or JN, eliminates E, leaving only A and D as possibilities. Lee is an option in both of those choices, so the only question is whether or not a diagram can be constructed in which Kimberly sits next to Jack without breaking any of the conditions.

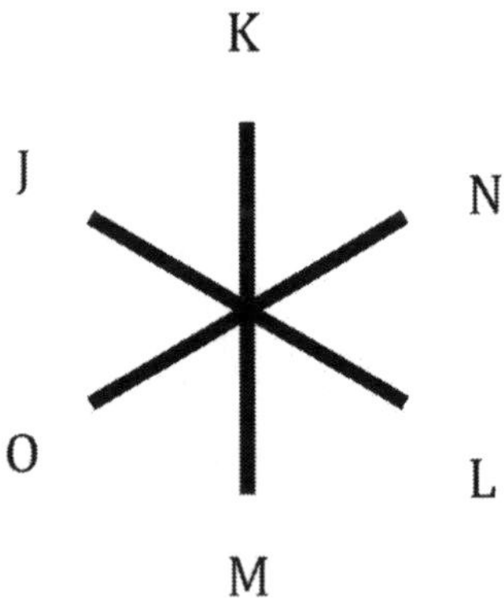

This is easy since the diagram from answer #8 shows that Kimberly can sit next to Jack in this scenario, making D the correct answer.

11. **A.** This one requires a diagram before any answer choices can be eliminated. First, place Jack and Nick next to each other on the diagram and Kimberly on the other side of Nick due to condition #3, KN. Lee must sit on the other side of Jack, since condition #1, ~(MJ), prevents Melissa from sitting there and condition #2, JO e/or JN, prevents Olivia from sitting there. Olivia and Melissa cannot be placed on the diagram as they could each go in either seat.

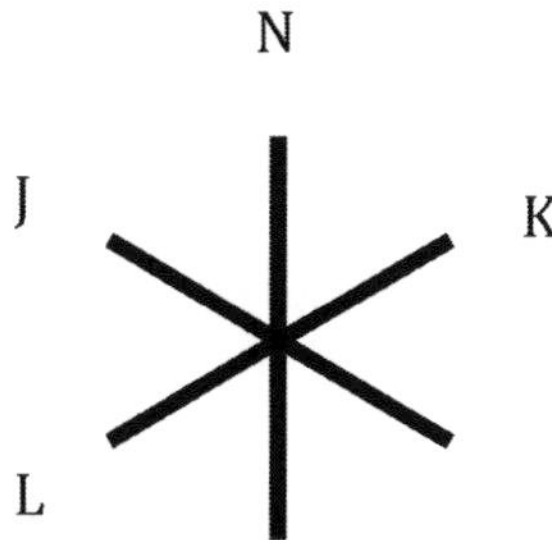

I. is false since Lee is sitting across from Kimberly, not beside her. Since Olivia and Melissa could go in either of the remaining seats, it cannot be determined whether II. or III. are true or false, and since the question asks which of the three MUST be false, the correct answer is only I, and thus A.

12. **C.** First place Olivia next to Nick on the diagram and Kimberly on the other side of Nick due to condition #3 – KN. Next Jack is placed next to Olivia due to condition #2 - JO e/or JN. Melissa cannot be placed next to Jack due to condition #1, ~(MJ), so Lee goes next to Jack and Melissa takes the other empty seat.

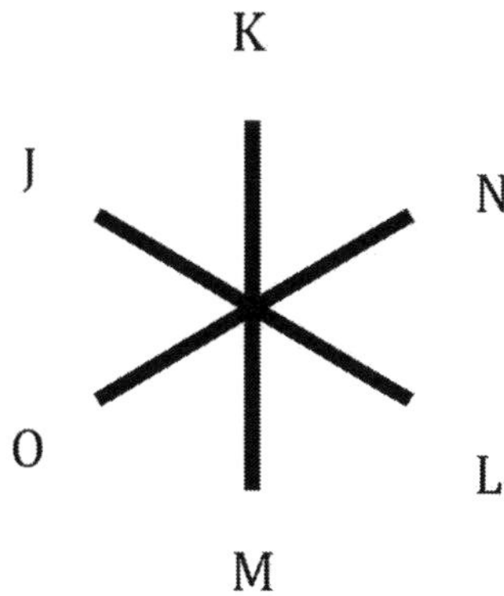

Now simply compare the diagram to the answer choices and only Olivia sits between Nick and Jack appears on the diagram making C the correct answer.

Cluster 3:

Rule 1 just gives the basic code and the rest of the rules simply state possible things that can happen, so there are no diagrams that can be setup beforehand.

13. **B.** The question asks which answer choice is not a valid code, so any answer choice that can be produced by using the rules is not the answer. A is incorrect since it is just the basic code, C is incorrect since it is the basic code plus rule 2, D is incorrect since it is the basic code plus rule 3, and E is incorrect since it is the basic code plus rule 4. This leaves B as the correct answer as there is no way to produce that code using the given rules.

14. **E.** V is at the front of the code under the basic code and rule 3. Using rules 2 and 4 can only get V into the middle of the code, not the end. Rule 3 places Y at the end of the code and rule 2 places W at the end of the code, so the correct answer is E.

15. **C.** First write out the basic code, V W X Y Z, and then check to see which of the rules have been applied and in what order. Note that the resulting code, X Y Z X Z Y V W, ends in V W, which means that the final rule to be applied is Rule 2 (so answer choices A and E can be eliminated). Next see that there is almost a repetition of the X Y Z, pointing to Rule 4, so we could write the code X Y Z V W X Y Z. However, in the code in the question, the Y and Z have switched places the second time these letters appear, meaning that Rule 3 must have been applied AFTER Rule 4, when the Y and Z were at the end of the code. So, we can write X Y Z V W X Z Y. Finally, apply Rule 2 as mentioned earlier, moving the V and W to the end of the code: X Y Z X Z Y V W. Thus, the correct order of rules is 4 3 2, which matches C.

16. **D.** The question asks which of the answer choices is not a code, so the answer choice that cannot be produced by using the rules is the correct answer. A can be produced by applying rules 5 and 3, B can be produced by applying rule 2 and then 5, C can be produced by applying rule 3, then rule 4, and then rule 5, and E can be produced by applying rule 5, then rule 4, and then rule 5 again. So, this leaves D as the only invalid code and thus the correct answer.

17. **B.** The question asks for a valid code, so any answer choice which cannot be produced using the rules is incorrect. The Z can't be moved to the front of the code by itself, so A is incorrect. X cannot be at the front of the code without both Y and Z (rule 2), making C incorrect. There is no way to switch the order of V and W, making D and E incorrect. Only B is a valid code, generated by using rule 4 and then rule 2.

Cluster 4:

To diagram this problem, translate the rules into symbols. For example, if lettuce is chosen, then pickles will also be chosen, translates into **L->P**. In all, the symbol translations of the conditions for this problem are:

Station #1	Station #2	Station #3	Station #3	Station #3

L->P

W->~P

B->~O

3 of the Healthy Options: Multigrain, Turkey, Lettuce, Tomatoes, and Onions

18. **A.** Because Pickles may not be chosen with a white bun, neither may Lettuce, since Lettuce requires Pickles to be chosen as well. With Lettuce and Pickles ruled out, the remaining three station #3 options must be chosen: Tomato, Onion, and Cheese. Similarly, with the requirement of the white bun, and with Lettuce already ruled out, the remaining three healthy options must be taken: Turkey, Tomato, and Onion. Given the constraints, this is the only combinations of ingredients that may be chosen along with a white bun:

W	Tu	To	O	C

19. **B.** This asks which one cannot be on the same burger, so if a burger can be made using all three of an answer choice's options, then it is incorrect. The following are sample burgers that can be made using the options given (some options may have multiple possibilities, so not all are listed).

For A:

W	Tu	C	To	O

For C:

M	Tu	O	To	C

For D:

M	B	P	L	To

For E:

M	C	To	O	C

For B, rule #2, L->P, means that Pickles must be chosen as a topping leaving a maximum of two healthy options which can be chosen. This violates rule #5, which requires 3 of the healthy options, and makes B the correct answer. It additionally violates rule #3, which states that Pickles cannot be chosen with a White bun.

20. **D.** First fill in the basic diagram with the given information.

M	C			

Due to rule #5 (include three of the healthy options), at least two of the remaining options must be healthy, as the Multigrain bun is also healthy. If Lettuce is one of the healthy options, then Pickles must be picked as well due to rule #2, L->P. The remaining option must be healthy and can be either Onions or Tomatoes, giving two possible combinations so far (**L P O, L P To**). If lettuce is not chosen, then both Tomatoes and Onions must be chosen to fill out the three healthy options. Either Pickles or Cheese can be chosen as the third option adding another two possible combinations (**To O P, To O C**). This makes a total of four possible combinations, which is answer choice D.

21. **C.** First fill in the basic diagram with the given information.

	B			

Since Beef is not a healthy option, three of the four remaining blanks must be filled in with healthy choices. We are only concerned with toppings, not bread, so we know that either two or three of the toppings must be healthy. Onions cannot be one of the toppings due to rule #4, B->~O, leaving us with Lettuce, Tomatoes, Cheese, and Pickles. Only Lettuce and Tomatoes are healthy, so we must choose both of these:

	B	L	T	

According to rule #2, L->P, Pickles must be chosen since Lettuce has been chosen, so we know the three toppings are Lettuce, Tomatoes, and Pickles, which is choice C.

Alternatively, you could check to see which answer choices violate the rules. Answer choices A and D violate rule #4, B->~O, and are incorrect. B violates rule #2, L->P, and is thus incorrect. E violates rule #5, 3 of the healthy options, as even if the multigrain bun was chosen, that would still only be two healthy options, making E incorrect. Only C does not violate any rules and is the correct choice.

22. **E.** First fill in the basic diagram with the given information.

	T	P	C	

Only one of the given choices is healthy, so according to rule #5, which requires three healthy options, we know that both remaining options must be healthy. The bread choice must be Multigrain and the topping must be Lettuce, Tomatoes, or Onions. The only answer choice that fits this is E.

Cluster 5:

The first step is to build a flow chart. This is done by translating the conditions into symbols and then combining them into a chart. Condition #1, If A is on duty, then neither B nor C is on duty, translates to **A->~(B or C)**. Condition #2, D and E cannot be on duty at the same time, translates to **D->~E** (E->~D also works). Condition #3, F can only be on duty if A is also on duty, translates to **F->A**. Condition #4, if C is on duty, then D is also on duty, translates to **C->D**. Conditions #1 and #3 can be connected since they both have A as a factor and conditions #2 and #4 can be connected since they both have D as a factor.

F -> A -> ~(B or C)

C -> D -> ~E

No further connections can be made. The C in the first and second lines cannot be connected in the flow chart as one is a C and the other is a ~C, but it will be important to remember that C is influenced by both while solving the problems.

23. **C.** Based on the flowchart, looking at the situation with A both on duty and off duty will have the greatest effect. Keep in mind that the question asks for the maximum amount of guards who can be on duty at the same time, so include anyone who could be on duty in the given situation. When A is on duty, F can be on duty as well (F->A), but neither B nor C can be on duty (A->~(B or C)). If C is not on duty, then either D or E can be on duty, but not both (D->~E). So if A is on duty, A, F, and either D or E can be on duty, a total of three guards. Now try it with A off duty, again trying to maximize the number of on-duty guards. If A is off duty, then F is off duty (F->A), but both B and C can be on duty (A->~(B or C)). If C is on duty, then D is on duty as well (C->D), but E is off duty (D->~E). So, if A is off duty, B, C, and D are on duty, again a total of three. In either case, the maximum number of guards who can be on duty at the same time is three, making C the correct answer.

24. **B.** If A is off duty, then F must also be off duty (F->A), eliminating D and E as answer choices. If D is off duty, then C must also be off duty (C->D), eliminating C as an answer choice as well. Both B (A->~B) and E (D->~E) can be on duty with A and D off duty, making them the complete list and B the correct answer choice.

Reading Comprehension, Section III

Questions 1–7

Synopsis: This passage discusses the significance of Federalist No. 10, one of the eighty-five Federalist Papers written by James Madison, Alexander Hamilton, and John Jay. The author begins by noting that Federalist No. 10 was not traditionally viewed as one of the most important Federalist essays but that it received more attention in the twentieth century due to its subject matter: the issue of dealing with factions. Given the rise in the importance and power of political parties, as well as various partisan groups, the author points out that it is hardly surprising for No. 10 to seem increasingly relevant. But the author is quick to note that it is erroneous to assume No. 10 had no relevance for its own era.

In the second paragraph, the author introduces the topic of the Anti-Federalists, the group that opposed the Federalists (of which Madison, Hamilton, and Jay were members) on the grounds that the Constitution would give too much power to a central government. More specifically, the Anti-Federalists believed that the United States could never truly be united and that the only way to unite in one sense would be by forcing some to abandon their beliefs. After the ratification of the Constitution, the Anti-Federalists were overruled and their group disbanded.

In the final paragraph, the author examines the reception to Federalist No. 10 in the late eighteenth century and beyond, after the demise of the Anti-Federalists. No. 10 received very little attention until the twentieth century, when scholars began considering the relevance, as well as the significance, of Madison's arguments, and applying them to the modern day. The author cites two historians with differing viewpoints and concludes that although many historians—by questioning the historical relevance of Federalist No. 10 versus its contemporary relevance—have missed the point altogether, No. 10 addresses issues that have plagued every government and society throughout history and thus is not limited in relevance to one era. As a final word, the author refocuses briefly on the Anti-Federalists, claiming that although they did not win the argument about the Constitution, history has suggested that their arguments were sound.

Question 1

Overview: Question 1 asks the student what the passage is doing in a broad sense. The student needs to consider the main point of the passage and how the author goes about arriving at his conclusions, reflecting on the overall goal of the passage. Is it comparative? Persuasive? Narrative? Or something else altogether? In reviewing the answer choices, the student must think clearly about the author's methods, so as not to confuse informational details with the broader purpose of the passage.

The Correct Answer:

C The author mentions in the first paragraph that Federalist No. 10 was not traditionally viewed as being a significant essay but has gained in scholarly importance over time. This establishes a time-honored view of the essay. But the author then takes a new approach to considering this essay by pointing out that it is not only relevant to the current era but is also relevant to the era in which it was written. The author notes that no historian has made this argument, so the author is essentially offering a new perspective on a scholarly argument that has been going on for some time. Thus, **answer choice (C)** is correct.

The Incorrect Answers:

A Although the author hints at contrasting viewpoints along the way—the traditional viewpoint that No. 10 is irrelevant versus the current viewpoint that it is significant, the viewpoint of Charles Beard versus the viewpoint of Douglass Adair—the overall format of the passage is not mainly one of contrast. The author's purpose is not to consider in detail the differences between these various contrasting views and the reasons behind him; rather, the author intends to offer a new perspective, as described above. Answer choice (A) is incorrect.

B The "traditional argument" is the argument that Federalist No. 10 had little relevance to the eighteenth century but is far more relevant in the modern era. The author notes in the second paragraph the presence of factions during the eighteenth century, and then states quite clearly in the last sentence that Federalist No. 10 addresses issues that are relevant to every era. Therefore, the author cannot be said to be defending the traditional argument, so answer choice (B) is incorrect.

D At no point does the author define any terms, other than to explain who the Anti-Federalists were, and this is clearly not the main point of the passage. Nor does this answer choice explain the author's format for developing the main point. Therefore, answer choice (D) cannot be correct.

E Although the author does consider the "popular" academic position (of the modern relevance of Federalist No. 10, but not the eighteenth-century relevance), the author does not necessarily challenge its validity. Although the author refers to Douglass Adair's opinion, there is no reason to believe that Adair's view is the popular one: indeed, considering the author's statements in the first paragraph about the current applicability of No. 10, it would seem that Adair's perspective does not necessarily mesh with the popular position. Answer choice (D), therefore, is incorrect.

Question 2

Overview: In question 2, the student must consider the author's main point (as opposed to the author's method, from question 1). This means that the student must combine all of the various pieces of information within the paragraph and formulate a statement of summary. The student would do well to take a few seconds to prepare mentally a brief summary, as this will help determine the correct answer. Simply put, the author is making two statements: (1) Federalist No. 10 contains arguments that are relevant to any time period, and (2) the Anti-Federalists were essentially right in their belief that factions would always exist. With these two points in mind, the student can find the correct answer quickly.

The Correct Answer:

A **Answer choice (A)** restates the summary sentences from above, noting that Federalist No. 10 has a universal application for all eras and that the Anti-Federalists understood the reality of factions. Answer choice (A) must be correct.

The Incorrect Answers:

B Answer choice (B), although stating information that can be derived from the passage, fails to offer a complete summary of the author's purpose in the passage. The student should watch for answer choices that provide correct information but that do not provide *enough* correct information. Just because the statement is true according to the passage does not mean that it offers a complete summary of the passage. Answer choice (B) is incorrect.

C Answer choice (C) summarizes the traditional argument regarding Federalist No. 10, as well as Douglass Adair's position. However, the author clearly indicates disagreement with this viewpoint in all three paragraphs, so the answer choice must also be incorrect. Answer choice (C) can be eliminated immediately.

D Answer choice (D) is slightly difficult, because the author *could* be suggesting that Federalist No. 10 (and thus the Federalists) did not appreciate the inevitability of factions. But the passage makes no clear comment about this at any point. The author suggests that Madison believed factions had to be quelled but does not mention the opinion of the Federalists on whether factions would always exist. The author states only that Anti-Federalists believed factions would always exist and would interfere with a nation's unity. Answer choice (D) is incorrect, because it has no unambiguous support in the passage.

E The author does suggest that the Anti-Federalists were right on one account (that factions were inevitable), but there is no mention at any point of human nature, nor can it be assumed that the author is referring to human nature when discussing the arguments of the Anti-Federalists. Answer choice (E), therefore, makes unsupported inferences, so it is incorrect.

Question 3

Overview: Question 3 asks the student to consider Douglass Adair's quotation about Federalist No. 10 being a "a document that was exclusive in application and in relevance to the time of its composition" and then infer one of the answer choices from it. The student should bear in mind that the question does not ask for the meaning of the quotation within the context of the passage, or even what the author's opinion of the quotation seems to be. This is not a trick question; it is just a fairly simple one, and that in itself might seem to be tricky.

The Correct Answer:

E Given the simple meaning of the quotation—that Federalist No. 10 is limited in relevance to the eighteenth century in which it was written—it can be inferred that Douglass Adair did not believe No. 10 to have relevance in any time period outside the eighteenth century. Thus, **answer choice (E)** is correct.

The Incorrect Answers:

A Although it is entirely possible that Douglass Adair believed all of the Federalist Papers to be limited in relevance to the eighteenth century, the quotation does not suggest this. Such a claim cannot be assumed from the quotation alone, so answer choice (A) is incorrect.

B Again, it is entirely possible that Douglass Adair disagreed with Charles Beard's position about the role of the Constitution on class exploitation, but the quotation under discussion makes no reference to that, nor does it suggest any commentary on Beard's own views. In fact, Adair's connection to Beard is only noted in that Adair paraphrases Beard's beliefs about the Constitution. No mention is made of Beard's own words on No. 10 or of Adair's opinion about Beard's thoughts on No. 10. Answer choice (B) is incorrect.

C Adair's comment about Federalist No. 10 is specifically related to the relevance of that essay to its own era. Clearly, Adair believes that the information within No. 10 relates to factions during the eighteenth century, and the Anti-Federalists were a faction and believed that factions were inevitable. But there is no evidence in the quotation to claim that Adair is agreeing with the Anti-Federalists in any way. He is simply remarking on the way that No. 10 should be applied historically. Answer choice (C) is incorrect.

D Adair makes no comment on current political situations, and there is nothing in his quotation to suggest that he would apply Federalist No. 10 to the modern era if problems like those of the eighteenth century reappeared. Answer choice (D) makes inferences that have no support in the passage, so it can be eliminated.

Question 4

Overview: In question 4, the student is asked to select an answer choice that is suggested by the passage. This means that the student is not looking for the main point of the passage but a statement that can be inferred from it (not a statement necessarily made explicitly in the passage). The student needs to keep the main point in mind, however (see question 2). In locating the correct answer choice, it is necessary to avoid any choices that step too far outside of the claims specifically given in the passage. (That is, a reasonable inference does not make assumptions that have no support in the passage.)

The Correct Answer:

B The passage notes in the second paragraph that the Federalists did win the primary argument for the Constitution, and states at the end of the final paragraph that the Anti-Federalists had the last word, suggesting that they were correct about factions. In the quotation from "Cato," the Anti-Federalist position indicates that this group believed it would be impossible for people of such varying differences to live comfortably together in the long term, suggesting that unity could be achieved only by force, and that such unity would not be real. **Answer choice (B)** encompasses this by stating that the Federalists succeeded in ratifying the Constitution, but that the Anti-Federalists were right about the impossibility of real long-term unity. Therefore, answer choice (B) is correct.

The Incorrect Answers:

A The author does state in the first paragraph that the Federalist Papers were "highly influential," and the author also says in the second paragraph that in writing them the Federalists contributed to the successful ratification of the Constitution. But the passage does not imply that the essays were an *essential* contribution, which would suggest that the Constitution could not have been ratified without them. Although this might be true, the passage makes no statement to support it clearly. So, answer choice (A) is incorrect.

C Although the author might very well believe that more Americans needed to listen to the Anti-Federalists, there is no such clear statement in the passage. What is more, the passage does not mention free speech at all, and although free speech is a freedom guaranteed by the Bill of Rights, the passage provides no reason to single out one freedom over others. Answer choice (C) is incorrect.

D The author states that upon the ratification of the Constitution, the Anti-Federalists "more or less ceased to exist, its members left with little choice but to accept the system that had been adopted," and that they were "silenced." But the author does not comment on irony or even suggest it, nor does the author imply that this was a *great* irony of the eighteenth century. Answer choice (D) is incorrect.

E Answer choice (E) is incorrect because it contradicts the statement in the first paragraph that Federalist No. 10 is now viewed in importance alongside those that are traditionally considered to be the most significant essays. In addition, the answer choice is too vague in its phrase "some of the others," offering little information about the essays to which No. 10 is being compared.

Question 5

Overview: In question 5, the student must consider which of the answer choices the author would most likely agree with, based on the statements made within the passage. As in question 4, the student needs to think carefully about what the passage says and what can be inferred from this, without straying too far from the actual statements made in the passage.

The Correct Answer:

C The author states that after the ratification of the Constitution, the Anti-Federalists "more or less ceased to exist, its members left with little choice but to accept the system that had been adopted"; the author also begins the last paragraph with the phrase, "With the silencing of the Anti-Federalist faction." These statements suggest that the Federalists were silenced, that is, that they were forced to remain quiet about some of their ideas after the Constitution was ratified. **Answer choice (C)** is correct.

The Incorrect Answers:

A Far from agreeing with the statement that Federalist No. 51, No. 78, and No. 84 remain the most important, the author clearly states in the first paragraph that many now see No. 10 as being of equal importance. Because the author does not contradict this statement anywhere in the passage, it can be assumed that the author agrees with the new importance afforded to No. 10. Answer choice (A) is incorrect.

B The author mentions Charles Beard's theories and explains why they were well received but makes no evaluative statement about them, either explicitly or implicitly. Answer choice (B) can be eliminated immediately.

D Although the author clearly disagrees with Douglass Adair's argument, there is no indication that the author thinks it is "intentionally misleading." Answer choice (D) is incorrect.

E The passage implies that the author agrees with the Anti-Federalists on at least one issue (that of factions), but the claim that the Anti-Federalists had a "more realistic appreciation of social and political challenges than the Federalists did" is a much broader, stronger claim. There is no evidence that the author would endorse this very claim. Therefore, answer choice (E) is incorrect.

Question 6

Overview: Question 6 asks the student to provide a definition for a word in the passage, considering the word within the context of the sentence in which it is located. A question that requires the student to select a definition usually means that the word will not be used as expected: in this case, the word *unkindred*, which usually signifies a non-relationship, is being employed differently, so the student must consider which of the answer choices best replaces the word in the sentence.

The Correct Answer:

C The sentence in which the word *unkindred* can be found is as follows: "the 'unkindred legislature' recommended by the Constitution would lead to the biblical example of the house collapsing because it has been divided against itself" (emphasis added). In other words, "Cato" is describing the legislature as "unkindred," noting that the differing interests of diverse Americans will create too much division. The correct answer choice, therefore, will need to provide a meaning that indicates variance or distinction that leads to division, and *disparate* is such a word. **Answer choice (C)** is correct.

The Incorrect Answers:

A Of the remaining answer choices, choice (A) is the most tempting because it encompasses the suggestion of many differences to which "Cato" is referring. In this case, however, *diverse* does not suggest a *negative* difference, so *diverse* would not replace *unkindred* as well as *disparate*, the word in answer choice (C).

B Although disorganization seems to be a secondary effect of the various differences that lead to disunity, the quotation does not suggest that the legislature itself is disorganized or that it is disorganization that causes factions. The word *disorganization*, therefore, implies more than can be inferred from the quotation, so answer choice (B) is incorrect.

D The quotation does not indicate that the legislature is unique but rather that it is filled with differences. Answer choice (D) cannot be correct.

E Although one of the results of disunity seems to be antagonism that creates factions, the quotation does not necessarily suggest that the legislature starts out as antagonistic. The correct synonym needs to indicate a cause (*disparity*) that creates an effect (*disunity and factions*), so *antagonism* is approaching the quotation from the wrong direction. Answer choice (E), therefore, is incorrect.

Question 7

Overview: The final question asks the student to consider the organization of the passage; that is, the way the author organizes and presents the information in order to make the argument. To answer this question, the student should review each paragraph quickly. Sentences to target include the first and last sentences of each paragraph. This question does not require any inferring; it is simply a matter of considering the arrangement of the information within the passage and comparing this arrangement to the answer choices. In several cases, the student might be able to eliminate answer choices by looking at the first item in the choice.

The Correct Answer:

E The layout of the paragraph is fairly simple: the author begins by considering an idea, follows this idea with some historical information, and then uses the historical information to argue in favor of a main point. **Answer choice (E)** describes this organization, so it is the correct answer.

The Incorrect Answers:

A Although the author does mention several theories in the final paragraph, the author does not begin the paragraph with these theories. And although the author does narrow the focus in the final paragraph, there is no sense that the focus is on one of the theories presented; in fact, the author presents an entirely new take on the topic. Answer choice (A) can be eliminated immediately.

B The author does begin the passage with the hint of a main point, but the historical information contained within the second paragraph is not a diversion. Instead, it offers the historical context for the author's primary argument in the final paragraph. Answer choice (B), therefore, is incorrect.

C The author does not begin the paragraph with a wide historical focus and then narrow to a contemporary one. In fact, the historical and contemporary focuses play off one another throughout the passage—with the author concluding that both are of equal relevance to a discussion of Federalist No. 10—so answer choice (C) cannot be correct.

D Answer choice (D) seems briefly promising, but it does not correctly describe the organization of the paragraph. Although the author hints at a thesis in the first paragraph, there is no statement of a clear thesis. Additionally, the author does not use the historical information to defend the thesis from the first paragraph; instead, the author uses it to make the primary argument in the final paragraph. The quotations in the passage place the opinions about Federalist No. 10 in the context of contemporary opinions, but the author does not suggest that these quotations come from leading authorities. Answer choice (D) is incorrect.

Questions 8–14

Synopsis: This passage discusses the linguistic issue of why there are not more Celtic influences in the English language. The author begins by discussing the linguistic influences that scholars already recognize and have identified—Old English (or the language of the Anglo-Saxons), Old Norse, French, and Latin—and then proceeds to explain that scholars consider the lack of Celtic words to be a mystery. When the Anglo-Saxons arrived in Britain, a considerable population of Celts lived there already. Yet there are very few Celtic words in the English language, leading scholars to wonder why the Celts appeared to make no linguistic impact on the Anglo-Saxons. The author notes that scholars have offered several theories. Some argue that the Anglo-Saxons did not need the Celtic words because they had enough of their own; a problem with this view is that the Anglo-Saxons borrowed plenty of words from other languages. Some scholars have suggested, then, that the Anglo-Saxons viewed the Celts as inferior people and thus avoided their language. The fact that the Celts ultimately migrated north and west—away from the Anglo-Saxons—seems to support this theory.

In the second paragraph, the author considers this theory and raises questions about it, citing linguistic scholar David Crystal, who points out that there is considerable evidence that the Anglo-Saxons gave their children Welsh (or Celtic) names. For example, there is a record of an Anglo-Saxon king and a renowned religious poet bearing Welsh names. It is unlikely that the Anglo-Saxons would deliberately choose names from the language of a group of people believed to be inferior, so Crystal points out that this theory does not bear up under scrutiny.

In the third paragraph, the author again cites Crystal with his suggestion that the English word *cross* might derive from Celtic sources. Again, it is unlikely that the Anglo-Saxons would adopt a word with such religious significance from a despised language. The author concludes by noting that the mystery of why there are so few Celtic words in the English language might never be solved, but that the theory that the Anglo-Saxons ignored Celtic words because the Celts were viewed as inferior ultimately does not have much historical or linguistic support.

Question 8

Overview: Question 8 asks the student to consider the main idea of the passage. This question does not ask for any inferences, so the student just needs to consider the author's argument and summarize it. Each paragraph contains a topic, and these topics ultimately contribute to a primary point. What the student needs to watch for in the answer choices are options that mention a supporting idea but that do not reflect the main point of the passage. The correct answer choice must encompass the evidence in the passage with a single statement.

The Correct Answer:

A Although the first paragraph seems to provide a great deal of information about the background of the English language, as well as theories about the lack of Celtic words, it is the final sentence of the first paragraph and the first sentence of the second paragraph that indicate the direction the passage will be taking. The author notes that one theory in particular seems to have support, but then goes on to say that a leading linguistic scholar disagrees with it. The rest of the passage explains Crystal's evidence that weakens the initial theory, and the final sentence of the third paragraph provides the main point: "It is unlikely that the mystery of the missing Celtic words will ever be solved satisfactorily, but what little evidence remains suggests that the mystery can no longer be written off as a case of a conquered people becoming linguistically obsolete." **Answer choice (A)** most closely summarizes this, so it is the correct answer.

The Incorrect Answers:

B Answer choice (B) is incorrect, because it focuses on a supporting piece of evidence Crystal has provided to undermine a theory, but that is not, in itself, the main point of the passage. Answer choice (B) is incorrect.

C Although the author does suggest that there might be considerable significance to the few Celtic words that are in the English language, the author does *not* claim or suggest anywhere that these words render other linguistic sources less significant. Additionally, the author does not indicate that there is any evidence contradicting the traditionally recognized influences. Answer choice (C) is clearly incorrect.

D, E As in answer choice (B), the example of the English changing German names during World War I, as well as the example of the occurrence of Welsh names among the Anglo-Saxons, is intended to give supporting evidence; such examples are not meant to represent the primary argument. In addition, answer choice (E) states, "of all the Celtic peoples the Welsh had the greatest linguistic impact on Anglo-Saxon daily life," an idea unsupported by the passage. Answer choices (D) and (E) are incorrect.

Question 9

Overview: In question 9, the student is asked to select a synonymous phrase for a word that is used in the passage. The student will need to consider the word itself, with its dictionary definitions, and then place the word within the context of the sentence and consider how it is being used. (If the student does not know the meaning of the word, the student should infer what basic idea is intended by considering the context in which the word appears.) In question 9, the word in question is *connotation*, which is defined as a connection, association, or secondary meaning. In the passage, the word is being used to convey the English concern that their names were connected to German names or assumed to be German. With this in mind, the student needs to consider the answer choices.

The Correct Answer:

D Of all the answer choices, **answer choice (D)** best conveys the idea of "connection" and "assumption" with the phrase *potential association*. As the passage notes, the English changed their names "to avoid sounding too Germanic." In other words, they feared the potential of their names being associated with German names. Answer choice (D), therefore, is correct.

The Incorrect Answers:

A Answer choice (A) offers a good option, but the passage does not suggest that the English knew there would be a *clear relationship*, nor does the word *connotation* in the context of the passage suggest a clear relationship. Instead, it suggests the possibility of a connection between English names and German names, a connection that answer choice (A) does not indicate. Answer choice (A) is incorrect.

B Although the fears of the English were about a linguistic matter (they were concerned that their names might be connected with German names), the phrase *linguistic origin* cannot replace the word *connotation* in meaning. Answer choice (B) is incorrect.

C Although the word *connotation* can, in some cases, indicate a definition that is more theoretical than it is concrete, there is nothing in the use of the word *connotation* in the passage to suggest that the English were concerned about a *theoretical definition*. Answer choice (C) is incorrect.

E Although the decision by some English people to change their names might have been based on emotion, the passage does not suggest this. Because there is no clear suggestion of emotion in the passage, answer choice (E) is incorrect.

Question 10

Overview: Question 10 asks the student to consider the purpose of the discussion of *cross* in the third paragraph. It was noted in the explanation for question 8 that the possible origin of the word *cross* represents supporting evidence for the main point of the passage. Therefore, the student should immediately recognize that the correct answer will indicate the way in which this discussion supports or points to the main argument. Recall that the main argument of the passage is that, despite the rarity of Celtic words in English, linguistic evidence suggests an influence on the English language from some Celtic words, so it is no longer possible to claim that the Anglo-Saxons deliberately avoided the people or the language in the belief that the Celts were inferior.

The Correct Answer:

E Bearing the main point of the passage in mind, **answer choice (E)** is the only answer choice to place the *cross* discussion within the context of this main point. Choice (E) notes that the information about the word *cross* offers evidence that the few Celtic words that exist in the English language are quite significant; this indicates that the Celtic influence might be more important than was previously thought. This point supports the main argument, so answer choice (E) is the correct answer.

The Incorrect Answers:

A The passage does not claim that many Celtic words influenced English; rather, the passage notes that there are few such Celtic words. Answer choice (A) is incorrect.

B The discussion of the word *cross* does suggest that an Old Irish (Celtic) word might have influenced an Old Norse word, but the passage does not indicate at any point that there were other Old Irish words that influenced Old Norse words. Answer choice (B) makes assumptions that are not supported by the passage, so it can be eliminated immediately.

C The discussion of the word *cross* does not illustrate that it would be wrong to assume that the Celtic language had a great influence on English. The author does not attempt to illustrate that one should not make such assumptions; rather, the author assumes that no one will make the assumption that the Celtic language had a very great influence on English. Answer choice (C) is incorrect.

D David Crystal's contribution to the passage is to show that there are signs of Celtic influence on the English language. The passage does not make any claim, however, that Crystal believes that Celtic words make up an *important part* of the English language. Answer choice (D), therefore, is incorrect.

Question 11

Overview: As in question 10, question 11 asks the student to consider the role of the example about English actions toward German names during World War I. And as with the discussion of the word *cross*, this particular information offers secondary details that support the main point of the passage. The student needs to consider the English/German names discussion within the context of the main point, as well as within the context of the statements immediately around it. The correct answer might or might not mention specifically the main point of the passage, but it will show that the example fits well with that main point.

The Correct Answer:

C The discussion of the English decision to change German or German-sounding names during World War I follows a paraphrased reference from David Crystal about the fact that the Anglo-Saxons would probably not have given their children Welsh names if those names were associated with something or someone negative. Since there is no immediate connection to Welsh names and German names, the student can assume that the author is intending to use this particular example to show how perceptions of peoples (whether they are Germans or Celts) influence the use of names associated with those peoples. **Answer choice (C)** expresses this idea and is thus the correct answer.

The Incorrect Answers:

A The passage makes no reference to human nature, and although it might be thought that associating names from certain linguistic backgrounds with either positive or negative qualities is a facet of human nature, there is not enough information in the passage to support this point. More specifically, the question of human nature is not related to the larger question of the impact of certain Celtic words in the English language. Therefore, answer choice (A) cannot be correct.

B If the discussion of the English response to German names were being used to support the traditional theory about Anglo-Saxons viewing the Celts as inferior, this argument might indeed undermine the theory of Welsh influence. But in the context of the second paragraph, it actually supports the point about Anglo-Saxons embracing certain Welsh influences, because it indicates clearly that the Anglo-Saxons did *not* avoid Welsh names. Answer choice (B) is incorrect.

D Answer choice (D) seems briefly promising, because the example of the English immediately follows this statement by the author: "it is unlikely that Anglo-Saxon parents would bestow Celtic names on their children if those names were closely associated with a despised language or a group of people deemed inferior." This seems to suggest that if the English during World War I did to the Germans what the much earlier Anglo-Saxons did *not* do to the Welsh, then the English might have viewed the Germans as inferior. But once again, this is not the main point of the illustration. Answer choice (D) is thus incorrect.

E The passage does not indicate at any point that English names might really be German. In fact, it seems to suggest just the opposite—that if many of the English changed German names, the names are now English. More to the point, however, this inference does not have a strong connection to the main point of the passage, and therefore answer choice (E) is incorrect.

Question 12

Overview: Question 12 asks the student to consider the author's tone toward the traditional argument that the Anglo-Saxons might have deliberately avoided Celtic words because they viewed the Celts as inferior. Certain key words in the passage will help discern whether the author's tone is one of vitriolic disagreement, patronization, or something else altogether. Such phrases include "Other scholars have ***suggested the theory***...," "leading linguistic scholar David Crystal ***disagrees***...," "the mystery ***can no longer be written off***..." All of these turns of phrase suggest a polite scholarly discussion in which one scholar (the author) disagrees with other scholars—firmly but not necessarily rudely. The student should select an answer choice that best reflects this.

The Correct Answer:

B **Answer choice (B)** is the only answer choice to present the best description of the author's tone: *scholarly disagreement*. The author is polite but holds to a certain view and defends that view. Answer choice (B), therefore, is correct.

The Incorrect Answers:

A The author might hold firmly to an opinion, but there is no tone of *insistence*, nor is the author *self-righteous* at any point. Answer choice (A) is clearly incorrect.

C The author clearly disagrees with the traditional viewpoint, but disagreement alone does not guarantee a patronizing attitude, and this passage does not suggest a patronizing tone at any point. Had the author mentioned the differing viewpoint repeatedly in order to belittle those who held it, the tone might be described as patronizing. As it is, however, the author mentions the viewpoint only twice and the scholars holding the view once, allowing the rest of the discussion to focus on evidence that supports his own perspective.

D The author's concern about the traditional viewpoint might be justifiable in his own mind, but the passage does not necessarily convey this tone. Instead, the tone is a scholarly one that leaves emotion at the door and relies on evidence. Answer choice (D) is incorrect.

E Although the author does disagree with the traditional viewpoint, there is nothing in the passage to indicate vitriol. Answer choice (E) can be eliminated immediately.

Question 13

Overview: In question 13, the student is asked to consider the primary purpose of the passage.

This is slightly different from considering the main point of the passage in that the student is looking from an even broader perspective without necessarily paraphrasing and summarizing details. However, knowing the main point is helpful in that the main point shapes the primary purpose of the passage. In this case, the author's final statement provides some indication of this: "what little evidence remains suggests that the mystery can no longer be written off as a case of a conquered people becoming linguistically obsolete." Clearly, the author is suggesting that there is evidence to counter a specific viewpoint while discouraging embracing this viewpoint without considering the evidence.

The Correct Answer:

A **Answer choice (A)** reflects the intention of the passage, as displayed in the final sentence: the author's purpose is to caution against making an historical judgment (the traditional viewpoint about the Anglo-Saxons deliberately avoiding Celtic words) without considering the further linguistic evidence (the Welsh names and the word *cross*). Answer choice (A) is thus correct.

The Incorrect Answers:

B The author does not necessarily indicate that the theory advocated is a new one; in fact, the author suggests that the leading authority David Crystal holds this theory, so the author is doing more to summarize Crystal's theory than to produce a new one. Answer choice (B) does not have enough support within the passage, so it is incorrect.

C The author is indeed discussing Crystal's opinion, but the purpose of the passage is not so much to defend his position but rather to caution against holding the traditional theory with respect to the linguistic evidence. Answer choice (C) is incorrect.

D The author does attempt to disprove a traditional theory, but there is no real focus on the linguistic evidence that supports this theory. (In fact, the author does not even mention the linguistic evidence that supports it and mentions only historical evidence of the relocation of the Celts.) Answer choice (D) is incorrect.

E The author discusses two of the opposing theories, but there is no comparison in the passage. Answer choice (E) cannot be correct.

Question 14

Overview: The final question for the second Reading Comprehension passage asks with which answer choice the author would likely agree. As with all questions like this, the student needs to consider what is stated directly in the passage and what can be inferred from these statements. The student should also take qualities such as tone into account.

The Correct Answer:

B The author notes in the first paragraph that there are few Celtic words in the English language and then implies in the second and third paragraphs that *although* there are few words, these words suggest a significant linguistic role (significant because the word *cross* itself, for example, has religious significance). **Answer choice (B)**, therefore, is correct.

The Incorrect Answers:

A Although the author suggests that *one word* in the English language might have a Celtic origin as opposed to an Old Norse origin, it cannot be inferred that the author believes there are more words (in English) of Celtic origin than of Latin or Old Norse origin. In fact, the author states several times that there are not many Celtic words in the English language, so the passage does not support the inference that one word is indicative of a much broader trend. Answer choice (A) is incorrect.

C The author uses the example of the word *cross* to indicate the potential for significant Celtic influences on English. Although this is related to the issue of how the English viewed the Celts (favorably or unfavorably), the passage does not indicate that the author believes that the origin of the word *cross* alone signifies how the English viewed the Celts. The author also cites David Crystal's mention of the Welsh names, so it cannot be inferred that the author believes that *cross* alone is significant in regard to the issue of how the English viewed the Celts. Answer choice (C) is incorrect.

D The author cites the information in answer choice (D) as one reason why some scholars believe that Anglo-Saxons did not absorb many Celtic words. However, the author also points out that this theory "is inconsistent with evidence that the Anglo-Saxons borrowed everyday words from other languages such as Old Norse and French." Answer choice (D) must be incorrect.

E The author notes that it is unlikely that the Anglo-Saxons would have given their children Welsh names if they believed the Celts to be inferior, but it cannot necessarily be inferred from this alone that the Anglo-Saxons *unquestionably* had a high opinion of the Celts. This strong claim goes well beyond anything stated or implied in the passage. Answer choice (E) is incorrect.

Questions 15–21

Synopsis: Questions 15–21 are based on a reading passage that discusses beauty and whether it can be objectively quantified. The author begins by presenting the general point that beauty has always fascinated people and then mentions that in the modern era scientists have begun considering beauty from a forensic perspective, asking whether beauty can be measured and quantified scientifically. The author writes that scientists believe that they *can* measure and quantify beauty, and their tests – based on the results from volunteers of many social and cultural backgrounds – indicate that there are some people who are definitely, consistently perceived as beautiful and some who are not. The author states that even infants are not immune to beauty and that studies indicate that babies are drawn to beautiful faces.

The author begins the second paragraph with a hint of caution, however. Although beauty might be quantifiable and objective, the response to beauty has potentially serious consequences. The author cites the research of psychologist Nancy Etcoff to show that beauty is often confused with goodness and that beautiful people are, in many cases, assumed to be good in some sense. Teachers tend to score attractive students higher; employers tend to award jobs to the attractive applicants; even voters tend to place their support behind the attractive candidate. The author's tone suggests that this is a concern worth looking into more closely.

In the third paragraph, the author discusses the question of whether people are looking at the beauty/character relation the wrong way around. Perhaps beauty and character (or personality) *are* related, but it is character or personality that affects beauty. Once again, the author cites Etcoff, this time with an anecdote about the notoriously unattractive writer George Eliot. Although author Henry James at first thought her ugly, he revised this view significantly after he had spoken with her and come to know her better. The author concludes by suggesting that scientists look more closely at the way that character affects beauty, or the perception of it, because character might play a much larger role in beauty than previously thought.

Question 15

Overview: Question 15 asks the student to summarize the main point of the passage by considering the author's central idea. The student should recognize that the primary point of the passage lies in the last part of the final paragraph, when the author recommends studying how character or other such personal qualities affect beauty: "Scientists studying the phenomenon of beauty would do well to turn their attention to the more intangible qualities that define beauty and to consider what lies beneath the skin in addition to what lies on it." The answer choice that best paraphrases this sentence will be the correct answer.

The Correct Answer:

B **Answer choice (B)** best summarizes the final sentence of the third paragraph by stating that scientists need to consider qualities other than those on the face in order to study beauty as accurately as possible.

The Incorrect Answers:

A Answer choice (A) is incorrect, because the passage makes no mention about society's claims about beauty or that society believes everyone to be uniquely beautiful. The passage does mention that scientists are testing beauty to see "whether beauty is simply a subjective perception," but this perception is not attributed to society. Answer choice (A) cannot be correct.

C Although the passage makes the suggestion that beauty *might* be related to character or personality, the author's main point is not to argue this but rather to suggest that scientists reconsider the way they study beauty. Answer choice (C) is incorrect.

D The author notes that scientists believe some people will always be perceived as beautiful, observing that beautiful people often receive privileges on the basis of their outward appearance. But this is not the author's main argument, so answer choice (D) is incorrect.

E At no point does the author indicate that scientists will be unable to quantify beauty; in fact, the author suggests that scientists have already been fairly successful in quantifying beauty (lines 9–17), so answer choice (E) contradicts statements that the author makes in the passage. Answer choice (E) is incorrect.

Question 16

Overview: Question 16 asks the student to select an answer choice that, on the basis of the passage, infers the author's belief. The student should keep the passage closely in mind and use only the direct statements of the passage to determine the correct answer. In many cases, wrong answer choices will contain bits of information that *seem* correct. But the question is not asking what the author seems to believe; the question is asking the student to infer a correct answer from what the author *does* say.

The Correct Answer:

E In the third paragraph, the author makes the following statements: "Character might affect beauty, and not the other way around," and "It may be that although physical features are indeed important in determining beauty, beauty itself is not simply 'skin deep' and can be defined by more than an arrangement of eyes, nose, and lips." From this, the student may deduce that the author is suggesting that personality might affect the perception of beauty. **Answer choice (E)** correctly summarizes the author's implied belief and is thus correct.

The Incorrect Answers:

A The author does note that, "Today, scientists are beginning to consider the question of beauty." However, this does not in itself imply that scientists have long ignored beauty (this is a stronger claim than what the author suggests) but only that today's scientific community has begun studying beauty. Answer choice (A) is incorrect.

B Although the author opens the third paragraph with the statement, "Scientists claim that a certain combination of features is universally considered beautiful," the author does not suggest anywhere that this is a view he supports. Answer choice (B) cannot be inferred as the author's belief and is thus incorrect.

C The author's comments that beauty is often associated with character suggest a tone of caution toward this issue, but the passage does not offer any indication that the author believes it should *never* be the case that beauty is associated with character. Answer choice (C) is incorrect, because it infers too much from the author's statements in the passage.

D The author does not claim that beauty is relative to cultural standards. Answer choice (E) can be eliminated immediately.

QUESTION 17

Overview: Question 17 asks the student to determine which answer choice best expresses the reasoning behind the author's argument. This question essentially requires the student to identify the main argument and then identify the reasons the author gives for that argument. All information necessary for identifying the correct answer is contained within the passage. The main point is that scientists, in their studies of beauty, should consider studying character or personality alongside their study of physical beauty. This suggests that the author's reasoning is that there must be something more than outward appearance that determines beauty. The answer choice that best expresses this idea will be correct.

THE CORRECT ANSWER:

C **Answer choice (C)** best summarizes the reasoning that inner qualities might affect outward appearance. This answer choice includes the author's statement from the first paragraph that beauty often seems mysterious, as well as alluding to the statements from the last paragraph about Henry James perceiving George Eliot as more beautiful after he had come to know her better. Answer choice (C) is correct.

THE INCORRECT ANSWERS:

A Although the author does encourage scientists to expand their approach to studying beauty, the author does not mention the idea of "definitive results" anywhere in the passage, nor is the author's focus on whether or not such results can be achieved. Answer choice (A) is incorrect.

B Despite the fact that the author mentions the scientific study about infants recognizing beauty, there is no indication in the passage that this is due to infants also recognizing character. What is more, this answer choice does not express the reasoning behind the author's main point, so it cannot be the correct answer. Answer choice (B) is incorrect.

D Although the author does not seem to support beautiful people receiving privileges just on the basis of their beauty, the author makes no mention of long-term consequences in society (mentioning only "interesting consequences"), so answer choice (D) has no support in the passage. In addition, answer choice (D) does not describe the reasoning behind the author's main point, so it can be eliminated immediately.

E Although the author does indicate the reasoning described in answer choice (E), this answer choice does not clearly express the reasoning behind the author's *main* point, relating instead to a secondary point. Answer choice (E), therefore, is incorrect.

Question 18

Overview: Question 18 asks the student to consider the discussion of how teachers respond to attractive students in classroom situations and then place this discussion within the context of the passage; in particular, the student is to identify the purpose of this information in the passage. First the student should place the discussion within the context of the main point and then examine it in relation to the surrounding sentences. The main point states that scientists should consider character along with physical features in studying beauty. The sentence immediately before the beginning of the teacher/student discussion is, "Beautiful people are often assumed to be better than unattractive people in terms of character or other traits." Therefore, the correct answer will reflect the idea that attractive people are often assumed to have better character (or other superior traits) than unattractive people.

The Correct Answer:

A **Answer choice (A)** best reflects the idea that character is often associated with appearance. Additionally, answer choice (A) is suggestive of the information that teachers scored attractive students higher, thereby perceiving their qualities on the basis of their looks. Answer choice (A), therefore, is correct.

The Incorrect Answers:

B Although the author does not indicate approval of the idea that beauty can determine character in the eyes of some, the author also does not explicitly discuss disapproval or express the view that beautiful people receive "unnecessary privileges." The information about teachers and attractive students in classroom situations is not intended to illustrate that there is a problem with unnecessary privileges; rather, it functions as evidence for the statement that perceptions of beauty influence perceptions of character. Answer choice (B) is incorrect.

C The author does not indicate anything about the character of the students except to say that it was perceived to be good based on the how the students appeared. This is clearly not the same as the claim that character affects how people appear (rather, it is the reverse). Answer choice (C) is incorrect.

D There is no discussion in the passage about youth affecting beauty (in the discussion of the school children, there is no claim that children are perceived as beautiful *because* they are young; in fact, the discussion explicitly mentions that some children are seen as less attractive, rather than as uniformly beautiful). The author does cite research showing that employers hire applicants based in part on the beauty of applicants and that voters choose candidates based in part on the beauty of candidates. But there is no support in the passage for the idea that youth is associated with beauty.

E Although the author does mention that there are some features universally deemed beautiful, there is no mention of the way teachers respond to beauty in students around the world. Nor does the author indicate that the studies he cites (regarding how teachers respond to attractive students) can be described as universal. Answer choice (E) infers more than the passage supports, so it is clearly incorrect.

Question 19

Overview: Question 19 asks the student to review the information about Henry James's meeting with George Eliot and to identify the purpose of this particular discussion, that is, what the author is trying to indicate by including it. To select the correct answer, the student needs to place the Henry

James/George Eliot discussion within the context of the main point as well as the surrounding sentences. The main point, of course, is that scientists should consider studying character or personality when studying beauty. In the sentence immediately before the anecdote about James and Eliot, the author notes, "Etcoff hints at the effect of character or personality in determining beauty." From this, the student can determine that the purpose of this particular section in the passage is to indicate that beauty is not always determined exclusively by outward appearance and that qualities of personality or character can be a significant part of the perception of beauty. The answer choice that best expresses this will be correct.

The Correct Answer:

A **Answer choice (A)** is the only answer choice that effectively conveys the idea that personality or character can affect the perception of beauty. Thus, it is the correct answer.

The Incorrect Answers:

B Although the author does say that George Eliot was "a woman who was generally considered to be very unattractive," the author does not make any suggestion that George Eliot would be judged differently today, even by the "scientific" tests referred to in the passage. In fact, the author notes that scientific studies show that perceptions of beauty based on outward appearance alone are universal, so there is no reason to think that Eliot would be judged differently today. Answer choice (B) is clearly incorrect.

C Although the author does tell the anecdote to indicate that Eliot's personality or character played a significant role in James's perception of her beauty, there is no clear suggestion that the *only* way to perceive her as beautiful was by interacting with her. Answer choice (C) makes inferences that are unsupported by the passage, so it is incorrect.

D The author makes no comment on James's standards of beauty. In fact, the placement of the story within the passage suggests that James is intended to represent the average person with a standard appreciation for certain physical features, so it is inaccurate to claim from the passage alone that James's standards were different than the standards of others. Answer choice (D) is incorrect.

E Although answer choice (E) is essentially correct in its statement, this statement does not, in and of itself, contribute to the author's reason for including the anecdote. The George Eliot/Henry James story contributes to the author's main point, as well as supporting the statements immediately surrounding it. Because answer choice (E) does not explain how the story does this, it is incorrect.

Question 20

Overview: In question 20, the student must consider the meaning of the word *phenomenon* within the context of the passage and select a synonymous phrase that best replaces it. As always with word replacement questions, the student must consider not only the word itself but the way that it is being used in the passage. It is entirely possible that several of the answer choices *could* be correct, but only one of them will be the best choice. In the passage, the word *phenomenon* as a description of beauty is being used to suggest something that is not so much astonishing or amazing but that does occur and is worthy of being studied. The correct answer choice will reflect this.

The Correct Answer:

B The phrase *intriguing occurrence* best replaces the word *phenomenon* as it is being used in the sentence, because it indicates something that does happen (*occurrence*) and that is worthy of study (*intriguing*). **Answer choice (B)**, therefore, is correct.

The Incorrect Answers:

A The passage does indicate that beauty is a *reality*, but it does not suggest anywhere that this reality is *unexpected*. Answer choice (A) has no support within the passage, so it is incorrect.

C The author does note that beauty is often mysterious, but this is not the same thing as strange. There is no indication in the passage that the author considers beauty strange. Answer choice (C), therefore, is incorrect.

D Although some might see beauty as abstract, the passage does not make any indication of this. What is more, the passage does not indicate that beauty is an *experience*, so answer choice (D) is incorrect.

E The author suggests in the passage that beauty can be studied scientifically, which aims at objectivity instead of subjectivity, so the phrase *subjective analysis* cannot be a correct replacement for *phenomenon*. What is more, *subjective analysis* does not make sense as a replacement for *phenomenon* in the sentence ("scientists studying the subjective analysis of beauty"), so it can be eliminated immediately.

Question 21

Overview: The last question of the third reading comprehension passage asks the student to consider the author's tone toward the issue of beautiful people receiving privileges or being judged as better on the basis of their beauty. The student should note that although the author indicates disapproval of this, there is no clear statement of anger toward it. Rather, the author's tone is largely one of giving information. Using expressions such as "interesting consequences," the author is not demanding that the reader believe one thing over another, or suggesting anger or combativeness. The correct answer choice will reflect the author's intention to provide information without strong emotion.

The Correct Answer:

D The phrase *informative interest* best expresses the author's tone, because it conveys the attitude that the author takes: one of providing information and suggesting mild interest but not a strong emotion such as insistence or anger. **Answer choice (D)**, therefore, is correct.

The Incorrect Answers:

A The author's tone is not one of combativeness; on this basis alone, answer choice (A) can be rejected. In addition, rather than sounding skeptical, the author indicates that the information cited about the issue is accurate. Answer choice (A), therefore, cannot be correct.

B The author does not mock the issue at any point, nor is there a tone of amusement, since the author takes the issue seriously. Answer choice (B) is clearly incorrect and can be eliminated immediately.

C The author does not directly encourage action. Nor does the author seem to give in and assume the problem is inevitable, so there is no sense of *quiet resignation*. Answer choice (C) cannot be correct.

E The author might very well be angry, but this tone is not apparent in the passage. And although the author's concern might be righteous, this does not suggest in itself that the author's tone is one of *righteous anger*. Answer choice (E), therefore, cannot be correct.

Questions 22–27

Synopsis: Questions 22–27 derive from two passages, each of which offers slightly different perspectives on the issue of free trade. The author of the first passage begins by quoting eighteenth-century economist Adam Smith and noting that Smith's arguments about the need for free trade remain relevant in the modern day. The author goes on to claim that most Americans support free trade (as well as outsourcing), and that the majority of economists recognize that free trade is necessary for economic growth, because it allows a society to import the items that it cannot make as cheaply, thereby focusing its resources on what it can produce in a cost-effective way. What is more, the author claims that in terms of trade and the United States, free trade also benefits its trading partners, particularly when those partners have smaller and/or weaker economies than the U.S. By importing the items produced in these countries, the U.S. is helping to improve the standard of living there by paying workers more than they might receive from traditional work in these economies. The author does note a downside, however. Citing Harvard economist Gregory Mankiw, the author points out that free trade often receives bad press during a weak economy, but suggests it is not an abundance of foreign imports that causes economic problems so much as a scarcity of exports. The author concludes by noting that a strong economy will have a healthy balance of imports and exports and that in a weak economy the U.S. should increase its manufacturing and export output in order to create stability.

The second passage takes a rather different approach to the question of free trade. The author begins by acknowledging that free trade is a good thing (it is a sound economic practice) and that most economists affirm its contribution to economic strength, particularly in a global economic system. At the same time, the author points out that *unrestricted* free trade has negative qualities. Citing the economist Ha-Joon Chang, the author notes that unrestricted free trade can create problems not so much for the U.S. but for its trading partners when they are smaller and weaker. Economies are always changing, and many times a small-business owner will find that the demand for his product is no longer enough to support his business. The U.S. has a strong welfare system, as well as plenty of government assistance for struggling business owners to get back on their feet; however, smaller and weaker economies seldom have any such programs or available assistance. As a result, small-business owners in many of these economies simply become poorer rather than wealthier, and their standard of living decreases rather than improves. The author also cites Swedish economist Peter Soderbaum, who points out that few economists take secondary factors into account when considering the value of free trade; these include factors such as environmental consequences, the changes to a culture, and even the disappearance of traditional lifestyles in some societies that can come as a result of free trade. But seldom are these factors calculated into the free trade equation. The author of Passage B concludes by encouraging economists to create a new system for analyzing benefits/detriments of free trade, a system that would include these factors and thus illustrate a far more accurate picture of the cost and value of free trade.

Question 22

Overview: Question 22 asks the student to consider which answer choice both authors would likely agree on. Considering the differences in conclusion between the two authors, there are few similarities in the passages except for the fact that both authors begin by claiming that free trade is a good thing, and that both note somewhere in their respective passages that at times free trade can raise questions and controversy. The correct answer choice will reflect this.

The Correct Answer:

C The author of Passage A states the following: "Harvard economics professor Gregory Mankiw argues that the majority of economists also recognize the importance of free trade," and, "Mankiw also cautions against faulting the free movement of imports into the U.S. during a time of economic weakness." The author of Passage B notes the following: "As most economists agree, free trade is a sound economic practice and necessary for the U.S. to function effectively in a global economy, but unrestricted free trade is fraught with potential dangers that few economists seem willing to acknowledge or address." Both authors agree that free trade (1) is an important element of economic strength and (2) is sometimes controversial. **Answer choice (C)** best expresses this, so it is the correct answer.

The Incorrect Answers:

A Although the author of Passage A suggests that free trade is *entirely* beneficial to trading partners and particularly beneficial to the smaller and weaker economies, the author of Passage B argues that free trade can be problematic for smaller and weaker economies. The two authors clearly do not agree on the statement in answer choice (A), so it is incorrect.

B The author of Passage A argues that in a weak economy the U.S. should increase manufacturing. This does perhaps suggest that the U.S. will thereby increase jobs. However, the author of Passage B makes no statement suggesting the government should create jobs, focusing only on the need for government assistance when business owners lose their businesses. It cannot be inferred that the author of Passage B is advocating job creation, so answer choice (B) is incorrect.

D The author of Passage B suggests that free trade can be beneficial for a larger and stronger economy but not necessarily for a smaller and weaker one. In contrast, the author of Passage A indicates that free trade benefits both trading partners, as long as the economies balance their imports and exports. It cannot be inferred that the author of Passage A believes free trade to be damaging to one economy and beneficial to another, so answer choice (D) is incorrect.

E The author of Passage A makes the argument in answer choice (E) quite clearly, but the author of Passage B makes no mention of exports, focusing instead on the idea that economists should create a new system for analyzing the peripheral dangers that free trade can cause. Answer choice (E), therefore, cannot be correct.

Question 23

<u>Overview:</u> Question 23 asks the student to select the answer choice that best summarizes Passage A. The author of Passage A focuses on the benefits of unrestricted free trade and notes toward the end that economies must balance imports and exports: "A balance of imports and exports is required to maintain a stable economy, and an increase in manufacturing for exports during economic weakness can actually bolster a struggling economy." The correct answer choice thus will reflect the author's focus on three areas: (1) free trade strengthens an economy, (2) free trade itself does not need to be restricted, but (3) economies need to balance imports and exports.

The Correct Answer:

D Answer choice (D) provides the best statement of summary for Passage A by including the three factors discussed in the Overview. Answer choice (D), therefore, is correct.

The Incorrect Answers:

A The author of Passage A *does* mention Adam Smith and argues that his claims in *The Wealth of Nations* were sound; but this is not necessarily the *main point* of Passage A. As the Overview indicates, the author's main point is a combined focus on the importance of free trade, the need to avoid restrictions, and the need to balance imports and exports. As answer choice (A) focuses on a secondary detail in the passage, it is incorrect.

B The author of Passage A definitely concludes with a focus on the importance of balancing imports and exports, but this is the final statement that rounds out the author's three-part focus. Because answer choice (B) fails to include the other two parts of this focus, it cannot be correct. Answer choice (B) can be eliminated.

C The author of Passage A does claim that economic weakness is not a result of unrestricted free trade, suggesting that it is instead a domestic problem (that is, related to a decrease of exports). However, answer choice (C) does not fully explain the author's main point. The author also states quite clearly that free trade *is* a good thing and that what is specifically needed is a balance between imports and exports. Because answer choice (C) does not convey this, it cannot be correct.

E Answer choice (E) reflects secondary details the author discusses: that the majority of Americans support outsourcing and the view that outsourcing can be good for economic growth. This, however, is clearly not the main point of Passage A, so answer choice (E) can be eliminated.

Question 24

Overview: In question 24, the student is asked to select the answer choice that best reflects the main point of Passage B. The author of Passage B acknowledges immediately that free trade is a good thing but qualifies the statement fairly early by raising questions about the problems with *unrestricted* free trade. Additionally, the author concludes by recommending that economists begin to consider the various effects of free trade, most of which they currently overlook. The correct answer choice will thus reflect this two-part focus: (1) unrestricted free trade can cause problems, and (2) economists need a different approach to free trade, an approach that considers the various effects of free trade.

The Correct Answer:

E By including details about the problems with unrestricted free trade and discussing the need for a new approach, **answer choice (E)** best expresses the two-part focus that is discussed in the Overview. Answer choice (E), therefore, is correct.

The Incorrect Answers:

A The author mentions in the first sentence that most economists will concede the value of free trade, especially in a global economy. But this is not the main point of the passage, and the author goes on to qualify the benefits of free trade very quickly. Answer choice (A), therefore, overlooks the main point of the passage and is incorrect.

B Answer choice (B) reflects the position of Swedish economics professor Peter Soderbaum. The author uses Soderbaum's views to *support* the main point but not necessarily to express the main point itself. Answer choice (B) is incorrect because it focuses on a supporting detail and fails to state the author's primary argument.

C, D Again, answer choices (C) and (D) reflect supporting details that the author uses to lead up to the main point, but that are not themselves the main point. The author claims that one of the problems with unrestricted free trade is that it can leave business owners with no recourse when their governments lack assistance programs; the author argues that these programs—welfare programs and financial assistance opportunities—are an important part of helping small-business owners survive in an evolving economy. But the author goes on to say that economists need to take these details into account for a new approach to free trade. Answer choices (C) and (D) are thus incorrect.

Question 25

Overview: Question 25 asks the student to consider how Passage B responds to Passage A and select the answer choice that best reflects this response. The student must consider how Passage B essentially *replies* to Passage A. Based on question 22, the student should recall that both authors agree on the fundamental importance of free trade, but the author of Passage B offers some qualifications on the benefits of free trade. So, Passage B responds by agreeing with Passage A in part but by then providing a different perspective. The correct answer choice will reflect this.

The Correct Answer:

B **Answer choice (B)** best expresses the statements made in the Overview: that Passage B concedes the importance of free trade but then goes on to offer a qualification and thus an alternate thesis. Answer choice (B) is correct.

The Incorrect Answers:

A Although Passage B does provide a different argument than Passage A, Passage B does not point out a specific flaw in the reasoning of Passage A. Rather, the two passages (though both begin with a focus on free trade) are essentially discussing related but different topics. Passage B would point out a flaw in the reasoning of Passage A if Passage B gave evidence that, for example, global free trade *is* a contributing factor to a weak economy. But it does no such thing. Passage B simply has a different focus. Answer choice (A) is incorrect.

C The authors of Passage A and Passage B ultimately address different concerns that arise with the issue of free trade; as a result, it cannot be said that the author's arguments in Passage A negate the claims that are made in Passage B. The author of Passage B is encouraging a new approach to studying the cost-value ratio of free trade, while the author of Passage A argues that the U.S. should increase exports during a weak economy to get the greatest benefit from free trade. The connection between these two ideas is not strong enough to support the statement made in answer choice (C), so it is incorrect.

D Both authors discuss free trade in the same way; they are simply addressing two different areas that free trade affects. What is more, the author of Passage B calls for a new approach to analyzing free trade but *not* necessarily a *new definition* of *free trade*. Therefore, it cannot be said from the information in either passage that the details about the secondary problems in Passage B undermine the definition of *free trade* in Passage A, so answer choice (D) is incorrect.

E Again, both authors address entirely different sides of the issue, and there is no information in Passage A to indicate that it assumes the truth of the argument in Passage B. Both authors basically start at the same point but go in very different directions, drawing conclusions that do not necessarily relate immediately to one another. Answer choice (E), then, must be incorrect.

QUESTION 26

Overview: Question 26 asks the student to consider the following statement by the author of Passage B: "It is historically significant that the U.S. was heavily protectionist until it became a world leader in the economy." The student must then define the word *protectionist* according to the immediate context of this statement as well as to the context of all of Passage B. What the author is essentially claiming is that the U.S. did not allow unrestricted free trade until it had built up a strong economy that could protect business owners from the very problems that the author of Passage B describes. In other words, the U.S. did *not* support unrestricted free trade until it could sustain it. The correct answer choice will reflect this in some way.

THE CORRECT ANSWER:

A **Answer choice (A)** best expresses the meaning of *protectionist* in the context of the sentence and of Passage B: "Protecting a domestic economy from unrestricted free trade." Answer choice (A), therefore, is correct.

THE INCORRECT ANSWERS:

B Far from suggesting support for unrestricted free trade, the word *protectionist* suggests a strong opposition to unrestricted free trade. So, answer choice (B) is incorrect and can be eliminated immediately.

C The author of Passage B acknowledges the reality of a global economy, but within the context of the passage, the sentence containing the word *protectionist* follows a discussion of smaller and weaker economies, not globalism. Answer choice (C) offers an incorrect definition in the context of the passage, so it is incorrect.

D, E The author of Passage B does mention the need for government programs to assist in the case of failing small businesses. But consider the statement containing the word *protectionist*: "It is historically significant that the U.S. was heavily protectionist until it became a world leader in the economy." The author mentions that the U.S. currently has such assistance programs in place, so it must have been heavily protectionist *before* it became a world leader in the economy not *since* it has become a world leader in the economy. Therefore, neither answer choices (D) or (E) provides a correct definition of *protectionist* in the context of the passage, so both must be incorrect.

QUESTION 27

Overview: The final question in the Reading Comprehension section asks the student to identify the author's tone regarding free trade in Passage B, as compared to Passage A. To answer this question correctly, the student should first identify the author's tone toward free trade in Passage A. Clearly, it is enthusiastic and very supportive. As has already been established, Passage B offers a qualification of the benefits of free trade, so the author's tone does not have the same note of enthusiasm or support. Instead, the author's support seems more tentative. The correct answer choice will reflect this in some way.

THE CORRECT ANSWER:

C The author's tone in Passage B could accurately be described as being more *cautious* toward the issue of free trade, so **answer choice (C)** is correct.

THE INCORRECT ANSWERS:

A, B, D, E In answering a question like question 27, the process of elimination becomes an important part of the strategy. To consider each incorrect answer choice in turn:

Answer choice (A) reflects an evaluative judgment the student should refrain from making for the purposes of the exam. Moreover, given the different foci of the passages, it is not obvious that one is more *sophisticated* regarding free trade than the other. Answer choice (A) must be incorrect.

Speculation suggests the lack of a clear conclusion, but since the author of Passage B offers a clear, specific recommendation, the author's tone cannot be described as *speculative*. Answer choice (B) must be incorrect.

The author of Passage B might very well be happy to debate someone on the merits of his claims, but his tone toward free trade is not so much one of debate as it is one of caution. (The author does not, for example, argue at length about an opposing viewpoint's claims, as might be expected in a debating tone.) Answer choice (D) has no immediate application to the author's tone, so it is incorrect.

As with *sophisticated*, the choice of *pragmatic* indicates an evaluative judgment but much less obviously an objective description of tone. Answer choice (E), therefore, is incorrect.

Logical Reasoning, Section IV

QUESTION 1

Overview: Question 1 presents a passage in which the student must consider the contrast between criticism and opinion. The passage begins by noting that a distinction must be made between criticism and opinion and then continues with an explanation of this distinction, concluding that criticism is not necessarily everyone's right to have or share but that opinion cannot be denied. The question then asks for the answer choice that can be inferred from the passage. An inference from a passage, of course, is not an outright statement of the passage, but an inference does *rely* on direct statements; therefore, the correct answer choice will be derived from specific comments made in the passage.

THE CORRECT ANSWER:

B **Answer choice (B)** makes the following statement: "Criticism and opinion are often confused with one another, because some mistake a negative opinion for criticism." The passage begins by noting that criticism and opinion need to be distinguished from one another, implying immediately that the distinction is *not* always made. Thus, the first part of answer choice (B) can be inferred from the passage. Additionally, the passage notes that people who criticize others are "hoping to effect a modification" in behavior and that criticism generally has a negative connotation. Although the author of the passage notes that opinion does not always have a negative connotation, if the opinion is itself negative such a connotation may be derived. From this, the student can correctly assume that a negative opinion is often confused for criticism, thus explaining the confusion that was stated in the first sentence of the passage. Answer choice (B) is correct.

THE INCORRECT ANSWERS:

A Although the passage begins with the implication that criticism and opinion are often confused with one another, there is no mention in the passage of *wording criticism as an opinion*, nor can this inference be derived from any of the statements made in the passage. The author does note the difference between the *purpose* behind criticism versus opinion, but the author makes no recommendation about offering criticism in such a way that it would be welcome. Answer choice (A) has no support in the passage and is thus incorrect.

C Clearly, the passage implies that people make the mistake of confusing opinion with criticism, but the passage does not mention phases of thought at any point, nor does the passage indicate that opinion is connected to criticism because of these phases of thought. In fact, the author notes quite clearly that criticism and opinion need to be distinguished from one another, suggesting that they are *not* related and thus cannot be connected by phases of thought. Answer choice (C) is incorrect.

D The author makes no mention of *different kinds of criticism*, instead discussing criticism as a whole rather than in separate forms. Answer choice (D) assumes information that is not in the passage, so it can be eliminated.

E Although the passage might very well go on to discuss the right to opinion as a component of freedom of speech, there is no such implication in the passage at this point, nor can such an idea be assumed merely from the information the passage provides. The author mentions only that "everyone should be entitled to *opinion*," but within the context of the passage this relates more to the purpose behind opinion rather than to abstract freedoms. Answer choice (E) is incorrect.

QUESTION 2

Overview: Question 2 describes a scenario about a department store that has hired a new person to represent its name. According to the passage, the company held certain standards for the new representative on the basis of the very positive public response to the previous representative. The company auditioned a number of applicants, and one applicant in particular was very interested in the job, explaining to the company how well she fit the image the company desired. The company agreed and hired her; the passage notes that this occurred without market research. Shortly afterward, the company featured her much less and then re-hired the former representative for the job. The question asks the student which answer choice best explains this action, based on the information provided in the passage. The student needs to consider two key points noted in the passage: (1) the popularity of the previous representative, and (2) the company's decision that at the time of hiring the new representative, no market research was required. These factors play an important role in what would affect the department store's decision, and the correct answer choice will indicate clearly that a situation involving one (or both) of these factors would change the company's view about the new representative.

THE CORRECT ANSWER:

A **Answer choice (A)** states that the department store chose to do market research after the fact and discovered that the new representative was not popular among customers. Instead of losing customers in order to keep an unpopular representative, the store apparently pushed her aside and re-hired the former—and very popular—representative. All of this fits two key pieces of information provided in the passage: first, that the former representative was very popular, and second, that when the company hired the new representative, it decided that "no market research was *then* required." The latter statement suggests that the company might well have decided that market research was required after the fact. Answer choice (A) takes into account both pieces of information and offers a solid explanation for the department store's decision, so answer choice (A) is correct.

THE INCORRECT ANSWERS:

B Answer choice (B) states that a tabloid magazine published an article questioning the new representative's character. Since the department store had a clear image requirement, this could very well affect its decision. But nothing in the passage suggests that there was such a tabloid magazine article, and it seems unlikely that the store would fire the new representative based solely on such an article, or more particularly that the store would slowly replace her, especially since the store had evidently hired the new representative in the belief that she had a good image. Answer choice (B) does not offer enough information to justify the company's decision, so it is incorrect.

C The actions of a competitor store and the popularity of their new representative could affect the department store's decision. But the passage does not say specifically that the new representative is unpopular, and the answer choice does not clarify among whom either representative is popular (or unpopular). If it turns out that the new representative of the other department store is more popular among customers of the first store, this might be a reason to question the long-term potential for their own representative. Answer choice (C) is unclear, however, and has no support in the passage, so it can be eliminated.

D Answer choice (D) essentially sums up what the passage tells us—that the department store believed it had made a mistake and decided to hire the former representative again—but it does nothing to provide a *reason* behind the belief about a mistake. Because answer choice (D) offers no clear indication of the company's motivation, it cannot be the correct answer.

E The passage indicates that the new representative was very interested in the position and believed that she would be good for it. This suggests that she would enjoy the job, rather than the opposite, and indeed nothing in the passage suggests she would *not* enjoy the job. Answer choice (E) is incorrect.

Question 3

Overview: Question 3 asks the student to identify the flawed reasoning in the passage by considering which of the answer choices offers similarly flawed reasoning. The passage presents the scenario of a snowstorm in Denver, with the added information that all of the news outlets in Denver have cautioned drivers to be careful on their way to work, noting that getting to work will take extra time. The passage concludes with the statement that because of these factors all the employees at First Community Bank of Denver will be late to work. To determine the correct answer, the student needs to determine the structure of the reasoning in the passage. The passage follows this line of thought: (1) a condition or problem is established and (2) thus everyone will be affected by the condition. The problem with this reasoning is that it does not allow for any anomalies. Suppose, for instance, several of the employees at First Community Bank of Denver decide to leave for work much earlier than normal in order to arrive at work on time. Suppose that the snowstorm affects certain parts of the city worse than others, so some employees will be able to get to work without as much trouble and can arrive on time. Suppose an employee lives in an apartment complex near the bank and can walk to work. None of these factors is considered; because the passage uses the inclusive pronoun "all," the passage's conclusion leaves no room for anomalies. The correct answer choice will reflect this.

The Correct Answer:

A **Answer choice (A)** is correct because it follows the pattern of reasoning given in the passage. First the answer choice claims that MSG can cause migraines; it then concludes that *everyone* who eats food with MSG should expect to develop a migraine. As with the passage regarding the snowstorm, the answer choice draws a conclusion about *everyone* from a general statement, without allowing for the possibility of variation (perhaps not everyone metabolizes MSG in the same way, for example).

The Incorrect Answers:

B Answer choice (B) does contain a flaw in the reasoning—that Theodore *must* be taller than Ferdinand because he is two years older—but this flaw does not match the flaw in the reasoning of the passage. If answer choice (B) stated that all people are taller than those two years younger, it would have approached the same flaw. Because it does not, answer choice (B) cannot be correct.

C Answer choice (C) does not contain a flaw in the reasoning. It states that a power outage in Chicago occurred in an area with 300,000 customers, so the majority of these people were without power. This would seem to be true. Additionally, it does not use the "all" argument.

D As with answer choice (B), answer choice (D) presents a scenario that involves only two people and in which the reasoning—although flawed—does not follow the pattern given in the passage. In addition to the fact that there is nothing to suggest that Nina *must* be angry with Edward, there is no suggestion that because of a general condition or statement of fact, *all* people must react or be affected in some way.

E Answer choice (E) is incorrect. Although the statement does indicate a general statement of fact (that lunch is served at noon) and draws a conclusion from that fact (some students must be hungry at noon), it does not claim that *all* students will be hungry.

QUESTION 4

Overview: Question 4 describes a situation in which the CEO of an automobile manufacturer announces plans to increase vehicle production due to an unexpectedly strong period in the economy. The passage adds that supplies for building vehicles currently have low prices and that the auto manufacturer hopes to use this time to produce vehicles in a cost-effective way. The implication is that this period of economic strength will not last and that the supplies will go up in price. This would make the vehicles *more* expensive for the manufacturer to build in the future, so by building them now the manufacturer will have the freedom to reduce production or even lower the selling price of the vehicles when an economic downturn strikes. To select the correct answer, the student needs to consider these details as the prevailing justification for the CEO's decision to increase vehicle production.

THE CORRECT ANSWER:

C If a recent study indicates that the steel used by the auto manufacturer is expected to increase in cost over the next few months, it would justify the auto manufacturer's decision to build cars while the economy is good and the cost of supplies is low. **Answer choice (C)** is correct.

THE INCORRECT ANSWERS:

A An increase in the price of the auto manufacturer's stock should do nothing to hinder or contribute to its decision to increase automobile production. In fact, the rise in the stock price is likely to occur as a result of the CEO's announcement, so this is likely an effect and not a cause of the decision to increase production. It is possible that the CEO is making the announcement to increase production in order to bolster a failing stock price; but as there is nothing in the passage to suggest specifically that the company is hoping to improve its stock price, this cannot reasonably be inferred as a cause of the decision. Answer choice (A) is incorrect.

B Although answer choice (B) could be a good option if it stated clearly that the car batteries in question are those used by the auto manufacturer, this answer choice does not make any such statement. As it is, the loss of the car battery company might have absolutely no effect on the auto manufacturer. Answer choice (B) is incorrect due to insufficient detail.

D The decision to merge with another auto manufacturer has no clear connection to the company's decision to produce more cars, based on the information within the passage. The fact that the second auto manufacturer has a surplus of vehicles would more likely motivate the original auto manufacturer to put an increase in production on hold. Therefore, answer choice (D) provides no justification for the CEO's announcement.

E As in answer choice (D), the expected rise in the price of oil—with the accompanying decrease in the expected purchase of new vehicles—is far more likely to motivate the CEO to put a hold on production and not to increase it immediately. It might be argued that a reduced incentive to buy new cars in the future would motivate the company to increase production now in the hopes that customers would buy them now. But this line of reasoning does not address the CEO's explicitly stated concern to build cars while the necessary supplies are low in cost. Answer choice (E) is incorrect.

QUESTION 5

Overview: Question 5 describes a situation in which an IT company is planning to open a new office in the city of Nizhny Novgorod, Russia, where IT is a major industry. The passage notes, however, that the economy has been in a state of weakness and that many residents are out of work. The IT industry is also weak, and a number of IT businesses that have been in the city for some time are now closing. However, the company opening the new office is confident of its success. The question asks the student to consider an explanation for why this is. To select the correct answer, the student needs to consider the details in the passage, reflecting what might set this particular IT company above the rest, even during an economic downturn.

THE CORRECT ANSWER:

A **Answer choice (A)** is the only answer choice that provides a sufficient explanation for why the IT company can be so confident of its success in spite of a struggling economy: its technology is up to date (and thus will be in demand), and it is able to keep its costs low (thus offsetting the economic weakness). Answer choice (A) also notes that the other IT businesses in Nizhny Novgorod have not kept their technology up to date, so this places the company with the new office at a distinct competitive advantage. Answer choice (A) is the correct answer.

THE INCORRECT ANSWERS:

B Although purchasing an existing building instead of building a new one creates an immediate financial advantage; it does not explain why the IT company with the new office can succeed where its competitors cannot. Answer choice (B) is incorrect due to insufficient details to explain the discrepancy.

C The employment opportunities offered by the IT company with the new office has some potential to explain its expected success. However, it is not clear from the answer choice *how* the company will pay new hires; that is, how the company can afford new hires. This answer choice alone does not provide a sufficient reason for the company's confidence in its financial success. Answer choice (C) cannot be correct.

D The presence of industrial scenery does not clearly contribute to a lack of business success, so answer choice (D) does not explain why the IT company with the new office can be confident of its success. Were the answer choice to include some information about *why* the industrial scenery has hurt other IT businesses and *how* it has added to their failure, this might be a good possibility. As it is, though, answer choice (D) cannot be correct.

E Far from explaining the reason for the IT company's confidence, answer choice (E) raises questions about the potential for its success by claiming that the company will immediately have large debts to pay off. Answer choice (E) is not correct and can be eliminated immediately.

QUESTION 6

Overview: Question 6 presents a statement from the member of a local school board, a statement in which the member argues that there should be computers in every classroom in the school district. The school board member claims that the city is one of few cities in the state that do not have computers in every classroom, and as a result the "schools are suffering." The speaker goes on to say that parents are moving out of the school district and that research indicates that students who attend schools with computers in every classroom have the highest rates of graduation and receive better-paying jobs than students who did not have computers in their classrooms. The question asks for the answer choice that best explains the flaw in the school board member's reasoning; specifically, what does the school board member *not* establish in reaching the conclusion that computers should be available in every classroom in this particular school district? The student must consider each point of evidence the school board member offers. These points are: (1) there has been a loss in student body in the school district because parents are relocating to another school district; and (2) schools that have computers in the classroom have the highest graduation rates and acquire higher-paying jobs. Because the school board member cites research to support the claim about graduation rates and higher-paying jobs, the problem clearly lies in the claim about parents moving out of the school district. The correct answer choice will address this.

The Correct Answer:

C As noted in the Overview, the correct answer choice must note that the school board member fails to explain that parents move out of the district *as a result of* the lack of computers in the school district classrooms. Because there could be many reasons for parents relocating, the school board member must explain the connection between the lack of computers and the fact that some parents relocate. **Answer choice (C)**, therefore, is correct.

The Incorrect Answers:

A Although funding is essential to the addition of computers to every classroom (and the reduced student body might suggest that the school district is losing funds instead of gaining them), the question of funding is not a part of the school board member's argument and thus does not contribute to the flaw in the reasoning. Answer choice (A) is incorrect.

B Answer choice (B) is related to answer choice (A) in the sense that it suggests a problem with adding computers to a school district that has a reduced student body. This in itself is a reasonable issue to raise. However, it is a secondary issue given the passage, just because the school board member's argument relies on the issue of parents relocating to new school districts (in addition to the claim about graduation rates and higher-paying jobs). Answer choice (B) is not correct because it does not address the immediate flaw in the member of the school district's reasoning.

D Although the school board member should ultimately provide specific documentation for the claim about graduation rates and higher-paying jobs, the school board member does make the general claim that "research" supports this allegation. What the member of the school board does not establish, however, is that there is any research that shows that parents relocate due to a lack of computers in the classroom. Answer choice (D) does not address this, so it is incorrect.

E Answer choice (E) has no connection to the school board member's claims, so it can be eliminated immediately. The school board member does say that the schools are suffering, but the evidence used to support this relates to parents relocating and research about academic and employment improvements for students who had studied with computers in the classroom.

Questions 7 and 8

Overview: Questions 7 and 8 are based on a passage about the presence of eating disorders in the fashion industry, particularly among models. The author notes that the fashion industry cannot ignore the reality of eating disorders but that there are a variety of objections to restrictions on the fashion industry, objections from both models and designers. Models often complain that they are naturally thin, while designers point out that eating disorders are not unique to the fashion industry; they claim that eating disorders are connected to personal concerns that cannot be addressed with rules regarding weight or BMI requirements. The passage concludes by noting that the industry is inclined to accept "awareness about eating disorders but not extra rules," that resources for dealing with eating disorders will be available, and that models should seek help when they realize they have a problem. Question 7 asks the student to determine the main point of the passage, while question 8 asks for the answer choice that best expresses the flaw in the fashion industry's reasoning.

Question 7

The Correct Answer:

D There are several important details in the passage that contribute to the main point: (1) the fashion industry is not happy with the idea of further restrictions about weight and eating disorders, (2) the industry wants to provide awareness about eating disorders, (3) the industry wants the models to initiate seeking help, though they will provide support. The correct answer will pull these three details into a summary statement. **Answer choice (D)** is the only answer choice to combine all three and thus restate the main point of the passage, so it is the correct answer.

The Incorrect Answers:

A Although the response from designers suggests that they believe eating disorders are related to factors other than fashion and thus cannot simply be eliminated by changing weight requirements among models, there is nothing in the passage to suggest that the industry as a whole believes eating disorders are "inevitable" and impossible to eliminate. Answer choice (A) cannot be correct.

B Answer choice (B) expresses one part of the discussion in the passage: the viewpoint of models and designers on the source of eating disorders. It does not, however, express the main point of the passage, which notes that the industry is open to providing awareness but wants models to initiate seeking help. Answer choice (B) is incorrect because it focuses on a secondary detail instead of the main point.

C As with answer choice (B), answer choice (C) expresses a supporting detail of the main point: that the industry tends to seek out models who are naturally thin and that they are not necessarily thin in an unhealthy way. But answer choice (C) does not go one step further to apply this to the bigger issue at hand, about how the industry would prefer eating disorders to be treated. Answer choice (C) is thus incorrect since it focuses on a secondary detail.

E There is nothing in the passage to suggest that rules for BMI will be ignored; in fact, the passage notes, "Some countries have gone so far as to establish rules that require models to maintain a certain BMI if they expect to walk the runways." This indicates that the rules for BMI *are* being observed, and that this is a source of frustration for designers and models in the fashion industry, because they believe that BMI is not a sufficient indicator of healthy weight. Answer choice (E) is clearly incorrect.

QUESTION 8

THE CORRECT ANSWER:

E Question 8 asks the student to consider *why* the reasoning in the fashion industry is vulnerable to criticism. This requires the student to consider three details carefully: (1) several countries have put BMI restrictions on models because they believe they are too thin to be healthy, (2) the industry admits that eating disorders exist but claims that they are based on *personal issues,* and (3) the industry wants to provide awareness but let the models seek help themselves. However, if an eating disorder is based on a personal issue, that very personal issue might prevent a person from seeking help; in putting the burden for seeking help on models themselves, the industry assumes that models are in fact able to do so. **Answer choice (E)** best expresses this idea, so it is the correct answer.

THE INCORRECT ANSWERS:

A The actions taken by several countries to establish BMI requirements indicate that public awareness might be involved in the issue, but the public is not actually mentioned in the passage, and the focus is almost entirely on the internal mood of the fashion industry toward eating disorders. Answer choice (A) infers details that cannot be supported by the passage, so it is incorrect.

B Although the designers note that the fashion industry tends to gravitate toward thin models—suggesting that thinness is part of the desired look or trend—there is no clear mention of thin models being part of a short-term trend in the fashion industry. Answer choice (B) infers details that are not supported within the passage, so it is not correct.

C, D The details in answer choices (C) and (D) are implied in the passage: that the fashion industry does not create eating disorders, that they exist elsewhere in society, that models are naturally thin and that most are not necessarily struggling with eating disorders. However, these details in particular do not represent the flaw in the industry's reasoning (in fact, they do more to support the reasoning than undermine it), so answer choices (C) and (D) are incorrect.

QUESTION 9

Overview: Question 9 presents the scenario of a warehouse company that has promised to pay its employees a 3% bonus each Christmas. In fact, this promise is treated as a guarantee and is included in the employee handbook. The company's new financial officer, however, claims that the company's budget will not support the Christmas bonus this year unless employees are willing to help out: the financial officer sends a memo to all employees, letting them know that the company *will* be able to pay the Christmas bonuses *if* the employees contribute by helping to generate advertising revenues. The question asks the student to decide which of the answer choices is true if the information in the passage is true. This is essentially a question about inference; the student must consider what the passage is saying and what can be inferred from it. Most important to note is the fact that the financial officer is more or less telling the employees that if they work harder to get the advertising revenues, they will get their bonuses. In essence, the financial officer is saying that the employees will receive the bonuses if they do something to bring the bonus money into the company—in other words, to work for their own bonuses.

THE CORRECT ANSWER:

B **Answer choice (B)** correctly deduces the implication of the financial officer's memo: that the employees will essentially be contributing to their own bonuses, making the bonus something less of a bonus. Thus, answer choice (B) is correct.

THE INCORRECT ANSWERS:

A The company's employee handbook guarantees a 3% Christmas bonus to its employees, and there is nothing in the passage to suggest that there is a codicil attached to this guarantee regarding whether the company's budget supports the bonus. By promising the bonus to employees, the company makes itself responsible to find a way to pay it, so answer choice (A) cannot be inferred from the passage and is thus incorrect.

C Given the information about the financial officer's memo, it may be inferred that the company has not had any trouble paying the Christmas bonus in the past. However, this in itself does not necessarily mean that the company will not have trouble paying it this year. What is more, nothing in the passage suggests that the company's current financial state is a result of corruption on the financial officer's part. Answer choice (C) does not have sufficient support within the passage and is thus incorrect.

D Although the financial officer might believe that downsizing would also benefit the company, there is no mention of this in the passage, nor can it be deduced from the information that is provided. Answer choice (D) is incorrect due to insufficient support.

E Although the employees might very well be planning to strike, there is nothing in the passage to suggest that this is the inevitable response or that a strike is imminent if the employees do not receive their Christmas bonus. Answer choice (E) cannot be supported by details in the passage, so it is incorrect.

QUESTION 10

Overview: Question 10 presents a statement from a philatelist (a stamp collector) who is discussing a very rare stamp, "the rarest stamp in the world," according to the philatelist: the Swedish Treskilling Yellow. The philatelist notes that the stamp is so rare because it was originally printed in error and only one remains. As of 1996, the Treskilling Yellow was sold for $2.06 million dollars and is now the most expensive stamp in the world. The philatelist concludes that it is thus the most valuable stamp in the world. The student must consider which of the answer choices represents the assumption on which the philatelist's conclusion depends. The first factor to consider is the conclusion itself—that the Treskilling Yellow is the most valuable stamp in the world. The second factor is the detail that supports the conclusion: (1) that the stamp is the only one of its kind to have been found, and (2) that it has sold for the highest price. According to the statements made by the philatelist, these details make the stamp the most valuable in the world, so the correct answer choice will reflect this.

THE CORRECT ANSWER:

D **Answer choice (D)** best summarizes the details noted in the Overview—that the philatelist considers the stamp to be the most valuable because it is unique and because it has sold for the most money. Therefore, answer choice (D) is correct.

THE INCORRECT ANSWERS:

A The information in the passage suggests that the philatelist's belief in the stamp's value is based in part on the fact that there is only one stamp known to be in existence. Therefore, answer choice (A) cannot be correct, because the philatelist's comments cannot be said to assume that a second stamp would sell for as much.

B Answer choice (B) is partially correct insofar as it expresses some of the information that supports the philatelist's claim: the original error that printed the stamp in a different color has contributed to its rarity and its desirability among stamp collectors. However, this is a supporting detail and does not necessarily indicate the primary assumptions on which the philatelist's argument depends. Answer choice (B) is not correct.

C Answer choice (C) offers a contrary assumption to answer choice (A): that the Treskilling Yellow would actually be *worthless* if a second stamp were found. But there is nothing in the passage to suggest that the philatelist believes this, so answer choice (C) can be eliminated due to insufficient support.

E The assumption that "the finest and costliest stamps in the world have originated from printing errors in Sweden" is utterly insupportable based on information in the passage. The philatelist notes only that *one stamp* is the costliest in the world, and this just happens to be because it is rare and because it is the result of a printing error. There is no further information about other rare and costly stamps, so answer choice (E) can be eliminated immediately.

QUESTION 11

Overview: Question 11 presents a passage that explains the early history of Karl Marx's *Das Kapital*. According to the passage, the book received very little attention upon its first publication, but in its later history became one of the most influential writings of the twentieth century. The student is asked to consider—within the context of the statements in the passage—which answer choice best explains the reason for the *eventual popularity* of the book. The student should note that the question does *not* ask for the reasons behind the initial unpopularity of the book, but rather what might have changed to make the book popular after Marx's death in 1883. This might seem like a question that requires a blind guess, but it is not. The necessary details for a correct inference are in the paragraph; the student must look closely and take them into account. The key sentence here is the last sentence of the passage: "After his death in 1883, however, there were growing changes in the international political climate, and *Das Kapital* grew in popularity, ultimately becoming one of the most influential political treatises of the twentieth century." This sentence suggests that the book's popularity did not occur until there was a change in the general attitude toward politics. Additionally, the sentence immediately before this suggests that Marx wrote his book before the public was ready to read it. Therefore, the correct answer will reflect the idea that Marx's book became popular after a change in political views in the world.

THE CORRECT ANSWER:

A **Answer choice (A)** best expresses the idea that Marx's book could not be popular until there was a significant change in the public political attitude. Therefore, answer choice (A) is the correct answer.

THE INCORRECT ANSWERS:

B, E Answer choices (B) and (E) provide a reason for why *Das Kapital* might not have been available to many readers, thus limiting the opportunities for its popularity. There is nothing in the passage, however, to suggest that *Das Kapital* was immediately popular with those who *could* read it, so neither answer choices (B) nor (E) offers a sufficient explanation of the book's eventual popularity. Both answer choices are incorrect.

C Answer choice (C) offers a possible reason for why few readers would be unwilling to take on such a massive tome, but it does not offer an explanation for the book's *eventual popularity*. What is more, it does not infer a reason from information contained within the paragraph, so it cannot be correct. Answer choice (C) can be eliminated.

D The reception from academics might very well have limited the opportunities early on for *Das Kapital* to be taught at the university level, but once again this does not explain the reason for the book's *eventual popularity*. Therefore, answer choice (D) is incorrect.

QUESTION 12

Overview: Question 12 offers historical information on the Black Plague, noting that although it destroyed up to 60% of Europe's population, the Plague might also have provided some positive contributions to European society. The author of the passage cites scholars who argue that the Black Plague, by decimating those who had traditionally ruled Europe, opened the door of opportunity for the development of a European middle class. The question asks students to consider which of the answer choices, if true, most clearly undermines this claim. To select the correct answer, the student must focus on the main point: some scholars argue that the Black Plague contributed to the development of a middle class in Europe. The correct answer choice will provide a reason that calls this claim into question.

THE CORRECT ANSWER:

E **Answer choice (E)** makes the claim that a "thriving middle class was already in development when the Black Plague first struck Europe in the 1340s." If this is true, it strongly undermines the claim that the Black Plague created an opportunity for the development of the middle class in Europe (because, presumably, such an opportunity was already there and had been taken advantage of). Answer choice (E) is correct.

THE INCORRECT ANSWERS:

A The passage states that it was the peasantry, freed from serfdom, who began building businesses and forming a middle class in Europe. Answer choice (A) claims that the Black Plague struck down very few of the peasantry (in contrast to the many members of the aristocracy who died). Far from undermining the passage, it offers secondary information that could be used to support it, so answer choice (A) is incorrect.

B The demographic information of male deaths versus female deaths is not clearly connected to the information in the passage, so it does not undermine the argument made in the passage; it is simply not clearly relevant. Nothing in the passage suggests that it was men only who built the middle class in Europe; even if this were a safe historical assumption, it cannot be assumed from the passage alone. Answer choice (B) cannot be correct.

C Like answer choice (A), answer choice (C) offers information to support the argument presented in the passage. If after the Black Death there was an increase in pre-industrial productivity, indicating a rise in new trades, it would follow that the argument has at least some evidence. Answer choice (C) is incorrect.

D Again, answer choice (D) presents information that strengthens the argument made in the passage by indicating that the aristocracy were weakened and lost the value of their lands during the ravages of the Black Plague. This would have provided freedom for many serfs, as well as given them the opportunity to purchase land at a low price. Answer choice (D) can be eliminated immediately.

Question 13

Overview: In question 13, a politician argues for ending trade with a major trading partner on the grounds that the trading partner engages in serious human rights violations. The politician notes that her country has always set a clear standard on the issue of human rights and that the only consistent path to take is one of ending trade with the trading partner. The question then asks for the answer choice that best expresses the assumption on which the politician's argument depends. To select the correct answer, the student first needs to identify the politician's primary claim: that despite the financial benefits of trade, the politician's country must end trade with a partner that is committing human rights violations, because the politician's country opposes any kind of human rights violations. It is important to note that the human rights violations are coming from a *chief* trading partner, so ending trade with that partner could create a void in the economy of the politician's country. Because the politician does not address this void, it is safe to assume that she believes the economic void will not compare with the moral void that would follow continued trade with the trading partner. The correct answer choice will reflect this assumption.

The Correct Answer:

C **Answer choice (C)** best expresses the assumption on which the politician's argument depends: the importance of holding up the standard of human rights is more important than the economic loss that would occur from ending trade with the trading partner. Therefore, answer choice (C) is correct.

The Incorrect Answers:

A The politician might very well hope that ending trade with the major trading partner will lead to an end in the human rights violations. She does mention that her country should "set the standard and encourage respect for human rights around the world." But this does not in itself suggest that the assumption for her conclusion is based on an expected end to human rights violations. The politician's statement indicates instead that she believes her country should be willing to end trade with the trading partner because it is the right thing to do and because her country "cannot risk practicing a double standard." It might be that the trading partner will end its human rights violations in order to resume trade with the politician's country. But nothing in the passage suggests that this is the primary assumption on which the politician's argument depends, so answer choice (A) is incorrect.

B The products currently being traded might very well be closely connected to the human rights violations, but there is nothing in the politician's statement that implies this. Answer choice (B) is incorrect due to insufficient information to support the assumption.

D The nature of the politician's responsibilities might contribute to her information about the trading partner that is committing human rights violations. But her responsibilities do not, in and of themselves, contribute to the assumption on which her argument depends. If anything, the politician is simply doing her job. Answer choice (D) is incorrect, because it is not immediately relevant to the assumption of the argument.

E Answer choice (E) describes more of a result rather than a cause; that is to say, it indicates a desired effect of ending trade with the trading partner but does not necessarily indicate the assumption on which the politician's argument depends. The politician notes, "We must instead set the standard and encourage respect for human rights around the world." So, she is encouraging her country to set an international standard that should be adopted internationally. But again, this is not the *assumption* on which her argument depends. Answer choice (E) is incorrect.

Question 14

Overview: Question 14 presents a letter to the editor of a Dublin-based newspaper, in which the writer claims that the Irish government should stop funding the teaching of the Gaeilge (or traditional Irish) language in Irish schools because this language has historically been used as the language of Irish revolutionaries. The letter writer posits that, because of this history, the language will divide rather than unite and thus should not be funded by the government. The question asks the student to identify the flaw in the letter writer's reasoning. The primary point to note is that the letter writer makes sweeping assumptions about the role of the language in contributing to events in Ireland's history. There is a comment in the beginning that this is the "traditional" language, indicating that this is the language of Ireland's past and an inherent part of its culture. But the letter writer then goes on to say that this traditional language is connected primarily to revolution and will thus create "unrest" and "division" in Ireland. Given that the letter writer offers no real historical data to support this, nor an explanation about why or how the language itself contributed to unrest and division, the correct answer choice will reflect the letter writer's failure to explain how past events will *inevitably* become current problems simply by teaching the language.

The Correct Answer:

B **Answer choice (B)** correctly explains the flaw in the letter writer's reasoning: that the historical events will occur again simply through the teaching of a language and that the language itself will contribute to unrest and division in Ireland. Answer choice (B), therefore, is correct.

The Incorrect Answers:

A, E Although the letter writer certainly fails to explain that language is an important part of a culture and offers people a link to their past, these options do not address the specific claims made by the author, i.e. do not point out a specific flaw in the author's own explicit reasoning. Answer choices (A) and (E) are incorrect.

C Rather than relying on obsolete sociological data, the letter writer fails to provide *any* data, making a claim about the role of the language in Irish revolutions without offering any historical information to support this claim. Answer choice (C) is clearly incorrect.

D Answer choice (D) is incorrect because the author does not focus on an *isolated historical event*, claiming instead that the language is "the language of revolution among the Irish and has done more throughout history to contribute to unrest and even open conflict in Ireland than it has done to bring about peace." This indicates a series of historical events rather than just one. Answer choice (D), then, is incorrect.

Question 15

Overview: Question 15 asks the student to consider a passage about a local farmer's interest in establishing a certified organic farm, and in particular the farmer's concerns about the cost of set-up. Since the passage notes that the certified organic farm requires fewer and less expensive supplies than a non-organic farm, and that the maintenance cost is relatively low, the student is asked to select an answer choice that best explains the farmer's concerns about cost. The correct answer choice will supply a clear explanation for where the cost is involved—some outside expense that is related directly to the *set-up* of the farm.

The Correct Answer:

D **Answer choice (D)** most clearly explains the reason for the farmer's concerns about cost. Although the cost of supplies and maintenance might be lower than that of a non-organic farm, the cost of the certification itself is very high, creating a financial burden for the farmer as he tries to establish the certified organic farm. Answer choice (D) is correct.

The Incorrect Answers:

A, C Although the demand in the community for organic food, as well as the presence of three other large organic farms, might affect the farmer's success in the long run, these factors do not affect the cost of set-up, which is the farmer's concern. Answer choices (A) and (C) provide irrelevant information, so both are incorrect.

B Answer choice (B) clearly contradicts the statement made in the passage: "A certified organic farm requires far fewer supplies than a non-organic farm." Therefore, answer choice (B) cannot be correct and should be eliminated immediately.

E The passage notes that the certified organic farm requires fewer supplies and that these supplies are less costly when compared to the supplies required on a non-organic farm. As a result, even if the supplies are unique and must be special-ordered, as answer choice (E) claims, they still should not contribute to the cost about which the farmer is concerned. Answer choice (E) is thus incorrect.

Question 16

Overview: In question 16, the student is asked to consider statements made in a commercial and to select an answer choice that exhibits similarly flawed reasoning. The commercial specifically states that the product being touted, Extra-Strength Spray-On Hair Growth, will enable men to re-grow the hair that they've lost, claiming that if men *do not* try the product, they will have *no chance* of re-growing their hair. The flaw in this reasoning is that the commercial assumes that there is no way a person will be able to re-grow his hair without using Extra-Strength Spray-On Hair Growth. But there could be other factors that will allow a person to re-grow hair (for instance, surgical implants, or another commercial hair growth product). The correct answer will mirror the structure of the argument given in the commercial. The structure is as follows: given one condition (use of Extra-Strength Spray-On Hair Growth), there is a positive result (hair re-growth); given the absence of the first condition (use of Extra-Strength Spray-On Hair Growth), there will be *no* chance for the positive result (hair re-growth).

The Correct Answer:

A **Answer choice (A)** offers the best comparison for similarly flawed reasoning. The answer choice claims that students who attend universities are more successful, so all students should attend universities in order to be successful and avoid failure. But this assumes that there is no way a student can be successful and avoid failure except by attending a university. The flaw in this is that there might be other ways a student could be successful (for instance, by attending a trade school, becoming an apprentice, or by getting a job). Answer choice (A) most closely mirrors the structure of the reasoning given in the commercial and is correct.

The Incorrect Answers:

B Answer choice (B) does not follow the same structure of the commercial; it does not first state that a positive result will follow from a certain action and then go on to claim that the only way to achieve that result is by following that action. Answer choice (B) is incorrect.

C Answer choice (C) states that ovens develop a buildup of food residue over time and thus should be cleaned immediately. But this answer does not explicitly indicate that a positive result will follow from a given action, in the way that the passage does. Answer choice (C) is not immediately parallel to the argument in the passage, so it can be eliminated.

D Answer choice (D) does not indicate that the only way to lessen toxicity is to buy green cleaning products, so the argument is not immediately parallel. Answer choice (D) is incorrect.

E Answer choice (E) bears no similarity to the passage. This answer choice states that Stan is unpopular because of his temper, so he will be removed from the team; the structure here is nothing like the structure of the argument given in the commercial, so answer choice (E) is incorrect and can be eliminated immediately.

Questions 17 and 18

Overview: Questions 17 and 18 discuss plans by the state of Hawaii to build a nuclear power plant in a town on the leeward coast of Oahu. The townspeople are not happy with this plan and have acquired a spokesperson to explain their concerns about the intended facility. According to the spokesperson, the town's primary fear is that the new nuclear power plant will create another incident like the Chernobyl disaster; the spokesperson cites details of that disaster, including its long-term effects. Question 17 asks for the answer choice that most undermines the spokesperson's claims; question 18 asks for the problem that most undermines the state's plans to build the facility. To answer question 17, the student should begin by noting the main point of the spokesperson's argument: the people of the town are opposed to the building of the nuclear power plant because they fear an explosion like the one that happened at Chernobyl. To answer question 18, the student needs to consider which answer choice has the greatest effect on the state's plans by taking into account the options among the answer choices—the answer choice that provides a clear problem with the construction or running of the plant will be correct.

Question 17

The Correct Answer:

C **Answer choice (C)** explains the problem with the spokesperson's argument. In a discussion of an event that occurred over two decades before, the spokesperson fails to consider whether technology has improved since then (particularly in light of the reasonable assumption that since the events at Chernobyl, nuclear engineers would be motivated to ensure that such an accident would not happen again). Because answer choice (C) states specifically that current nuclear power plants are designed to prevent similar accidents, answer choice (C) is correct.

The Incorrect Answers:

A Answer choice (A) approaches a part of the problem in the spokesperson's argument, but it does not undermine it completely. This answer choice suggests that the fears of the people in the town are not justified, but offers only a vague claim that they *cannot be applied.* Without further information to explain *why* they cannot be applied (such as the correct answer choice provides), this is simply not enough to undermine the argument effectively. Answer choice (A), therefore, is incorrect.

B The role of the spokesperson as a paid lobbyist against nuclear power might motivate him to speak on the town's behalf, but this does not necessarily undermine his argument in any way. If anything, it simply explains why he was hired. Answer choice (B) is incorrect.

D, E Although answer choices (D) and (E) offer explanations for why there should be support for the intended nuclear power plant, they both fail to offer a clear statement that *undermines the argument* of the spokesperson. In fact, both answer choices (D) and (E) essentially create red herrings (that is, change the subject) by diverting the spokesperson's argument in a different direction and thus failing to address the substance of the argument. Therefore, answer choices (D) and (E) are incorrect.

QUESTION 18

THE CORRECT ANSWER:

E **Answer choice (E)** indicates the most serious problem that could undermine the state's plans to build the new nuclear power plant. If the facility needs cold water to cool the reactor core, the extra energy required to cool the reactor would add extra expense to the construction and maintenance of the facility, potentially damaging its chances of being a viable energy alternative. Answer choice (E) is correct.

THE INCORRECT ANSWERS:

A The opinion of the community regarding the budget is a legitimate issue. The community's fears alone, however, do not necessarily indicate the most serious problem that could undermine the construction of the plant. Regardless of how well founded (or not) those fears are, these fears can be allayed, or the project might proceed in spite of them. (This contrasts with the answer choice (E): if the statement this answer choice describes were true, it is very unlikely that the plant would be built.) Answer choice (A) is correct.

B Although the value of the jobs that the plant will bring into the community is a worthwhile consideration, answer choice (B) offers too little detail to present a problem that is as serious as the problem indicated in the correct answer choice. Therefore, this answer choice is incorrect.

C Answer choice (C) does raise questions about the connection between state officials and the managers of the nuclear power plant, but this alone does not necessarily mean that there is corruption involved. Answer choice (C) does not contain enough information to undermine the state's plans and is thus incorrect.

D The plans of the local builder do not by themselves necessarily present a problem as serious as the problem described in the correct answer choice; again, the latter would almost certainly prevent the building of the plant, while this is not true of answer choice (D). Answer choice (D) is thus incorrect.

QUESTION 19

Overview: In question 19, the student is given information about the female earless seal and the events surrounding gestation and breeding. According to the passage, the female earless seal gestates for anywhere from nine to eleven months (depending on the variety of earless seal) and gives birth to and nurses only one pup at a time. The passage notes that during a bad season up to three female earless seals in a colony will die three months after giving birth, although all of the pups usually survive. Considering that other female seals cannot nurse orphaned pups—since each lactating female can nurse only a single pup—a natural expectation is that the pups would die with their mothers, since they have no one to nurse them. However, the pups all survive. The question asks the student to select an answer choice that best explains this discrepancy.

The Correct Answer:

D **Answer choice (D)** indicates that the mother seals nurse the pups only up to a month at the longest, suggesting that after a month the pups are capable of locating food for themselves. This answer choice thus provides a sufficient explanation for why the mother seals might die three months after giving birth, while the pups survive: the pups are finished nursing by this point and can find their own food. Answer choice (D) is correct.

The Incorrect Answers:

A Answer choice (A) contradicts the statement in the passage that the mother seals give birth to and nurse only one pup at a time and then use most of their energy to nurse that single pup, fasting while lactating. Answer choice (A) cannot be correct.

B Answer choice (B), although interesting, is irrelevant to explaining the discrepancy. The question asks for a reason that the pups survive although the mothers do not; answer choice (B) simply diverts from this point to say that very often the mothers do not die. Moreover, answer choice (B) ignores the statement in the question about the reason for mothers dying *during a bad season*. Answer choice (B) is clearly incorrect and can be eliminated immediately.

C Answer choice (C) does not explain why seal pups survive even when their mothers die. It is not surprising that some female seals do not give birth (for instance, because they are not sexually mature). The existence of such seals alone does not explain why more pups survive (there is nothing in the passage to suggest they would nurse the orphaned pups, for example).

E As with answer choice (B), answer choice (E) ignores the central question by offering interesting but irrelevant information. The question asks for a reason for the discrepancy between mother seals dying three months after giving birth while the pups survive. Answer choice (E) merely provides information about some of the mothers living up to six months. Because this is unrelated to why pups live when mothers die, answer choice (E) is incorrect.

Question 20

Overview: Question 20 presents information about William Paley, a Christian apologist remembered for developing the watchmaker analogy: if a person came upon a watch and knew nothing about watches, would that person believe the watch to have simply appeared or to have no designer behind it? Paley thought not. Paley argued that a watch contains such complex mechanisms that a person would naturally assume the watch to have an intelligent designer. Similarly, the universe displays a vast complexity, and according to Paley we can assume that it has an intelligent designer as well. The passage notes that Paley's argument is often thought to be flawed. The question asks the student to identify the flaw in the reasoning by selecting an answer choice that best expresses the nature of the logical fallacy. (The student does not need to know specific details about logical fallacies; within the answer choices there are enough details to help the student select the correct answer.)

The Correct Answer:

B Paley's analogy is weak because it does not establish a clear comparison between a watch and the universe. In other words, there is not enough similarity between a watch and the universe to create a strong and effective analogy (for instance, a watch is small and the universe is vastly larger; a watch does not last very long, relatively speaking, and the universe has existed for a very long time). **Answer choice (B)** is thus correct.

The Incorrect Answers:

A There is nothing within Paley's analogy to suggest he is creating a distraction; rather, he is making a specific comparison between two items. Answer choice (A) is incorrect.

C Nothing in the passage suggests that Paley is attacking any person on personal grounds. Answer choice (C) is clearly incorrect.

D Paley uses a comparison between a watch and the universe, but at no point does his argument clearly appeal to the sympathies of others. In this particular example, an appeal to sympathy might consist of an attempt to win over supporters by appealing to religious views. As the passage does not indicate that Paley does this, answer choice (D) cannot be correct.

E Paley does not at any point appeal to any specific authority. An appeal to authority involves a clear appeal to an outside source, such as religious figures or biblical claims. Paley clearly does not do this in the passage. Answer choice (E) is incorrect.

Question 21

Overview: Question 21 presents information about the condition of plant growth in Iceland. According to the passage, the Icelandic climate forbids much new plant growth and delays normal plant growth considerably. Apparently, only one species of tree exists in Iceland, because previous residents in past centuries cut down most of the trees, and few have been able to grow back. Additionally, the passage notes that the plant life is exceedingly delicate and that off-road vehicles are not allowed in certain places, while hikers are expected to avoid stepping on certain plants. The question asks the student to identify which of the answer choices is most correct given the statements made in the passage. The student is essentially being asked to make an inference. Note that this question does *not* ask for the main point of the passage, so the statement that is correctly inferred will not necessarily be the primary focus of the passage; it will simply be something that can be deduced from what is stated in the passage.

The Correct Answer:

E Of all the answer choices, **answer choice (E)** is the only one that can correctly be inferred from the information in the passage. The author states that "little plant growth will be able to survive" in Iceland, that "plants require a long period of time to grow in Iceland," and that "plant life in Iceland is also notoriously delicate." This suggests that off-road vehicles have the potential to destroy plant life, leaving plants unable to grow back for long periods of time or, in some cases, unable to grow back at all. Therefore, answer choice (E) is correct.

The Incorrect Answers:

A The passage notes quite explicitly, "Because of both the severe cold and the severe heat, plants require a long period of time to grow in Iceland." This indicates that the extreme heat of the volcanoes would not encourage plants to grow any better than the extreme cold of other parts of Iceland. Answer choice (A) is incorrect.

B The passage states that the plant life is "notoriously delicate" and that it takes years for plants to grow back. Answer choice (B) contradicts this, so it cannot be correct. Therefore, answer choice (B) can be eliminated immediately.

C The passage does state that one species of tree survives in Iceland, but it does not identify that species or imply what it might be. Answer choice (C) is incorrect.

D Although the information in answer choice (D) might be accurate, there is nothing in the passage to suggest that it is. The passage notes only that Iceland's climate forbids extensive plant growth and that plants can take a very long time to grow. Therefore, the details in answer choice (C) cannot be inferred from the passage, so it must be eliminated. Answer choice (C) is clearly incorrect.

Question 22

Overview: Question 22 presents details about the Highland Cattle, the shaggy breed of cattle iconic to the Scottish landscape. The author mentions that the Highland Cattle are strong and "resilient" and that they have lived in Scotland for an extensive period of time. The author also notes that the Highland Cattle have traditionally lived in the wild, are well-used to the harsh Highland climate and might live up to twenty years and give birth fifteen times. The question asks what inference can be drawn from the statements in the passage. Note that this question does *not* ask for the main point, so the student must look at each answer choice carefully to decide which is most likely to be correct.

The Correct Answer:

C The author states specifically, "The Highland Cattle are most common in the remote areas of the Highlands where they live and breed wild, and they are known for their hardy ability to withstand the elements." The author also states in the previous sentence that the Highland Cattle have lived in the Scottish Highlands for "unknown centuries." This suggests that the cattle have found a way to adapt to the harsh northern climate of Scotland during the centuries that they have lived there and have thus learned to survive in that climate. **Answer choice (C)**, therefore, is correct.

The Incorrect Answers:

A The author of the passage notes that the Highland Cattle have traditionally lived wild in the Scottish Highlands, but there is nothing in the passage to suggest that the cattle are not good for human consumption and can be used only for grazing. Answer choice (A), then, cannot be inferred from the passage and is thus incorrect.

B Although the passage indicates that the Highland Cattle are native to Scotland and have adapted to the climate of Scotland, the passage does not necessarily suggest that this is the *only* breed that can survive in Scotland. The author focuses almost exclusively on the cattle in the Highland region of Scotland; other breeds might very well be able to survive in southern parts of Scotland. Answer choice (B) states details that are not supported by the information in the passage, so it can be eliminated.

D The author of the passage makes no mention of the interaction between Highland Cattle and human residents of the Highlands, so answer choice (D) cannot be inferred from the information in the passage. It can be eliminated immediately.

E The passage does not make claims on the availability of food for the Highland Cattle, so this answer choice cannot reasonably be inferred. (Rather, as the author notes that Highland Cattle have lived wild in the Highlands for "unknown centuries," it stands to reason that the availability of food has been adequate). Answer choice (E) is incorrect.

Question 23

Overview: Question 23 gives information about the vision deficiency known as colorblindness, wherein sufferers have varying degrees of an inability to distinguish color. The author explains that colorblindness is believed to originate from a mutation of the X chromosome. The author also states that men have an XY chromosome makeup, while women have an XX chromosome makeup. The question asks for a statement that may be inferred from the passage, based on the information contained within it.

THE CORRECT ANSWER:

D At the end of the passage, the author notes, "Men carry a single X chromosome, possessing an XY-chromosome makeup, while women carry two X chromosomes, thus having the potential to combat colorblindness with an extra X chromosome." This suggests that men are more likely to be colorblind than women because men have only a single X chromosome. Of all the answer choices, **answer choice (D)** can best be inferred from the passage, so it is correct.

THE INCORRECT ANSWERS:

A The author makes no comment on the population percentage of colorblindness sufferers, so it is impossible to infer safely that colorblindness is a rare condition. The student might know from prior knowledge that colorblindness *is* a fairly rare condition, but the question asks what can be inferred from the passage, not what the student already knows to be true. As answer choice (A) cannot be inferred, it cannot be correct.

B Again, the information contained within answer choice (B) might well be true, but it cannot be inferred from the passage. The author notes only that colorblindness "limits the ability of the sufferer to see certain colors clearly. The condition may affect a person in varying degrees, ranging from mild colorblindness with a red or green color deficiency to complete colorblindness with no ability to distinguish any colors beside dim shades of brown." This in itself does not suggest clearly that colorblindness sufferers would be able to see camouflage well, so answer choice (B) is incorrect.

C The author does not discuss the way that colorblindness is passed on, much less the fact that colorblindness is a hereditary condition. Although the author does imply that women are less likely to be colorblind than men, the author does *not* necessarily imply that women alone pass the condition on. Answer choice (C) cannot be inferred from the passage, so it is incorrect.

E As with answer choice (C), the author does not discuss whether colorblindness is an inherited condition. So, it is impossible to determine from the passage if the author also believes that colorblindness can be tested at birth. Answer choice (E) infers details that are not supported by the passage, so it is incorrect.

QUESTION 24

Overview: Question 24 presents information about the historic location of Jamaica Inn, which was also the setting for a book of the same name by Daphne du Maurier. According to the author, the real Jamaica Inn is set on Bodmin Moor, in Cornwall, and in du Maurier's book the owners of the inn are participating in the criminal act of wrecking (luring ships to the coastline for the purpose of destroying and plundering them). The author of the passage notes that ghost stories are believed to be the source for du Maurier's book, but that the story of wrecking does match actual events that occurred along the Cornish coast during the time setting of the book *Jamaica Inn*. The question asks the student to identify which of the answer choices best summarizes the main point of the passage. The student should first identify the main point of the passage: although not completely historic in its plot, du Maurier's *Jamaica Inn* discusses real historic events that occurred in Cornwall. The answer choice that reflects this most clearly will be correct.

The Correct Answer:

B **Answer choice (B)** best restates the information above: that du Maurier took some creative license with plot but used historic events for her story about Jamaica Inn. Answer choice (B), therefore, is the correct answer.

The Incorrect Answers:

A The author makes no mention of literary historians, mentioning only that Daphne du Maurier's story of *Jamaica Inn* is "hardly an historic textbook" but contains accurate historic information about events on the Cornish coast. Answer choice (A), therefore, infers details that are not supported by the passage and do not reflect the main point; so, answer choice (A) is incorrect.

C The passage does indicate that the information in answer choice (C) is correct: lights *were* lit along the coastline to lure ships in. This information, however, is *not the main point* of the passage and reflects only a supporting detail. Answer choice (C), then, cannot be correct.

D The author does not discuss Daphne du Maurier's other books, nor is there any information in the passage to imply anything about the setting for other du Maurier books. Nor, of course, does this detail express the main point of the passage (The fact that this piece of information is true is irrelevant; the question is asking for the main point of the statements in the passage.) Answer choice (D) is incorrect.

E Answer choice (E) directly contradicts a statement made in the passage: "This being said, wrecking was a real activity in Cornwall during the eighteenth and nineteenth centuries." Therefore, answer choice (E) can be eliminated immediately for ignoring key information in the passage.

Question 25

Overview: The final question in the second Logical Reasoning section of the test discusses discoveries made by psychologists about the differences between the way adults and children learn to play the piano. The author states that the learning differences are due largely to differences in mind development: children's minds develop in such a way that they learn "certain skills more quickly and more effectively than adults." At the same time, the motor skills of children develop differently, so they do not learn to play as quickly as adults might; however, their minds allow them to *recall* the pieces better than adults can. Finally, the author notes that adults retain muscle memory and can reproduce the pieces merely by remembering the fingering of the pieces, implying that children actually retain a better memory of the piece itself and the notes and do not have to rely only on muscle memory. The question then asks which of the answer choices *cannot* be concluded from the passage. This means, of course, that four of the answer choices are implied in the passage, so the student needs to consider each answer choice carefully.

The Correct Answer:

C The author states early in the passage, "the piano is an instrument that knows no one age for learning and presents multiple opportunities for the successful attainment of musical skills." This suggests that the piano is *one* instrument that both adults and children can learn to play. This does not imply, however, that the piano is the *only* instrument that adults and children can learn to play. **Answer choice (C)** cannot be concluded from the passage, so it is the correct answer.

THE INCORRECT ANSWERS:

A The author states the information in answer choice (A) directly in the passage: "It does, however, offer a variety of challenges both to children and to adults—due to the differences in mind development." So, answer choice (A) can be inferred from the passage and is thus incorrect.

B At the end of the passage, the author notes, "At the same time, adults are more likely to retain the muscle memory of the pieces that they learn and reproduce them blindly, just by allowing their fingers to recall the correct notes." Therefore, answer choice (B) is clearly a conclusion that can be drawn from the passage and is thus incorrect.

D In the second sentence of the passage, the author states, "In particular, the piano is an instrument that knows no one age for learning and presents multiple opportunities for the successful attainment of musical skills." This means that answer choice (D) is a conclusion that can be drawn from the passage. So, answer choice (D) can be eliminated as incorrect.

E The author notes in the passage, "How quickly children learn is often limited by their motor skills." This suggests that the fully-developed motor skills of adults allow them to learn the hand and finger movements more quickly than children, so answer choice (E) is a conclusion that can be drawn from the passage. Answer choice (E) is thus incorrect.

Writing Sample Topic

How to Approach the Sample Essay

There is no right or wrong answer for the writing sample, and LSAC does not actually give the essay a score. But the law schools to which the students apply will receive a copy of the essay, so students need to shape a response that indicates their writing skills to these schools. There are several important considerations to keep in mind when developing the essay:

1. Schools want to know that students have strong communication skills, so the essay should be clear and concise and provide a solid response to the topic, with a strong development of each paragraph.
2. The essay should stay entirely on topic: students should not veer off the point by including unnecessary examples or by failing to address the primary focus of the topic. The key is to remain relevant and answer the topic question with clear exposition.
3. Essay writing establishes that a student is able to develop persuasive ideas and organize them effectively. Schools look for these skills, so the essay provides students with the opportunity to indicate an ability to make a credible and well-developed argument in written form.

Practice Test #2

Section I

Time – 35 minutes

25 Questions

Directions: The questions in this section are based on the reasoning contained in brief statements or passages. For some questions, more than one of the choices could conceivably answer the question. However, you are to choose the best answer; that is, the response that most accurately and completely answers the question. You should not make assumptions that are by commonsense standards implausible, superfluous, or incompatible with the passage. After you have chosen the best answer, blacken the corresponding space on your answer sheet.

1. **Sleep Specialist: Insomnia is a sign of potentially serious health risks and should not be ignored, especially in women. Doctors often diagnose women with depression when in reality they are suffering from insomnia as a result of sleep apnea. Sleep apnea is a condition in which the sleeper briefly stops breathing and thus wakes up repeatedly during the night to take a breath. It is seldom misdiagnosed in men because they snore, and doctors thus recognize signs of sleep apnea. In women, however, doctors may fail to identify sleep apnea and instead lean toward a diagnosis of depression. All women who have received a diagnosis of depression should see a female doctor to be reevaluated for insomnia and sleep apnea.**

   The reasoning in the sleep specialist's conclusion is flawed because it does which of the following?

   (A) The sleep specialist claims that women do not snore, with the result that doctors cannot identify sleep apnea correctly.
   (B) The sleep specialist assumes that the doctors who provided the false diagnoses of depression were male.
   (C) The sleep specialist fails to explain the health risks that may come from misdiagnosed insomnia.
   (D) The sleep specialist incorrectly argues that sleep apnea is a sign of depression.
   (E) The sleep specialist ignores other causes of sleep apnea and thus undermines the main point of the argument.

2. ***Adelaide:*** **Mainstream cleaning supplies are dangerous for people, because they contain toxic chemicals such as phosphates. Young children are especially at risk for asthma and other diseases from these airborne chemicals, plus some of the cleaning products can imitate estrogen and cause severe health problems for women. Natural cleaning products are safe and effective, however, so people should consider switching to healthier and more environmentally friendly cleaning alternatives.**

   ***Marcel*:** **But natural cleaning products are not as strong as the mainstream products and often fail to provide the same level of cleanliness. If parents keep the cleaning products out of reach, the products will not create a serious risk for children. And the mainstream cleaning products are cheaper and thus more economical for families to purchase.**

   Marcel responded to Adelaide's argument by doing which of the following?

   (A) Ignoring the main point that Adelaide is making and redirecting his focus to different topics
   (B) Ceding the main point of Adelaide's argument but suggesting a problem that Adelaide fails to address
   (C) Relying on apocryphal and unsupported information to formulate a separate argument
   (D) Raising an argument that Adelaide does not clearly address and offering an alternative take on the topic that Adelaide is discussing
   (E) Overlooking important details of Adelaide's argument and thus failing to counter her claims with sufficient objection

3. **The Russian *Domostroy* is a set of principles that dates from the fourteenth century and was intended to guide upper-class Russians in the establishment of solid family life. The *Domostroy* utilized quotes from the Old Testament as well as traditional Russian stories. Today the *Domostroy* has strongly negative connotations due to its suggestions of an exclusively patriarchal tone, and at least two nineteenth-century Russian novelists referenced it as a negative feature of medieval Russian life. The negative associations overlook the significance of the Domostroy, however, by failing to appreciate its importance to Russian families and its necessity for ensuring the stability of the Russian merchant class.**

   Which of the following best summarizes the main point of the passage above?

   (A) The *Domostroy* is a valuable tool for scholars who are studying medieval family life in fourteenth-century Russia.
   (B) The *Domostroy* was once an important feature of life among upper-class Russians but now has clear negative connotations.
   (C) The *Domostroy* was particularly odious to nineteenth-century Russian novelists who were eager to leave medieval expectations of Russian family life in the past.
   (D) The *Domostroy* contained references and advice that were useful only to the upper classes in fourteenth-century Russia.
   (E) The *Domostroy* has negative connotations now but may be valued for its contribution to Russian family life and the survival of a merchant class in Russia.

4. **Since 1978, the Hawaiian green turtle has been listed among endangered species. In the nineteenth century and in the early part of the twentieth century, the Hawaiian green turtle was considered a delicacy and was frequently caught for its value as a luxury food item. Its shell and other nonedible features were also considered valuable on the open market. Today the green turtle is heavily protected, and there are strict laws against capturing or harming the large turtles. The green turtles remain on the endangered species list, however, and there are signs that the green turtle population is not increasing as quickly as had been hoped.**

   Which of the following best explains the anomaly of the ongoing diminishment of the green turtle population in spite of the endangered species status?

   (A) The Hawaiian green turtle is omnivorous but has lately been forced to live primarily as a vegetarian.
   (B) The Hawaiian green turtle is known for its very long life, with females living up to 750 years, but it has not been living as long in recent years.
   (C) The Hawaiian green turtle has faced problems among its species, such as tumors that target the young turtles in particular.
   (D) The Hawaiian green turtle navigates its migration habits based on ocean currents, and the onset of global warming has altered the traditional currents.
   (E) The ghost crab is a traditional predator of the Hawaiian green turtle hatchlings at their nesting sites in the French Frigate Shoals.

QUESTIONS 5 AND 6 REFER TO THE FOLLOWING PASSAGE:

The 1936 North American heat wave remains one of the hottest and most destructive on record, causing serious environmental and economic problems. Beginning in June of 1936 and lasting only through the summer, temperatures rose sharply across the United States, attacking the Midwest and Southwest in particular. Even in Canada, scientists recorded dangerously high temperatures. Air conditioners did not have common distribution in homes and businesses until some years later, and the heat-related deaths rose to upwards of 5,000 people. Not surprisingly, the heat caused problems for the most vulnerable members of society. The temperatures were so high, in fact, that the soil was depleted of necessary bacteria, and the crops withered away, leaving a serious shortage of corn and wheat. The drought that accompanied the heat wave stripped the soil of all nutrients, and the upper layers of the soil quite literally blew away, developing into serious dust storms in the Midwest.

5. **Which of the following may be assumed strictly based on the information provided in the passage above?**

   (A) The heat wave of 1936 damaged the crops seriously, but the temperatures returned to normal the next year, so farmers did not have problems with the crops in 1937.
   (B) The temperatures did not rise as high in Canada as they did in the United States, and thus the damage in Canada was not as extreme as it was in the United States.
   (C) It is certain that fewer people would have died in the 1936 heat wave had air conditioners been common in homes.
   (D) The problems from the heat wave of 1936 were exacerbated because the United States was in the midst of the Great Depression.
   (E) Because of the damage to the crops from the heat wave in 1936, prices of crops such as corn and wheat rose very high.

6. **All of the following may be assumed from the information in the passage above EXCEPT:**

(A) The temperatures noted during the North American heat wave of 1936 remain some of the highest ever recorded.
(B) Because extremely hot summers generally follow very cold winters, the winter of 1936 remains one of the coldest on record.
(C) The unusually high temperatures during the 1936 heat wave ceased to be a problem by October of 1936.
(D) By killing essential bacteria that the soil needed to remain intact, the heat left the upper layers of the soil vulnerable to wind.
(E) The heat had the biggest impact on the very old and the very young, among others.

7. **Psychologist: Violence in video games can have a severe effect on children, even impelling them towards committing violent acts. A recent study indicated an incident in which an eleven-year-old boy played a video game that contained excessive images of violence, and then he perpetrated a violent crime similar to the one portrayed in the video game. Violent video games thus lead to violence among children, and they should be carefully restricted.**

The weakness in the psychologist's argument is similar to the weakness in which of the following examples of reasoning?

(A) A homeschooled student has won the national spelling bee due to the excellent education received at home. Therefore, homeschooling is shown to be a valid form of education, and all homeschooled students may be expected to excel.
(B) A popular home decorating program offers excellent do-it-yourself tips for those who would like to decorate their own homes without employing an expensive designer. Therefore, all homeowners planning to redecorate can utilize the resources of this program to decorate their homes.
(C) A university known for its strong program for training elementary school teachers has over 200 students graduated and ready to enter the school system. Due to the value of the skills provided in the university's program, the school system can expect that all of the graduates will make excellent teachers.
(D) A well-known celebrity has experienced positive results from taking a rather questionable supplement not yet approved by the FDA. Due to the significance of the celebrity's results, our nutritional supplement company will begin stocking this product.
(E) Studies show that music classes broaden the minds of students and provide increased awareness for other subjects. Therefore, schools should begin adding music classes to the curriculum to benefit students.

8. **Political changes have had a significant impact on the art of the Communist country of North Korea. Early art forms were dominated by influences from the Soviet Union and China, but today North Korean art indicates a more relevant cultural influence from its own revolutionary material. Films and sports have proven to be the most popular forms. On the other hand, North Korean artists who fled North Korea and relocated to Europe and the United States have continued to produce art that indicates outside influences. Many of these artists have melded their own traditional techniques and images with those of Western artists to produce art that is a unique combination of East and West. The North Korean expatriates are particularly known for turbulent images of landscapes.**

   The author of the passage above suggests which of the following about early North Korean art?

   (A) All early North Korean art was primarily political in its topic and focus.
   (B) Unlike the artists who have left North Korea and moved to the West, artists remaining in North Korea do not paint landscapes.
   (C) North Korean art initially took its cue from other Communist states until it developed its own artistic traditions.
   (D) It took many decades of imitating the artistic techniques of other cultures for North Korean artists to generate a uniquely North Korean style.
   (E) North Korean artistic techniques are unlike any in the world, thus making it difficult for North Korean artists to formulate a style for the early North Korean state.

9. **A family is looking into purchasing and installing solar panels at their home in order to apply an alternative energy resource and thus reduce their energy bills. The solar panels store up sunlight each day and convert it to energy for the home, with the more sunlight absorbed creating a surplus of energy for the home and offsetting energy bills. At present, however, the cost of investing in solar panels is comparatively greater than the return investment in decreased energy bills. Because of the expense that is required to produce and market the solar panels, the initial cost can sometimes take more than a decade to realize in energy cost advantage. The family is still planning on investing in the solar panels, however, believing that they will see a return fairly quickly.**

   Based on the information contained within the passage, which of the following, if true, most supports the decision by the family to invest in solar panels?

   (A) The government is now offering incentives to homeowners who invest in solar panels.
   (B) Coal is believed to be the most inexpensive source of energy, and producers expect to see a drop in coal prices soon.
   (C) Silicon is a chief proponent of solar panels for many manufacturers, and silicon production is expected to rise considerably within the next few months.
   (D) With the sharp rise in energy costs, consumer demand for solar panels has increased quickly, with several new manufacturers to begin production soon.
   (E) The family lives in Southern California, where they receive a large amount of sunlight each day.

10. Despite the strict social structure of medieval society, the medieval pilgrimage, made famous by Geoffrey Chaucer's *The Canterbury Tales*, provided an opportunity to lower the social bar. During the pilgrimage, all of the pilgrims were expected to remain together in the same inn during a break in the journey. All talked together, and all worshipped together. In Chaucer's vision of the pilgrimage, each of the pilgrims is asked to tell four tales, with the winner decided by popular vote. Social standing was not a prerequisite for a good story, and each had equal right to the reward. Nevertheless, *The Canterbury Tales* also indicates that the social structure did not disappear entirely on the pilgrimage: each of the pilgrims is initially introduced by order of social position—from the knight to the parson—and the tales are told in the order of introduction. While Chaucer's account is largely fictional, the historicity of his presentation remains unchallenged.

Which of the following best summarizes the main point of the passage above?

(A) Chaucer's *The Canterbury Tales* records the details of medieval pilgrimages authentically.
(B) The pilgrimage provided an opportunity for social barriers to vanish, however temporarily, during the Middle Ages.
(C) As indicated in *The Canterbury Tales*, storytelling was a traditional means of polite entertainment during the medieval pilgrimage.
(D) The medieval pilgrimage presented an opportunity for a relaxed social structure, but as *The Canterbury Tales* indicates, this social structure did not cease to function altogether.
(E) The medieval pilgrimage offered a chance for people from all walks of life to join together in a common activity, regardless of social position.

11. The mistral is a powerful katabatic wind that sweeps through parts of Europe annually and contributes to the climate of Provençe, a large region in the South of France. Katabatic winds are created by the confluence of high-pressure systems and low-pressure systems when the combination of these systems moves downward from a higher elevation and pushes forcefully through a lower elevation. These winds are most notable around mountainous areas, developing into the very powerful blasts that come off the mountain slopes. In Europe the height of the Alps, in combination with the high-pressure winds off the North Atlantic and the low-pressure winds off the Mediterranean, create the formidable mistral that usually blows through Provençe in the winter, forcing the people of that region to adapt: bell-towers remain open in Provençe, and houses face south. At the same time, the air in Provençe is comparatively clear, and the people generally face fewer respiratory problems.

The statements made in the passage above imply which of the following about the mistral?

(A) The powerful winds of the mistral blow impurities and pollution out of the air, leaving it clean.
(B) There are katabatic winds like the mistral around any mountain chain, and the people who live in mountainous areas must learn to adapt to the powerful winds.
(C) Katabatic winds are unique to the South of France, because of the specific geophysical features of that part of Europe.
(D) The mistral is so powerful that it is known to damage structures frequently, requiring adaptation in construction.
(E) The mistral blows through most of Europe, but it is strongest in Provençe.

12. **The Acholi are a traditional agricultural people native to Northern Uganda with culture and traditions that are different from those of the people of Southern Uganda, the Baganda. While the Acholi have always been farmers, the Baganda built up a monarchy and cities over a period of centuries. When the British colonists arrived in Uganda, they chose to utilize the Acholi as a labor force and for lower-ranking military purposes, while they settled their primary colonies in the more familiar political establishment of Southern Uganda. Today, Southern Uganda remains heavily developed and industrialized, while Northern Uganda struggles with regionalized conflicts and has been war-torn for many decades.**

    The passage suggests which of the following about the Acholi people in Northern Uganda?

    (A) The monarchy of the Baganda people in Southern Uganda utilized the Acholi people as a labor force and as soldiers for the military.
    (B) The British viewed the lifestyle of the Baganda people as superior to that of the Acholi, due to the Baganda's development of cities and a monarchy system.
    (C) Because the Acholi people have traditionally been farmers, they were unfamiliar with war until the British arrived.
    (D)The British are entirely responsible for the wars that continue to plague the Acholi people of Southern Uganda.
    (E) The Acholi people welcomed the opportunity to abandon their traditional agricultural lifestyle with the arrival of the British.

13. **The majority of linguistic scholars recognize that language will inevitably evolve over time. What causes this change, however, is the subject of great debate. One respected scholar claims that it is the colloquial, or nonstandard, usages within a language that drive its change and development. In other words, it is not formal speech but rather slang that acts as a catalyst for language evolution. Other scholars argue that it is geographical isolation that leads to the formation of one language, and it is the eventual mingling with other languages and gradual globalization that cause languages to evolve and perhaps even to merge into a single language.**

    The passage supports which of the following claims?

    (A) Colloquial and nonstandard usages have been recognized as significant factors in language evolution.
    (B) Linguistic scholars will probably never be able to come to agreement about what contributes to language evolution.
    (C) With the advent of globalization, different languages will ultimately disappear and fuse into one.
    (D) All languages have a common origin and have gradually evolved into individual languages due to geographical isolation.
    (E) Regardless of the reason for language evolution, languages are recognized to be dynamic and will not remain static.

14. Small Bookstore Owner: Online merchants, including online booksellers, are putting small, local shops out of business through artificially low prices that smaller businesses cannot maintain. These local businesses, such as the local bookstore that I own, have always been an important part of the community and have traditionally offered a place for members of the community to gather in a safe, neutral place for discussion. It would be a mistake to allow these important features of community life to disappear simply because items are cheaper to purchase online. Citizens should demand that restrictions should be placed on online merchants to prevent the eradication of local small businesses.

The small business owner's reasoning about the importance of small, local businesses is based on which of the following assumptions?

(A) The value of community life provided by small businesses outweighs the extra cost that the small, local storeowners must charge for merchandise.
(B) The majority shift to online purchasing is not inevitable if consumers return to purchasing most items in small, local stores.
(C) The artificially high prices of small, local stores are justified due to the overhead costs of storeowners.
(D) The small, local bookstores provide a better venue for community life than other locations and should thus be retained even if other small shops fail.
(E) The government is entirely responsible for keeping small, local businesses alive in a community.

15. *Johan*: Global warming has been sold to the general population as a serious threat, but in reality, there is very little scientific proof that the earth is experiencing anything more than normal climate change over long periods of time. There is scientific truth to the argument that the climate is changing and that the earth is slightly warmer now than it was several decades ago, but there is no proof that this is due to human activity or to environmental pollutants. In reality, the earth experiences gradual climate shifts that result in warmer and cooler climates. We are currently in one of those shifts.

***Andrian*: It is impossible to believe that governments would spend billions of dollars on research to prevent global warming if it were scientifically proven to be a case of normal climate change. Most scientists seem to agree that the earth's climate is changing, and given the output of pollution from mankind, it stands to reason that the pollution has affected some climate change.**

Which of the following best characterizes Andrian's response to Johan's argument?

(A) Andrian ignores the substance of Johan's argument and instead delivers an ad hominem, or personal, attack against Johan.
(B) Andrian relies on faulty evidence to back up his rebuttal to Johan.
(C) Andrian disputes the starting point of Johan's argument but fails to address the evidence that Johan uses in support.
(D) Andrian focuses only on one part of Johan's argument but does not sufficiently challenge the second part of Johan's argument.
(E) Andrian attacks a secondary point of Johan's argument but does not counter the main point effectively.

16. A pharmaceutical company has come under public scrutiny for manufacturing a controversial drug. Tests indicate that the drug provides the advertised results, but there are potentially serious side effects that clearly outweigh the positive results. After extensive further testing, the CEO of the pharmaceutical company has announced that the drug is now safe: "With the approval of the FDA, our new drug may now be marketed and sold to hospitals around the country to respond to a serious medical problem that doctors have been unable to address effectively before now."

Which of the following, if true, most seriously calls into question the pharmaceutical company's claim that their drug is now safe?

(A) Records indicate that the pharmaceutical company has lied in the past about the safety of controversial drugs that it has manufactured.
(B) The pharmaceutical company is receiving a large government grant to enable its improvement of the drug.
(C) The board of the pharmaceutical company is currently under federal investigation for charges of marketing fraud.
(D) A competitor pharmaceutical company is in the process of manufacturing a drug that will offer similar results but without the side effects.
(E) The FDA approval required the altering of certain ingredients within the controversial drug, and there is no evidence that the company made the changes.

17. Ballet Instructor: The Cecchetti style, developed by Enrico Cecchetti in Italy, remains the purest method of classical ballet. While we acknowledge the value of the Russian Vaganova method and the French style of dance, our studio utilizes the Cecchetti method because of its use of consistent teaching and strong technical preparation. The daily regime of similarity in practice and repetition in steps yields the strongest results, and we believe that this will ultimately provide a basis of solid technique. From there, dancers are able to develop personal artistry in their performance. As a result, we proudly offer classes in the Cecchetti style, and many of our dancers have gone on to pursue professional careers.

In making the argument about the value of the Cecchetti style, the ballet instructor assumes which of the following?

(A) The Russian Vaganova method and the French style are both inferior to the Cecchetti method of teaching.
(B) The best professional dancers in the world have been trained in the Cecchetti method.
(C) Developing strong technique is more important than developing artistry in dancers.
(D) Individual artistic style is developed best when built upon a foundation of strong technique.
(E) All ballet schools should shift their teaching styles to the Cecchetti method in order to produce the strongest technical dancers.

18. Unique to the region of Brittany in Northern France, the Breton language descended from the family of Celtic languages known as *Brythonic*. These languages include Welsh and the now-obsolete language of Cornish. After the Anglo-Saxon settlement of Britain, many of the Brythonic peoples relocated: to Wales, to Cornwall, and across the English Channel to Brittany. For a time during the Middle Ages, Breton functioned as a status language for those traveling between Britain and Armorica (or Brittany). After the twelfth century, French became the official language of all France, including Brittany, and the Breton language slowly died out. There are current attempts to revive it but to little avail, and the French government has consistently refused requests to add it as an official language within France.

Which of the following best summarizes the main point of the passage?

(A) The Breton language was once an elite language but has lost much of its status since the Middle Ages.
(B) Formerly an important language between Britain and Northern France, Breton has declined over time despite attempts to revive it.
(C) Given its historical importance as a language of unity between France and England, the French government should recognize Breton officially.
(D) There have been a variety of attempts to revive the Breton language, but it is rapidly on the decline due primarily to the French government's refusal to recognize it.
(E) Given the fact that Breton is a sister language to Welsh and Cornish, the native Breton speakers in Northern France are essentially Celtic.

QUESTIONS 19 AND 20 REFER TO THE FOLLOWING PASSAGE:

In 1997, Colorado doctor Steven Bratman coined the term *orthorexia nervosa* to refer to an eating disorder in which the sufferer has an unhealthy addiction to consuming only healthy foods for the purpose of achieving a holistic lifestyle. According to Dr. Bratman, who actually suffered many symptoms of the condition, those who develop orthorexia nervosa do not begin the road to an eating disorder in the same way that those suffering from anorexia nervosa or bulimia do. Instead, they begin with the best of intentions as they pursue the healthiest diet possible. Along the way, however, their pursuit of health can develop into a dangerous obsession that ultimately harms the body more than it helps, and those with orthorexia nervosa suffer from an eating disorder as serious as anorexia nervosa or bulimia. At present, orthorexia nervosa is not officially recognized as an eating disorder among the medical community, but in the last decade more doctors have come to recognize the legitimacy and seriousness of this condition.

19. The passage supports which of the following claims?

(A) Orthorexia nervosa is a more serious condition than anorexia nervosa or bulimia, because the sufferer begins with the good intention of consuming a healthy diet.
(B) Because it is not currently recognized as an official eating disorder, orthorexia nervosa should not be included under insurance coverage at this time.
(C) Given the seriousness of the condition, orthorexia nervosa should be classified as an eating disorder alongside anorexia nervosa and bulimia.
(D) Because sufferers of orthorexia nervosa begin their condition in the pursuit of a holistic lifestyle through the healthiest possible diet, the condition does have some benefits.
(E) The causes and problems associated with orthorexia nervosa require more medical research before it can be officially classified as an eating disorder.

20. Which of the following may be inferred from the passage above?

(A) The example of Dr. Steven Bratman suggests that orthorexia nervosa is more common among professionals than among any other demographic.
(B) The increase in the number of doctors who now recognize orthorexia nervosa indicates that the medical community is coming to acknowledge the condition.
(C) Unlike other eating disorders, orthorexia nervosa is more of a problem among adults who are concerned with eating well than among teens concerned with being thin.
(D) With the advent of increased interest in healthy and holistic lifestyles, orthorexia nervosa has only manifested itself as an eating disorder in the last few decades.
(E) The medical community in general is resistant to the idea of recognizing orthorexia nervosa as an eating disorder, and only a few doctors diagnose it.

21. Though universally popular and worn every day by women around the world, perfume is known to have several potentially serious health risks. The majority of perfumes contain chemicals such as ethyl acetate and acetone, both of which are recognized as respiratory allergens. At the same time, the majority of allergic reactions to perfumes manifest themselves in skin irritations and, in some cases, severe topical problems. Linalool, a suspected skin allergen, is a perfume ingredient, but it is almost never used in the form that causes topical reactions in perfume wearers.

Which of the following helps to resolve the apparent conflict between the chemical ingredients of perfume and the manifestation of skin allergies?

(A) The inhalation of chemicals that are frequently used in perfumes can cause skin irritation.
(B) Scientists have recently discovered a chemical combination that will enable perfume makers to use non-allergenic ingredients.
(C) When combined with antioxidants, linalool does not manifest itself as a skin allergen in perfumes.
(D) Very few people are actually allergic to perfume, so severe allergic reactions to perfume are rare.
(E) Most perfumes contain either ethyl acetone or acetate, but not both in combination.

22. American author Gertrude Stein is credited with labeling the post-World War I generation a "lost generation." Over time, the phrase came to refer in part to the generation of writers who came to literary maturity after the war. Literary scholars have noticed a trend among these writers. The end of World War I facilitated a turn in the literary consciousness and a definite movement toward modernism in literature, often notable for throwing off the restraints of tradition and conveying an overall sense of emptiness and indifference. Modern literature had been developing prior to the war but was not yet firmly established. Another scholar, however, has also noted an unexpected trend: post-World War I authors have produced more fantasy literature than any other generation in history.

Which of the following may be inferred from the statements made in the passage above?

(A) Post-World War I literature is among the bleakest and most apathetic in all of literary history.
(B) All post-World War I authors rejected the traditions of the past to embrace non-traditional forms of literature.
(C) Literature became the primary outlet of frustrated veterans who had experienced the horrors of World War I.
(D) Relatively few soldiers survived World War I, and those who did were greatly altered by the experience.
(E) The experiences of World War I prompted many authors to turn to literary forms that were not as common before the war.

23. After the publication of *Origin of Species*, Charles Darwin sent a copy to his friend and former tutor Adam Sedgwick, an early geologist who strenuously opposed the idea of natural selection. Sedgwick's response to Darwin was both cautious and kind: he encouraged his friend and one-time pupil to beware of embracing natural selection and claimed that the theory had no scientific proof to back it up. In a later letter to another friend, however, Sedgwick was far more candid about his views. He claimed to be appalled by Darwin's theories and stated forthrightly that they were, without a doubt, untrue and even dangerous.

Based on the information provided in the passage, which of the following best accounts for the difference in tone between Sedgwick's letter to Darwin and his later letter to a friend?

(A) Sedgwick was a notorious flatterer and was more interested in maintaining his friendship with Darwin than in telling him the truth about his own views.
(B) Darwin was acquainted with the recipient of Sedgwick's letter, but Sedgwick was not aware of this and did not know that Darwin would find out eventually.
(C) Sedgwick became angrier about the popularity of Darwin's theories over time and chose to vent his feelings in the later letter.
(D) Sedgwick was hesitant to use his position as a former teacher in order to chide Darwin so openly.
(E) Darwin's response to Sedgwick's original letter was one of open disagreement, and Sedgwick responded by dismissing Darwin's theories to another friend.

24. In 1918, an influenza pandemic struck the globe, leaving at least 20 million people dead. Some have estimated that the number of people killed during the influenza outbreak might reach upwards of 100 million. This particular strain of influenza occurred during the summer months, an unusual case since most flu outbreaks occur in the fall and winter. What makes the 1918 influenza pandemic so fascinating to scientists, however, is that it struck healthy young adults the hardest and took most of its victims from this demographic, leaving young children and older adults otherwise unscathed.

Which of the following best explains the anomaly between the expected victims and the actual demographic that was struck the hardest during the outbreak?

(A) Because the influenza pandemic occurred during World War I, some have suggested that the soldier deaths were combined with influenza deaths.
(B) Governments were unable to acquire vaccines in time to immunize the general population, leaving many vulnerable to the disease.
(C) The 1918 strain is believed to have created a cytokine storm, in which a virus attacks healthy immune systems far more severely than weak immune systems.
(D) Many of the soldiers who caught influenza were already weakened from their service on the front and could not resist the virus.
(E) It is now believed that the influenza strain was manufactured as a biological weapon to be used on soldiers during World War I.

25. Near the city of Budapest in Hungary sits Lake Balaton, the largest lake in central Europe and one of the primary bodies of water in the landlocked country of Hungary. Lake Balaton has had a significant impact on the climate of the surrounding area: it is believed to create an environment for considerably more precipitation than in other regions of Hungary, and the climate itself resembles that of a Mediterranean region, despite the fact that Hungary lies several hundred miles from the Mediterranean Sea. What is more, the soil around Lake Balaton is dense in volcanic ash residue, which is known for containing rich nutrients, and the lake releases small amounts of secondary radiation, providing extra sunlight in the region. Wine is a popular export from the Lake Balaton area.

Which of the following may be inferred from statements made in the passage above?

(A) The volcanic ash is the result of an extinct volcano that permanently affected temperatures near Lake Balaton.
(B) Because of its Mediterranean climate, Lake Balaton is a popular tourist destination for Hungarians and non-Hungarians alike.
(C) Lake Balaton has created a climate and environment that are excellent for vineyards and wine production.
(D) Due to the environmental effects of Lake Balaton, the area around the lake is the greenest and most fertile in Eastern Europe.
(E) Because of the climate, the region of Lake Balaton has a large number of immigrants from Mediterranean countries who bring their knowledge of wine production.

Section II

Time – 35 minutes

24 Questions

Cluster 1:

On a busy road there are six fast food restaurants: McDonalds, Burger King, Jack in the Box, Sonic, Wendy's, and Taco Bell. All the restaurants are on the same side of the road, which runs from west to east, and are next to each other except for the fact that there is a dry cleaner's separating the three on the east from the three on the west.

McDonalds is at an end of the road.
Sonic is to the immediate west of Taco Bell.
McDonalds is not next to either Taco Bell or Sonic.
Burger King is to the west of Wendy's and Sonic, and not next to McDonalds.

1. **Which one of the following stores CANNOT be next to Jack in the Box?**
   (A) Taco Bell
   (B) Burger King
   (C) McDonalds
   (D) Wendy's
   (E) Dry Cleaners

2. **If Burger King is next to Jack in the Box, then Wendy's CANNOT be next to:**
   (A) Dry Cleaners
   (B) Sonic
   (C) Taco Bell
   (D) McDonalds
   (E) End of the street

3. **If Jack in the Box is east of Wendy's, then which one of the following must be false?**
   (A) Burger King is at the end of the street.
   (B) Sonic is to the west of the dry cleaners.
   (C) McDonalds is the east of the dry cleaners.
   (D) Jack in the Box is west of McDonalds.
   (E) Wendy's is next to Taco Bell.

4. **Which one of the following is a possible arrangement of the stores from west to east?**
   (A) McDonalds, Jack in the Box, Wendy's, dry cleaners, Burger King, Sonic, Taco Bell
   (B) McDonalds, Jack in the Box, Burger King, dry cleaners, Wendy's, Sonic, Taco Bell
   (C) Burger King, Jack in the Box, Wendy's, dry cleaners, Sonic, Taco Bell, McDonalds
   (D) Burger King, Sonic, Taco Bell, dry cleaners, Wendy's, McDonalds, Jack in the Box
   (E) Burger King, Taco Bell, Sonic, dry cleaners, Wendy's, Jack in the Box, McDonalds

5. **If Wendy's is next to Sonic, then which one of the following pairs of restaurants must be next to each other?**

   (A) McDonalds and Burger King
   (B) Taco Ball and Wendy's
   (C) Jack in the Box and Burger King
   (D) Sonic and Burger King
   (E) Jack in the Box and Wendy's

6. **If the McDonalds is on the west end of the street, then which one of the following must be false?**

   (A) Burger King is east of Jack in the Box.
   (B) Wendy's is west of Jack in the Box.
   (C) Taco Bell is east of Burger King.
   (D) Jack in the Box is west of Sonic.
   (E) Burger King is next to the dry cleaners.

Cluster 2:

A square serving cart has a total of eight attachments for gallon ice cream containers. There are two attachments on each side and each attachment is directly opposite another one. There are eight different ice cream flavors—Chocolate, Vanilla, Strawberry, Lemon, Pistachio, Banana, Mocha, and Oreo—currently attached to the serving cart.
The Lemon is directly across from the Banana.
The Chocolate is immediately to the left of and on the same side of the cart as the Vanilla.
The Strawberry is next to the Pistachio.

7. **If the Lemon is not next to either the Vanilla or the Chocolate, then which one of the following must be true?**

   (A) Either the Strawberry or the Pistachio is next to the Vanilla.
   (B) Either the Chocolate or the Vanilla is directly across from the Mocha.
   (C) The Banana is next to the Mocha and the Oreo.
   (D) The Oreo must be next to the Lemon.
   (E) The Pistachio is directly across from either the Chocolate or the Vanilla.

8. **If the Mocha is directly across from the Chocolate, then which of the following flavors could be next to the Strawberry?**

   I. Oreo
   II. Lemon
   III. Vanilla

   (A) I only
   (B) II only
   (C) III only
   (D) I and II only
   (E) II and III only

9. **If the Banana is next to the Vanilla and the Oreo is next to the Lemon, which one of the following must be false?**
   (A) The Mocha is next to the Oreo
   (B) The Banana is next to the Strawberry.
   (C) The Banana is between the Vanilla and the Pistachio.
   (D) The Vanilla is directly across from the Mocha.
   (E) The Chocolate is directly across from the Strawberry.

10. **If the Strawberry is to the immediate right of the Banana, then which one of the following is possible?**
   (A) The Pistachio is next to the Lemon.
   (B) The Banana is next to the Chocolate.
   (C) The Mocha is next to the Strawberry.
   (D) The Lemon is next to the Strawberry.
   (E) The Vanilla is next to the Pistachio.

11. **If the Chocolate is next to the Banana, which is next to the Oreo, what is the maximum number of distinct arrangements of the eight flavors around the serving cart?**
   (A) 2
   (B) 3
   (C) 4
   (D) 5
   (E) 6

12. **If the Mocha is next to the Chocolate, which one of the following is a complete and accurate list of the flavors that could be next to the Lemon?**
   (A) Mocha
   (B) Mocha, Oreo
   (C) Mocha, Oreo, Vanilla
   (D) Mocha, Oreo, Strawberry, Pistachio
   (E) Mocha, Oreo, Strawberry, Pistachio, Vanilla

Cluster 3:

A code generator forms codes by combining the letters L, M, N, O, and P using the following rules:
A code may be three to five letters long and the letters may be used multiple times in a code.
If M appears in a code, then it is immediately next to N.
L can only be the first or last letter in a code.
O and P cannot be next to each other in a code.
P can only appear in the second or fourth spot in a code.

13. **Which one of the following is a code?**
   (A) M N L O
   (B) O P N M L
   (C) L M N M
   (D) L O M N P
   (E) L P M O N

14. In the sequence – N M, which of the following could replace the dash at the beginning to make a code?

I. L
II. P
III. M

(A) I only
(B) II only
(C) III only
(D) I and II only
(E) I and III only

15. Which one of the following is NOT a code, but could be made into one by adding a single letter to its beginning?

(A) N O
(B) L N P
(C) O M
(D) N P
(E) M N L O

16. If the fifth rule is eliminated, then which of the following is a code when a P is added to the beginning of it?

(A) L M N P
(B) N P L
(C) O M N
(D) M P L
(E) M N M O L

Cluster 4:

Representatives from six different corporations – F, G, H, I, J, K – meet at a business conference. During the time they are at the conference they decide which of the other corporations, if any, they want to do business with.
K uses unsavory business practices and so only J is willing to do business with it, but K is willing to do business with any of the other corporations.
F is here only for the presentations and is uninterested in doing business with any of the others, but has quality products and all the other corporations want to do business with it.
G doesn't want to do business with three of the other corporations, two of which are I and J.
J wants to do business with all the other corporations except for G.
H and I want to do business with each other and two other corporations, one of which is J.

17. A business partnership is a pair of corporations who want to do business with each other. How many business partnerships were created at this conference?

(A) 1
(B) 2
(C) 3
(D) 4
(E) 5

18. If the two corporations who weren't a member of any business partnership at the end of the conference decide to do business with each other, which two corporations would make up this new partnership?

(A) F and G
(B) H and J
(C) K and G
(D) F and I
(E) G and H

19. Of the following corporations, which ones have one, and only one, business partnership desire that is unreturned?

I. K
II. H
III. G

(A) I only
(B) II only
(C) III only
(D) I and II only
(E) II and III only

Cluster 5:

A group of nine people—R, S, T, U, V, W, X, Y, and Z—go out to dinner. They are seated in the same section of the restaurant, but not at the same table. There are three tables available: the first table has four seats, the second table has 3 seats, and the third table has two seats.
R and S sit at the same table.
T and U sit at the same table.
Z sits at the two-person table.
X and Y do not sit at the same table.

20. Which of the following is a valid seating arrangement for the three-person table?

(A) R, S, Z
(B) T, U, R
(C) V, X, Z
(D) W, X, U
(E) T, U, W

21. If R, S, and V sit at the three-person table, then which of the following can sit at the two-person table?

(A) T and U
(B) Z and W
(C) Z and Y
(D) Z and T
(E) W and X

22. If V and W sit at the four-person table, then which of the following cannot be true?

(A) R sits at the four-person table.
(B) X sits at the four-person table.
(C) U sits at the three-person table.
(D) X sits at the two-person table.
(E) Y sits at the three-person table.

23. If S, T, and X sit at different tables, then how many valid seating arrangements are there?

(A) 2
(B) 3
(C) 4
(D) 5
(E) 6

24. If neither X nor Y sits at the two-person table, then which of the following cannot be true?

(A) V sits with Y.
(B) X sits with S.
(C) W sits with X.
(D) R sits with T.
(E) W sits with Z.

Section III

Time – 35 minutes

27 Questions

Directions: Each passage in this section is followed by a group of questions to be answered on the basis of what is stated or implied in the passage. For some of the questions, more than one of the choices could conceivably answer the questions. However, you are to choose the best answer; that is, the response that most accurately and completely answers the questions, and blacken the corresponding space on your answer sheet.

Passage 1A

Although it has come under heavy criticism in recent years, the genetic modification of food offers extraordinary opportunities to feed an ever-growing world population, particularly in developing nations. Where some see the unethical altering of nature's perfect work, scientists see the prospect of eliminating the problems that plague farmers and the chance to produce enough food to eradicate world hunger. Among the nations that produce the bulk of agriculture, the governments have created strict regulations concerning the types of genetic modifications that are allowed and the labeling methods for genetically modified food. In Australia and New Zealand, for example, the governments verify that the food is safe for human consumption, and the use of genetically modified food is restricted to ingredients within other food rather than the commercial sale of the food itself. This means that genetically modified food cannot be sold illegally and that consumers are always made aware of what they are purchasing and eating. For those who ask about the need for genetic modification, the answer is quite simple: farmers around the world face similar problems with pests that attack and destroy a crop, the degrading of food before it can reach its intended destination, and the gradual diminishing of food's nutritional quality in recent years. Genetic modification can solve these problems. Scientists have discovered that it is possible to make food resistant to pests and even to rotting, and they are learning new ways of increasing the vitamin content of food so that it retains the nutritional value of previous eras. Perhaps genetic modification is not the perfect answer. Perhaps it would be better to return to a time of small farms where consumers can shop and buy what they can get locally. But unfortunately, this only helps those who have access to such farms. In reality, much of the world is facing ongoing hunger and even starvation due to limited resources and poor nutrition. With genetic modification, scientists are—for the first time in history—making it possible to make world hunger a thing of the past.

Passage 1B

In some cases, the benefits of something questionable can outweigh the negative qualities, but in the case of the genetic modification of food, the negative qualities swamp the benefits. Genetic modification undoubtedly has value. Crops face fewer natural predators, and some produce is receiving an infusion of vitamins not seen in generations. Without question, these are real benefits. But questions do arise about the long-term safety of food that has been genetically modified. No generation has grown up consuming genetically modified food, so the claim that such food is safe cannot be verified for several decades at the earliest. When scientists alter the chemical structure of food for the purpose of removing pests and increasing a crop size, they also alter the unique nutritional content of that food. Consuming such food over the course of one's life could create serious problems in later years, and these problems are not yet fully understood—but the prospect of them is definitely known. The human digestive system is designed to process food in its natural chemical structure. When that chemical structure it altered, the digestive system no longer recognizes it. In 1999, the Hungarian scientist Árpád Pusztai discovered that rats that had been fed genetically altered potatoes suffered severe intestinal problems and even immune deficiency, whereas the rats that ate unmodified potatoes experienced no negative results. This is one example, of course, and no human can be expected to live exclusively on potatoes, genetically modified or otherwise. But large portions of the world consume vast quantities of individual crops: rice, wheat, and corn. With the chemical altering of these crops, there is a very real risk that humans will experience negative and irreversible consequences from the chemical altering of the food—just as Pusztai found with the rats. World hunger is a serious problem, but genetic modification does not necessarily provide the best or the most effective solution. As Pusztai himself said, knowing now that there are potentially serious results with genetic modification, we will not have an excuse in several decades, and when previously unknown illnesses arise and populations suffer, we cannot say that we were unaware of the possibility for negative consequences.

1. The author of Passage A would agree with which of the following statements?

(A) Given the problems with world hunger and even starvation, the benefits of genetically modified food justify overlooking the risks.
(B) Hoping for an ideal scenario of returning to the days of small farms and locally purchased produce is futile.
(C) Due to the restrictions that governments have imposed and the labels that are now required, the genetically modified food available to consumers is likely to be safe.
(D) With the advent of genetically modified food, world hunger will cease to be a problem within decades.
(E) The scientific advances of genetically modified food will ultimately remove all questions of its safety for human consumption.

2. Which of the following best expresses the main point of Passage B?

(A) Given the current knowledge of potential risks, genetically modified food might create long-term problems and should be reconsidered as a solution to world hunger.
(B) Genetically modified food is unethical, because it alters the chemical structure of what is already perfect in nature.
(C) There are far more negative qualities than benefits to genetically modified food, so the ongoing scientific pursuit of genetic modification should be abandoned.
(D) The problem of world hunger cannot be solved through the genetic modification of food.
(E) Scientists know of far too many risks for governments to continue supporting and investing in the genetic modification of food.

3. **The author of Passage A and the author of Passage B would agree with which of the following statements?**

(A) Scientists will ultimately be able to find a safe way to mass produce food and thus end world hunger.
(B) The fact that lab animals have experienced negative results from the testing of genetically modified food does not guarantee that humans will experience negative results.
(C) It is impossible to know now how genetically modified food will affect future generations.
(D) The problems of pests, rotting, and vitamin deficiency can no longer be ignored and require intense international discussion.
(E) There is an ongoing need to address the issues of large-scale hunger and crop problems.

4. **Passage B differs from Passage A in that the author's approach to the question of addressing world hunger is more:**

(A) Tenacious
(B) Circumspect
(C) Dubious
(D) Ethical
(E) Denunciatory

5. **It may be inferred that the author of Passage B holds which of the following opinions?**

(A) Árpád Pusztai's experiment with lab rats and potatoes is conclusive in demonstrating the potential risks of consuming genetically modified food.
(B) The genetic modification of food does offer important benefits, but the benefits do not necessarily justify the risks.
(C) There are a number of important alternatives to genetic modification that will solve the problems now facing farmers without altering the chemical structure of food.
(D) Genetic modification alters food beyond all physical recognition.
(E) There are serious ethical questions that arise with the consideration of feeding genetically modified food to human beings.

6. **Whereas the author of Passage A uses the word *safe* __________, the author of Passage B uses it __________.**

(A) Conclusively...doubtfully
(B) Forcefully...jokingly
(C) Decisively...angrily
(D) Questionably...usefully
(E) Traditionally...flippantly

Passage 2

The study of art history would not be complete without a study of the many art mysteries that persist. Some of these mysteries remain unsolved, having accompanied the artists to their graves. Other mysteries only seem impossible to solve. With the keen eyes of researchers and the enthusiastic enterprise of detectives, art scholars are beginning to study these mysteries more closely and to provide some relevance for modern art lovers. One such mystery, long relegated to the realm of the unknowable, is that of *The Gates of Hell*, a bronze sculpture from famed French sculptor Auguste Rodin. At present, Rodin's apparently finished sculpture sits in the courtyard of the Musée Rodin in Paris, where many of Rodin's works of art are housed. The massive doors stand over nineteen feet tall, extend over thirteen feet in width, and depict a rather gruesome series of writhing figures representing the horrors of hell. The initial inspiration is believed to have been Lorenzo Ghiberti's *Gates of Paradise*, which dates from 1336 and is currently in Florence. In 1880, Rodin was commissioned to create a set of doors for the planned Museum of Decorative Arts in Paris. He immediately went to work on the doors, bearing Ghiberti's work in mind: but then something went wrong.

The underlying problem was that the Museum of Decorative Arts never actually came into being. Funding ran out, and the plan was abandoned, leaving Rodin with a partially finished set of doors and the death of a dream. The project, it turns out, had been an important one for Rodin, because it would have allowed him to explore in sculpture a favorite piece of literature—that of Dante's medieval masterpiece *Inferno*. The evidence on the doors still indicates Rodin's early thought processes. At the top of the doors is a seated figure leaning over a clutched fist, meant to represent Dante himself and now famous as Rodin's stand-alone sculpture *The Thinker*. There are figures indicative of the characters Ugolino, who was placed in hell for devouring his own children, and Paulo and Francesca da Rimini, who were sent to hell for their adulterous relationship. Ultimately, Rodin decided to continue work on the project even though it would not appear in the Museum of Decorative Arts. But Rodin's decision to continue work on the doors is not the real mystery behind *The Gates of Hell*. What is so curious about this sculpture is that it is not the one that Rodin chose to exhibit. Inside the museum, visitors can see what Rodin viewed as his "finished product" of *The Gates of Hell*, a curiously abstract set of doors with no obvious focal point and unclear representation. The identifiable figures from the other door have virtually disappeared, replaced by indefinite images. Compared to the set of doors now on display at the museum, this seems highly unfinished.

The link that seems to unite Rodin's shift from the early doors to the later abstract doors may be explained in the shift in thinking that occurred in the late nineteenth century. Sculpture, long viewed as a respected art form, acquired the reputation of being outdated. French critic Charles Baudelaire wrote an essay entitled "Why Sculpture Is Boring" that seemed to encompass the developing attitude toward sculpture. Many art aficionados began to question sculpture's ability to find its place in the art world, with the gradual movement to more abstract qualities that now define modern art. Sculpture seemed so solid and traditional: clean lines and clear form. Realizing this, Rodin reconsidered his earlier plan of the doors and decided to envision them anew. Gone were the recognizable figures from Dante and in their place the complex swirls and unknown images. This unusual sculpture became the version that Rodin later exhibited to the public and displayed as his finished work of art. In exhibiting these doors, Rodin actually created one of the first truly modern sculptures, and he established precedents for later sculptors to envision the abstract possibilities of their medium. As it turns out, the real mystery in Rodin's *The Gates of Hell* is not why the later set of doors appears to be unfinished but why it is not the set of doors exhibited by the museum in a place of honor as Rodin's achievement of modern sculpture.

7. **The discussion of Dante and Rodin's allusion to Dante's *Inferno* is intended to do which of the following in the passage?**

(A) Demonstrate the importance of previous influences and indicate the way that Rodin's vision of *The Gates of Hell* changed in time
(B) Contrast the styles and influences of traditional sculpture with the styles and influences of what would become modern sculpture
(C) Indicate the role that medieval influences played in much of Rodin's early work
(D) Argue for the need to research Rodin's sources more closely before drawing conclusions about the intention behind his work
(E) Suggest the value of combining disciplines so that art scholars, literary scholars, and historical researchers could work together for a common goal

8. **Which of the following best describes the organization of the passage?**

(A) The author opens with an anecdote, proceeds with the explanation of historical research, and concludes with an abstract reflection.
(B) The author introduces a problem, provides historical background to explain it, and uses the historical research to offer a solution.
(C) The author poses a hypothetical scenario, references a historical situation, and recommends a conclusive action.
(D) The author begins with an issue that needs to be addressed, compares several historical examples, and concludes by explaining the solution.
(E) The author begins *in medias res* (in the middle of things), backtracks to explain the origin of the issue, and combines the details to redefine the problem.

9. **Which of the following best expresses the central argument of the passage?**

(A) Rodin's abstract work on the later, and final, version of *The Gates of Hell* makes him the first modern sculptor and the father of modern sculpture.
(B) Solving the mysteries that remain in the art world is possible, as the case of Rodin's *The Gates of Hell* indicates.
(C) The version of *The Gates of Hell* that currently sits outside the Musée Rodin in Paris is inaccurately shown to be Rodin's preferred version.
(D) Rodin's exhibited version of *The Gates of Hell* is the version that he considered the final and most complete set of doors, and it strongly influenced modern sculpture.
(E) Had the Museum of Decorative Arts come into existence, Rodin might never have explored the more abstract forms of sculpture that became the later version of *The Gates of Hell.*

10. **Which of the following best explains the reasoning behind the author's statement that the "real mystery" concerning Rodin's *The Gates of Hell* is why the second set of doors is not on primary display at the Musée Rodin?**

(A) Because Rodin chose to exhibit the more abstract set of doors, that was the sculpture that he personally recognized as his most complete work.
(B) The Musée Rodin's decision to showcase the earlier and more traditional set of doors reflects a rejection of Rodin's developing aesthetic as a sculptor.
(C) Because of the original allusion to Lorenzo Ghiberti's *Gates of Paradise*, the Musée Rodin has chosen to focus on Rodin's earlier work over his later work.
(D) Rodin's *The Gates of Hell* is a true masterpiece, whereas the earlier version of the sculpture offers little artistic value for connoisseurs of Rodin's work.
(E) Showcasing Rodin's earlier version of *The Gates of Hell* robs art lovers of the full trajectory of Rodin's work as an artist.

11. The author's tone in the last sentence of the passage may best be described as:

(A) Sarcastic
(B) Pedantic
(C) Sagacious
(D) Insistent
(E) Reflective

12. It may be inferred that the author of the passage is claiming that:

(A) Because it was a favorite piece of literature, Rodin referenced Dante's *Inferno* in many of his works of sculpture.
(B) Rodin felt that Lorenzo Ghiberti's *Gates of Paradise* was incomplete without an accompanying vision of hell, so he set out to create *The Gates of Hell.*
(C) The abstract elements that Rodin incorporated in the final set of doors influenced later modern sculptors.
(D) Rodin single-handedly returned relevance to sculpture by reworking *The Gates of Hell* to be more abstract.
(E) The failed Museum of Decorative Arts handicapped Rodin's creative impulse for some time by making it difficult for him to complete the sculpture he was working on.

13. The author of the passage would probably agree that

(A) Rodin's sculpture now known as *The Thinker* is more famous than it should be, taken out of the context of *The Gates of Hell.*
(B) The public reception to the later and more abstract version of *The Gates of Hell* was largely confusion, so the Rodin Museum has chosen not to showcase it.
(C) The failure of the French government to build the Museum of Decorative Arts had affected many other artists besides Rodin.
(D) Most mysteries in the art world arise out of incomplete information, and time spent in research can locate important clues for solving all of these mysteries.
(E) Despite Baudelaire's opinion, sculpture is not necessarily boring, as the history of Rodin's *The Gates of Hell* indicates.

Passage 3

The morning cup of coffee. The afternoon soda. The energy drink to provide that much-needed boost. The familiar ingredient in all three? Caffeine. First identified by German-born chemist Friedrich Ferdinand Runge in 1819, caffeine is a xanthine alkaloid that occurs naturally in certain beans and leaves. Historians officially credit Runge with the discovery, but in reality, the powerful effects of caffeine have been recognized for centuries. Around 3000 BC, the Chinese emperor Shennong is said to have noticed the stimulating effect of caffeine after boiling some tea leaves. It is believed that around 600 BC, the Mayans were consuming cocoa for its value in providing extra energy. In the ninth century AD, an Ethiopian goatherd named Kaldi is said to have observed that goats were highly active after grazing on coffee beans, and by the fifteenth century, Yemeni Sufis utilized coffee to prevent them from falling asleep during prayers. Runge's discovery is primarily in his work of isolating and identifying caffeine as a separate ingredient for the first time. A possibly apocryphal account of the event suggests he did so because his friend Johann von Goethe requested it.

The effects of consuming caffeine are wide-ranging and vary by person, with weight and metabolism playing a role. Research also indicates that some individuals are able to develop a unique tolerance for caffeine that others of a similar size and metabolism might not have. Not surprisingly, though, the most significant variable in the effects of caffeine seem to be the amount consumed. Studies suggest that small doses of caffeine can have very positive effects, improving the rate of activity in athletes and even eliminating breathing problems connected to apnea in infants. Large doses of caffeine, however, can have effects ranging from mildly negative to highly severe. As mentioned before, individuals who consume steady amounts of caffeine can develop a tolerance for caffeine, but it might come at a price. Consistent consumption of caffeine in beverages such as coffee can produce a tolerance in less than three weeks, and the tolerance can become a dependence with negative effects when caffeine is not consumed. Caffeine influences the adenosine receptors in the central nervous system, and these receptors naturally dilate blood vessels in the brain. Lack of expected caffeine can cause an unnatural response in the adenosine receptors, creating too much dilation and producing severe headaches. Additionally, scientists have found that caffeine withdrawal can contribute to feelings of nausea and mild depression.

What is more, excess caffeine use over time can create a variety of increasingly severe health concerns. Caffeine causes an increase of stomach acid, which can lead to ulcers and other gastrointestinal conditions. Caffeine intoxication occurs when an individual consumes more caffeine than the body can process in a normal amount of time (three to four hours), thus causing the individual to develop extreme nervousness, irregular heart rate, insomnia, and even manic depression. An overdose of caffeine can actually cause death, although this is rare with caffeine occurring in its natural forms—such as coffee and tea—and is generally connected to the consumption of caffeine tablets. Caffeine has also been linked to the possible risk of Parkinson's disease in men, an increased risk of miscarriage in pregnant women, and potentially negative effects on memory retention. Before you dump out that cup of tea or vow to quit the coffee habit, though, consider that caffeine in moderation is not entirely bad: some studies indicate that caffeine actually improves brain performance when related to short-range thought processes, and there is strong evidence that caffeine might reduce the risk of heart disease in certain patients. And if nothing else, caffeine withdrawal is now recognized as a health disorder, so there is treatment available to help with that daily fix.

14. Which of the following best expresses the author's main argument?

(A) Friedrich Ferdinand Runge is mistakenly credited with the discovery of caffeine as a stimulative substance in 1819.
(B) The consumption of caffeine involves too many health risks that ultimately outweigh the benefits.
(C) Caffeine, an ingredient known to ancient man, occurs naturally and remains a popular stimulant in various beverages.
(D) Caffeine can be beneficial as well as risky, so it needs to be consumed in moderation.
(E) The consumption of caffeine offers significant health benefits and should thus remain a part of the daily diet.

15. Based on the information provided in the passage, the author would agree with which of the following statements?

(A) Johann Wolfgang von Goethe is responsible for Runge's work in the discovery of caffeine.
(B) Caffeine intoxication occurs very rarely and has never been linked to drinking coffee or tea.
(C) Individuals who will be performing mental activities that require short-range thought processes might benefit from consuming small amounts of caffeine.
(D) Because caffeine withdrawal is now considered to be a health disorder, insurance companies should provide benefits for those suffering from it.
(E) Even mild amounts of caffeine can create problems with excess stomach acid and severe gastrointestinal concerns.

16. The passage suggests that the author believes which of the following?

(A) Studies indicate that there are enough health benefits to consuming caffeine, as long as it is consumed in reasonable quantities, based on individual tolerance.
(B) Due to the effects of caffeine withdrawal, individuals who consume caffeine regularly should not stop consuming it at the risk of developing severe side effects.
(C) Because of the risk of Parkinson's disease, men should not consume caffeine at all.
(D) The Chinese emperor Shennong should be credited as the real discoverer of caffeine.
(E) As caffeine tolerance can vary, some people require far more than three weeks to develop a tolerance for the stimulant.

17. The author uses the word *unique* in line 17 to connote which of the following?

(A) Unexpected
(B) Individual
(C) Surprising
(D) Valuable
(E) Unlikely

18. The author uses the historical information about caffeine to:

(A) Suggest the historical inaccuracy of attributing the discovery of caffeine to Friedrich Ferdinand Runge
(B) Prove that caffeine occurs naturally in beans and leaves around the world
(C) Indicate that the use of beverages containing caffeine for the stimulative effects is not a recent development
(D) Confirm the significance of Friedrich Ferdinand Runge's work in isolating and identifying caffeine
(E) Explain the value of scientific research in establishing what ancient civilizations already knew

19. The passage implies which of the following about caffeine and its effect on adenosine receptors?

(A) The adenosine receptors usually act to prevent headaches, and caffeine can conflict with this.
(B) The adenosine receptors also control the part of the brain related to depression, so depressions often accompanies the headaches that occur with caffeine withdrawal.
(C) Due to the different levels of tolerance among individuals, most overweight people do not experience severe headaches during caffeine withdrawal.
(D) The use of caffeine has proved valuable in medical research for dilating the blood vessels connected to the adenosine receptors.
(E) The adenosine receptors adapt to the extra stimulation of caffeine but are unable to respond normally when the individual stops consuming caffeine.

20. The author's tone in the final sentence may best be described as

(A) Ironic
(B) Acerbic
(C) Mollified
(D) Perturbed
(E) Querulous

Passage 4

Recent concerns about the modern system of education in the United States have led many to research and pursue alternative methods of education. In some cases, methods have simply been rediscovered, and one of the past decade's most popular discoveries is known as classical education. The origins of classical education are unclear, but most recognize that it dates back to medieval Europe. It derives its primary source from Ancient Greece. Classical education as it is taught today is divided into two distinct primary levels: the trivium and the quadrivium. The quadrivium is generally equated with post-secondary education, and there are several colleges and universities in the United States now offering studies that reflect a traditional quadrivium breakdown of astronomy, arithmetic, music, and geometry. While this might sound limiting, these studies are actually much broader when applied to a current university setting. The modern quadrivium might include such areas as natural science, business, fine arts, and engineering. Furthermore, quadrivium subjects are all taught within the larger framework of history. In classical education, history is viewed as the subject that links the other studies together. As the study of history encompasses the study of all that has occurred, every other subject falls into its historical place, thus providing the scholar with an appreciation for the development of each field over time.

Whereas the quadrivium is equated with post-secondary study, the trivium is understood to be primary and secondary studies. It is then divided into the three sections of grammar, dialectic, and rhetoric, with history again creating the framework of context for the various studies. The grammar stage might best be associated with the elementary level, where students focus on the development of basic language and math skills and receive the foundational knowledge on which their education will be built. The dialectic stage most closely parallels the junior high level and focuses student learning on logical reasoning, taking the foundational studies of the grammar level and developing them further. The rhetoric stage is generally equated with the high school level. In the rhetoric stage, students begin to explore abstract thought, taking all of the skills learned in the earlier stages and honing them with rhetoric and composition. Persuasive reasoning often becomes the primary focus of the rhetoric stage.

Having vanished into the history of the Middle Ages, classical education made an unexpected reappearance when English scholar and novelist Dorothy L. Sayers presented an essay entitled "The Lost Tools of Learning" at Oxford University in 1947. In the essay, Sayers encourages educational reforms, arguing that medieval education produced a stronger student and was far more successful than the educational systems that followed the Middle Ages: Sayers notes in particular that despite the high rates of literacy in Europe and elsewhere, people today are more vulnerable to media manipulation, have little ability to formulate serious arguments in a debate, and are no longer capable of distinguishing the good literature from the bad. Sayers posits that whatever its limitations, the classical system of the Middle Ages produced a stronger thinker and a more rounded individual. Some educators took notice, and an eventual rebirth of classical education ensued with a particular focus among homeschooling parents. But there are skeptics to the system of classical education made popular in recent years. Dr. George Bugliarello of Polytechnic University argues that the strict liberal arts focus of the classical trivium can no longer prepare the modern student adequately, because students also need a strong background in science and technology. As Dr. Bugliarello indicates, the modern world has a greater focus on science and technology than the medieval world, and any education limited in these areas will only handicap a student in the long run. Perhaps there is a balance to be found in the perspectives of both Sayers and Bugliarello, and the classical education of the next few decades will find a way to fuse the strengths of the past with the needs of the future.

21. Which of the following most clearly expresses the author's main point?

(A) Classical education derives from medieval traditions of learning and was rediscovered in the twentieth century when Dorothy Sayers presented an essay on it.
(B) The traditions of classical education still have value today but should be combined with modern educational needs to be of full benefit to students.
(C) Classical education is a medieval form of learning that comes from an earlier Greek tradition and is composed of a trivium and a quadrivium.
(D) History is the most important subject in the classical curriculum, because it links all of the other subjects together.
(E) The current approach to classical educational has begun to incorporate many modern subjects.

22. In lines 42–47, the arguments that Dr. George Bugliarello make concerning the need for the study of science and technology in the classical curriculum suggest which of the following about traditional classical education?

(A) Classical education no longer has any relevance for modern students, and the current system of education should simply be reformed.
(B) The modern system of education provides the ideal balance of traditional studies with the study of science and technology.
(C) Dr. Bugliarello is currently in the process of developing a program of science and technology that will fit into the classical system.
(D) All students who receive a traditional classical education will have virtually no training in science and technology.
(E) Because it is based on medieval educational needs, classical education tends to minimize the study of science and technology in favor of other subjects.

23. The word classical, as used to identify the traditional system of education that the author discusses, is most similar to which of the following?

(A) Thorough
(B) Elitist
(C) Humanistic
(D) Superior
(E) Ideal

24. Which of the following may be inferred from the importance of the study of history to the classical curriculum?

(A) The study of history is ubiquitous in all subjects, but the classical system of education is the only system to recognize this clearly.
(B) The focus on history constitutes the most unique quality of the system of classical education.
(C) The study of history provides a framework into which the other subjects fit correctly, because it explains the chronological development of information.
(D) Because the study of history is inherent to a classical system of education, teachers seldom mention history as a separate part of the study.
(E) The public education system has failed largely due to its choice of alienating history to a distinct subject.

25. The author includes information about the quadrivium in the first paragraph of the passage to indicate which of the following?

(A) The successful ability of colleges and universities to adopt and update the quadrivium and the potential for making the trivium relevant to modern needs
(B) The extension of problems with the current system of education to the university level
(C) The value of the traditional four subjects of the quadrivium and the problems that ensue from ignoring them at the post-secondary level
(D) The way that most colleges and universities have handicapped students by allowing them to focus on one subject instead of studying a range of subjects
(E) The importance of returning the four subjects of the quadrivium back to the university curriculum

26. Which of the following may be inferred from Dorothy Sayers's argument about the problems with modern education in comparison to medieval education?

(A) The modern system of education needs to teach students how to resist media manipulation.
(B) The current system of educational should stop focusing on literacy rates and focus instead on producing stronger thinkers.
(C) If educators would have adopted the reforms that Sayers suggested back in 1947, the current public education system would not need to be reformed today.
(D) The medieval system of education taught students how to recognize bad reasoning and think logically, qualities that are lacking in modern education.
(E) Homeschooling is ideal for incorporating classical education because of its focus on the individual student.

27. Which of the following best describes the author's opinion about the potential for merging elements of classical education with the study of science and technology?

(A) Vehement
(B) Optimistic
(C) Diffident
(D) Incredulous
(E) Impatient

Section IV

Time – 35 minutes

25 Questions

Directions: The questions in this section are based on the reasoning given in brief statements or passages. It is possible that for some questions there is more than one answer. However, you are to choose the *best* answer; that is, the response that most accurately and completely answers the question. You should not make assumptions that are by commonsense standards implausible, superfluous, or incompatible with the passage. After you have chosen the best answer, blacken the corresponding space on your answer sheet.

1. **Concerned about the ongoing downturn in the economy, the head of a large charitable organization recently began reviewing receipts to see how the economic problems have affected the donations that the organization has received. Much to his surprise, the amount received in donations has not changed at all—the charitable organization has continued to receive the same amount as before the economic slump. The head of the organization knows that the regular donors are typically faithful with sending in their donations, but he is still surprised to find that the organization is not having any trouble meeting its donation goals.**

   Which of the following best explains the anomaly between the expected decline in charitable donations and the actual receipt?

   (A) The wealthier members of society are generally the largest source of charitable donations, and they will always have extra money for non-profit organizations.
   (B) The charity made the decision to lower its expectations for donations, so the amount received was accurate, based on the adjustment for anticipated donations.
   (C) The charity is now receiving federal money, so the losses that it sustains during the economic downturn are covered under government subsidies.
   (D) People generally feel more obligated to give in a time of economic loss, even if they do not have as much disposable income as they do in a healthy economy.
   (E) Charitable donations function as tax deductions, so those who usually give to the charitable organization have strong incentive to give during economic weakness.

2. **Geophysicist: Although scientists do not entirely agree on the causes of geomagnetic reversal, they do agree that the process has the potential for significant changes on the earth. A geomagnetic reversal occurs when the magnetic field of the earth adjusts in its orientation, so that the magnetic north becomes the magnetic south, and vice versa. What is more, studies indicate that the magnetic field is gradually losing its strength and that we might expect to see a reversal within the next few millennia. While this might not seem significant, the reversal of the magnetic fields would occur over a long period of time, leaving the earth potentially unprotected from the sun's radiation.**

   Reviewing the information in the passage above carefully, which of the following represents the geophysicist's primary argument?

   (A) While there will be a few effects of a geomagnetic reversal, the negative effects will be limited.
   (B) Geomagnetic reversals have occurred within the period of human existence on the earth, and since mankind has survived, there is no reason to fear human eradication from geomagnetic reversal.
   (C) Scientists do not fully understand the causes or results of geomagnetic reversal, but there is evidence that the process should not be ignored.
   (D) Given the severe possibilities that may arise from a geomagnetic reversal, governments should begin funding studies of this process.
   (E) The current placement of magnetic poles on the earth has little effect on the natural functions of the earth.

3. **While black or green tea tends to be the leaf of choice among connoisseurs, recent studies have indicated there are significant benefits to drinking white tea. White tea is considerably more delicate and rarer than black or green tea and has fewer producers. Because it is unprocessed and unfermented, white tea has very high levels of catechins, which are known for having antibiotic qualities and delaying aging. Additionally, white tea has elevated levels of theobromine, a substance that can improve circulation. To produce white tea, basic tea leaves are picked when they are very young, so white tea contains considerably less fluoride than black or green tea and much higher levels of theanine, which is known for its relaxing qualities. Research indicates that white tea has an amount of caffeine comparable to that of either black or green tea.**

   The reader can infer each of the following from the passage EXCEPT:

   (A) Some companies process black tea but not white tea.
   (B) White tea is usually derived from the same leaves as black or green tea, but it is picked when it is younger, and the leaves are not processed or fermented.
   (C) Research suggests that white tea has extra benefits that black or green tea do not always have.
   (D) Fluoride is a necessary ingredient for tea, so most white tea producers add fluoride to the tea that they sell.
   (E) The increased levels of theanine in white tea could have the potential to be used for therapeutic purposes.

4. *Angelica*: **The cultural development of the Roaring Twenties is a direct result of the social breakdown that occurred during World War I. The soldiers and other young people witnessed the dishonesty of authority figures regarding the war, its causes, and the nature of patriotism, and the Roaring Twenties became a backlash against authority, with the defiance of traditions and moral expectations. This became the tone of the Modern Age, so the Roaring Twenties may be called the start of modernism.**

   Luca: **While the 1920s generation embraced the mood of modernism more thoroughly than previous generations, it is more correct to note that the Modern Age had already begun in the mid-nineteenth century, as philosophers and political thinkers started questioning traditional religious authorities and raising questions about the nature of morality.**

   Luca responds to Angelica's comment by doing which of the following?

   (A) Acknowledging a part of the argument but suggesting the need for revision.
   (B) Criticizing the substance of the argument and calling the conclusion into question.
   (C) Demonstrating the logical fallacy embedded in the argument.
   (D) Questioning the possibility of arriving at any real conclusion regarding the topic.
   (E) Offering a point-by-point disagreement and providing alternate views.

5. **The island of Sark is the smallest of four islands in the southwestern area of the English Channel. Sark is a part of the British Crown. Until 2008, it was considered the last remaining feudal state in Europe, its government under the Seigneur and functioning as a fiefdom granted by the British monarch. Sark is a tiny island, with only two square miles of land and a population of only 600 people, most of whom are past middle age. It has no airport, and airplanes are not allowed to fly over; Sark may be reached by ferry alone. The fragile landscape and climate of the island are heavily influenced by its location in the English Channel, and its residents are committed to maintaining a natural quality with a focus on sustainable activities. Sark has a "horses-only" policy, and no cars or other motor vehicles are allowed there.**

   Based on the statements made in the passage, which of the following offers the best explanation for the "horses-only" policy on Sark?

   (A) As the island is only two square miles, most of the residents can walk or ride easily enough to get from one location to another.
   (B) Most of the residents on Sark are accustomed to the laws forbidding motor vehicles and have no interest in changing them at this time.
   (C) Sark is composed of several very small and self-contained villages, and there is little need for the residents to go from one place to the other frequently.
   (D) Due to the delicate environment of the island, the residents of Sark are concerned about the pollution that motor vehicles could bring with them.
   (E) Because the island of Sark was a feudal state for so long, many of the laws are arbitrary and have no relevance to contemporary society.

6. **The name *Japan* is generally considered to be an exonym, or a name that is given to a country from outsiders but is not the name with which inhabitants identify their country. The Japanese call their nation *Nippon* or *Nihon*, both of which mean "the sun's origin." The name "Japan" is believed to have come from the Portuguese word *Giapan*, which is a derivation of the Malay word *Jepang* and is thought to have originated with the Mandarin word *Cipangu*. The Portuguese established ongoing trade with the Far East during the sixteenth century, and the name that they adopted for the country now known in English as Japan has stuck. This particular usage exists in at least nine other languages.**

   Which of the following may be inferred from statements made in the passage above?

   (A) As the name Japan is an incorrect usage, the name should be adjusted to reflect the way that the Japanese people refer to their country.
   (B) At least ten languages can trace the exonym Japan back to its likely Mandarin roots.
   (C) It would be an insult for non-Japanese to refer to Japan as Nippon or Nihon, because both names are sacred to the Japanese people and their language.
   (D) The name Japan is Mandarin in origin and carries the same meaning as Nippon or Nihon.
   (E) Exonyms are rare, and the name Japan is one of very few examples.

7. **Farmer in Norway: Two decades ago, it became clear that the greylag goose population was on the decline due to the encroachment of cities and the destruction of their native nesting sites. The government provided official protection for the diminishing greylag goose, but with the result that farmers are now inundated with geese on their farms. These geese graze on crops and are causing an increasing number of problems for farmers who are unable to do anything to drive off or destroy the invading geese. As the greylag goose population has clearly increased, the government should now remove the official protection status to allow farmers to protect their crops.**

   The reasoning in the farmer's argument is subject to which of the following flaws?

   (A) He fails to offer an alternative solution to the problems that farmers are facing with the greylag geese.
   (B) He relies on questionable data to present his argument about the need to lift the protection status.
   (C) He fails to note that lifting the protection status of the greylag goose could send it back into endangerment, and he suggests a solution that does not fully consider both sides of the issue.
   (D) He declines to compare the situation with the greylag goose to comparable situations in which an endangered species has experienced a population explosion.
   (E) He sides too openly with his fellow farmers who are struggling with excessive geese on their farms and fails to demonstrate objectivity.

8. **When making a logical argument, it is essential to distinguish between theory and fact and to recognize the place of each. Theory suggests an idea or a hypothesis that might be true, but it requires the support of fact in order to verify it. Fact is the evidence or the proof that makes a theory valid; without fact, that theory is merely a concept for consideration and an idea that has potential. Theory is not always unacceptable in a logical argument, but that theory must be based on comparable facts from similar situations or examples. A logical argument founded on a theory usually ends in speculation, while a logical argument that builds on a theory with comparable facts can prove to be highly effective.**

   Which of the following does the passage above imply?

   (A) Fact is always more important and more valuable than theory when making a logical argument.
   (B) While theory has a place in a logical argument, it is generally better to avoid it altogether.
   (C) Theory is basically equivalent to speculation and, as such, can undermine the strength of a logical argument.
   (D) Theory should never be confused with fact, at the risk of making a logical argument that is entirely false.
   (E) Theory has a place in a logical argument, but only if fact can be proven based on an analogous scenario.

9. **A large corporation is currently in the middle of turnover, as many of the older employees are retiring around the same time. With a weak economic situation, the corporation has to consider its hiring options carefully. Most of the retiring employees have been with the company for many years and have acquired knowledge and skills that would require the corporation to hire additional employees to take over their positions. The CEO of the corporation has decided not to replace all of the retiring employees, however. Instead, the corporation will be hiring fewer employees. The corporation does not expect to see a reduction in the work output, but it does plan to see a reduction in salaries.**

   Which of the following best explains the decision by the corporation to hire fewer employees?

   (A) The corporation is relocating many of the jobs to an overseas branch, thus reducing the jobs required at its primary U.S. location.
   (B) Many of the retiring employees will continue to work part-time to fill in the gaps with the reduced number of jobs.
   (C) The corporation is working with a headhunting firm in order to bring on versatile workers who will accept diverse employment requirements for a lower salary.
   (D) The corporation has reviewed the open positions in the company, and the CEO feels as though many of those positions are outdated and can be eliminated.
   (E) The corporation is reducing its pay for employees and is altering the retirement plan available to retiring employees in order to save money.

10. Editorial from Local Art Instructor: Studies indicate that art lessons can be of particular benefit to elementary school children, because art allows children to explore creative skills in ways that other programs do not. Art allows children to pursue creativity without fear of restriction, but more importantly, art encourages the development of different areas of the brain, thus providing the student with a well-rounded mind. This development will provide the further benefit of improving the performance of students in other subjects. Elementary schools in Japan have recently begun adding a daily art program for students, and the student test scores in math and science have improved considerably.

Which of the following undermines the statements that the art instructor makes in favor of the local elementary schools adopting art programs?

(A) The local elementary schools focus more on math and science programs, because they receive exclusive government funding for good test scores.
(B) The art instructor is closely connected to a non-profit organization that focuses on bringing art programs into the school system.
(C) Many other elementary school subjects allow for the development of creative skills.
(D) Elementary schools in Japan have recently adopted a new math and science curriculum, and the students in all of the schools have responded well to it.
(E) All of the local elementary schools have had extensive art programs in the past, but the students did not enjoy the programs, so they were dropped.

Questions 11 and 12

It is believed that the earliest precursor to the modern-day camera derives from the camera obscura, usually credited to the Arab scientist Abu Ali Al-Hasan Ibn al-Haitham in the eleventh century. Working in an early version of a dark room, Ibn al-Haitham studied the movement of light and discovered that he could reproduce images by reflecting light through pinholes. Prior to Ibn al-Haitham, though, the Chinese philosopher Mozi had already begun developing a variety of a pinhole camera in the fourth century BC. Later in that same century, both Aristotle and Euclid remarked on the placement of light when projected through pinholes. What is more, the Arab mathematician Abu Yusuf Ya'qub Ibn Ishaq al-Kindi became the first to project images with an early type of camera obscura in the ninth century. As a result, although Ibn al-Haitham is often credited with the creation of the camera obscura, he is also recorded as having said that he did not invent it.

11. The claims made in the passage above, if true, support which of the following statements?

(A) Though Ibn al-Haitham is given credit for inventing the camera obscura in the eleventh century, it was invented by Mozi in the fourth century BC.
(B) Ibn al-Haitham's development of the camera obscura in the eleventh century was the result of discoveries in previous centuries that contributed to his research.
(C) The Greek philosophers Aristotle and Euclid developed their experiments on the pinhole camera from the writings of the Chinese philosopher Mozi.
(D) Ibn Ishaq al-Kindi is unfairly overlooked as the real inventor of the camera obscura.
(E) Though usually considered a modern development, the camera was really invented in the eleventh century.

12. The passage above implies all of the following EXCEPT:

(A) In developing the camera obscura, Ibn al-Haitham stole research from previous scientists and philosophers and claimed it as his own.
(B) Centuries before the camera obscura was fully developed, scientists and philosophers had been experimenting with the reflection of light through pinholes.
(C) The first recorded research about the study of light and pinholes appears to come from the Chinese philosopher Mozi.
(D) Ibn al-Haitham recognized that his accomplishment in inventing the camera obscura was founded on previous centuries of research into light reflection.
(E) Prior to Ibn al-Haitham's invention in the eleventh century, Ibn Ishaq al-Kindi had developed a forerunner to the camera obscura.

13. Political Activist: Given the current economic state, the U.S. government should strongly consider nationalizing some banks. The recent economic situation has become so dire that leaving the banks private will soon be academic. International law requires that when a government nationalizes the bank, it must compensate the owner for the full value of the assets that are assumed. The recent inflow of federal money into the majority of banks in this country, however, means that the government has basically compensated the owners, and official nationalization is simply the next logical step so that the banks are fully protected under the U.S. government.

Which of the following most undermines the argument that the political activist makes in the passage above?

(A) The voters in the U.S. are still divided on the issue of nationalization, and there does not seem to be enough support to merit it.
(B) A small percentage of banks in the U.S. are still solvent and have not received federal funding.
(C) The federal funding that the banks in the U.S. have received has not entirely covered the debts that the banks now hold on the account books.
(D) The U.S. government is heavily in debt to other nations, and the nationalized banks in the U.S. might represent necessary collateral to pay off that debt.
(E) The nationalization of several banks in the United Kingdom was not as successful as the government had hoped it would be.

14. German composer Ludwig van Beethoven is remembered both for his masterpieces of Classical and Romantic music and for the tragic loss of his hearing that still did not preclude him from composing. The exact cause of Beethoven's deafness has never been determined, but historians and scientists have suggested several reasons, the most influential of which has become the discovery of very high rates of lead in Beethoven's hair. Lead poisoning can manifest itself in a variety of ways, including irregular behavior, inexplicable rage, and deafness. Beethoven is recorded as having suffered all of these symptoms. Some, however, still question lead poisoning as a sufficient diagnosis.

Which of the following best explains the reason for why lead poisoning remains an unsatisfactory diagnosis for some?

(A) Beethoven had contracted typhus as a child, and this disease can often leave the sufferer with deafness.
(B) Beethoven is known for having frequently dunked his head in icy water in order to maintain alertness, a habit that could have weakened his hearing over time.
(C) Lead poisoning almost never manifests itself in the type of deafness that Beethoven suffered, and his other symptoms are not unique to lead poisoning.
(D) It is believed that Beethoven developed tinnitus, which made it difficult for him to hear music or to have intelligible conversations.
(E) Some argue that Beethoven's deafness was simply hereditary and that his irregular behavior and rage is the result of his artistic temperament.

15. Inflation has traditionally been viewed as a negative cycle for an economy, whereas deflation has been seen as a time for the economy to return to healthier price levels. In recent years, though, economists have begun to view low inflationary development over time as healthy for the modern economy, due to the fact that inflation signals growth of money supply and increased prices. These increased prices become increased value for businesses and eventually trickle down to consumers as employees. Although prices are actually higher, consumers have more liquidity and thus spend more, helping to balance the economy. Many economists believe that inflation can sustain an economy that is struggling with recession.

Which of the following may be inferred from statements made in the passage above?

(A) Modern economists would prefer a severe state of inflation to a severe state of deflation.
(B) Historically, cycles of deflation have signaled low economic growth, while cycles of inflation have signaled high economic growth.
(C) Inflation is good for an economy domestically, but an increase of money supply usually corresponds with lower exchange rates and decreased international value.
(D) While low rates of inflation can be of benefit to an economy, higher rates of inflation can have devastating effects on a healthy economy.
(E) Consumer prices are lower during deflation, but this does not help an economy in recession, because consumers have less liquidity and are thus spending less.

16. A popular electronics company that is known for producing innovative technology recently began heavy marketing for a new music-playing device. The company is excited about the new device, because it is much smaller than previous devices and is very light and highly portable, allowing the listener to carry it easily, without any cumbersome pieces or cords. After three months on the market, however, the device is not selling well, and the company is forced to admit that its competitor's product is still selling much better, in spite of the fact that the competitor's product is heavier and does not offer the same qualities of portability.

Considering the passage above carefully, which of the following provides the best reason for the failure of the new device to take off with the public?

(A) Consumers have become accustomed to using the competitor's device and dislike the style of the new device.
(B) The competitor is planning to update its popular device soon, so the new device from the first company will have major rivalry among the public.
(C) The popular company that produced the new device hired a marketing firm that failed to inform the public sufficiently about the benefits of the new device.
(D) The new device requires that owners purchase and download music in a unique form, as it is incompatible with other forms and does not allow for conversion.
(E) The president of the popular electronics company is currently in talks to leave and become president of the competitor company.

17. Psychiatrist: Having counseled day traders for several years now, I have come to realize that they could benefit greatly from the behavioral training techniques that modern psychiatry has embraced. One of the biggest challenges for day traders is recovering from losses and developing the ongoing self-discipline and conscious discretion to trade without the fear of loss. In order to achieve success, day traders must utilize the trading techniques that they have learned and maintain the trading plan that they develop. The behavioral training system I have created, including hypnosis and other subconscious techniques, will help traders get over their fears and return to trading without anxiety.

On which of the following assumptions is the psychiatrist's argument founded?

(A) All behavioral training includes degrees of hypnosis in order to modify the negative behavior of the participant.
(B) Hypnosis and other subconscious behavioral techniques can be applied to an activity that requires ongoing self-discipline and conscious discretion.
(C) All day traders develop fear after big losses, so all day traders struggle with utilizing their trading techniques and maintaining their trading plans.
(D) It is impossible for day traders to trade successfully without the modification of negative behavior through behavioral training.
(E) A successful trader does not begin trading without careful training in trading techniques and development of a trading plan.

18. It is believed that the diamond was originally discovered and extracted in India as much as 6,000 years ago. The word *diamond*, however, derives from the Greek αδαμας, or *adámas*, which means "unbreakable" or even "untamed," and has made its way into Western literature through the Greek tradition. Having heard rumors of exceptionally strong stones, the Greeks developed a mythology about an unbreakable stone that was known as *adamant*. By the Middle Ages, this came to be recognized as the diamond. Over time, the legendary adamant came to take on a mystical quality that passed into certain forms of medieval literature and even today has an allegorical place in some genres.

The statements made in the passage above support which of the following claims?

(A) Given the legendary status of the adamant, it might have been better if the diamond and its actual qualities had remained a mystery.
(B) Because the adamant was originally associated with mythical qualities, it retains figurative attributes that are still valuable for some writers.
(C) The diamond and the adamant are essentially the same gem, and the two terms can be interchanged.
(D) The Greek word *adámas* is based on an ancient word of India that meant the same thing but has now been lost to history.
(E) Although the Greeks were mistaken about the mystical qualities of diamonds, they were right to identify them as unbreakable.

QUESTIONS 19 AND 20

Beginning in the mid-nineteenth century, discussion about the possibility of life on Mars developed in earnest. From his research, English scientist William Whewell observed that Mars might have a geophysical landscape similar to that of Earth, complete with bodies of water, land masses, and possibly even intelligent life forms similar to humans. Scientists had already determined that Mars experienced days that spanned virtually the same length of hours as on Earth but with seasons that were approximately double the length due to Mars's axial tilt in combination with its highly elongated orbit. In the late nineteenth century, scientists noticed what appeared to be canals on Mars's landscape, and some even suggested that these canals were created by earlier civilizations. It took the research of American astronomer William Wallace Campbell in 1894 and the work of scientists with more powerful telescopes in the early twentieth century to debunk the canal theory with the discovery that the atmosphere of Mars is entirely devoid of water and oxygen.

19. The passage above strictly implies which of the following about the speculation of the canals on Mars?

(A) All life forms, whether human or otherwise, must have water and oxygen in order to survive.
(B) The scientists who believed that earlier civilizations had built canals on Mars also believed that the civilizations were composed of alien life forms completely unlike human beings.
(C) The canals on the surface of Mars have some other substance than water flowing through them.
(D) William Wallace Campbell is responsible for debunking the myth about canals and earlier civilizations on Mars.
(E) As there is no water or oxygen within the atmosphere of Mars, the canals had been mistaken for some other feature on Mars's landscape.

20. Which of the following may be inferred from statements made in the passage above?

(A) Although the presence of life forms on Mars has not been proven, scientists still hold out for the possibility that life does or can exist there.
(B) After the work of William Wallace Campbell and other astronomers in the early twentieth century, it has been shown conclusively that life has never existed on Mars.
(C) With limited telescopic equipment, early scientists made too many assumptions about the similarities between Mars and Earth.
(D) Due to the similarity in the length of a day in Mars and on Earth, Mars experiences a year similar in length to Earth.
(E) Because Mars is lacking in water and oxygen, it is also lacking in many other essential elements for the survival of life forms.

21. Medical Sales Agent: This new device that our company has developed will offer tremendous advantages to both surgeons and patients. The surgeon will now be able to perform previously complicated and very invasive procedures quickly and non-invasively. What is more, patients will be able to schedule outpatient procedures, where they were formerly required to remain in the hospital for several days. We have tested this device at several area hospitals, and many of the surgeons and patients have offered positive feedback. As a result, we may say with confidence that this device will be universally useful to all surgeons and patients.

Which of the following is most similar to the logical fallacy within the medical sales agent's argument?

(A) If you leave your car in the driveway and do not park it in the garage, it will become rusty from exposure; Edward's car is rusty, so he must not park it in the garage.
(B) You must purchase this new type of hand lotion, because if you do not you will always regret how dry your skin is.
(C) You cannot purchase that SUV, because the owner of the only SUV dealership in town has not made known his opinion on using animals for medical research; so, you cannot buy a vehicle without knowing his beliefs on that issue.
(D) If you do not enroll your child in an advanced preschool, your child might fall behind the other students in elementary school; therefore, it is essential that you enroll your child in an advanced preschool.
(E) Within the western district of a large state, 80% of the voters dislike a piece of proposed legislation; therefore, it must be a poor piece of legislation that will offer no benefits to anyone in the state.

22. Within the last few decades, scientists have begun to pay much closer attention to the dangerous effects of ground-level ozone, which occurs when strong sunlight combines with nitrous oxide and volatile organic compounds. Scientists in Los Angeles have long since believed that the location of the city, sitting in a natural basin with little circulation and receiving large amounts of sunlight, has made it vulnerable to high levels of ground-level ozone. Scientists in Chicago, however, have found that the Windy City also has high levels of ground-level ozone although it sits on a flat, open plain. These scientists believe that advective heating, which is caused by winds drawing in large amounts of warmth but not circulating them out, is the cause of the increased amounts of ground-level ozone in Chicago. Los Angeles receives strong winds off the Pacific Ocean.

The passage above implies which of the following statements?

(A) It is possible that advective heating from ocean winds and not the location of Los Angeles is what makes Los Angeles so vulnerable to ground-level ozone.
(B) Since it is known as the Windy City, Chicago receives an amount of wind comparable to Los Angeles.
(C) Ozone is a necessary element when it occurs naturally in the upper regions of the atmosphere, but it is very dangerous when at ground level.
(D) The combination of chemicals that creates ground-level ozone creates dangerous respiratory concerns.
(E) Chicago receives a large amount of wind, but because the city is on a flat-open plain the wind is able to circulate out more easily.

23. Psychologist: The media in America believes that its role is to inform the public about current events, whether positive or negative, and to maintain an objective stance in the presentation. It is clear from watching any news program, however, that the media is far from objective in selecting the news that it will report. A recent report in a major psychological journal has indicated that Americans feel more stress after watching a news program than before it. When graphic images accompany a negative story, the stress level gets even higher. When the news program presents a positive story, however, the stress level goes down. The media should begin focusing on presenting more positive stories in order to provide an uplifting contrast to the negativity.

Which of the following best describes the flaw in the psychologist's reasoning?

(A) The psychologist unfairly attacks the media for failing to provide objective news, but without offering any proof for the accusations.
(B) The psychologist accuses the media of subjectivity in selecting stories but then suggests that the media continue to be subjective by selecting different stories.
(C) The psychologist mistakenly confuses two separate arguments and attempts to combine them into a single argument.
(D) The psychologist does not indicate clearly enough that the public responds well to positive stories and fails to prove that a balance of stories will be of benefit.
(E) The psychologist does not distinguish among types of negativity in news stories and does not indicate clearly what it is that causes the most stress in viewers.

24. The hearing organs of unborn babies begin to develop after less than four weeks of pregnancy, and by four months an unborn baby can actually hear. At six months in the womb, infants are able to hear clearly, and some biologists believe that they are already developing a partiality for certain kinds of music. A number of companies have begun marketing prenatal listening devices so that parents can instill a love for classical music in their unborn child, and research has indicated that classical music has very positive effects on the mind development of unborn babies. Some research suggests, however, that the baby is most likely to respond positively to the mother's musical preference, because her favorite music is most likely to relax her.

The passage above implies which of the following about playing music for unborn babies?

(A) Because unborn babies can hear music clearly by the sixth month of pregnancy, astute parents should begin to introduce their child to music in the womb.
(B) Studies indicate that the best music to play around unborn babies is classical, because it has the most positive effects on prenatal development.
(C) Although classical music has positive benefits on unborn babies, parents should play music that is most comfortable for them and particularly for the mother.
(D) Because unborn babies can begin to develop musical partiality at six months, the baby will definitely develop a taste for whatever music its mother likes best.
(E) Given that an unborn baby's music preferences can develop by six months, the baby can make its dislike for music very clear to its mother.

25. Dating from the ninth century AD, the Cyrillic alphabet is credited to the brothers Cyril and Methodius, natives of Thessalonika who became missionaries to the Slavic peoples. They utilized a type of Greek script in combination with the Glagolitic alphabet, an obsolete Slavic form, in order to create a writing system for sounds not existing in Greek. Today the Cyrillic alphabet is used for six Slavic languages and at least five non-Slavic languages in nations that stretch from Eastern Europe to Mongolia. At the political peak of the Soviet Union, Cyrillic was used for more than fifty languages, but many languages have rejected the use of the Cyrillic alphabet since the USSR's collapse. At the beginning of 2007, the Cyrillic alphabet was recognized as one of three official alphabets for the European Union, the other two being Latin and Greek.

The passage above implies all of the following EXCEPT:

(A) The brothers Cyril and Methodius developed the Cyrillic alphabet as a part of their missionary work to the Slavic peoples.
(B) The Slavic peoples were not literate and had no alphabet prior to the missionary work of Cyril and Methodius.
(C) The languages that abandoned Cyrillic might have associated the alphabet with negative qualities of the Soviet Union.
(D) The European Union recognized Cyrillic as an official alphabet, because it has a significant presence in European nations.
(E) The Greek alphabet alone did not suffice in recording the language system of the Slavic peoples.

Writing Sample Topic

(35 Minutes)

Fashion Now is a major fashion magazine that has traditionally led the industry in identifying and popularizing trends. In recent months, an economic downturn has led to a decrease in sales, and the magazine has struggled to retain readers. The editors began including celebrity faces on the covers in place of models and focusing more on fashionable celebrities, but this did little to improve sales. As a final resort, the editors have made the decision to redesign the magazine. Two different redesign options have been proposed. Write an argument for the editors choosing one redesign proposal over another, based on the following criteria:

- The magazine editors want to retain as many current subscribers as possible, because ongoing subscriptions represent the bulk of the magazine's income.
- The magazine editors want to bring in new subscribers by appealing to new demographics.

The first proposal redirects the entire focus of *Fashion Now* toward the "green" movement, notably the areas of sustainability and ethical fashion. The green movement has become increasingly significant in the fashion industry, and many designers have begun to utilize techniques related to sustainability, even as they reject fashion techniques that are considered to be unethical. As the movement gains momentum, more and more designers are embracing green elements, but no fashion magazine has led the way for an industry-wide adoption of it. This proposal would utilize all recycled materials in the magazine production and offer paperless issues for readers. This proposal hopes for *Fashion Now* to represent the fashion of the future for current readers and for a previously untapped audience that places a high value on the green lifestyle.

The second proposal returns *Fashion Now* to its fashion-only origins by eliminating the celebrity faces and focus. In recent years, most fashion magazines, including *Fashion Now*, have become increasingly commercialized, with excess advertisements and minimal focus particularly directed on the fashion industry itself. Instead, the trend has been to shift most attention to the way that fashion is represented among celebrities. This proposal rejects the shift and hopes to make *Fashion Now* the unquestioned leader in discussing fashion as a concept by reigniting the enthusiasm for style and design among fashion connoisseurs and by limiting the celebrity focus. Additionally, the second proposal hopes to make fashion accessible to all readers. This proposal would drop the price per issue and add the discussion of fashion for every income in order to bring in readers who believe that they cannot afford to adopt new trends.

LSAT Answer Key

SECTION I

Question	Question	Question	Question
1. B	8. C	15. C	22. E
2. E	9. E	16. E	23. D
3. E	10. D	17. D	24. C
4. C	11. A	18. B	25. C
5. E	12. B	19. C	
6. B	13. E	20. B	
7. A	14. A	21. A	

SECTION II

Question	Question	Question	Question
1. A	7. E	13. C	19. B
2. D	8. B	14. E	20. E
3. E	9. D	15. A	21. C
4. B	10. A	16. B	22. B
5. C	11. C	17. D	23. E
6. B	12. D	18. A	24. D

SECTION III

Question	Question	Question	Question
1. C	8. E	15. C	22. E
2. A	9. D	16. A	23. C
3. E	10. A	17. B	24. C
4. B	11. E	18. C	25. A
5. B	12. C	19. E	26. D
6. A	13. E	20. A	27. B
7. A	14. D	21. B	

SECTION IV

Question	Question	Question	Question
1. E	8. E	15. E	22. A
2. C	9. C	16. D	23. B
3. D	10. D	17. B	24. C
4. A	11. B	18. B	25. B
5. D	12. A	19. E	
6. B	13. D	20. C	
7. C	14. C	21. E	

LSAT Answer Explanations

Logical Reasoning, Section I

QUESTION 1

<u>Overview</u>: Question 1 asks the student to determine the answer choice that highlights the flaw in the reasoning in the sleep specialist's conclusion. The sleep specialist begins by claiming that insomnia is a serious condition and that women, in particular, should be on guard for signs of it. The sleep specialist goes on to claim that many doctors miss insomnia and instead diagnose women with depression. There is a discussion of sleep apnea (resulting from insomnia) that follows, and the sleep specialist concludes that any woman who has been diagnosed with depression should acquire a second opinion from a female doctor to see if she is actually suffering from insomnia. The student must keep in mind the focus on flawed reasoning *in the conclusion itself* in order to locate the correct answer: the conclusion is that women who have been diagnosed with depression should see female doctors about being tested for insomnia.

THE CORRECT ANSWER:

B This is a fairly simple question that might seem deceptively difficult, largely because it *is* so simple, so the student needs to beware of thinking too hard about it. Clearly, the primary problem with the reasoning is the sleep specialist's conclusion that women who have been diagnosed with depression should see *female* doctors and try to be tested for insomnia. There is nothing in the sleep specialist's previous claims to suggest that the doctors who misdiagnosed women were male; in fact, the sleep specialist claims that insomnia is much more difficult to diagnose in women in general. While it might stand to reason that a female doctor would be more likely to consider a correct diagnosis of insomnia, this line of reasoning is too tenuous to be reliable, given only statements made in the passage. The sleep specialist does not offer any legitimate indication that female doctors diagnose women correctly any more often than their male colleagues, so the conclusion remains flawed. **Answer choice (B)** is correct.

THE INCORRECT ANSWERS:

A The sleep specialist claims that snoring in men has enabled doctors to recognize sleep apnea more quickly, but the sleep specialist does *not* claim that women do not snore, nor can this be clearly inferred from the passage. More importantly, however, this argument is not an immediate part of the *conclusion*, and it does not contribute to the flaw in the sleep specialist's reasoning. Answer choice (A) is incorrect.

C The sleep specialist begins the passage with the claim that insomnia can lead to "potentially serious health risks." It is true that the sleep specialist does not expand this argument much further by explaining what these risks happen to be, but that is unimportant since it does not contribute to the purpose of the passage. Instead, the sleep specialist is attempting to show that doctors often miss a diagnosis of insomnia in women and that women should consider being tested for this condition. As a result, answer choice (C) does not indicate a flaw in the sleep specialist's conclusion, so it cannot be correct.

D At no point does the sleep specialist claim that sleep apnea is or has been linked to depression. In fact, the sleep specialist makes a clear distinction between sleep apnea as a result of insomnia and depression. Answer choice (D) therefore cannot be correct.

E The focus of the sleep specialist's discussion is insomnia in women and the need for doctors to diagnose this condition correctly in them. The mention of sleep apnea is raised in conjunction with insomnia, but it is not the focus. As a result, there is no need for the sleep specialist to discuss other causes of sleep apnea. Answer choice (E) is clearly incorrect.

QUESTION 2

Overview: Question 2 asks the student to review two comments, one from Adelaide and one from Marcel, and then to determine which answer choice best describes the way in which Marcel responds to Adelaide. Adelaide claims that people should stop using mainstream cleaning products and switch to natural cleaning supplies due to the potential health and environmental risks that mainstream products can cause. Marcel argues that natural cleaning supplies do not clean as well and that the mainstream products should be used but kept out of reach so that children cannot get to them. The student should notice right away that Marcel's response seems to miss the point of Adelaide's argument altogether. She claims that the mainstream products contain airborne chemicals (thus calling into question the value of just putting products out of the reach of children), and she claims that natural cleaning supplies are effective (thus contradicting Marcel's claim that they do not clean as well).

THE CORRECT ANSWER:

E **Answer choice (E)** correctly notes that Marcel's response overlooks important details within Adelaide's argument (i.e., the detail about the airborne chemicals and the detail about the natural products being effective) and as a result fails to offer a worthwhile objection. Answer choice (E) is correct.

THE INCORRECT ANSWERS:

A Marcel's response does not necessarily ignore Adelaide's main point: He *does* counter her claims that people should switch from mainstream cleaning products to natural cleaning products. What is more, his response also does not redirect the focus to different topics. So, answer choice (A) cannot be correct.

B At no point does Marcel cede the main point of Adelaide's argument. He does raise the question of cost—which Adelaide does not discuss directly—but this makes answer choice (B) only half correct. Answer choice (B) may be eliminated.

C It is possible that Marcel's information is apocryphal and unsupported, but the information given within the two comments does not provide enough detail for the reader to make the determination that it *is* or *is not*. Marcel does not claim to have support for his arguments, but then again neither does Adelaide. As a result, answer choice (C) is largely irrelevant as an option, functioning primarily as a red herring, and it should be eliminated immediately. *Note*: The student should take care to avoid getting caught up in answer choices such as these that seem less clearly incorrect than other answer choices.

D The only argument Marcel raises that Adelaide does not *directly* address is that of cost: he claims that natural cleaning products cost more than mainstream products. But this does not, in itself, offer an alternative take on the topic that Adelaide is discussing. It should also be noted that Adelaide's comments about the health and environmental risks of mainstream products contain the implication that these dangers are worth the increased cost of the products. Students familiar with this topic might try to argue that many natural cleaning products can be very cheap, but as this is not clearly a feature of Adelaide's argument, it cannot be used against Marcel's claims in this question. Adelaide does not mention inexpensive natural products, and Marcel raises the concern of cost, so it *can* be argued that Marcel makes an argument that Adelaide does not clearly address. As mentioned before, however, this is not enough to suggest that Marcel is offering an alternative take: he is merely trying to undermine Adelaide's claims.

QUESTION 3

Overview: Question 3 provides information about the *Domostroy*, a book of family principles dating from fourteenth-century Russia, and the student is asked to identify the answer choice that best summarizes the main point of the passage. The student should approach any question about the main point from a specific perspective. To locate the main point, it is best to find an answer choice that draws all of the information from the passage into a single statement. Any answer choice that summarizes only part of the passage or paraphrases one comment in the passage is incorrect. In this passage, the main point is that the *Domostroy* is largely seen to be negative today (or since the nineteenth century), but that it remains an important compilation due to its role in shaping Russian families and keeping the merchant class in Russia intact through the Middle Ages. The correct answer choice will reflect this.

THE CORRECT ANSWER:

E **Answer choice (E)** correctly summarizes the main point by targeting the two primary thrusts of the passage: (1) the *Domostroy* is unpopular now, but (2) is still valuable because it had a heavy influence on Russian families and ensured the survival of the Russian merchant class. Answer choice (E), therefore, is the correct answer.

THE INCORRECT ANSWERS:

A Answer choice (A) might be inferred from the passage: due to the information that it contains and to its role in shaping the Russian merchant family during the Middle Ages, historians might very well find this book to be useful. But the passage itself does not say this anywhere, so answer choice (A) cannot function as a summary of the main point and is incorrect.

B The passage *does* claim that the *Domostroy* was an important feature in upper-class Russian family life and that it now has negative connotations. But this fails to include the important statement at the end of the passage about the way that the *Domostroy* contributed to the stability of the merchant class. Answer choice (B) contains insufficient information and is thus incorrect.

C Again, the passage *does* claim that at least two Russian novelists utilized references to the *Domostroy* negatively, but this is certainly not the main point of the passage and is used within the passage primarily to indicate the modern point of view. Answer choice (C) cannot be correct.

D The passage claims that the *Domostroy* contained information that was useful to the upper-class Russian families. It does not claim or imply, however, that it contained information useful *only* to upper-class Russian families. What is more, this is clearly not the main point of the passage, so answer choice (D) is incorrect and may be eliminated.

QUESTION 4

Overview: In question 4, the student is given information about the Hawaiian green turtle and asked to identify the answer choice that best explains the anomaly between the endangered species status of the green turtle (which should protect it from species diminishment) and the actual species diminishment that continues to occur. The passage contains information about the history of the Hawaiian green turtle, suggesting that the Hawaiian green turtle is well protected under its endangered species status. As a result, there is no clear information in the passage itself to indicate a reason for the ongoing diminishment of the species, so the student must consider each of the answer choices in turn to see if it suffices to explain the anomaly. This makes question 4 somewhat more challenging, and the student must pay careful attention to each answer choice to see if it makes sense within the context of the information that is provided.

The Correct Answer:

C If there are tumors attacking the species and targeting the younger turtles, it is clearly arguable that the younger turtles are dying off and, thus, that the turtle population is not increasing in spite of endangered species protection. Put another way: if the tumors are attacking the younger turtles, it means that there is less chance for reproduction and less opportunity for the turtle population to grow. **Answer choice (C)** is correct.

The Incorrect Answers:

A Answer choice (A) provides an interesting piece of information: the Hawaiian green turtle is omnivorous but has recently begun to live as a vegetarian due to available food. A closer look, however, shows that this answer choice does not provide enough information to explain the anomaly. If the turtles are living as vegetarians, they might still be getting enough to eat. And if they are omnivorous, they should be able to live as vegetarians without it creating mass starvation among them. Because answer choice (A) does not contain the suggestion that there is a shortage of vegetation for the turtles to eat, it is insufficient and cannot be correct.

B Answer choice (B) also contains interesting information, but it does not provide enough detail to explain sufficiently the diminishment of the Hawaiian green turtle population. There is no information about a shorter life span among the female turtles, nor is there any information about their range of reproduction age (i.e., whether they are dying while they are still in their reproductive years). As a result, answer choice (B) cannot be correct.

D Answer choice (D) contains no explanation about why the changes in ocean currents from global warming have contributed to a decrease in the Hawaiian green turtle population. Without the further details, answer choice (D) contains no context and simply offers information that does little to explain the anomaly. This answer choice is incorrect and may be eliminated.

E At first glance, answer choice (E) does provide information that could explain the diminishment of the Hawaiian green turtle population: ghost crabs are consuming the hatchlings at the nesting site in the French Frigate Shoals. Upon a closer look, however, there is information to indicate that the ghost crab is a "traditional" predator of the green turtle hatchlings, so this does nothing to explain the more recent reduction of the green turtle population. Answer choice (E) is incorrect.

Questions 5 and 6

Overview: Questions 5 and 6 refer to the passage that discusses the history of the North American heat wave in 1936, a climate phenomenon that caused massive problems for most of North America, including crop shortages and even several thousand deaths. Question 5 asks the student to determine which of the answer choices may be assumed *strictly based on information provided in the passage*. This means that the answer choice cannot infer information that has no support in the passage. Question 6 then asks the student to locate the answer choice that *cannot be inferred*. This means, of course, that four of the answer choices are implied from the details in the passage, but one of them is not.

Question 5

The Correct Answer:

E To arrive at the correct answer in question 5, the student has to sort through a variety of details. The first sentence states that the heat wave caused "serious environmental and economic problems." Further down, the author of the passage notes that there was a "serious shortage" of corn and wheat due to the damage from the heat wave. From this, the student may correctly infer that shortages created a price increase (i.e., "economic problems"). **Answer choice (E)** may be inferred from the details in the passage, so it is correct.

The Incorrect Answers:

A The passage states very clearly that the heat wave damaged crops severely and that it lasted only through the summer. But the passage does not contain enough information to suggest that temperatures were normal the next year or that farmers had no problems with crops in 1937. What is more, there are a variety of factors besides weather that can affect crops, so it would be assuming too much to claim that crops were good in 1937, even if the temperatures were normal. Answer choice (A) cannot be correct.

B The author of the passage claims that scientists in Canada "recorded dangerously high temperatures." While there is no immediate comparison to temperatures in the United States, there is nothing to suggest that the high temperatures in Canada caused fewer problems. Answer choice (B) assumes what is not implied in the passage, so it is incorrect.

C Answer choice (C) provides a seemingly good option. The author of the passage claims that air conditioners were not universal and that many died in the heat. This suggests that air conditioners might have been of assistance in helping those suffering in the heat. But the passage also states that the heat wave "caused problems for the most vulnerable members of society." Even in the highly air-conditioned twenty-first century, heat waves target and kill the most vulnerable members of society. Furthermore, it is too much to assume from the statements made in the passage that air conditioners would certainly have prevented deaths, however likely that may seem. They might have, but there is not enough information to determine the point decisively. Answer choice (C) makes inferences that do not have enough support from the passage, so it cannot be correct.

D The passage claims that the heat wave caused "serious environmental and economic problems." The fact that the United States was also suffering the Great Depression would probably add to this, but there is simply not enough information in the passage to infer this specific piece of information. The heat wave, in and of itself, caused many severe problems. The Great Depression was a separate problem, but it is not addressed, nor does the author of the passage make any reference to outside factors that exacerbated the problems from the heat wave. Answer choice (D) seems like a good option, but it simply has no support in the passage.

Question 6

The Correct Answer:

B **Answer choice (B)** is the only answer choice that *cannot* be inferred from information in the passage. The author of the passage makes no comment on the tradition of hot summers following cold winters, and there is definitely no mention of the winter of 1936 and the temperatures that were recorded during that season. Answer choice (B), therefore, is correct.

The Incorrect Answers:

A The passage notes that the heat wave of 1936 "remains one of the hottest and most destructive on record." From this, it may be assumed that the temperatures noted during the heat wave remain some of the highest of record. Answer choice (A) may certainly be inferred, so it cannot be correct.

C The author of the passage claims that the heat wave of 1936 lasted "only through the summer," so it may be assumed that the heat was no longer a problem by October (i.e., the fall) of 1936. The passage supports the information in answer choice (C), so it cannot be correct.

D The author of the passages states that the heat "stripped the soil of all nutrients" and that the "upper layers of the soil quite literally blew away." From this, the reader may assume that the heat and reduced nutrient quality of the soil made it vulnerable to the wind, so answer choice (D) may be inferred from the passage and is therefore not correct.

E The passage claims that the heat wave "caused problems for the most vulnerable members of society." The most vulnerable members of society include the very old and the very young, so it is safe to assume that these demographics may be included among those who suffered most from the heat. As a result, the passage implies answer choice (E), so it is incorrect.

Question 7

Overview: Question 7 presents statements made by a psychologist about the potential dangers of violent video games. The psychologist cites an incident in which an eleven-year-old boy played a violent video game and then committed an act of violence that resembled the violent crime in the video game. As a result, the psychologist concludes, violent video games can lead to violence and should be restricted. The question then asks the student to compare the weakness in the psychologist's reasoning with the answer choices and locate a similarity. The student should first identify the problem with the psychologist's reasoning: in this case, the weakness follows the line of reasoning that one event makes a trend. In other words, one example of a child playing violent video games and committing an act of violence guarantees further such events; therefore, violent video games should be restricted. The psychologist does not provide multiple accounts but instead offers only one incident and tries to build a case for a larger conclusion based on it. The correct answer choice will reflect a similar problem.

The Correct Answer:

A **Answer choice (A)** correctly provides a statement with a similar weakness. A homeschooled student who received a good education at home won a national spelling bee; therefore, all homeschooled students must be similarly equipped with a good education.

Again, the weakness is that a case is built upon a single example, with a single example representing a trend. Answer choice (A) is correct.

The Incorrect Answers:

B The weakness in answer choice (B) is the suggestion that one program can be of universal benefit to all homeowners who are planning to redecorate. This, however, is not the same as the problem of one example creating a trend. Had the answer choice claimed that because one homeowner benefited all would benefit, the weakness would be comparable. As it is, though, answer choice (B) is incorrect.

C The weakness in answer choice (C) is, in many ways, similar to the weakness in answer choice (B). Answer choice (C) claims that a university has an excellent program for training elementary school teachers; therefore, all of the students who graduate from the program will be good teachers. Had the answer choice claimed that because one student who graduated from the program was a good teacher all would be, the weakness would be similar. Again, it is not, so answer choice (C) is incorrect.

D What makes answer choice (D) incorrect is primarily the presentation of the statement. The claim is made that a single celebrity benefited from a "questionable" product not yet approved by the FDA. As a result, a nutritional supplement company has decided to begin stocking the products. On the one hand, this implies that the company believes the product to be beneficial. *But no specific recommendation is made based on the celebrity's experience.* Instead, a decision is made to sell the product. Because the nutritional supplement company does not follow up with a statement of who would benefit, answer choice (D) does not contain enough similarities to be correct and may be eliminated.

E Answer choice (E) bears virtually no similarity to the statements made in question 7. This answer choice claims that because music classes are shown to "broaden the minds of students and provide increased awareness for other subjects" all schools should incorporate them. There is no suggestion of a single incident making a trend; in fact, the answer choice suggests that a study has been done, a study that might very well have included many students. Answer choice (E) cannot be correct.

Question 8

Overview: Question 8 begins with information about the history of North Korean art, with its early influences from Russia and China and its eventual development of its own artistic voice. The question asks the student to select an answer choice that is suggested by statements made in the passage. Choosing an answer choice based on implication can be very challenging, so the student must keep the details of the passage in mind when reviewing the separate answer choices and *must* eliminate an answer choice that is not clearly suggested by direct statements made in the passage. The key to answering this type of question is the ability to point to a sentence, more than one sentence, or a phrase that provides the link between the correct answer choice and the passage itself.

The Correct Answer:

C The passage states up front that North Korea is a Communist country, that the art of that country has been influenced by political changes, and that North Korean art was originally "dominated by influences from the Soviet Union and China." What is more, the passage goes on to claim that "today North Korean art indicates a more relevant cultural influence from its own revolutionary material." From this, the student may infer that North Korean art initially used the styles and influences of other Communist countries until it had developed its own art. **Answer choice (C)** is correct.

The Incorrect Answers:

A The author notes that "political changes have had a significant impact" on North Korean art, but there is not enough information in the passage to indicate that *all* North Korean art is political. Answer choice (A) is too general, so it may be eliminated immediately.

B The author claims that expatriate North Korean artists favor "turbulent images of landscapes," but there is nothing in the passage to suggest that the artists who have remained in North Korea do not paint landscapes. This might very well be true, but because the passage does not imply it, answer choice (B) cannot be correct.

D The author of the passage suggests that North Korean artists originally took the style and subject of their material from countries like the Soviet Union and China, but there is not enough information in the passage to imply that the North Korean artists also took the specific artistic techniques from these countries, nor that this practice continued for "many decades." The passage does talk about the artistic techniques of expatriate North Korean artists, but answer choice (D) is not clear. In fact, answer choice (D) suggests a long-term absorption of artistic techniques from other countries, so this is entirely irrelevant to the passage. Answer choice (D) may be eliminated.

E Answer choice (E) is largely irrelevant to the information in the passage, focusing on the unique qualities of North Korean artistic techniques, something that the passage does not mention or imply.

Question 9

Overview: In question 9, the student is presented with a scenario in which a family is considering the purchase of solar panels, which are very high in cost. The passage explains the value of having solar panels: they store up sunlight and convert it to energy, thus reducing the cost of energy bills. Unfortunately, the cost of solar panels can be prohibitive, and it can take years to see a return on the investment. The family has decided, however, to invest in the solar panels in the belief that they will see a return quickly enough to make the cost of the panels worthwhile. The question then asks the student to select an answer choice that best explains the family's decision within the context of the information in the passage.

The Correct Answer:

E There are several details in the passage that point to **answer choice (E)** as the correct answer. For one, the passage notes that the solar panels store up sunlight, and the more sunlight that is stored, the more energy is saved for the purpose of reducing the cost of energy bills. Additionally, the family believes that it *will* see a rather quick return on the investment of the solar panels. This should immediately point to location as a significant factor. If solar panels need more sunlight to help with the cost of energy bills, and the family is convinced that the investment will be worthwhile, it stands to reason that they live in a place where they will receive enough sunlight to make the solar panels a good investment. Answer choice (E) offers this explanation, so it is correct. *Note:* Again, this is a fairly simple question, so the student should not step into the trap of thinking too hard about it. The most obvious explanation is the correct one in this case, and the problems with the other answer choices will demonstrate this.

The Incorrect Answers:

A Answer choice (A) seems promising at first glance but not upon closer inspection. The family believes that it will see a *return on the investment fairly quickly*. This suggests that something significant will make the purchase of solar panels worthwhile. Answer choice (A) merely says that the government is offering incentives. There is no information about the type of incentives or the value of them in comparison to the solar panels. Without more information, answer choice (A) does not offer enough detail to explain the family's decision, so it is incorrect.

B In bringing up the mention of coal—which is not discussed or implied in the passage—answer choice (B) has no clear relevance to the passage, so it may be eliminated immediately.

C, D Answer choices (C) and (D) both deal with the supply/demand ratio. In answer choice (C), the increased production of silicon suggests that the production of solar panels is expected to rise in the near future, with the added possibility of reduced cost. That is interesting information, but it has no relevance for the family that is purchasing solar panels *now*. Answer choice (C) cannot be correct, so it may be eliminated. As for answer choice (D), it too suggests that an increased production of solar panels will reduce the cost over time, but that means nothing for the family that is in the process of purchasing solar panels right now. Answer choice (D) may also be eliminated.

Question 10

Overview: Question 10 is another question that requires the student to select an answer choice best summarizing the main point. Again, the student must look for the answer choice that draws out the primary focuses of the paragraph and combines them into a single statement. In question 10, the author of the passage notes several important facts: (1) the medieval pilgrimage was an "opportunity to lower the social bar" because the pilgrims all lived and journeyed together, (2) Geoffrey Chaucer's *The Canterbury Tales* is a story about the tales that pilgrims tell during the medieval pilgrimage, and (3) *The Canterbury Tales* suggests that social structure still remained in place even on the pilgrimage. The correct answer choice will incorporate all of these elements.

The Correct Answer:

D Considering the explanation in the Overview above, **answer choice (D)** best brings all three elements together in a summary statement of the passage. Answer choice (D) is correct.

The Incorrect Answers:

A, C While the author of the passage does mention Chaucer as describing the medieval pilgrimage, there is no mention of whether or not Chaucer's account is *authentic*. As the author seems to rely on it for making the point about the retained social structure, it stands to reason that the story has some authenticity; but this is not a question about inferences but rather about the main point. Answer choice (A) cannot be said to summarize the main point, so it is incorrect. As for answer choice (C), the author of the passage does not discuss whether or not storytelling was a common means of entertainment on the medieval pilgrimage. Such an argument might be inferred from the passage, but it is not the main point. Answer choice (C) is also incorrect.

B, E The author does make a point similar to the ones in answer choices (B) and (E), but neither is the main point; they are only a part of it. Therefore, answer choices (B) and (E) contain insufficient summaries and are incorrect.

Question 11

<u>Overview</u>: In question 11, the student must consider a passage that discusses the mistral, a strong wind most famous in the southern part of France. The author of the passage explains the causes and effects of the mistral in some detail. The author notes that the mistral is a type of katabatic wind, or a wind that develops from a combination of high-pressure and low-pressure systems and pushes in a downward direction from high elevation to low elevation. Due to the location of southern France, with the low-pressure winds off the Mediterranean Sea and the high-pressure winds from the Alps, the people of Provençe in the South of France receive the strong winds of the mistral. The question asks for the answer choice that is most implied by statements made in the passage. As with all questions of this variety, the student must keep the specific comments of the passage in mind. The correct answer will reflect a sentence or two in the passage, and the student should be able to point back to the passage and know exactly which sentence or sentences may be claimed for the inference. The student should keep a close eye on the wording of the answer choices in comparison to the wording of the passage, because even a single word can make a difference in whether or not an answer choice is correct.

The Correct Answer:

A At the end of the passage, the author states that "the air in Provençe is comparatively clear, and the people generally face fewer respiratory problems." This suggests that the mistral wind—which is described as "powerful," "strong," and "formidable" in the passage—actually contributes to the cleanliness of the air by literally blowing pollution and impurities away. The passage thus implies the statement made in **answer choice (A)** very clearly, so answer choice (A) is correct.

The Incorrect Answers:

B In the second sentence of the passage, it is noted, "Katabatic winds are created by the confluence of high-pressure systems and low-pressure systems when the combination of these systems moves downward from a higher elevation and pushes forcefully through a lower elevation." This suggests that katabatic winds are not necessarily unique to the South of France and that other regions of the world might experience such winds. The author of the passage goes on to explain the ways that the people of Provençe have adapted to the mistral, but there is not enough in the passage to argue that all peoples around the world who experience katabatic winds *must* learn to adapt; nor is there a guarantee that they have learned. What is more, the passage does not claim clearly that katabatic winds exist around *any* mountain chain, just that they may occur under certain conditions. There is simply not enough information in the passage to derive the inference made in the second part of answer choice (B), so it is not correct.

C As mentioned above in the explanation for answer choice (B), the author does leave open the possibility that katabatic winds exist in other parts of the world: "Katabatic winds are created by the confluence of high-pressure systems and low-pressure systems when the combination of these systems moves downward from a higher elevation and pushes forcefully through a lower elevation." Even though the author claims that the topographical qualities of Provençe make it ideal for katabatic winds, the author does *not* claim that katabatic winds are unique to the South of France, so answer choice (C) must be incorrect.

D The author claims that the people of Provençe have had to alter the construction of some buildings: "Bell-towers remain open in Provençe, and houses face south." The author does *not* claim or imply, however, that the mistral damages structures *frequently*. Instead, the author suggests that the people of that region have long since learned how to live with the mistral, so their structures are not necessarily damaged as much anymore. Answer choice (D) is incorrect.

E Any student who is familiar with the mistral will know that the information in answer choice (E) is actually correct: the mistral *does* blow through other parts of Europe, but it is strongest (and most famous) in the South of France. But this question is not a test of what the student already knows; it is more important that the student is able to focus on and digest the information in the test itself, independent of outside knowledge. In reality, there is nothing in the passage to suggest that the mistral blows through other parts of Europe but is specifically strongest in Provençe. Yes, the author indicates that the mistral might exist in other places, but those places are not noted or implied in any detail, except for the general remark about the mistral occurring "in Europe." In reality, there is not enough information in the passage to argue confidently that the mistral blows through *most* of Europe or that it is strongest in Provençe. Answer choice (E), therefore, cannot be correct.

Question 12

Overview: Question 12 provides information about the Acholi people, a tribe in Northern Uganda that is known for its traditional agricultural lifestyle and is very unlike the Baganda people of Southern Uganda. The author of the passage contrasts the Acholi and the Baganda, noting that the Baganda developed cities and a monarchy, but the Acholi have always been farmers. When the British began arriving in Uganda, they focused their colonization among the Baganda and used the Acholi people as servants and as soldiers. The author concludes by mentioning that Southern Uganda today has some stability, with its industrialization, while Northern Uganda still struggles with regional wars. The student is asked to select the answer choice that is implied, from the passage, about the Acholi. Again, it is important to focus on what the passage says specifically and to select an answer choice that has an immediate antecedent in the passage.

The Correct Answer:

B The author does not state outright that the British took a superior view of the Baganda over the Acholi. But the author does claim, "When the British colonists arrived in Uganda, they chose to utilize the Acholi as a labor force and for lower-ranking military purposes, while they settled their primary colonies in the more familiar political establishment of Southern Uganda." This suggests that the British were familiar with the social and political organization of Southern Uganda and made the assumption that the Baganda people were superior to the Acholi because they were more developed. The fact that the British chose to use the Acholi only for different forms of service indicates that they did not view their qualities as highly. **Answer choice (B)** may be inferred from the passage, so it is correct.

The Incorrect Answers:

A Although the author of the passage claims that the *British* used the Acholi as servants and as military fighters, there is not enough information in the passage to indicate that the Baganda did the same. In fact, the author states that the Acholi have traditionally been farmers and thus indicates that they did not take up the different types of service until the British arrived. Answer choice (A) is not clearly implied in the passage, so it is not correct.

C Answer choice (C) is a potentially tricky rewording of statements made in the passage. Yes, the author claims that the Acholi were an agricultural people, and probably continued to be until the British arrived. But there is not enough information in the passage to argue that the author claims the Acholi people to be unfamiliar with war. The fact that the Acholi are still struggling with regional conflicts suggests that there have been regional differences among the Acholi for some time but that these differences were minimized before the Acholi became official soldiers among the British. Answer choice (C) has no clear implication in the passage, so it is not correct.

D As with answer choice (C), answer choice (D) seems to have potential, depending on how the student chooses to read the author's tone in the passage. There seems to be a hint of disapproval about the British colonization, and it is all too easy to read this as a way of placing blame on the British. But the student should beware of reading too much into this tone, because it is unreliable. The only real implication made about the Acholi people is that the British did not necessarily view them to be as superior as the Baganda because the Acholi were farmers. There is simply not enough information in the passage to argue that the British are *entirely responsible* for the conditions among the Acholi today. Too much is left out of the passage, including information about how long Uganda has been independent of Britain (or even that it *is* independent of Britain) and what political events have occurred in recent years. Answer choice (D) is tempting, but it ultimately does not have enough support in the passage, so it must be eliminated.

E The passage does not provide enough information about the response from either the Acholi or the Baganda to the British colonization, so there is clearly not enough information to support the claim that the Acholi welcomed the opportunity to abandon their agricultural lifestyle (or, in converse, to suggest that they despised colonization). Answer choice (E) is incorrect.

Question 13

Overview: Question 13 begins with a passage explaining the challenge of understanding the evolution of language. The author of the passage mentions that linguistic scholars do not necessarily agree on what causes the evolution of language. One claims colloquial distinctions, while others suggest that geographical divisions are most responsible. The passage concludes with the add-on statement that as the world becomes more global and geographical divisions give way to globalization, languages might ultimately join and become a single language. The question asks the student to select an answer choice that is supported by claims made in the passage. In this question, the passage is organized somewhat differently from previous passages, in that in begins with a general statement about the difficulties of reconciling two features. It continues with one side of a contrast and actually concludes with the other side of the contrast without a clear hint of a reconciliation or a return to the opening statement. So, the student needs to beware of assuming too much about the author's preference for one side of the issue or the other.

The Correct Answer:

E Since the passage does not offer a clear conclusion about the reconciliation for the two contrasting views of language evolution, the student is left with selecting an answer choice that is *clearly* suggested from the passage. The passage opens with the following two sentences: "The majority of linguistic scholars recognize that language will inevitably evolve over time. What causes this change, however, is the subject of great debate." From this, it may be inferred that (1) languages are dynamic and do not stop evolving, and (2) even scholars who do not agree on the reason for the change can agree that change does occur. The rest of the passage supports these inferences, so **answer choice (E)** is correct.

The Incorrect Answers:

A Recognizing that answer choice (A) is incorrect requires a careful look at the wording. The author claims, "One respected scholar claims that it is the colloquial or nonstandard usages within a language that drive its change and development." And yet the answer choice indicates that colloquial and nonstandard usages are *recognized* to be *significant factors* in language evolution. One scholar does not make a general recognition among linguists, and while this scholar might be correct, the passage does not necessarily support this claim. Answer choice (A) is incorrect.

B The author of the passage indicates that linguistic scholars do not *currently* agree on what causes language evolution. There is nothing in the passage to suggest, however, that linguistic scholars will *never* agree. Answer choice (B) assumes more than the passage implies, so it is incorrect.

C The end of the passage suggests that some scholars believe there will be an end to individual languages and a resultant global language. The passage does *not* imply, however, that this is a universal opinion or that it is the reconciliation of the contrasting ideas. It is simply one idea, so it does not function as anything more than a single theory in the passage. Answer choice (C) assumes too much, so it cannot be correct.

D The passage is focused primarily on language evolution and not language origin(s), and there is nothing whatsoever in the passage to suggest that all languages derive from a single source. Answer choice (D) may be eliminated.

Question 14

Overview: Question 14 presents a statement made by a small bookstore owner about the impending failure of many small businesses due to the advent of online booksellers. The small bookstore owner claims that local businesses are a significant part of a community and that they contribute more than just the products that they sell. The small bookstore owner then concludes with the statement that people should require that online booksellers face restrictions to prevent the complete collapse of local bookstores. The question asks the student to select an answer choice that best explains the assumption on which the small bookstore owner's reasoning is based. To locate the correct answer, the student needs to focus on several features of the small bookstore owner's argument: (1) Online booksellers have low prices that local bookstores cannot maintain, (2) local businesses, such as local small bookstores, offer important qualities for a community, and (3) small bookstores may not have prices as low as online booksellers do, but they provide intangible benefits for a community. From this, the student should be able to see that the small business owner's assumption is that the intangible qualities of local businesses are more valuable than the savings that people will receive from purchasing books online. The correct answer will reflect this.

The Correct Answer:

A **Answer choice (A)** correctly reflects the explanation in stating that the small bookstore owner's assumption is about the intangible qualities of community life that small businesses allegedly provide and how these outweigh the extra costs the small businesses must charge. Answer choice (A) is correct.

The Incorrect Answers:

B Answer choice (B) sounds tempting, but it applies an irrelevant statement to the small bookstore owner's reasoning and, thus, has no immediate connection to the actual statements that the small bookstore owner makes. Answer choice (B) should be eliminated immediately.

C The small bookstore owner *does* make a statement about online booksellers and their "artificially low prices," but this does not immediately mean that the prices charged in small, local shops are *artificially* high. There is a definite implication that the prices charged in the local shops are higher, but there is not enough in the passage to indicate that they are unreasonably so. Answer choice (C) puts words in the small bookstore owner's mouth that cannot be inferred from the passage, so it is incorrect.

D The small bookstore owner does not necessarily claim that local bookstores alone provide an important venue for community life. In fact, the small bookstore owner seems to be making a statement about *all* local small businesses and uses the bookstore as an immediate example. Answer choice (D), therefore, is irrelevant to the passage and is incorrect.

E Answer choice (E) does offer—in part, at least—an assumption in the small bookstore owner's reasoning. The small bookstore owner says, "Citizens should demand that restrictions be placed on online merchants to prevent the eradication of local small businesses." These restrictions would almost certainly come at the government level, so the small bookstore owner is holding the government partially responsible for assisting in this situation. But this is not immediately connected to the *assumption* about the importance of small, local businesses. Additionally, answer choice (E) claims that the government is *entirely* responsible, while the small bookstore owner clearly places some responsibility at the citizen level. Answer choice (E) cannot be correct.

Question 15

Overview: Question 15 presents a conversation between Johan and Andrian about global warming. Johan argues that global warming is essentially a normal feature of climate change and that the earth experiences such climate shifts periodically. He claims that human actions and environmental pollution have not caused global warming and that the earth is simply going through an expected climate change. Andrian responds by claiming that if scientists really recognized global warming to be a normal feature of climate change, governments would not be spending so much money on preventing global warming. Andrian goes on to say that since the earth's climate is changing, and man has been releasing an increasing rate of pollution into the environment, it stands to reason that the argument about man's contribution to global warming is correct. The student is then asked to identify which of the answer choices best characterizes Andrian's response to Johan.

The student should recognize at once that Andrian's response to Johan has very little substance to it. He initially disagrees with Johan but then uses a circular argument to explain his point. What is more, he does not address any of Johan's primary points of support and, as a result, his (Andrian's) argument makes little sense as a response to Johan. While the question itself does not necessarily point to identifying a flaw in Andrian's reasoning, the correct answer will need to reflect this failure on Andrian's part.

The Correct Answer:

C **Answer choice (C)** accurately explains Andrian's response and the problem with it: he disagrees with Johan but does absolutely nothing to target and undermine Johan's points of support. Answer choice (C), therefore, is correct.

The Incorrect Answers:

A At no point does Andrian attack Johan personally, and there is not part of his response that could be perceived as a personal attack, so answer choice (A) must be incorrect.

B Andrian relies on virtually no evidence to back up his line of reasoning, and while this in itself could be deemed faulty, it cannot be said that he actually *relies on faulty evidence*. Answer choice (B) is also incorrect and may be eliminated.

D Andrian *does* focus on disagreeing with Johan, but Johan's argument is not divided into two parts, so it cannot be said that Andrian focuses on one part but ignores the second part. Johan's argument is a single statement about man's contribution to global warming, and Andrian only focuses on disputing Johan's point that man has had no part in it (with no supporting evidence on Andrian's part except for a hypothetical statement that governments would not spend money on something nonexistent). Answer choice (D) is incorrect.

E Again, Johan's argument is not actually divided into two parts: it is a single argument with several points of support. So Andrian cannot be said to attack the secondary part and overlook the main part. Answer choice (E) is also incorrect.

Question 16

Overview: In question 16, the student is given information about a pharmaceutical company that has manufactured a controversial drug and is attempting to market it. The studies that have been done on the drug indicate that it does offer the results claimed but that it also creates serious side effects. After more testing, the CEO of the pharmaceutical company makes a statement that the drug is safe and will be marketed and sold with the approval of the FDA. The question asks the student to select the answer choice that most seriously undermines the statements made by the CEO of the pharmaceutical company. Each answer choice will have to be considered individually, but there are several points within the passage on which the student needs to focus: (1) the drug is controversial and has potentially serious side effects, (2) the pharmaceutical company has done further testing, and (3) the CEO does not actually claim that the FDA *has* approved the drug but that it will be marketed and sold "with the approval of the FDA." This final point might be the most significant, since the CEO's wording is suspiciously confusing—"with the approval of the FDA" suggests a conditional approval that could affect the safety of the drug and the ability of the pharmaceutical company to market it legally.

The Correct Answer:

E As suggested in the Overview above, **answer choice (E)** offers a statement that indicates a conditional approval from the FDA. This approval is based on the altering of ingredients in the drug, and there is nothing to indicate that the company *has* altered the ingredients. So the drug would probably not be safe, and the CEO is making claims that seem to be deliberately obscure. Answer choice (E) is correct.

The Incorrect Answers:

A Although previous behavior may indicate future actions, there is no guarantee that just because the company has lied in the past it is lying again. Answer choice (A) offers far too tenuous a reason to undermine the CEO's claims, so it is not correct.

B The presence of government money is largely irrelevant to the accuracy of the CEO's claims in this case. Furthermore, if the company were receiving government money, it is more likely that they would be willing to make the drug as safe as possible since someone else would be paying the bill, and the company would be required to submit to yet another level of government oversight. Answer choice (B) actually functions more in support of the CEO's claims, so it is not correct.

C As in answer choice (A), the fact that the board of the pharmaceutical company is being investigated for marketing fraud does not necessarily mean that they are committing marketing fraud in *this* case. The connection between the two events is too uncertain to be valid, so answer choice (C) is incorrect.

D The fact that another pharmaceutical company is in the process of manufacturing a similar drug does more to support the CEO's claims than to undermine them, because the original pharmaceutical company would be more likely to produce a safe drug with a competitor on the market. Answer choice (D) is also incorrect.

QUESTION 17

Overview: Question 17 presents a statement that is made by a ballet instructor regarding the specific style that the studio employs in teaching its ballet students. The ballet instructor claims that although the others styles—Russian Vaganova and French—are certainly worthwhile, the Cecchetti style is preferred at the studio for consistency and the development of excellent technique. The ballet instructor goes on to say that based on strong technique, the dancers are more able to develop artistry in their dance, and the instructor concludes by vouching for the success of the method in saying that many dancers from the studio have become professional dancers. The question asks the student to determine which of the answer choices most clearly represents the assumption on which the ballet instructor's argument about the value of the Cecchetti style is based. The student should already be able to determine the correct answer without reviewing the answer choices, because buried in the middle of the ballet instructor's comment is the assumption: "The daily regime of similarity in practice and repetition in steps yields the strongest results, and we believe that this will ultimately provide a basis of solid technique. From there, dancers are able to develop personal artistry in their performance." There is a dual-layer statement in here that what young dancers need is technique first, because they will be able to develop individual artistry based on technique. The correct answer will reflect this.

THE CORRECT ANSWER:

D **Answer choice (D)** accurately explains the assumption that the ballet instructor makes: individual artistry can develop best when a dancer has had a good foundation of solid technical training. Answer choice (D), therefore, is correct.

THE INCORRECT ANSWERS:

A Answer choice (A) might very well be an *inference* about the ballet instructor's opinion regarding the Russian Vaganova method and the French style. But this is not the *assumption* on which the belief in the Cecchetti method is based. The ballet instructor founds the belief in the Cecchetti method on the qualities of the method itself and not necessarily on the lack of qualities in the other methods. Answer choice (A) cannot be correct.

B The ballet instructor does claim that the studio has produced a number of dancers who have gone on to a professional level. The ballet instructor does *not* claim, however, that the best dancers in the world have been trained in the Cecchetti style, nor is this in any way an assumption on which the support for the Cecchetti style is based. Answer choice (B) is incorrect.

C The ballet instructor clearly values both technique and artistry. The statements made distinguishing the two qualities are intended to suggest that one cannot be developed without the presence of the other. Far from undermining artistry, this suggests that it is equal to technique and that the two qualities must work in conjunction with one another. Answer choice (C) is incorrect.

E Answer choice (E) is certainly not an assumption on which the ballet instructor's comments about the Cecchetti style are based, and it is not even an inference to be drawn from the passage. So, it may be eliminated at once.

Question 18

Overview: Question 18 presents information about the Breton language of Brittany, focusing primarily on its history and its current status in the northern part of France. The author of the passage notes that Breton is a Celtic language in origin (similar to Welsh), that it was at one time a language spoken by the elite, but that it is now spoken only by a few people in Brittany and is not officially recognized as a language of France. The question then asks the student to select an answer choice that best summarizes the main point of the passage, so the student needs to condense and distill in order to determine what the passage is saying. The student should note specifically that the passage does *not* offer opinion but rather fact, so any answer choice that leans toward shaping an opinion must automatically be incorrect.

The Correct Answer:

B **Answer choice (B)** accurately summarizes the overall point of the passage: Breton was an important language at one time but has since declined in spite of the fact than some people in Brittany are trying to revive it. Answer choice (B) is correct.

The Incorrect Answers:

A, D Answer choices (A) and (D) partially summarize the passage, but neither summarizes it in full. Answer choice (A) includes the important information about how Breton was at one time a "status language." But answer choice (A) fails to bring in clearly the information about how attempts have been unsuccessful to revive Breton, focusing instead on a vague comment about how the language has lost its status. Answer choice (D) focuses on the other half of the passage, with information about how there have been efforts to revive Breton, but it ignores the historical information altogether. This choice also makes the unsubstantiated claim that the decline is due to the government's refusal to recognize Breton as an official language. Answer choices (A) and (D), therefore, must be incorrect.

C Answer choice (C) offers a statement of opinion that the passage does not support, so it must be eliminated immediately, as noted in the Overview above.

E Answer choice (E) functions as an inference, but it is not a summary of the passage, so it, too, must be eliminated.

Questions 19 and 20

Overview: Questions 19 and 20 are based on a passage that discusses the eating disorder known as orthorexia nervosa, which has only recently begun receiving attention among doctors. The condition was first identified by Colorado doctor Steven Bratman and results from an obsessive desire to eat healthy foods. This pursuit of healthy eating can ultimately backfire and become an eating disorder, one that Bratman himself experienced. According to the passage, most doctors do not yet officially recognize orthorexia nervosa, but more doctors are becoming aware of the condition and are beginning to diagnose it. Question 19 asks the student to identify the answer choice that represents a claim supported by the passage, and question 20 asks the student to identify an inference that may be drawn from information in the passage. In answering these two questions, the student needs to distinguish between a claim that is supported and an inference. A supported claim is generally a statement of opinion that derives support from statements made in the passage, whereas an inference is a statement that is *implied* in the passage. The student should be careful to focus on the distinction between opinion and implication when answering these two questions.

Question 19

The Correct Answer:

C The passage indicates strongly that orthorexia nervosa *is* an eating disorder, and as a result, the passage offers support for the statement that the condition *should be* classified as an eating disorder along with the other currently recognized eating disorders. **Answer choice (C)** is correct.

The Incorrect Answers:

A The passage indicates that orthorexia nervosa is as serious an eating disorder as anorexia nervosa or bulimia, but there is nothing in the passage to support the claim that it is *more* serious. The author of the passage indicates that the condition begins with good intentions, but that does not necessarily make it more serious, and the author does not question the seriousness of the other conditions in comparison to the seriousness of orthorexia nervosa. Answer choice (A) is incorrect.

B Far from calling into question the official recognition of orthorexia nervosa, the author of the passage indicates support for it. And while there is no mention of insurance in the passage itself, there is also no reason to believe that the author would encourage official recognition at the medical level but not among insurance companies. Answer choice (B) is incorrect.

D Answer choice (D) has absolutely no support in the passage. The author comments on the fact that orthorexia nervosa often begins with good intentions, but there is no indication that the condition has any benefits. Instead it is described as "unhealthy" and a "dangerous obsession that ultimately harms the body more than helps it." Answer choice (D) may be eliminated.

E Although the reason for the delay in recognizing orthorexia nervosa among medical professionals might very well be due to the lack of research on the condition, the author does not seem to support the need for more delay in recognizing it officially. Instead the author seems more concerned with seeing the condition acknowledged for its severity. Answer choice (E) is also incorrect.

Question 20

The Correct Answer:

B **Answer choice (B)** accurately reflects the implications of the passage—that the increasing number of diagnoses of the condition among doctors suggests acknowledgement of the condition among medical professionals. Answer choice (B) is correct.

The Incorrect Answers:

A The passage does mention that Dr. Bratman suffered symptoms of orthorexia nervosa, but there is no clear mention of a demographic for those who develop the condition—except that it develops among people who are pursuing a lifestyle of healthy eating. So it is assuming too much to infer that other professionals have suffered from the condition. Answer choice (A) is incorrect.

C The author of the passage claims clearly that those who develop orthorexia nervosa are primarily concerned with eating healthy foods. But the author does *not* identify these people as primarily being adults, and there is not even enough information in the passage to support the claim that teenagers are the primary sufferers of other eating disorders. Answer choice (B) assumes too much, so it may be eliminated.

D The author of the passage does not offer a time frame for the onset of orthorexia nervosa, mentioning only that the name was coined in 1997. The condition could very well have been in existence, but unnamed, for decades or even centuries, so it cannot be inferred that it is only a recent development. Answer choice (D) is incorrect.

E The author comments that a number of doctors have begun to diagnose the condition, but there is no clear mention about the response of the medical community in general. It might very well be true that most medical professionals are loathe to embrace the condition as an official eating disorder, but the passage is unclear, so this cannot be clearly inferred. Answer choice (E) is incorrect.

Question 21

Overview: In question 21, the student is given information about the potential health and environmental risks of perfume. The author of the passage claims that perfume contains chemicals that are known to be allergens. These allergens can cause various topical reactions, both minor and severe. The passage concludes with a comment that the chemical linalool is frequently used in perfume and is also known to be a skin allergen but that perfume manufacturers seldom use it in the form that causes direct topical reactions. The question then asks for the student to determine the answer choice that best explains this anomaly: linalool, which causes topical reactions in perfume wearers, is not used in the form that *does* cause topical reactions. This question might sound confusing at first, but there really is only one possible explanation for why an ingredient known for topical reactions upon application, in a certain form, can cause topical reactions when it is not in that form. The student needs to bear in mind that perfume, by its nature, is applied topically *as an inhalant.* Even though the passage mentions the topical qualities of perfume several times, there is no mention of reactions caused from inhalation of perfume. This should suggest to the student that the correct answer will provide some explanation of allergic—and likely topical—reactions from inhaling perfume.

The Correct Answer:

A As discussed in the Overview, the correct answer provides a clear link between the inhalation of perfumes (and the chemicals that are contained within them) and the topical reactions that some people have from perfumes—in spite of the fact that the chemicals are not necessarily supposed to create topical reactions. **Answer choice (A)** is correct.

The Incorrect Answers:

B Answer choice (B) is interesting but largely irrelevant. The passage is not focused on the potential for nonallergic reactions from perfume ingredients in the future, but rather on the current reactions from certain ingredients. Answer choice (B) cannot be correct.

C Again, answer choice (C) is interesting, but it does little to explain the problem of topical reactions from ingredients that are not supposed to cause topical reactions in certain forms. Answer choice (C) functions primarily as a red herring, so it should be eliminated.

D Answer choice (D) ignores the situation discussed in the passage and the question: while many people might not have allergic reactions, *some people do*. And question 21 is concerned with those who do. Answer choice (D) cannot be correct.

E Both ethyl acetone and acetate are mentioned in the passage, but answer choice (E) does not offer any clear explanation about how the mention of them in this answer choice links them to the question that has been asked. Answer choice (E) is also irrelevant and must be eliminated.

QUESTION 22

Overview: In question 22, the student is given a passage that discusses the various literary developments among the post-World War I generation. The passage begins with Gertrude Stein's comment that this was a "lost generation," and the author of the passage goes on to explain that many of the post-war writers began turning toward modernism in literature by "throwing off the restraints of tradition and conveying an overall sense of emptiness and indifference." The author does note that modern literature was in development prior to the start of World War I but that it became far more prevalent after the war. Additionally, the author concludes by noting that one scholar has argued for an increase in fantasy literature after World War I, more in fact "than any other generation in history." The question asks the student to determine which of the answer choices might best be inferred from statements made in the passage. As always with inference questions, the student must focus on locating an answer choice that can point directly back to a statement or more than one statement made in the passage. Any answer choice that pushes the inference beyond the information provided will not be correct, because it assumes more than the passage offers.

THE CORRECT ANSWER:

E The discussion of the rise of modern literature and the mention of the rise of fantasy literature after World War I—in conjunction with the explanation that both forms were in existence but not necessarily prevalent prior to the war—suggests that the war itself contributed to the genres in which the "lost generation" chose to write. **Answer choice (E)** best explains this and is, therefore, correct.

THE INCORRECT ANSWERS:

A The author of the passage does mention that post-World War I modern writers are often known for "throwing off the restraints of tradition and conveying an overall sense of emptiness and indifference." This does *not* mean, however, that their writing is among the bleakest and most apathetic in all of literary history, nor can this be inferred from the information provided in the passage. Answer choice (A) assumes too much, so it cannot be correct.

B The passage indicates that *many* post-World War I authors rejected literary conventions of the past. The passage does *not* indicate, however, that *all authors* rejected the literary conventions of the past. The word "all" is far too universal to be inferred from the information in the passage, so answer choice (B) must be incorrect.

C The author of the passage *does* imply that a number of post-World War I authors were veterans who had experienced the horrors of the war. But there is nothing in the passage to suggest that veterans focused primarily on literature as an outlet after the war. Answer choice (C) assumes too much, so it must be eliminated.

D The passage certainly implies that World War I left the soldiers with strong impressions, but there is simply not enough information in the passage to indicate the number of soldiers to have survived the war. The initial part of answer choice (D) cannot be inferred from the passage, so it must be incorrect.

QUESTION 23

Overview: Question 23 records an account of Charles Darwin's relationship with his friend and former tutor Adam Sedgwick, particularly after the publication of Darwin's *Origin of Species*. Sedgwick was not a supporter of natural selection, a theory that Darwin developed and propounded in *Origin of Species*. (The student should note that this is not stated outright but is implied in the statement, "...he encouraged his friend and one-time pupil to beware of embracing natural selection," which suggests the topic of Darwin's book.) In writing to Darwin, Sedgwick's response was "both cautious and kind," and he warned Darwin against the theory. When he wrote to another friend about the book, however, Sedgwick chose stronger words and vehemently opposed Darwin's theories as "untrue and even dangerous." The question then asks the student to identify an answer choice that explains—based on the information in the passage—why Sedgwick's response to Darwin was less candid. The student should recognize immediately that there is a limited amount of information in the passage to account for the differences in Sedgwick's remark. The passage claims that Sedgwick "strenuously opposed" natural selection and that he was a "friend and former tutor" to Darwin. This leaves the student with only two real options: (1) Sedgwick was *so* opposed to the theory of natural selection that he shared his feelings honestly with his friend, or (2) Sedgwick always opposed the idea but still respected Darwin as a friend and former student and thus felt the need to maintain that respect despite the different opinion. Option 1 provides an explanation in part, while option 2 provides an explanation in full. The correct answer should reflect the second option.

THE CORRECT ANSWER:

D Based on the information provided in the Overview above, **answer choice (D)** best explains Sedgwick's different comments to Darwin. As a personal friend and as a one-time figure of authority to Darwin, Sedgwick was concerned about using that position to express his full criticism of Darwin's theory. Answer choice (D) is correct.

THE INCORRECT ANSWERS:

A Answer choice (A) would only be a good explanation if the passage had provided enough information to justify it. As it stands, however, the author of the passage is silent on the question of Sedgwick's ability to flatter. Answer choice (A) assumes too much, therefore it is incorrect.

B Again, answer choice (B) assumes information that cannot possibly be inferred from the information in the passage, so it should be eliminated at once.

C Answer choice (C) is tricky, because it provides a perfectly valid situation: Sedgwick might have written to Darwin initially with a tone of kindness but grew more frustrated over time and vented his irritation to a friend. The problem with this, however, is that the passage does not explain how much time elapsed between the letter to Darwin and the letter to the unnamed friend. It was simply "later," which could have been a matter of hours, days, weeks, and so forth. What is more, the passage does not contain enough detail to suggest that Sedgwick's feelings about the theory grew more strongly in opposition over time. In fact, the author of the passage makes it clear from the start that Sedgwick always opposed the theory of natural selection, so the reader cannot infer that he grew increasingly upset about it. Answer choice (C) cannot be correct.

E The author of the passage provides no information about Darwin's response (if any) to Sedgwick's letter, so it is impossible to infer what Sedgwick's reaction to such might have been. Answer choice (E) is clearly incorrect, so it may be eliminated.

Question 24

Overview: Question 24 presents information about the devastating influenza outbreak of 1918, an outbreak that according to some records might have killed as many as 100 million people. The author of the passage notes several anomalies that made this particular outbreak of influenza so unusual: (1) it occurred during the summer, and (2) it killed more strong young adults than children and elderly people. The question then asks the student to identify the answer choice that provides the best explanation for the anomaly of the influenza killing so many healthy young adults, when the disease usually strikes the very young and very old the hardest. To select the correct answer, the student must consider each answer choice carefully, in turn. The key to answering this question accurately will be in identifying an answer choice that takes all of the information in the passage and adds something to it that *clearly* explains the immediate issue without leaving other questions unanswered. The incorrect answer choices will add potentially valuable information but will also leave confusions about the information that has been provided.

The Correct Answer:

C **Answer choice (C)** explains that the *type* of virus causing the 1918 influenza outbreak is what is believed to have caused the disease to strike the unexpected demographic. Furthermore, answer choice (C) leaves no remaining questions or confusions (except for a possible interest in simply acquiring more information). It explains clearly that the virus has been linked to a specific variety known especially for doing just what the 1918 influenza outbreak did. The reader does not need further information or statistics in order to gauge the explanation in this answer choice; it is clear enough in itself. Answer choice (C), therefore, is correct.

The Incorrect Answers:

A Answer choice (A) offers a believable explanation about soldier deaths being combined with influenza deaths, but this does not in itself explain why the virus attacked so many young people. It only suggests that the number of deaths recorded from influenza might be inaccurate due to the war occurring at the same time. What is more, this answer choice leaves the student with a variety of questions about what this really means. Were there more soldier deaths and fewer influenza deaths? Vice versa? Were soldier deaths included among the "healthy young people" who died? This answer choice is too vague to be valid, so it must be incorrect.

B The key phrase in answer choice (B) is "general population." There is no indication from this answer choice that the governments immunized the young children and the very old but not the healthy young people. The answer choice merely says that the governments were unable to provide vaccines for everyone. Again, answer choice (B) is too vague and leaves too many unanswered questions to be correct, so it may be eliminated.

D Answer choice (D) does offer a possible explanation, except that the passage notes the virus to have attacked "healthy young adults." If the immune systems of soldiers were already weakened, they would not fall into this category. What is more, there is not enough information about the number of soldiers who were serving or who caught the disease to justify this particular answer choice as the clear explanation for why the disease targeted so many young adults. Answer choice (D) cannot be correct.

E Answer choice (E) sounds good, but it is entirely misleading. Once again, the information about the numbers among soldiers is vague, and the passage itself suggests that there *were* young children and older adults who caught the disease—just not as many as might be expected. So, it stands to reason that plenty of young adult civilians caught it as well, leaving this answer choice to be largely irrelevant without further information. Answer choice (E) should be eliminated.

QUESTION 25

Overview: Question 25 presents the student with information about Lake Balaton, a very large lake in Central Europe (the largest in that region, in fact) and a very important body of water to the nation of Hungary, which is landlocked. The author notes that Lake Balaton plays a significant role in the climate of that area, creating an almost Mediterranean quality to a region of Hungary that is hundreds of miles from the Mediterranean Sea. Additionally, the soil of the Lake Balaton area is unique with its quality of volcanic ash—which is usually very high in nutrients—and the lake itself gives off extra sunlight through secondary radiation. The author of the passage concludes by noting that the wine of the area around Lake Balaton is very popular. The question asks the student to select an answer choice that may be inferred, requiring once again that the student choose an answer based on *specific* statements in the passage. If the student cannot point directly to a comment in the passage as support for the inference, it must be incorrect.

THE CORRECT ANSWER:

C The author of the passage notes several features of the region: (1) the climate is similar to that of the climate near the Mediterranean Sea, (2) the soil around the lake is rich in volcanic ash, and (3) the lake gives off secondary radiation and, thus, extra sunlight. With this, the author then makes the statement that the area is known for its wine. The immediate inference is that the lake itself has created a region that is good for wine. **Answer choice (C)** is correct.

THE INCORRECT ANSWERS:

A The author of the passage does note that the soil around Lake Balaton contains volcanic ash. But the author makes no mention of a volcano itself, and it is assuming too much that there is/was a volcano that is now extinct. There is reason to believe that a volcano once affected the region, but there is simply not enough information to make the statement that it "permanently affected temperatures." Answer choice (A) cannot be correct.

B, E The climate of the Lake Balaton region would suggest it as a popular tourist destination, but the passage does not provide enough detail to indicate *who* the tourists might be. Similarly, answer choice (E) assumes far too much about the way that the climate might affect migration (if any) to the region. Neither answer choice (B) nor answer choice (E) is clearly implied, so both must be incorrect.

D The area around Lake Balaton is implied to be very fertile, but the passage makes no comparison to other fertile areas in Europe. The author notes only that Lake Balaton is the largest lake in Central Europe; it might not necessarily have the greenest and most fertile region. Answer choice (D) cannot be inferred, so it is incorrect.

Analytical Reasoning, Section II

Cluster 1:

There are seven possible spaces for stores on the side of the road.

1	2	3	4	5	6	7

To begin diagramming, start with the most restrictive condition, which is stated in the question itself and puts the dry cleaners in the middle space.

			D			

The most restrictive condition is condition #1, McDonalds is at the end of the street. This means that there are possible spaces for McDonalds, #1 or #7.

M			D			
			D			M

The next step combines conditions #2 and #3, Sonic is to the immediate west (left) of Taco Bell and neither of them is next to the McDonalds. This actually gives two possible locations for Sonic and Taco Bell in each of the current diagrams.

M			D	S	T	
M			D		S	T
S	T		D			M
	S	T	D			M

The final condition is condition #4, the Burger King is to the west (left) of Wendy's and Sonic and not next to McDonalds. For the first two diagrams, this is easy. Burger King cannot be next to the McDonalds, so it can't be in space #2. Sonic is already in the diagram, but a space also needs to be left for Wendy's to be east of Burger King leaving only space #3 for Burger King. Putting both Burger King and Wendy's into the first two diagrams.

M		B	D	S	T	W
M		B	D	W	S	T

In the second two diagrams, Burger King cannot be in space #6 because that would put it next to McDonalds, and it cannot be in space #5 or #3 as that would put it to the east of Sonic rather than the west. This forces Sonic and Taco Bell in diagram #3 to move one space east to match diagram #4 to get Burger to the west of Sonic in both cases.

B	S	T	D			M
B	S	T	D			M

Diagrams #3 and #4 are now identical and the temptation may be to combine them, but Wendy's and Jack in the Box can be in either space #5 or #6, so keep them separate to represent this.

B	S	T	D	W	J	M
B	S	T	D	J	W	M

Putting Jack in the Box in the only empty space in diagrams #1 and #2, the final diagrams are:

Diagram #1

M	J	B	D	S	T	W

Diagram #2

M	J	B	D	W	S	T

Diagram #3

B	S	T	D	W	J	M

Diagram #4

B	S	T	D	J	W	M

1. **A.** Start with the first answer choice and move down the list comparing each one to the four diagrams. The first one, A, is actually the correct answer. All the other answers are next to Jack in the Box in one of the diagrams.

2. **D.** Burger King is next to Jack in the Box only in diagrams #1 and #2, so reference only those. Wendy's is next to Taco Bell and the end of the street in diagram #1 and the dry cleaners and Sonic in diagram #2, so McDonalds and D is the correct answer.

3. **E.** Jack in the Box is only east (right) of Wendy's in diagram #3. In that diagram, Burger King is at the end of the street, Sonic is west (left) of and McDonalds is east (right) of the dry cleaners, and Jack in the Box is west (left) of McDonalds. However, the Wendy's is not next to Taco Bell, making E the correct answer.

4. **B.** Just look at each answer choice and see which one matches a diagram. B is the only arrangement of stores that does, matching diagram #2, making it the correct answer.

5. **C.** Wendy's is only next to Sonic in diagram #2. This makes it easy to look at each of the pairs in the answer choices and see that only C, Jack in the Box is next to Burger King, is a correct pairing.

6. **B.** Diagrams #1 and #2 have McDonalds on the west end of the street making this a bit more difficult to check than the last one. But Wendy's can be either on the west (left) or east (right) side of Jack in the Box, while all the other answers state relationships that are true in both diagrams, so B is the correct answer.

Cluster 2:

To diagram this problem, translate the conditions into symbols. Condition #1, the Lemon is directly across from the Banana, translates into **L<->B**. Condition #2, the Chocolate is immediately to the left of, and on the same side of the cart as, the Vanilla, translates into **C<-V**. Condition #3, the Strawberry is next to the Pistachio, translates into **SP**. So the symbol translations of the conditions for this problem are:

L<->B

C<-V

SP

Next, draw a visual representation of the serving cart. The questions states that the ice cream is attached two to a side around a square serving cart with each container directly across from another one:

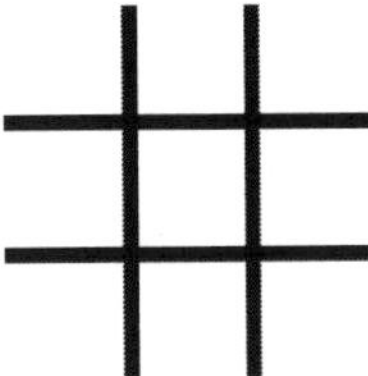

Then add condition #2 to the diagram; it could be put on any side of the serving cart, but for ease of use, put it on the south side.

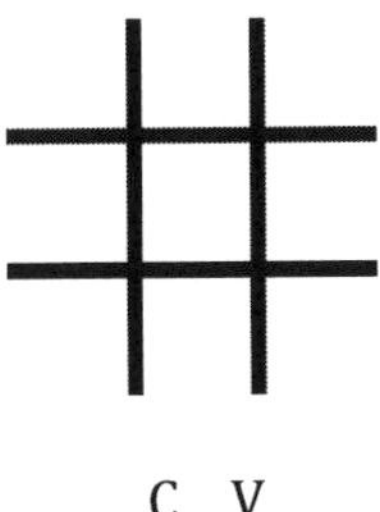

This will be the basic diagram to use to solve the questions. Conditions #1 and #3 are much less restrictive and can fit into the diagram in a number of different ways, so wait to add them until the additional restrictions from the individual problems can narrow down the options.

7. **E.** Due to condition #1, L<->B, neither the Lemon nor the Banana can be on the north side of the cart as both spots on the south side are already taken. This leaves one of the two flavors on the west and the other directly across from it on the east, but the question adds the restriction that the Lemon can't be next to either the Chocolate or Vanilla, eliminating the two spots on the sides closest to the south side and leaving two possible diagrams:

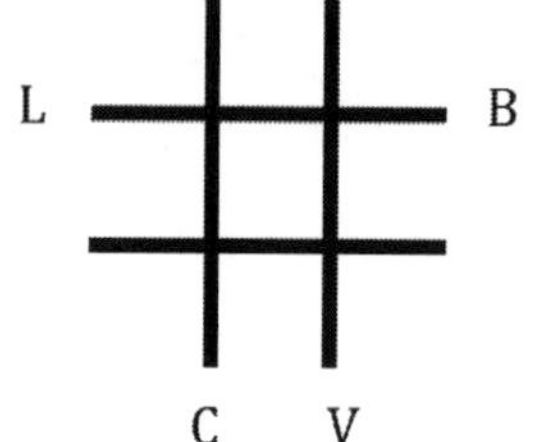

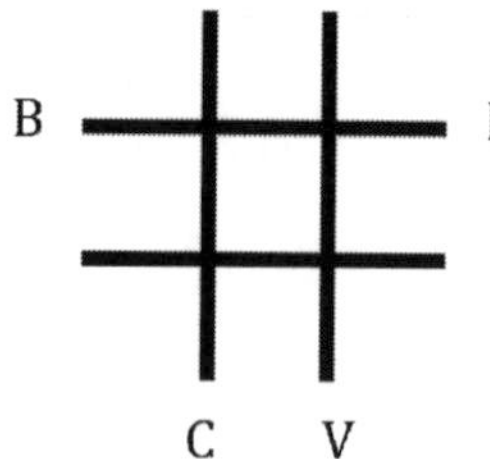

And since condition #3 says that the Strawberry and Pistachio must be next to each other, that means that they are in the two spots on the north side creating four possible diagrams.

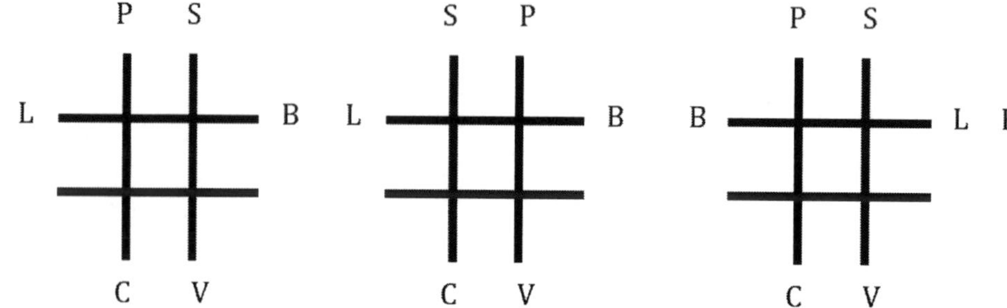

This could be repeated for the Mocha and Oreo making eight possible diagrams, but that is not necessary to solve the problem. The Strawberry and the Pistachio must on the north side as shown in all four diagrams, meaning they cannot be next to the Vanilla, so A is incorrect. Both north side spots directly across from the Chocolate or the Vanilla are already taken, meaning that Mocha cannot be directly across from them, making B incorrect. The Banana is next to either the Strawberry or the Pistachio in all four diagrams, meaning that it cannot be next to both the Oreo and the Mocha, making C incorrect. The Oreo can be next to the Lemon, but it could also be next to the Banana, and since the question asks for "must," this makes D incorrect. In all four diagrams, the Pistachio is directly across from either the Chocolate or the Vanilla, making E the correct answer.

8. **B.** First, place the Mocha directly opposite the Chocolate in the basic diagram.

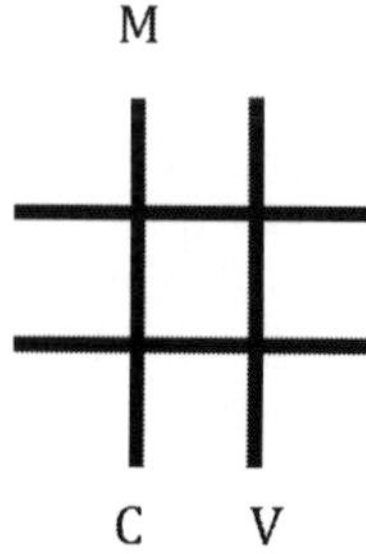

Condition #3, SP, means that the Strawberry and the Pistachio must be placed in a pair of consecutive empty spots. The pair on the west side of the serving cart won't work as this would violate condition #1, L<->B, as would the pair on the east side of the cart. The only consecutive pair that meets both condition #1 and condition #3 is the upper east spot and remaining north spot. This produces two possible diagrams:

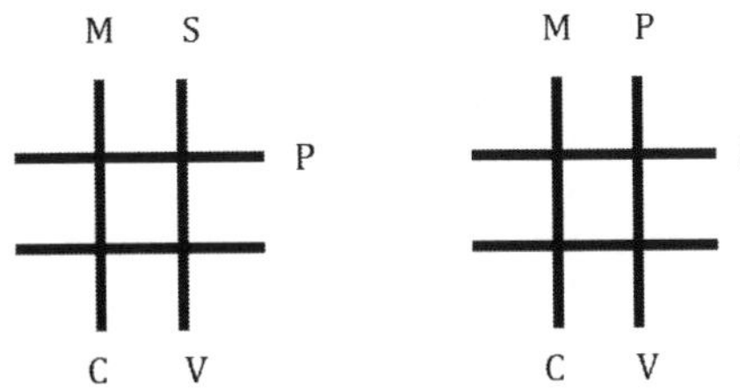

The Lemon and Banana must be in the lower east and lower west spots to satisfy condition #1, L<->B, leaving the upper west spot for the Oreo. Since the Lemon and the Banana could be on either side, this leaves four possible diagrams.

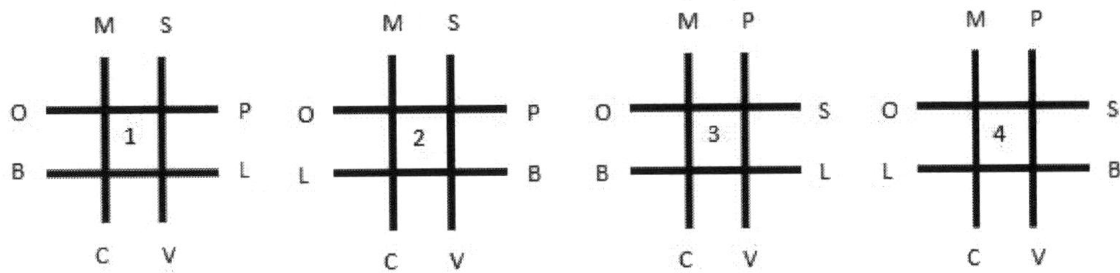

The question asks which of the following—Oreo, Lemon, and Vanilla—could be next to the Strawberry. Looking at the diagrams, of those three only the Lemon is ever next to the Strawberry (diagram #3). The Lemon is II, making II only or B the correct answer.

9. **D.** The question states that the Banana is next to the Vanilla, so place the Banana and the Lemon on the basic diagram following condition #1, L<->B.

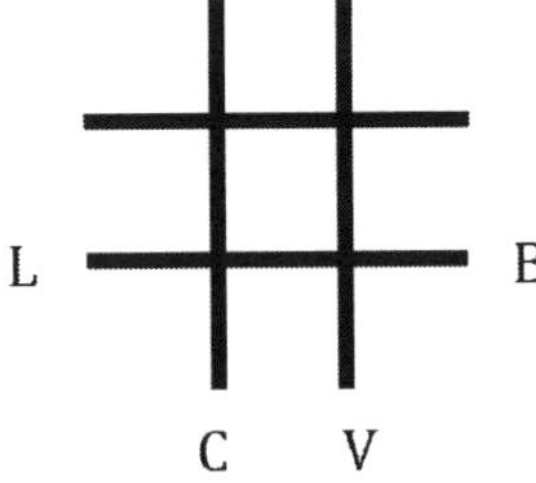

Next, the question also states that the Oreo is next to the Lemon, so add that next.

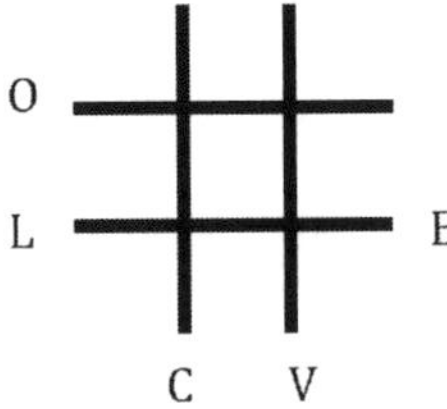

And finally condition #3, SP, gives the Strawberry and Pistachio two possible spots, either both spots on the north side or the upper east spot and the rightmost north spot, with the Mocha filling in the final spot. But the Strawberry and Pistachio can fit in either spot in the two possible configurations making a total of four final diagrams.

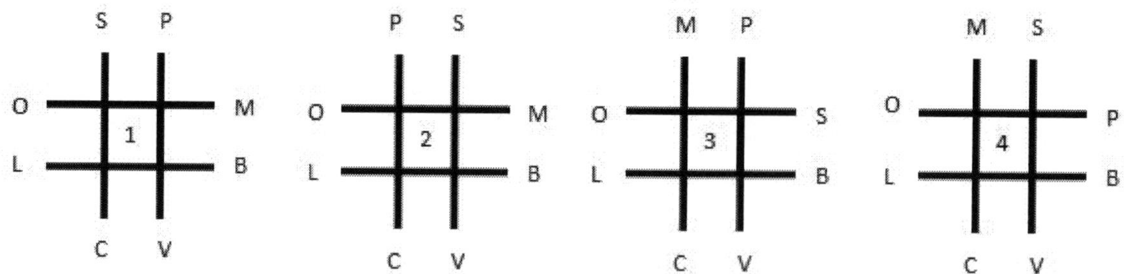

The questions asks which answer choice must be false, so compare each one to the four diagrams and the correct answer is the one that appears in none of them. The Mocha is next to the Oreo in diagrams #3 and #4, making A incorrect. The Banana is next to the Strawberry in diagram #3, making B incorrect. The Banana is between the Vanilla and the Pistachio in diagram #4, making C incorrect. The Chocolate is directly across from the Strawberry in diagram #1, making E incorrect. However, the Vanilla is not directly across from the Mocha in any of the diagrams, so D is the correct answer.

10. **A.** Since the south side is already taken, the Lemon and Banana can only be directly across from each other in either the lower or upper west and east spots due to condition #1, L<->B. Additionally, the Banana must be on the east side of the cart as there is no possible configuration on the west side that would satisfy condition #3, SP, while placing the Strawberry to the immediate right of the Banana.

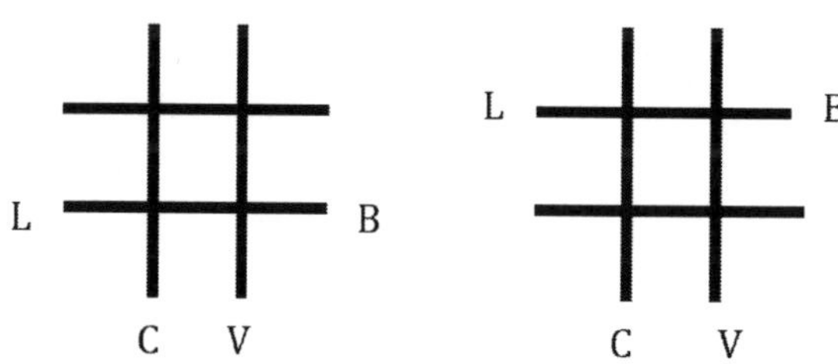

Add the Strawberry and the Pistachio to the right of the Banana in the diagrams.

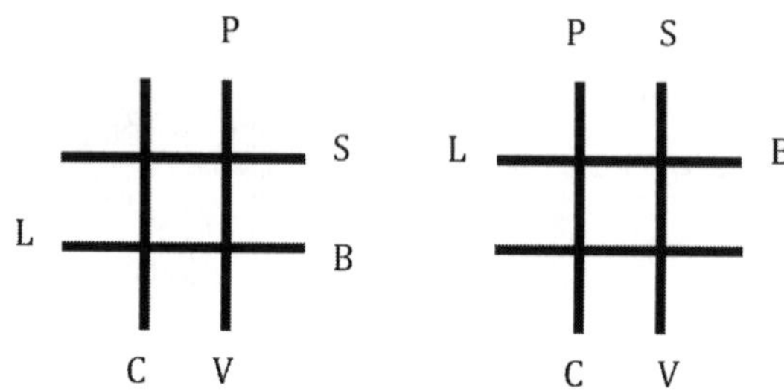

The Oreo and the Mocha can go in either of the two open spots in each of the diagrams, so there are four final possible diagrams.

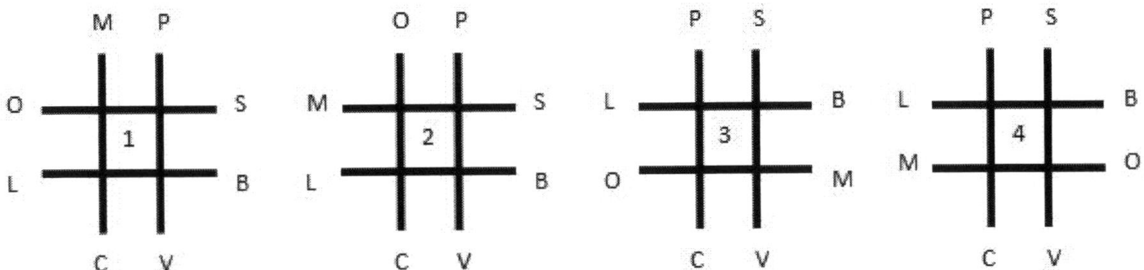

The question asks which of the answer choices is possible, so the answer choice that appears in one of the diagrams is the correct answer. Of the five answers, only A, where the Pistachio is next to the Lemon, appears in the diagrams (#3 and #4), making that the correct answer.

11. **C.** Place the Banana next to the Chocolate and the Oreo next to the Banana on the basic diagram and then put the Lemon directly across from the Banana due to condition #1, L<->B.

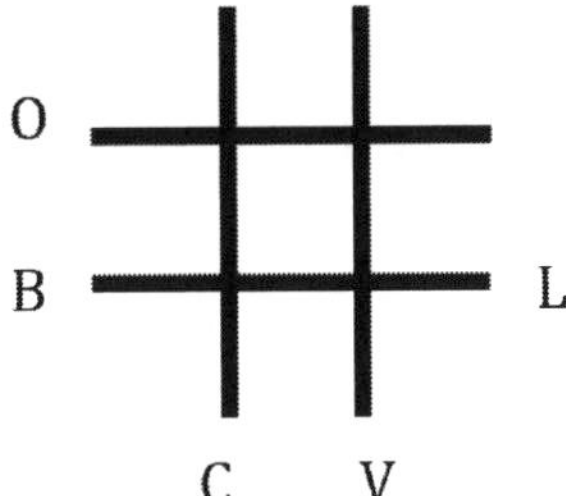

The Strawberry and the Pistachio must be next to each other due to condition #3, meaning that the Mocha cannot be in the middle empty spot. So, the Mocha must be in one of the two spots at the end and the Strawberry and Pistachio can be in either of the two remaining spots. This produces four possible diagrams.

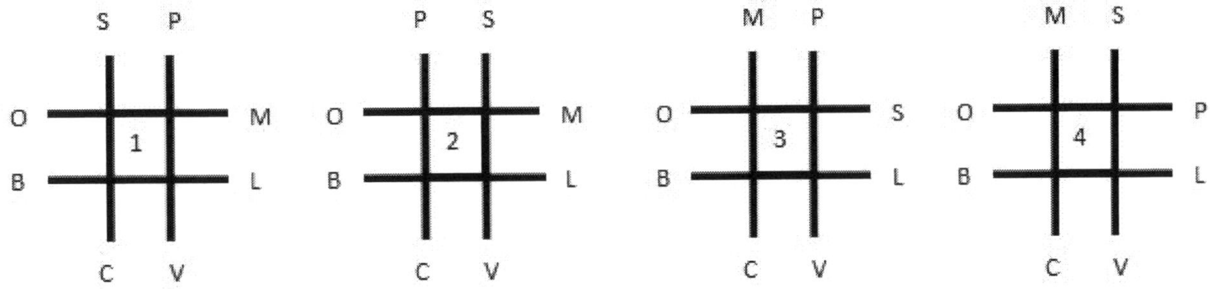

With four possible arrangements possible, the correct answer is C.

12. **D.** Place the Mocha next to the Chocolate in the basic diagram.

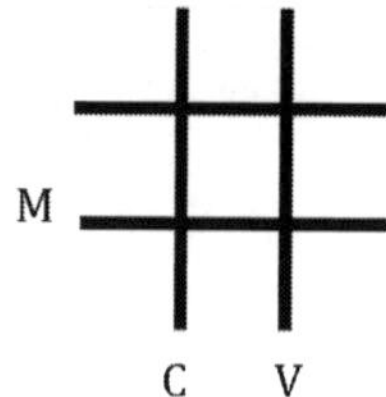

This leaves only two possible locations for the Lemon and the Banana pair to meet condition #1, L<->B.

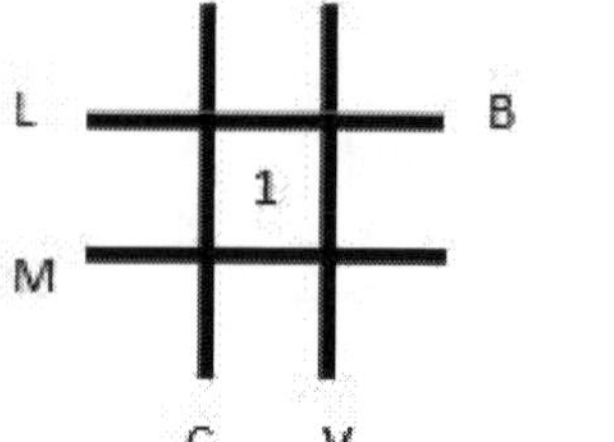

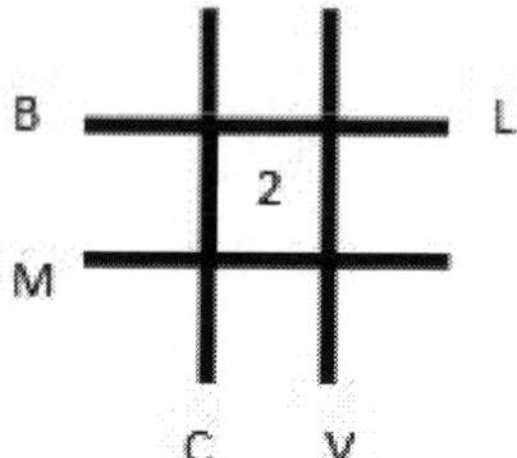

The problem can be solved just using these two diagrams. Due to condition #3, SP, the Strawberry and Pistachio must be on the north side and the Oreo must be in the remaining spot on the east side.

The question asks for all the flavors that could possibly be next to the Lemon. There are a total of seven flavors other than the Lemon. The Chocolate is not in any of the answer choices and the Mocha is in all of them, so that only leaves five other flavors. The Oreo can be next to the Lemon in diagram #2, making A incorrect. In neither diagram #1 or #2 is the Lemon next to the Vanilla, making C and E incorrect. In both diagram #1 and #2, both the Strawberry and Pistachio can be next to the Lemon, making B incorrect and leaving D as the correct answer.

Cluster 3:

The first step is to translate the rules into symbols. Rule #1, a code is three to 5 letters long, translates into - - - **to** - - - - -. Rule #2, if M appears in the code then it is next to N, translates into **M->MN**. Rule #3, L can only be the first or last letter of the code, translates to **L = First/Last**. Rule #4, O and P cannot be next to each other in the code, translates to **~(OP)**. Rule #5, P can only appear in the second and fourth spots of the code, translates to **P = #2,#4**. So, the symbol translations of the conditions for this problem are:

- - - to - - - - -
M->MN
L = First/Last
~(OP)
P = #2,#4

13. **C.** This is a simple matter of comparing each answer choice to the rules and seeing which doesn't break any of them. A breaks rule #3, L = First/Last. B breaks rule #4, ~(OP). D breaks rule #5, P = #2,#4. Finally, E breaks rule #2, M->MN. Only C doesn't break any rules and is thus the correct answer.

14. **E.** L N M makes a valid code due to rule #3, L = First/Last. M N M makes a valid code due to rule #2, M->MN. However, P N M breaks rule #5, P = #2,#4, since P is in spot #1. So numbers I and III both work and E is the correct answer.

15. **A.** Adding a letter to B would violate rule #3, L = First/Last. C already breaks rule #2, M->MN, and no letter added to the beginning could rectify this. Adding a letter to D would push P into the third spot, violating rule #5, P = #2,#4. And there is no letter that could be added to E to change the fact that it is violating rule #3, L = First/Last. Adding L, N, M, or O to the beginning of A makes a valid code, making this the correct answer.

16. **B.** Adding a P to the beginning of A violates rule #3, L = First/Last. Adding a P to the beginning of C violates rule #4, ~(OP). D is already violating rule #2, M->MN, and adding a P to the beginning will not rectify it. And adding a P to the beginning of E violates rule #1, - - - to - - - - -. However, adding a P to the beginning of B violates no rules, making it the correct answer.

Cluster 4:

The first step is to build a flow chart. This is done by connecting the six corporations with arrows based on who they want to do business with and who wants to do business with them. A single-sided arrow denotes a corporation wanting to do business with another, with the arrow originating at a corporation and pointing at the corporation it wants to do business with. A double-sided arrow denotes that each corporation in the pair wants to do business with the other. First, arrange the corporations so that they can be connected to one another in a clear diagram.

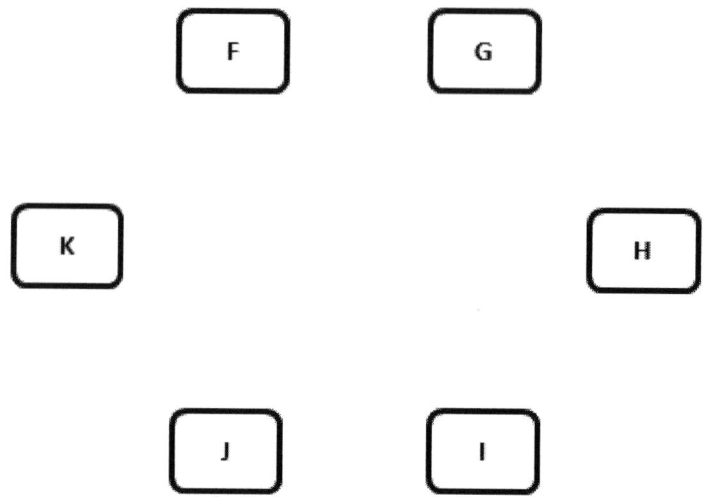

Now add the conditions to the flow chart one by one. The first condition is that K wants to do business with all of the other five corporations, but only J wants to do business back to K. So, add arrows from K pointing to F, G, H, and I and a double-sided arrow between K and J.

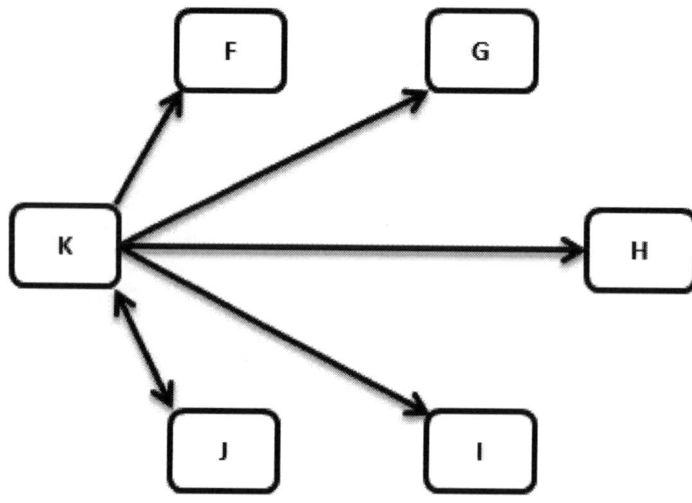

The second condition is that while F doesn't want to do business with any of the other corporations, all the other corporations want to do business with it. So, add arrows pointing to F from all the other corporations, note that the arrow from K to F is already there.

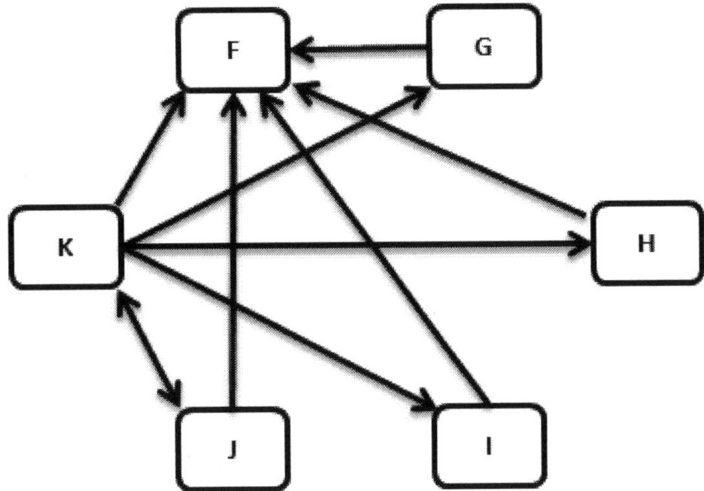

The third condition is that G does NOT want to do business with three of the other corporations, two of which are I and J. From condition #1, G doesn't want to do business with K, so we know that the three corporations are I, J, and K. That leaves G wanting to do business with F and H. There is already an arrow from G to F, so just add the one from G to H.

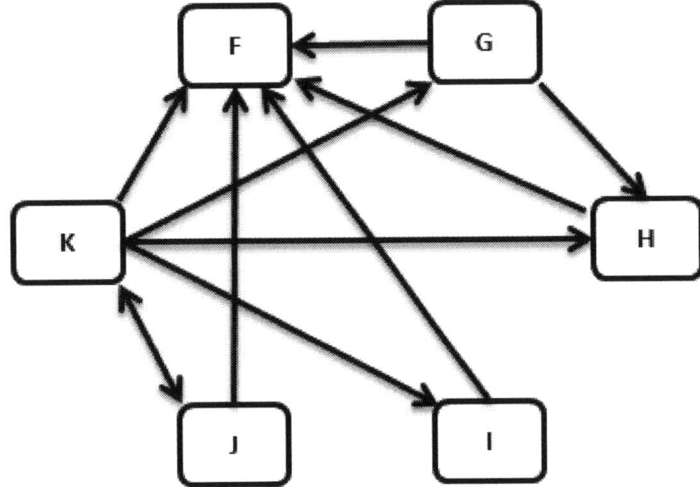

The fourth condition is that J wants to do business with all the corporations except for G. There are already arrows from J to K and F from previous conditions, so just add the ones from J to H and I.

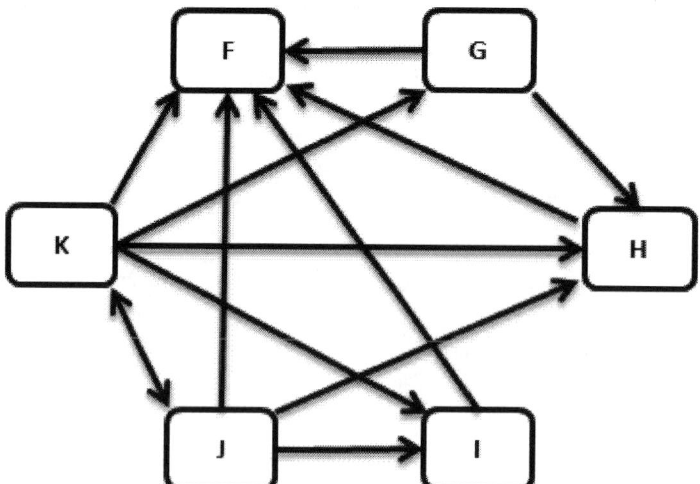

The final condition is that H and I want to do business with each other and two other corporations, one of which is J. H and I want to do business with F from condition #2, so that is the other corporation along with J. J already wants to do business with H and I from condition #4, so those arrows need to be changed to double sided. Additionally, add a double-sided arrow between H and I.

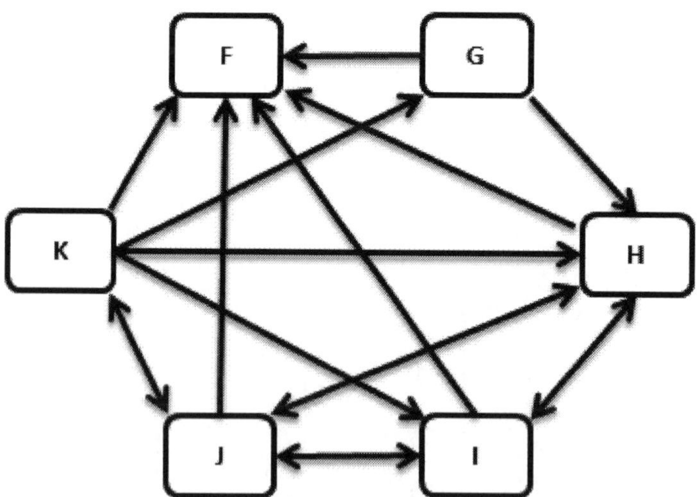

This is the final flow chart of all the conditions.

17. **D.** A business partnership is a pair of corporations who want to do business with each other which is denoted in the flow chart as a double-sided arrow. So, solving this question is a simple task of counting the double-sided arrows: K<->J, J<->H, H<->I, and I<->J. So, the correct answer is 4, or D.

18. **A.** Once again this involves the double-sided arrows. The question asks for the only two corporations that don't have a double-sided arrow connected to them. Looking at the flow chart this is F and G, making A the correct answer.

19. **B.** K has unreturned business partnership desires with F, G, H, and I, so A and D can be eliminated. G has unreturned business partnership desires with F and H, so C and E can be eliminated. Only H has one, and only one, unreturned business partnership desire (with F), making B the correct answer.

Cluster 5:

The problem states that there are nine people seated at three tables: a four-person table, a three-person table, and a two-person table. This can be represented as:

Next, it lists four conditions that need to be translated into symbols. Condition #1, R and S sit at the same table, translates to **R = S**. Condition #2, T and U sit at the same table, translates to **T = U**. Condition #3, Z sits at the two-person table, translates to **Z = 2**. Condition #4, X and Y do not sit at the same table, translates to **X ≠ Y**. So, the symbol translations of the conditions for this problem are:

R = S
T = U
Z = 2
X ≠ Y

And since only the third condition allows placement of a person into it, the basic diagram is:

	Z

20. **E.** Check each answer against the conditions for violations. Answer choices A and C violate condition #3 (Z = 2), B violates condition #1 (R = S), and D violates condition #2 (T = U). This leaves E, or T, U, W, as the correct answer.

21. **C.** First, fill in as much of the diagram as possible with the given information.

R	S	V

	Z

Immediately notice that neither A nor E is correct as both of them violate condition #3 (Z = 2). Next, notice that D is incorrect as well due to condition #2 (T = U). To decide between B and C, the diagrams will need to be filled in. Answer B:

T	U	X	Y

R	S	V

W	Z

And answer C:

T	U	X	W

R	S	V

Y	Z

Doing this it becomes clear that answer B violates condition #4 (X ≠ Y), making C the correct answer.

22. **B.** First, fill in the diagram with the given information.

V	W									Z

Notice that there is not room for one of the R/S or T/U pairs at the two-person table and that there is room for only one of them at the three-person table. This means that one of these pairs must take the remaining two spots at the four-person table. Looking at the answer choices, B puts X, who is not a member of either of the pairs, at the four-person table, meaning it cannot be true and making B the correct answer.

23. **E.** In diagramming this problem, notice that S and T are both part of the pairs from the first two conditions, meaning that neither of them can take the single spot at the two-person table. So either:

R	S				T	U			X	Z

Or:

T	U				R	S			X	Z

Since X is at the two-person table, no conditions restrict the placing of the remaining 3 people. So each one of those three remaining people could take the last spot at the three-person table putting the other two at the four person table. This makes 3 variations for each of the two versions of the diagrams, for a total of 6, so E is the correct answer.

24. **D.** The given information is easy to diagram:

X/Y					X/Y					Z

Looking at the diagram, notice that with either X or Y taking up one spot at the four-person table, the two pairs (R/S and T/U) cannot be seated at the same table; one pair must be at the four-person table and one pair at the three-person table. Thus, there is no way for R and T, both members of a different pair, to be seated at the same table, and D is the correct answer.

Reading Comprehension, Section III

Questions 1–6

Synopsis: Questions 1–6 relate to two passages, each of which has a distinct perspective on the issue of genetically modified food. The author of the first passage acknowledges that there is controversy regarding the consumption of genetically modified food but argues that the need for the modifications is great and that governments have provided "strict regulations" to avoid the abuse of genetically modified food, thus ensuring safety among consumers. Referencing the decisions made in Australia and New Zealand—decisions that limit the sale of genetically modified food to *ingredients* in other products, rather than the open sale of genetically modified produce—the author suggests that governments are aware of potential problems but are focused on making sure consumers only receive genetically modified food that is safe. The author then goes on to explain that genetic modifications can help to remove problems that have been frustrating farmers, such as pest invasion that leads to limited crop size and early rotting before produce can reach the market. Passage A also states that genetic modification can infuse produce with the nutritional elements that have gradually disappeared over time. Given the problems of food shortages in some parts of the world, the author argues that genetic modification is of great value. The author recognizes that refocusing agriculture on small farms and providing consumers with the means of shopping for healthy produce locally is a worthwhile goal. However, the author also argues strongly that this strategy is limited in practicality to certain locations and that as a solution it does little to benefit the much larger regions of the world where people are experiencing severe hunger because of a lack of available food. In conclusion, the author of Passage A claims that in developing the means of genetically modifying food, scientists might also discover the means of ending world hunger.

The author of Passage B provides a perspective on the issue of genetically modified food that counters the perspective of Passage A quite strongly. While admitting that there is some value in the genetic modifications that scientists have already made (citing the reduction of pests and the addition of nutritional elements), the author of Passage B argues that there are just too many potential risks to overlook in making genetically modified food widely available to the public. The author cites a study from 1999 by the Hungarian scientist Árpád Pusztai, which showed that rats that consumed genetically modified potatoes experienced gastrointestinal problems and immune deficiency concerns. While admitting that humans are unlikely to live on genetically modified potatoes alone (suggesting that the rats in Pusztai's study did not eat other foods), the author raises a concern for many people around the world who eat large quantities of certain foods that are currently being modified genetically. By mentioning this, the author suggests that people could very well experience negative effects, simply due to the balance of their diet. As a result, the author concludes that this constitutes sufficient cause to question the safety of genetically modified food. Mentioning a comment from Árpád Pusztai, the author argues that it will not be acceptable to say, decades from now, that we were ignorant of the dangers. We know of the dangers now, the author says, and we need to be careful.

Question 1

Overview: Question 1 of the Reading Comprehension section asks the student for the answer choice with which the author of Passage A would agree. This is largely an inference question, so the student needs to consider each answer choice carefully to determine which one best expresses an implication that is made in Passage A. And as always, the student needs to be able to locate a sentence or more than one sentence that correctly links the statement in the answer choice back to the passage.

The Correct Answer:

C A few sentences into Passage A, the author claims, "Among the nations that produce the bulk of agriculture, the governments have created strict regulations concerning the types of genetic modifications that are allowed and the labeling methods for genetically modified food." The author goes on to cite the governments of Australia and New Zealand as examples, noting that these particular governments have regulated genetically modified food to the extent that it appears only as ingredients and cannot be sold openly to consumers. From this, it is clear that the author of Passage A is *not* necessarily claiming that *all* governments regulate genetically modified food this way but that the governments of Australia and New Zealand function as specific instances representing the types of regulations in place among other governments. As a result, it may be inferred that the author believes these types of regulations to ensure that the genetically modified food available to consumers is safe. **Answer choice (C)** is thus correct.

The Incorrect Answers:

A The author of Passage A notes that some view genetic modification as "the unethical altering of nature's perfect work," but there is no real discussion of actual risks. It might be assumed from this that the author weighs the benefits over the risks, except for the fact that the author really does not reference risks. The more correct inference is that the author of Passage A views the risks as unimportant or insignificant and does not even feel it is necessary to mention them. Answer choice (A) assumes just a little too much from the passage, so it is incorrect.

B The author states, "Perhaps it would be better to return to a time of small farms where consumers can shop and buy what they can get locally," but then goes on to point out that this does not provide a solution for much of the world's population and is thus irrelevant. The author does *not* suggest, however, that hoping for such a thing is futile. It is possible to infer that the author would support the vision of small farms and locally-grown produce in some places but that the idea cannot be supported on a larger scale. Answer choice (B) puts words in the author's mouth, so to speak, so it cannot be correct.

D The author claims, "With genetic modification, scientists are—for the first time in history—making it possible to make world hunger a thing of the past." The author is thus saying that scientists *might* be able to eradicate world hunger, but the author is not putting a time limit on this goal and is certainly not claiming that it will definitely happen. Answer choice (D) assumes too much, so it cannot be correct.

E Answer choice (E) is tempting, because it reworks several of the author's points and tries to put them together in a slightly different way. The author says, "Among the nations that produce the bulk of agriculture, the governments have created strict regulations concerning the types of genetic modifications that are allowed and the labeling methods for genetically modified food." This suggests that the governments *consider* the genetically modified food currently being sold as ingredients as safe for human consumption. The author suggests throughout the passage that scientists are continuing to work on genetic modification. From this, it may be assumed that scientists are certainly interested in keeping the genetically modified food safe (if nothing else, for the purpose of receiving government approval), but there is nothing in the passage to indicate that scientists *will ultimately* be able to make it safe. This appears to be a goal, but there is no guarantee that it will happen. Answer choice (E) cannot be correct.

QUESTION 2

Overview: Question 2 asks for the main point of Passage B. The student needs to review the passage quickly and consider the primary topics that are discussed. The author discusses several important themes: (1) the negative effects of genetic modification outweigh the benefits, (2) there is no long-term data available to indicate the consequences of eating genetically modified food, (3) genetic modification alters food in such a way that the digestive system cannot identify it, (4) genetic modification cannot function as a safe solution to world hunger, and (5) knowing the *possibility* for long-term effects negates the validity of excuses in the future. All of this indicates that the author's main point focuses around the potential for serious effects deriving from the consumption of genetically modified food and the fact that scientists know enough about these effects now to be wary of considering it safe for human consumption and as a way to remove hunger concerns from populations. The answer choice that best paraphrases this will be correct.

THE CORRECT ANSWER:

A **Answer choice (A)** accurately restates the summary indicated in the Overview above: there is current knowledge of potential risks, so the long-term consumption of genetically modified food carries a very real possibility of risks of which scientists are aware. As a result, it is not necessarily a good solution to world hunger. Answer choice (A) is correct.

THE INCORRECT ANSWERS:

B Answer choice (B) reflects a statement that is made in Passage A: "*Where some see the unethical altering of nature's perfect work*, scientists see the prospect of eliminating the problems that plague farmers and the chance to produce enough food to eradicate world hunger" (emphasis added). Passage B is clearly opposed to genetically modified food, in contrast to Passage A's support of it. This does *not* mean, however, that the statement from Passage A may be assumed to be the perspective of the author of Passage B. In fact, the author of Passage B never mentions ethics. The author of Passage B does mention that genetic modification alters the chemical structure and the "unique nutritional content" of food, suggesting that it is safest in its natural form. But the author makes no mention of nature making something "perfect": again, that is taken from Passage A. Answer choice (B) then attempts to indicate that the author of Passage B holds the opinion that the author of Passage A disputes, but that is assuming more than the author of Passage B implies. What is more, this is definitely *not* the main point of Passage B. Answer choice (B), therefore, is incorrect.

C The author of Passage B argues that "the negative qualities swamp the benefits" in the discussion of genetically modified food and that "genetic modification does not necessarily provide the best or the most effective solution." This would suggest that the author of Passage B might not see any value in the continued work on genetic modification of food. But this is an assumption without clear support in the passage, and it is certainly not the main point of Passage B. Answer choice (C) is incorrect.

D The author of Passage B does claim that "genetic modification does not necessarily provide the best or the most effective solution." But this is only a part of the author's primary point and fails to discuss the reason *why* the author believes genetic modification to be a poor solution. As the *why* part is essential to the author's argument, answer choice (D) cannot be correct.

E There is clear discussion in Passage B that scientists are aware of the risks involved with the consumption of genetically modified food. But the author of Passage B does not mention governments anywhere clearly, so it cannot be assumed that the author is arguing against government funding for genetic modification. Answer choice (E) assumes too much and definitely does not offer a summary of the author's main point, so it is incorrect and may be eliminated.

QUESTION 3

Overview: Question 3 asks the student to select an answer choice about which the author of Passage A *and* the author of Passage B would be in agreement. Given that their opinions are so clearly different on the issue of the genetic modification of food, the student should review each passage quickly to see if there is any point on which the two do agree. The author of Passage B mentions that there are *some* benefits to genetic modification, but none of the answer choices reflect this kind of conditional statement. Embedded in the statement made in Passage B, however, is an acknowledgement that the problems facing farmers—pests and nutritional dearth of crops—are worthy of discussion. Additionally, the author of Passage B mentions the problem of world hunger, and since this is a clear concern that the author of Passage A addresses, it stands to reason that both agree to some extent that world hunger is an important issue. So, both authors seem to agree that pest problems (leading to crop shortages), vitamin deficiencies in crops, and world hunger are important issues. The answer choice that mentions any (or all) of these concerns will be correct.

THE CORRECT ANSWERS:

E **Answer choice (E)** correctly notes that both authors seem to agree on the need for discussion regarding hunger and crop problems, as demonstrated in the Overview above. So, answer choice (E) is correct.

THE INCORRECT ANSWERS:

A Answer choice (A) reflects the opinion of the author of Passage A ("With genetic modification, scientists are—for the first time in history—making it possible to make world hunger a thing of the past.") But the author of Passage B makes no mention of science ending world hunger and suggests only that it is a subject meriting discussion. Answer choice (A), therefore, cannot be correct.

B Answer choice (B) offers a perspective that does not appear in either passage. The author of Passage A does not mention lab animals, and the author of Passage B indicates that the study by Hungarian scientist Árpád Pusztai indicates the potential dangers to humans who consume genetically modified food. Answer choice (B) makes assumptions that are not implied in either passage, so it is incorrect.

C Answer choice (C) reflects the opinion of the author of Passage B, but it certainly does not reflect the opinion of the author of Passage A. In fact, the author of Passage A argues that the regulations provided by governments indicate the safety of food, so there is no mention of effects on future generations. Answer choice (C) cannot be correct.

D Answer choice (D) comes very close to reflecting the views of both authors in that it mentions the need for some type of discussion about the problems with growing crops. But it bears mentioning that the author of Passage B never talks about the problem of rotting, so it cannot be added to the list of crop concerns that the author of Passage B discusses. Additionally, answer choice (D) also goes a little too far by adding the mention of *intense international discussion*. This statement infers too much about *how* both authors feel that the problems need to be addressed, so answer choice (D) is ultimately incorrect.

Question 4

Overview: Question 4 asks the student to identify the way that the author of Passage B discusses the problem of world hunger. A contrast to Passage A might prove useful. The author of Passage A is very certain about the need to utilize genetic modification in eliminating world hunger. In other words, the author of Passage A is quite certain that world hunger can be removed and that there is a means of eliminating it. In reviewing Passage B, however, the student will probably notice that while the author of Passage B recognizes the importance of discussing this issue, the author is more cautious about the approach. Caution, in fact, is a word that defines much of the tone of the author in Passage B, and the author's point of view on addressing world hunger is certain (that it should be addressed) but also cautious (in considering the solutions). To be sure, the student should review each answer choice to eliminate the ones that do not fit, but it is likely that the correct answer choice will reflect caution or something related to it.

The Correct Answer:

B The word *circumspect* suggests discretion, prudence, and, yes, caution. This accurately reflects the author's tone, so **answer choice (B)** is correct.

The Incorrect Answers:

A To be *tenacious* is to be persistent and determined. This does not describe the tone of Passage B in any way, so answer choice (A) cannot be correct.

C The word *dubious* indicates doubt, and while the author of Passage B expresses clear doubt about the overall values of consuming genetically modified food, there is no real doubt expressed about the discussion of addressing world hunger. Answer choice (C) does not offer a valuable description of the author's tone, so it is incorrect.

D To define the tone of Passage B's author as *ethical* would be for the student to make a statement of judgment about the two authors. Recognizing the differences between the authors is one thing; indicating a preference is another—and it is not necessary in this test. Answer choice (D) provides an option that the student does not really have in answering the question correctly, so it should be eliminated.

E The word *denunciatory* suggests that the author of Passage B is angry and wants to denounce the issue of world hunger. This does not reflect the author's words or tone in any way, so answer choice (E) cannot be correct.

Question 5

Overview: Question 5 asks the student to infer an opinion that the author of Passage B might hold. Again, this is an inference question, specifically regarding statements made in Passage B, so the student should approach it accordingly. The real challenge in question 5 is in selecting what turns out to be a fairly simple answer, so the student should not think *too* hard about the answer choices. The answer choice that *seems* to be correct in this case, probably is. Question 5 is a good exercise in clearly interpreting the information that is presented in the passage and in recognizing that simple answers can, in fact, be correct.

The Correct Answer:

B The author of Passage B *does* acknowledge certain benefits to the genetic modification of food: "Genetic modification undoubtedly has value. Crops face fewer natural predators, and some produce is receiving an infusion of vitamins not seen in generations." But the author also reflects repeatedly that these benefits alone do not justify or outweigh the risks.

Answer choice (B) is clearly the answer, so the student should not be afraid of looking for a correct answer that is more challenging.

The Incorrect Answers:

A The author of Passage B references Árpád Pusztai's experiment as an example of negative effects, but there is nothing in the passage to indicate that this experiment, in and of itself, is conclusive. Instead, the author utilizes it just as the author of Passage A cites the government regulations in Australia and New Zealand as examples. More to the point, the author of Passage B even mentions that Árpád Pusztai's work is not the final statement, because no one expects humans to eat potatoes exclusively, as the rats ate them. Answer choice (A) assumes more than the passage implies, so it cannot be correct.

C The author of Passage B states, "World hunger is a serious problem, but genetic modification does not necessarily provide the best or the most effective solution." This would imply that there are or might be other solutions to the issue of world hunger. This does *not* imply, however, that the author of Passage A believes *there are a number of important alternatives* or that they will solve the problems now facing farmers. Answer choice (C) infers too much, so it is incorrect.

D The author of Passage B argues that genetic modification alters food beyond the ability of the digestive system to recognize it. There is *no* mention, however, of the *physical* appearance being altered, nor can the student infer that the author of Passage B is discussing the physical appearance. Answer choice (B) cannot be correct.

E The author of Passage B does not mention ethics at all, and there is not enough detail in the passage to indicate that the author is focused on the ethics of genetically modified food—just the scientific and long-term health concerns. While it might be argued that health concerns and that knowing of potential health problems represent ethical concerns, this is more of a judgment call than a definite indication of the passage. Answer choice (E) is not *clearly* implied, so it cannot be correct.

Question 6

Overview: Question 6 requires that the student evaluate two different elements: the way that the author of Passage A uses the word *safe* and the way that the author of Passage B uses it. The answer choices include two modifiers, so the student will need to get both correct in order to select the correct answer. Obviously, any answer choice in which only one of the modifiers is correct will ultimately be incorrect. The best approach to answering this question is for the student to review the usages of the word in each passage and decide on the modifiers that seem most accurate before sorting through the answer choices.

In Passage A, the author says, "Among the nations that produce the bulk of agriculture, the governments have created strict regulations concerning the types of genetic modifications that are allowed and the labeling methods for genetically modified food. In Australia and New Zealand, for example, the governments verify that the food is **safe** for human consumption..." Here the author seems to be indicating that the word *safe* is intended to be decisive and clear. There is no question about whether or not the food is actually safe; because of the government regulations that are in place, the food actually is safe, according to the author of Passage A.

In Passage B, however, the author says, "No generation has grown up consuming genetically modified food, so the claim that such food is **safe** cannot be verified for several decades at the earliest." Clearly, there is a degree of concern about the label of *safe* in this case. Far from using it decisively, the author is raising questions about it, expressing doubt. At this point, the student should note words such as *decisive* and *doubtful* as options. In reviewing the answer choices, any option that offers similar words is likely correct.

THE CORRECT ANSWER:

A **Answer choice (A)** includes the word *doubtfully*, and the word *conclusively* is close enough to the word *decisively* to indicate the correct answer, as demonstrated in the Overview above. As both modifiers are accurate, answer choice (A) is correct.

THE INCORRECT ANSWERS:

B The author of Passage A is decisive but not necessarily *forceful*—a word that takes the author's tone to something of an extreme. What is more, there is nothing that suggests a *joke* in the way that the author of Passage B uses the word *safe*. The author is ironic perhaps, but not joking. Answer choice (B) may be eliminated.

C Answer choice (C) is accurate in that it utilizes the modifier *decisively* to describe the tone of Passage A's author, but it also uses the word *angrily* to describe Passage B's usage of *safe*. There is nothing in the passage to suggest that the author of Passage B is angry—just concerned—so answer choice (C) must be eliminated as being only partially correct.

D The word *questionably* has a variety of possible meanings: it can reflect the subject or the object—that is to say, it can mean that the subject is *questionable* (i.e., potentially incorrect/inappropriate) or the subject is expressing a *question* about the object. The actual usage in answer choice (D) is unclear. What is more, there is very little in Passage A to reflect either usage of *questionable*, so from this alone answer choice (D) may be eliminated. As for *usefully*, this reflects a judgment statement on the part of the reader, so it cannot apply. Answer choice (D) is incorrect.

E There is no clear indication of what a *traditional* usage of *safe* might be, unless it is to use the word quite literally. But the author of Passage B is definitely not *flippant* in the usage—again, just ironic perhaps—so answer choice (E) cannot be correct.

QUESTIONS 7–13

Synopsis: The second passage in the Reading Comprehension section of the test presents the history of Auguste Rodin's sculpture *The Gates of Hell*. The author of the passage begins the first paragraph by noting that there is something of an "art mystery" surrounding the sculpture, but the author chooses not to explain what this mystery is right away, offering only a hint by saying, "Rodin's apparently finished sculpture sits in the courtyard of the Musée Rodin in Paris." From this, the student may deduce that the completion of the sculpture will play some role in the mystery. The author provides no other information, however, choosing instead to explain the history of the sculpture and Rodin's inspiration in crafting it. According to the author, *The Gates of Hell* was commissioned for a Museum of Decorative Arts that was being planned for Paris. Rodin drew from his love of Dante's *Inferno*, as well as his appreciation for Lorenzo Ghiberti's fourteenth-century masterpiece *Gates of Paradise* (currently in Florence), to begin the plans for the sculpture of the underworld that he intended to make for the Museum of Decorative Arts.

As the author notes at the beginning of the second paragraph, the Museum of Decorative Arts did not make it past the planning stage, so Rodin's vision of the doors of hell also lost its initial momentum, and this was apparently a great blow to Rodin, who had been very excited about the project. Rodin continued to work on the sculpture, though, and the author suggests that several individual pieces from it were displayed publicly (independent of the set of doors themselves); the most famous of these individual sculptures is *The Thinker*, which was actually intended to represent the figure of Dante. It is in the second paragraph that the author finally introduces the mystery noted at the beginning. As the author explains, what is so interesting about *The Gates of Hell* is that Rodin did not view the set currently on display outside the Musée Rodin as the final version of the doors, despite the fact that it appears to be complete. Inside the museum is the true finished set—a very abstract sculpture that lacks most of the clear images of the other set and appears to be incomplete. It is this set that Rodin chose to exhibit when he revealed his final work to the public.

In the final paragraph, the author explains Rodin's reasoning. It turns out that sculpture underwent something of a shift in consciousness during the latter part of the nineteenth century. The author Baudelaire claimed that it was "boring" and no longer relevant, because it was not adapting to the shift toward modern art with its movement toward abstract imagery. The author indicates that Rodin was concerned about this and decided to rework *The Gates of Hell*, revising it from a traditional sculpture to a modern one. As a result, the second version of the doors proved to be far more "unfinished" in appearance, even though it was, in fact, the finished version. The author of the passage goes on to note that Rodin's work in early modern sculpture has proven to be of important influence to many later sculptors, and the author concludes by pointing out that the actual mystery is not about why there is a second set of doors but rather why the second set is not the set on primary display at the Musée Rodin.

QUESTION 7

Overview: In question 7, the student is asked to select an answer choice that best explains the allusion to Dante and his *Inferno* in the passage. The most effective approach to answering this question is for the student to review that portion of the passage quickly and to formulate a reason even before looking over the answer choices. By looking over the answer choices first, the student runs the risk of reading answer choice options *into* the passage, instead of the other way around. By reviewing the passage first and preparing a brief explanation, the student has a much better opportunity of selecting the correct answer.

In the passage, the author notes the following in the second paragraph: "The project, it turns out, had been an important one for Rodin, because it would have allowed him to explore in sculpture a favorite piece of literature—that of Dante's medieval masterpiece *Inferno*. The evidence on the doors still indicates Rodin's early thought processes. At the top of the doors is a seated figure leaning over a clutched fist, meant to represent Dante himself and now famous as Rodin's stand-alone sculpture *The Thinker*. There are figures indicative of the characters Ugolino, who was placed in hell for devouring his own children, and Paulo and Francesca da Rimini, who were sent to hell for their adulterous relationship." Further on, the author notes, "Gone were the recognizable figures from Dante and in their place the complex swirls and unknown images." From these statements made in the passage, the student may deduce that the mention of Dante is intended to do two things: (1) describe Rodin's early influences, and (2) prepare for the later changes as Rodin's interest in modern sculpture developed. The answer choice that encompasses a similar explanation will be correct.

THE CORRECT ANSWER:

A **Answer choice (A)** is most similar to the explanation provided in the passage above, in that it accounts for Rodin's initial influence and provides some historical detail against which to place his eventual movement into modern sculpture. Answer choice (A), then, is correct.

The Incorrect Answers:

B While it might be argued that the allusion to Dante functions as a compare and contrast scenario between Rodin's early work and his later work, it *cannot* be argued that the author's mention of Dante serves as a general compare and contrast between traditional and modern sculpture. The passage is focused primarily on Rodin's influences, and answer choice (B) extrapolates too much about the similarity between Rodin's influences and those of other sculptors. Answer choice (B) cannot be correct.

C The author mentions Dante's *Inferno* as an influence on *one* piece of Rodin's work, but there is no mention of other sculptures. Although the author claims that Dante was a "favorite piece of literature," there is not enough information to argue that he utilized other medieval writings in general within his earlier work. Answer choice (C) is not correct.

D The author does discuss the need for research in order to solve the mysteries of the art world: "With the keen eyes of researchers and the enthusiastic enterprise of detectives, however, art scholars are beginning to study these mysteries more closely and to provide some relevance for modern art lovers." In the case of Rodin, however, the author does not suggest that Rodin's immediate sources were ever in doubt; instead, the author is calling into question the accuracy of placing the earlier and more traditional set of doors on primary display at the Musée Rodin. Answer choice (D) takes an earlier statement in the passage and applies it incorrectly to the author's purpose, so it cannot be correct.

E At no point does the author mention or indicate the *separate disciplines* of art, literature, and history; and while the author does incorporate elements from all three in the passage, they fall under the implied field of art study. There is a distant indication that the study of art includes some knowledge of literature and history, but there is not enough information in the passage to suggest that the author is arguing for combined resources among the different fields for a common goal. Answer choice (E) misreads the information that is actually in the passage and assumes too much from it, so it is incorrect.

Question 8

Overview: In question 8, the student is asked to select an answer choice that best explains the *organization* of the passage. In questions such as this, the student should begin by determining a system of organization *before even reviewing the answer choices* and then going on to select the answer choice that best matches this. As in question 7, if the student tries to read through all of the answer choices before formulating a solid answer from personal review, there is a risk of reading the answer choices into the passage; in this case, the student could actually feel as though three or four of the answer choices might be correct, when a few moments of preparation would have made it easier to eliminate the incorrect options. As for the organization of the passage, it is divided into three paragraphs, and it is likely that the answer choices will divide up the organization into three parts. The student needs to decide what each part does.

Clearly, the first paragraph introduces the situation and explains the problem, but there is a catch to this. The author does not begin at the beginning, so to speak, choosing instead to *throw the reader headlong into the issue* that will be discussed without even explaining the problem or mystery that needs to be solved in the first paragraph. The second paragraph goes on to *offer some historical detail that provides context* for the problem. And the third paragraph utilizes the details that have been provided, as well as the explanation of the problem itself, in order to *revise the vision of the original problem and explain how it should be reconsidered*. The answer choice that most closely identifies the three parts of the passage in this way will be accurate.

THE CORRECT ANSWER:

E **Answer choice (E)** mirrors the three parts presented in the Overview above: (1) the opening paragraph does send the reader diving into the problem *in medias res*, (2) the second paragraph provides the history, and (3) the third paragraph revises the approach to the problem. Answer choice (E), therefore, is correct.

THE INCORRECT ANSWER:

A An *anecdote* is an amusing story. The author's tone might be somewhat playful at times, but there is no hint of an anecdote in the opening paragraph. (Had the author mentioned the mysteries of the art world and then included a brief example of a mystery that was solved, there might be reason to identify an anecdote. As it is, though, the first paragraph is devoid of one.) What is more, the final paragraph does *not* necessarily end in an *abstract reflection*. The author mentions abstract art, but the author's focus does not necessarily become abstract at any time. Answer choice (A) cannot be correct.

B At first glance, answer choice (B) seems like a tried-and-true explanation of the passage's organization. The author introduces the problem of mysteries in the art world, provides some historical information about the mystery of Rodin's two sculptures, and offers a concluding remark at the end. Taking a closer look, however, it becomes clear that this is just a little too easy and that the pieces do not fit quite that nicely. In reality, the author does *not* introduce the mystery/problem in the first paragraph; the author waits until the second paragraph to do so. What is more, the author does not actually use the historical information of the second paragraph to offer a real solution in the third paragraph. Instead, the author redirects the focus to provide the reader with a new appreciation for the issue under discussion. The solution, if any, is only vaguely implied: the Musée Rodin should reconsider placing the later set of doors as the main display instead of the earlier and more traditional set. But the author does not actually state this and instead offers it as a final thought for consideration instead of a solution. As a result, answer choice (B) attempts to force a standard template on the passage without taking anomalies into account, so it cannot be correct.

C Far from beginning with a hypothetical scenario, the author begins with the very concrete statement that mysteries remain within the world of fine art. And while the author does reference the historical situation of Rodin's two different versions of *The Gates of Hell*, the author definitely does not recommend a conclusive action at the end of the passage. Answer choice (C) is thus incorrect.

D The author does begin with an issue that needs to be addressed (ongoing mysteries in the art world), but the author does *not* follow this up with a comparison of several historical examples; and there is no real solution within the concluding paragraph. Answer choice (D) cannot be correct.

QUESTION 9

Overview: Question 9 asks the student to identify the answer choice that best expresses the central point of the passage. The student will be best served by defining the main point quickly and then comparing this point to the answer choices. The student should also locate a sentence (or more than one sentence) that consolidates the main point and place this against the answer choices. Additionally, it is important to recognize that the question asks for the *central argument*: this means that the correct answer choice will be in the format of an argumentative statement; in other words, the central argument will be a statement that requires the rest of the passage to prove it.

In reviewing the passage, the student should recognize that the author discusses several important points: (1) there is something of a mystery about why Rodin crafted two sets of doors for *The Gates of Hell*, (2) the earlier set of doors seems to be more complete, (3) traditional sculpture fell out of favor during the late nineteenth century because it did not seem to adapt to modern techniques, (4) Rodin ultimately decided to redesign the doors for *The Gates of Hell* to reflect the evolution of art toward more abstract images, (5) Rodin exhibited the more abstract and seemingly unfinished set of doors, and (6) Rodin's early abstract piece became influential in modern sculpture. In the final paragraph, the author says, "This unusual sculpture became the version that Rodin later exhibited to the public and displayed as his finished work of art. In exhibiting these doors, Rodin actually created one of the first truly modern sculptures, and he established precedents for later sculptors to envision the abstract possibilities of their medium."

From all of this, it becomes clear that the author's main point is not so much the solution to a mystery but rather the fact that Rodin's second set of doors—the abstract set that appears to be unfinished and the one that he decided to exhibit—is actually the set he considered complete and final, and this work would go on to influence modern sculptors. The correct answer choice should incorporate these elements to create a similar kind of summary.

THE CORRECT ANSWER:

D **Answer choice (D)** best summarizes the explanation provided in the Overview above: the author's primary argument is to point out the significance of the set of doors that *appears* to be unfinished, in contrast to the set that appears to be complete. What is more, the author is making a statement about Rodin's purpose and the importance of Rodin's choice in exhibiting one set over the other. Answer choice (D) is correct.

THE INCORRECT ANSWERS:

A The author does note that Rodin's later version of *The Gates of Hell* was to have an influence on later modern sculptors, and the author suggests that Rodin might deserve the title of being the first modern sculptor. The author makes *no* comment, however, about Rodin being the *father of modern sculpture*. This statement functions as more of an inference, and it has little support in the passage. What is more, answer choice (A) fails to take other important elements of the author's argument into account, so it cannot be correct.

B The author's purpose in mentioning art mysteries is largely to set up the information in the passage. More importantly, the author's focus is on *one* art mystery—the two versions of *The Gates of Hell*—and is not a general discussion of the way that art scholars solve art mysteries. Answer choice (B) places too much focus on peripheral information from the paragraph, so it cannot be correct.

C The author's final statement and the historical detail that leads up to it suggest that the author would agree with the statement that the Musée Rodin should substitute the later version of *The Gates of Hell* for the earlier version. This, however, is more of an inference on the part of the reader rather than the author's primary argument. The author is more focused on proving that the later version is Rodin's preferred version and not on arguing for the removal of the currently displayed version. Answer choice (C) focuses too much on the author's implication over the primary details, so it is not correct.

E Answer choice (E) is an entirely hypothetical statement. The author states that the Museum of Decorative Arts "never actually came into being," and "Ultimately, Rodin decided to continue work on the project even though it would not appear in the Museum of Decorative Arts." The only inference that can be drawn from these statements is that Rodin was committed enough to sculpting the doors that he wanted to continue even without a specific museum to display them. Claiming from this that Rodin would never have arrived at a place of working on abstract sculpture cannot be deduced from these statements or from any information in the passage. It is entirely possible that Rodin would have worked on different abstract pieces or that he would have reworked *The Gates of Hell* even if they were on display at the Museum of Decorative Arts. The real point, however, is that these ideas are merely hypotheses; and while hypothesis can function as argument, it requires evidence. There is no such evidence in the passage, so answer choice (E) may be eliminated as incorrect.

QUESTION 10

Overview: Question 10 asks for the answer choice that best explains the reasoning behind the author's comments about the "real mystery" of Rodin's *The Gates of Hell*, mentioned in the final sentence. The author says, "As it turns out, the real mystery in Rodin's *The Gates of Hell* is not why the later set of doors appears to be unfinished but why it is not the set of doors exhibited by the museum in a place of honor as Rodin's achievement of modern sculpture." To explain the reasoning behind this statement is simply to answer the question, *Why does the author say this?* Question 9 asks for the central argument, so the student has already identified the main point of the passage. The author's final statement just mentioned follows the sentences that have already been noted as contributing to the central argument. The student should thus deduce that the author's reasoning is closely connected to the main point and is probably derived from it. In other words, the author says this *because of the main point*. The answer choice that links the reasoning to the main point will be correct.

THE CORRECT ANSWER:

A **Answer choice (A)** accurately—and quite literally—provides a *because* to explain the reasoning behind the author's final statement. The author suggests that the real mystery is not why Rodin created a second set of doors but rather why this set of doors is not on primary display *because* that is the set Rodin recognized as his final and most complete version. This answer might seem too easy, but this is another case of a simple question demanding a simple answer. The student should not allow simplicity to get in the way of clear thinking.

THE INCORRECT ANSWERS:

B The author's statement seems to question the choice by the Musée Rodin to display the more traditional set of doors instead of the later set, but there is no implied explanation on the part of the author as to why the museum would do this. More importantly, though, answer choice (B) does not provide a clear reason why that flows smoothly from the author's central argument, so it cannot be correct.

C Answer choice (C) offers an explanation for the Musée Rodin's choice to display the original set of doors instead of the more modern set, but again it does not clearly link the author's central argument to the author's final statement. What is more, answer choice (C) is entirely hypothetical and has no support within the passage, so it cannot even function as an accurate inference. Answer choice (C) is incorrect.

D Answer choice (D) functions primarily as a statement of opinion, and not even an opinion that the author seems to imply in the passage. It is obvious that the author values Rodin's later version of *The Gates of Hell*, due to its significance as an early piece of modern sculpture. But the author does not necessarily imply that the original version is lacking in artistic merit. The real problem with answer choice (D), of course, is that it does little to link the author's central argument to the author's concluding remark. Answer choice (D) may be eliminated.

E Again, answer choice (E) may be described as an opinion, but it is not necessarily an opinion that may be inferred from the author's statements, nor does it connect the main argument of the passage with the author's final comments. Answer choice (E) is also incorrect.

QUESTION 11

Overview: Question 11 asks the student to identify the author's tone in the final sentence of the passage. Answering questions of this variety requires that the student keep several considerations in mind. *Tone* can be a somewhat subjective quality, but the student needs to be careful about projecting personal opinion on the author's tone. The student needs to make an effort to read the author's tone *within the context of the passage* and not within the context of the student's own opinion about the tone. In some cases, the process of elimination might work best: any answer choice that casts an outside point of view on the passage or specific word/sentence within it is probably incorrect. For instance, answer choices such as "inappropriate," "astute," "useful," "enlightened," and so forth are not descriptions of the author's actual tone in the passage but rather personal opinions on the part of the reader, and any answer choices that contain these kinds of words are automatically incorrect. The student would do well to recognize and eliminate them right away.

Additionally, any answer choices that lean toward extreme descriptions are also likely to be incorrect. Modifiers such as "infuriated," "elated," etc. are all *too* strong. LSAT Reading Comprehension sections contain fairly balanced passages in terms of tone, and few include passages that are extreme in any way. As a result, extreme descriptions of an author's tone should be cordoned off as unlikely. (In rare cases, such a description *might* be correct if it describes a particular element of the passage, so the student should not necessarily eliminate it altogether. But more often than not, these types of answers—when describing an author's tone—will be incorrect.)

To answer question 11 correctly, the student needs to review the final sentence and decide how the author's tone could best be described in comparison to the answer choices. A brief perusal of the sentence suggests that the author's tone is not extreme in any way, so extreme options may be eliminated. Additionally, the author's tone offers a hint of a suggestion for future action but not in a strong or insistent way. The author seems more focused on making a thoughtful final statement. The answer choice that encompasses this quality will be correct.

THE CORRECT ANSWER:

E **Answer choice (E)** describes the author's tone as *reflective*, and this most closely parallels the description provided in the Overview above. Answer choice (E), therefore, is correct.

THE INCORRECT ANSWERS:

A In this case, *sarcastic* would not be a description that projects the reader's opinion onto the passage, so answer choice (A) is not incorrect on that account. But there is nothing within the final sentence to justify a description of sarcasm. The author's tone might indicate an error that has been made in showcasing one piece of artwork over another, but that alone does not determine sarcasm. Answer choice (A) lacks support in the passage, so it is incorrect.

B To be *pedantic* is to be fussy or to nitpick about little details. The author has just presented a passage full of information explaining the history of *The Gates of Hell* and the reason why the later and more abstract sculpture is the one that Rodin intended to display as his final work. So, the author's concluding sentence falls in line with the author's previous remarks and is hardly pedantic. Answer choice (B) is incorrect.

C Answer choice (C) falls into the category of a projection of the reader's opinion, so it may be automatically eliminated. To describe the author's tone as *sagacious* (or *wise*) is to place a statement of individual judgment on it. Answer choice (C) cannot be correct.

D As mentioned in the Overview above, the author's tone might lean toward a hint of a recommended action, but there is certainly nothing *insistent* about it. Answer choice (D) may be eliminated as incorrect.

Question 12

Overview: Question 12 is an inference question, so the student needs to read each answer choice closely and be sure to select the answer choice that has *clear implication* in the passage. Any answer choice that assumes more than the passage suggests is immediately incorrect.

The Correct Answer:

C The author says, "In exhibiting these doors, Rodin actually created one of the first truly modern sculptures, and he established precedents for later sculptors to envision the abstract possibilities of their medium." The use of the word "precedents" indicates that Rodin utilized techniques or provided an aesthetic for future modern sculptors to incorporate. **Answer choice (C)** may thus be inferred from a statement that is made in the passage, so it is correct.

The Incorrect Answers:

A The author mentions that Dante's *Inferno* was a "favorite piece of literature" for Rodin, but there is nothing in the passage to indicate that he incorporated elements from Dante in other works of art. It is, of course, entirely possible that he did, but without specific references to other Rodin sculptures, there is no reason to infer this. Answer choice (A) is incorrect.

B In terms of historical information, answer choice (B) is technically correct: Rodin wanted to create an accompanying set of doors for Ghiberti's *Gates of Paradise*. But in terms of information within the passage, there is nothing to suggest this clearly. The author mentions only that Ghiberti was an inspiration. Answer choice (B) is thus incorrect.

D The author suggests that Rodin's work on the later version of *The Gates of Hell* provided a new modern focus for sculpture. There is not enough in the passage to assume, however, that Rodin *single-handedly returned relevance to sculpture* through his work on the project. Answer choice (D) infers more than the passage implies, so it must be eliminated as incorrect.

E The author claims that the failed Museum of Decorative Arts was the "death of a dream" for Rodin, because, "the project...had been an important one for Rodin." But the author then goes on to say that Rodin continued work on the project in spite of the fact that the museum would not be built, so there is no reason to believe that the loss of the museum handicapped Rodin's creative impulse in any way. Answer choice (E) is clearly contradicted in the passage, so it is incorrect.

QUESTION 13

Overview: Question 13 is somewhat challenging to answer, because it requires that the student utilize inference and extend it just a little beyond what the passage states. The question asks for the answer choice with which the author would most likely agree. This is largely inference, but in this case, it also includes a degree of argument, so the student must select an answer choice that provides a statement of argument that the author would support—based on the information in the passage. The student will have to tread very carefully in order to avoid over-reading (or under-reading) certain parts of the passage.

THE CORRECT ANSWER:

E The author mentions Baudelaire to provide some historical context for the gradual decline of sculpture's reception during the late nineteenth century. The author does not offer a stated opinion about Baudelaire's essay, but an opinion is definitely implied. Given that the author has written a passage concerning an art mystery and has provided a great deal of detail about a particular work of sculpture, it stands to reason that the author would disagree with Baudelaire: sculpture is very interesting, as the history of *The Gates of Hell* would attest. **Answer choice (E)** may thus be inferred and argued from the passage, so it is correct.

THE INCORRECT ANSWERS:

A The author indicates that the sculpture of *The Thinker* is a famous and easily recognizable work of art, but there is not enough information in the passage to suggest that the author has a negative opinion about this. It might be argued that the author believes *The Gates of Hell* deserves more public recognition, but even this is not clear, as the author's focus is ultimately on *which version* of the sculpture receives attention. The author might believe that *The Gates of Hell* is already well known. Answer choice (A) thus assumes too much and requires too many accompanying hypotheticals, so it cannot be correct.

B The author makes no mention of the public's reception to Rodin's later sculpture, so there is no way to assume accurately that the public was confused by it. At the most, it might be inferred that there was public surprise over such an unusual piece, but since the public had not seen the earlier piece (that Rodin chose never to exhibit), even this assumption is tenuous. Answer choice (B) is incorrect.

C The author mentions only Rodin in connection to the failed Museum of Decorative Arts. From common sense alone, it may be assumed that other artists would have been involved at some point, but since the museum failed before it was even built it is impossible to argue that any—much less *many*—were affected. Answer choice (C) infers more than the passage implies, so it is incorrect.

D Regarding the solving of mysteries in the art world, the author makes the following remarks: "The study of art history would not be complete without a study of the many art mysteries that persist. Some of these mysteries remain unsolved, having accompanied the artists to their graves. Other mysteries only seem impossible to solve. With the keen eyes of researchers and the enthusiastic enterprise of detectives, art scholars are beginning to study these mysteries more closely and to provide some relevance for modern art lovers." What this indicates is that there are some mysteries that can be solved, and there are some mysteries that will never be solved. It is arguable that the mysteries of the art world arise out of incomplete information (as do all mysteries), but the author states quite clearly that some of these mysteries will always have incomplete information. The passage contradicts answer choice (D) quite clearly, so it is incorrect.

Questions 14–20

Synopsis: Questions 14–20 refer to the third passage of the Reading Comprehension section of the test, namely a description of caffeine, its history, and its effects. The opening paragraph introduces the reader to the official discovery of caffeine in 1819, with a German chemist named Friedrich Ferdinand Runge credited with identifying the drug. The author goes on to note, however, that foods and beverages (such as beans and leaves) containing caffeine have been recognized for their stimulative effects for several millennia. The author cites the emperor of China around the year 3000 BC, the Mayans in 600 BC, an Ethiopian goatherd in the ninth century AD, and the Sufis of Yemen in the fifteenth century AD—all historically known for appreciating the power of caffeine, even if they did not actually know caffeine by name or as a specific ingredient.

In the second paragraph of the passage, the author describes the various effects of caffeine. As the author points out, tolerance to caffeine varies by individual, with weight, metabolism, and, most importantly, amount consumed playing the biggest roles. Scientific studies indicate that small amounts of caffeine can be beneficial for athletes and for infants suffering from apnea. Large amounts of caffeine, however, can quickly create negative effects: caffeine dependence can result from caffeine tolerance, and those who stop consuming caffeine after developing a dependence on it might experience headaches, nausea, and depression.

The third paragraph continues with the description of the negative effects that can ensue from consuming too much caffeine. According to the author, caffeine contributes to stomach acid, so excess amounts of caffeine can cause gastrointestinal concerns. Those who consume more caffeine than their bodies can process in a normal period of time might experience caffeine intoxication, which is marked by nervous behavior, rapid heartbeat, sleeplessness, and so forth. In some cases, caffeine intoxication can cause death. The author goes on to note that studies have indicated a link between caffeine consumption and Parkinson's disease in men, and the author points out that pregnant women are at a heightened risk for miscarriage if they consume caffeine.

At the same time, the author continues on a more ambivalent note. Despite the negative effects of caffeine, research suggests that there are distinct positive effects, as long as caffeine is consumed in small amounts. It has been suggested that caffeine could boost mental performance and reduce the risk of heart disease. The author concludes with a dry tone by pointing out that caffeine withdrawal—as well as the symptoms that accompany it—is now recognized to be a legitimate health disorder, so those who need their caffeine just might have medical support.

Question 14

Overview: Question 14 asks the student to select the answer choice that best expresses the author's main argument. The student needs to bear the details of the passage in mind, as well as the author's primary argument in order to arrive at the correct answer. In the first paragraph, the author focuses largely on the history of caffeine and its discovery. This is useful information for establishing context, but because the author does not end here, the main point of the passage is not necessarily going to be focused merely on the history of caffeine.

More specifically, the main point of the passage will distill all of the details of each paragraph into a single statement that indicates *why* the author is writing the passage and *what* the author is trying to say with all of the different details. Perusing the rest of the passage, the student might note that there does not seem to be a single sentence that seems to represent or reflect a main point. In some passages, there will be such a sentence. In this passage, however, the student must consolidate the various pieces of information into a single statement. As noted before, the first paragraph alone cannot offer a main point, because it does not include the important details about the effects of caffeine. What is more, the first paragraph functions primarily as context, with the rest of the passage moving into the real point that the author wants to make.

Reviewing the author's different twists and turns throughout the second and third paragraphs, the student will probably realize that the author counters positive and negative effects frequently, mentioning that caffeine definitely has negative effects, but it also has positive effects if consumed in moderation. This, then, seems to be the author's primary point: caffeine has both positive effects and negative effects, so individuals should utilize moderation when consuming it. The answer choice that most closely reflects this will be correct.

The Correct Answer:

D **Answer choice (D)** most closely states the argument as indicated in the Overview above: the author's main argument seems to be that there are positive effects and negative effects to drinking caffeine, so it should be consumed in moderation. Answer choice (D) is correct.

The Incorrect Answers:

A The author does mention that there was appreciation for the stimulative effects of caffeine long before Friedrich Ferdinand Runge isolated the drug in 1819. The author does not claim Runge to be the first person to discover or recognize caffeine, however, claiming instead that historians see him as the "official" discoverer of caffeine, because he actually identified it as a unique ingredient. This suggests that Runge receives credit for linking the same ingredient in different beans and leaves and not that he is mistakenly believed to be the first to recognize the stimulative effects of these products. What is more, the discussion of Runge does not encompass the author's main argument and functions more as a set-up for the passage, so answer choice (A) cannot be correct. Answer choice (A) may be eliminated.

B The author does mention a number of health risks connected to the excessive consumption of caffeine. But the author also clearly states that there are definite benefits to consuming caffeine: "Before you dump out that cup of tea or vow to quit the coffee habit, though, consider that caffeine in moderation is not entirely bad: some studies indicate that caffeine actually improves brain performance when related to short-range thought processes, and there is strong evidence that caffeine might reduce the risk of heart disease in certain patients." This suggests that the author is *not* arguing for the elimination of caffeine consumption but rather encouraging a balanced approach to consuming it. Answer choice (B), therefore, cannot be correct.

C Answer choice (C) might function as the main point of the first paragraph, but it hardly represents the main argument for the entire passage. Additionally, it is a mere statement of fact rather than an argument. Answer choice (C) cannot be correct.

E Answer choice (E) is more or less the opposite approach to answer choice (B): it claims that because caffeine has health benefits (as demonstrated by the author), it should be a part of the daily diet. The problem with this is that the author implies a balanced approach to consuming caffeine, but there is no clear information about *how* the author defines balance. It might be daily caffeine for some people, and it might be more infrequent for others. Placing all of the information in the passage together, the author suggests that caffeine consumption should vary by person, and the author makes no general remark about how often it should be consumed. Answer choice (E) assumes too much—and it certainly does not represent the main argument of the passage—so it cannot be correct.

Question 15

Overview: Question 15 asks the student to choose the statement with which the author would likely agree. The student needs to review each answer choice and select the option that is most closely inferred from information provided in the passage. Any answer choice that infers more than the author *clearly implies* in the passage cannot be correct.

The Correct Answer:

C In the final paragraph, the author comments, "some studies indicate that caffeine actually improves brain performance when related to short-range thought processes." In other words, those who will be performing activities requiring this form of thinking might very well benefit from consuming caffeine. The answer choice does *not* say that individuals *will* benefit but rather that they might. This is an accurate inference from the passage, so **answer choice (C)** is correct.

The Incorrect Answers:

A In the first paragraph, the author says, "Runge's discovery is primarily in his work of isolating and identifying caffeine as a separate ingredient for the first time. A possibly apocryphal account of the event suggests he did so because his friend Johann von Goethe requested it." An *apocryphal* account is one that is not necessarily true, so the author is suggesting a potential lack of evidence for this story. What is more, the author indicates that if the story is true, Runge pursued the work at the behest of a friend, but *Runge is still responsible for the work itself.* Answer choice (A), therefore, cannot be correct, because the passage does not indicate that the author would agree with the statement.

B In the third paragraph, the author says, "An overdose of caffeine can actually cause death, although this is rare with caffeine occurring in its natural forms—such as coffee and tea—and is generally connected to the consumption of caffeine tablets." This means that caffeine-related deaths from overconsumption of coffee and tea are uncommon but that they might very well have occurred. Answer choice (B) claims that they *never* occur, and this cannot be inferred as something with which the author would agree. Answer choice (B) is incorrect.

D The author's final comment about caffeine withdrawal now being considered a health disorder might stretch so far as to imply that insurance companies would consider paying for it. But there is nothing in the last sentence of the passage to indicate that the author is arguing in favor of it. Answer choice (D) assumes too much, so it is incorrect.

E The author mentions, "Caffeine causes an increase of stomach acid, which can lead to ulcers and other gastrointestinal conditions." This would suggest that any consumption of caffeine leads to some kind of increase in stomach acid. But there is not enough in the sentence to suggest that the increase in stomach acid is excessive or that it generates severe gastrointestinal concerns. In fact, the author's statements in the second paragraph of the passage would indicate that there are various individual factors involved in the severity, not the least of which is the amount of caffeine that is consumed. Answer choice (E) assumes more than the passage implies, so it is not correct.

Question 16

Overview: Question 16 is similar to question 15 but with a slight rewording: the student must now select an answer choice that reflects the author's belief, based on information in the passage. This is basically another form of an inference question, so the student should approach it in the same way, reviewing each answer choice and considering statements in the passage that imply the information in the answer choice.

The Correct Answer:

A **Answer choice (A)** makes a similar statement as the main argument as demonstrated in question 14, but this makes it no less correct for question 16. Although there is not a single sentence that suggests answer choice (A), there are various comments within the passage to imply the author's support for the statement made in answer choice (A): the author indicates that caffeine tolerance varies by individual, implying that individuals should be careful to consume an amount of caffeine that is well within the personal range of tolerance, and the author mentions several times that there are different health benefits associated with caffeine, so it should not necessarily be discouraged for human consumption. All of this points to the author's belief in the benefits of caffeine consumed in moderation, so answer choice (A) is correct.

The Incorrect Answers:

B Answer choice (B) offers an interesting—albeit inaccurate—twist on the author's words. The author notes, "Lack of expected caffeine can cause an unnatural response in the adenosine receptors, creating too much dilation and producing severe headaches. Additionally, scientists have found that caffeine withdrawal can contribute to feelings of nausea and mild depression." This indicates that there can be uncomfortable or even serious problems that result from not consuming caffeine once a dependency on it has developed. But this does *not* necessarily mean that the author is arguing for a continued dependence on caffeine because the negative side effects are too serious. The author mentions a number of other side effects that caffeine consumption could cause, and there could be a variety of reasons for the individual to stop consuming caffeine, regardless of the side effects. What is more, there is no reason to believe that headaches, nausea, or even mild depression are serious enough to require ongoing dependency. Clearly, answer choice (B) takes the author's statement and assumes an extreme action based on them, an action that the statement does not imply. The author is merely providing information; the decision to consume caffeine or not to consume it is left up to the individual. Answer choice (B) is incorrect.

C As with answer choice (B), answer choice (C) takes the author's words and assumes an extreme response based on them. The author mentions, "Caffeine has also been linked to the possible risk of Parkinson's disease in men..." A *possible risk* does not necessarily guarantee a risk for all men or even the eventual development of the disease. Again, the implication is that the risk is individual and that individuals should take this into account. At the most, the author might be implying that doctors should be more aware of early signs of Parkinson's in men who consume caffeine, but even this is not clearly implied. Answer choice (C) cannot be correct.

D The author takes the history of caffeine back to the Chinese emperor Shennong, noting that he became aware of stimulative effects when some leaves were boiled. This alone does not mean that Shennong discovered caffeine or that there was no one earlier to recognize the effects of the leaves. And because the author does not say that Shennong's experience was the first experience of caffeine in tea leaves, it can only be assumed that this is the first example the author chooses to mention. More importantly, though, the author does not imply that Runge is incorrectly credited with the actual discovery of caffeine. The author says, in fact, that historians credit him *officially*, but this is because Runge was the first to isolate the specific ingredient (whereas others recognized the stimulative effects of different products). Answer choice (D) cannot be correct.

E The author claims, "Consistent consumption of caffeine in beverages such as coffee can produce a tolerance in less than three weeks." The author makes no mention of caffeine tolerance requiring longer in other people, and even though the author mentions the importance of individual response to the drug, it may be assumed that the author discusses three weeks as the greatest amount of time required. It is entirely possible that caffeine tolerance takes much longer in others, but there is not enough information in the passage to imply this clearly, so answer choice (E) is incorrect.

QUESTION 17

Overview: Question 17 asks the student to identify the connotation of the word *unique* in the following sentence: "Research also indicates that some individuals are able to develop a **unique** tolerance for caffeine that others of a similar size and metabolism might not have." The word *unique* is subject to a variety of different nuances, depending on its usage, so the student should take a moment to consider what it is that the author is trying to say. The author seems to be indicating that some individuals have a distinct tolerance specific to their biological makeup. The student will probably notice that the word *individual* is an option among the answer choices, so this seems as though it might be a good option. A quick review of the other answer choices will indicate that *individual* is, in fact, the best comparative meaning for *unique* in this particular case. A final litmus test is whether or not the word can be replaced in the passage without much confusion; there is no doubt that *individual* fits the connotation of *unique* very closely.

THE CORRECT ANSWER:

B As explained in the Overview above, the word *individual* best describes the meaning of the word *unique* in the context of the sentence from the passage. **Answer choice (B)** is correct.

THE INCORRECT ANSWERS:

A The author does not indicate that the tolerance for caffeine developed by different individuals is *unexpected* in any way, though perhaps intriguing, so replacing the word *unique* with the word *unexpected* only confuses the information in the passage. Answer choice (A) is incorrect.

C To say that this is *surprising* is inaccurate, since the passage shows no emotion and does not convey that this tolerance took researchers by surprise. Answer choice (C) can be eliminated.

D While the caffeine tolerance might be perceived as *valuable* by some, this would be a judgment statement rather than a direct suggestion from the passage. Answer choice (D) cannot be correct.

E The passage does not indicate the number of individuals with this unique tolerance, so the reader has no way of knowing how likely or unlikely it is. Answer choice (E) is also incorrect.

QUESTION 18

Overview: In question 18, the student is asked to place the historical information about caffeine within the context of the passage and to determine the author's purpose in including this information. As mentioned before, the first paragraph provides a background of sorts to introduce the student to caffeine and to explain how it has been used over time. This paragraph does not contribute extensively to the main argument of the passage, but it completes the passage by indicating that people have been consuming caffeine for its stimulative effects for many centuries. In fact, this more or less summarizes the author's goal in including the first paragraph: to provide some historical context and to suggest that people have been consuming caffeine for its effects for many centuries. The answer choice that best expresses this will be correct.

The Correct Answer:

C **Answer choice (C)** best summarizes the author's intention with the first paragraph: to explain that caffeine consumption is not a modern innovation and to indicate that its effects within certain products have been known to many for some time. Answer choice (C) is correct.

The Incorrect Answers:

A At no point does the author claim or suggest that Runge is mistakenly credited with discovering caffeine. At most, the author indicates that he is historically credited with the official discovery, *because he was the first to identify it as a separate ingredient*. This does not mean, however, that the credit he has received is inaccurate. If anything, it simply means that some further historical information is required to explain the full story, and the author provides that further historical information. Answer choice (A) cannot be correct.

B The author's mention of tea leaves from China, cocoa among the Maya in Mexico, and coffee beans in Ethiopia and Yemen definitely indicate that these beans and leaves seem to occur naturally in different parts of the world. But is the author's purpose in mentioning these varying places to indicate the universality of certain beans and leaves? Without a doubt, the answer is *no*. The author intends to show that the use of these products for their stimulative effects has occurred around the world. As a result, answer choice (B) cannot be correct.

D Clearly, the author believes that Runge's work is of some significance. But mentioning the other historical information about caffeine consumption does not necessarily confirm Runge's discovery so much as place it in a larger context. Answer choice (D) is incorrect.

E Answer choice (E) offers an interesting option, but it does little to explain the historical detail within the context of Runge's research and the passage as a whole. At most, answer choice (E) functions as a red herring, or an answer choice that seems all right and does not immediately send up red flags of incorrectness but also does not have a clear link to the passage. Answer choice (E) may be eliminated.

Question 19

Overview: In question 19, the student is asked to select an answer choice that best explains the implication in the author's discussion about the adenosine receptors and how caffeine affects them. The author states the following: "Caffeine influences the adenosine receptors in the central nervous system, and these receptors naturally dilate blood vessels in the brain. Lack of expected caffeine can cause an unnatural response in the adenosine receptors, creating too much dilation and producing severe headaches." In other words, the adenosine receptors must become accustomed to the effects of caffeine (thus developing a caffeine tolerance of their own), because when caffeine is withdrawn, the adenosine receptors no longer behave normally and can cause headaches. The author does not specify *how* caffeine affects the adenosine receptors, although there is the suggestion that caffeine influences the natural dilation to some degree. The primary indication in this statement is that the adenosine receptors grow accustomed to caffeine and thus, devoid of caffeine, cannot perform their natural function without causing some discomfort. The answer choice that indicates this will be correct.

THE CORRECT ANSWER:

E **Answer choice (E)** best expresses the author's implication regarding the adenosine receptors: they adapt to the caffeine and are then unable to respond normally when the caffeine is withdrawn. Answer choice (E) is correct.

THE INCORRECT ANSWERS:

A The author claims only that the adenosine receptors "naturally dilate blood vessels in the brain." When there is caffeine withdrawal, the adenosine receptors dilate too much, and the added dilation causes headaches. There is no mention of what effect the adenosine receptors have in regular activity on the prevention of average headaches—just that a disruption of their normal activity can lead to the development of a headache. Answer choice (A) attempts to make connections that the author does not clearly make, so it acts as a red herring in this case and should be eliminated. Answer choice (A) cannot be correct.

B The author mentions depression as a possible side effect of caffeine withdrawal, but there is no clear connection between the adenosine receptors and depression. The only side effect linked to the adenosine receptors is headaches, so answer choice (B) cannot be correct.

C Answer choice (C) makes assumptions that are not implied and contributes outside information that has no support within the passage. The author *does* mention weight as a possible factor in determining caffeine tolerance. But this alone is not enough to argue that people who are overweight will not experience severe headaches during caffeine withdrawal. In fact, it may be argued that the headaches experienced by overweight people will be comparable to those experienced by people of average weight, because the proportion of caffeine to body weight will be the same, even if the exact amount of that caffeine is not. In other words, an overweight person might (with the emphasis on *might*) be required to consume more caffeine to develop the tolerance, but in the case of withdrawal the adenosine receptors will be affected the same way. Answer choice (C) is thus incorrect.

D The author links caffeine to medical research in the case of preventing apnea in infants and the risk of heart disease in adults. But the author does not mention, nor can it be assumed, that medical researchers have utilized caffeine to assist with dilation. There is simply not enough information in the passage to suggest it, so answer choice (D) cannot be correct.

QUESTION 20

Overview: In question 20, the student is asked to select an answer choice that most closely describes the author's tone in the last sentence. As with all questions of this variety, the student must beware of projecting a personal opinion onto the author's tone. The correct answer choice will be a word that describes the tone within the context of the passage, and devoid of outside opinion. In the Synopsis, it was mentioned that the author's tone is "dry." Reviewing the sentence, it is clear that the author has a slightly tongue-in-cheek tone: not entirely negative, but certainly a bit playful. The phrase "if nothing else" and the mention of "that daily fix" hint distantly of satire on the author's part, but again the author is not so much indicating disapproval as amusement. The best word might be something such as ironic or satirical, and a quick review of the answer choices makes this likely. The student should, of course, review the other answer choices, but it should not take long to eliminate any incorrect options.

THE CORRECT ANSWER:

A The word *ironic* best describes the author's tone in the last sentence of the passage, as indicated in the Overview above. **Answer choice (A)**, therefore, is correct.

THE INCORRECT ANSWERS:

B An *acerbic* tone is angrily biting, and this hardly describes the author's tone in the final sentence, so answer choice (B) may be eliminated.

C A tone that is *mollified* has been pacified or calmed down. As there is no indication the author needed to be mollified at any point in the passage—especially since the author makes no earlier demand in the passage for caffeine withdrawal to be labeled as a health disorder—answer choice (C) has no immediate relevance. Answer choice (C) may thus be eliminated.

D The author might be slightly amused to find that caffeine withdrawal has been identified as a health disorder, but there is no indication that the author is *perturbed*, or excessively concerned, about this. Answer choice (D) cannot be correct.

E A tone that is *querulous* would be described as *cantankerous* or extremely *fussy*. This is certainly not a good description of the author's tone in the final sentence or in any other sentence of the passage, so answer choice (E) cannot be correct.

QUESTIONS 21–27

Synopsis: The final passage of the Reading Comprehension section presents a discussion of the form of education known as "classical" education, which has become increasingly popular in recent decades. In the first paragraph of the passage, the author provides historical information to explain the origins of this form of education, noting specifically that it developed during the Middle Ages and utilized traditions of Greek education. The author mentions that classical education is generally divided into two sections, that is, the trivium and the quadrivium. According to the author, the quadrivium, with its four-part focus on astronomy, arithmetic, music, and geometry, is generally considered today to be the post-secondary studies. As the author points out, a number of colleges and universities now offer a version of the quadrivium. The author concludes the first paragraph by mentioning the importance of history to classical education, because history is believed to link all subjects and all studies by providing context.

In the second paragraph, the author goes on to explain the trivium, divided into the grammar stage, the logic or dialectic stage, and the rhetoric stage. The author explains each briefly. The grammar stage is usually associated with elementary studies, the logic stage with junior high, and the rhetoric stage with high school. The author stresses that each stage builds on the previous, with the grammar stage laying the framework of knowledge and the logic and rhetoric stages developing this knowledge with gradually more difficult studies. And the author notes that history is once again very important to the trivium.

The final paragraph provides the context for how classical education became popular once again after it was left behind with the Middle Ages. As the author notes, the English academic/writer Dorothy L. Sayers presented an essay that sparked interest in classical education, by arguing that the modern system of education does not prepare students sufficiently and leaves the student vulnerable to manipulation due to weak reasoning skills. Dr. George Bugliarello of Polytechnic University, however, points out that the classical curriculum is weak in the study of science and technology and that the classical system does not offer enough science training for students in the modern world. The author concludes by suggesting that there is "a balance to be found in the perspectives of both Sayers and Bugliarello."

QUESTION 21

Overview: Question 21 asks the student to identify the answer choice that best expresses the author's main point. Considering the passage in full, it is obvious that the author's goal is to inform the reader about classical education by explaining its history and traditional sections of study. In the Reading Comprehension section, however, the main point (or main argument) is seldom just a statement of description. The author will have an angle, so to speak, sometimes indicated in a sentence or two and sometimes entirely implied. In the fourth passage of the Reading Comprehension section, the author does provide a statement that suggests the main point. In the last sentence, the author says, "Perhaps there is a balance to be found in the perspectives of both Sayers and Bugliarello, and the classical education of the next few decades will find a way to fuse the strengths of the past with the needs of the future." In other words, the author is indicating that classical education has value, but it also needs to be updated to suit the requirements of educating the modern student. The answer choice that most closely encompasses this idea will be correct.

THE CORRECT ANSWER:

B **Answer choice (B)** summarizes the author's statement in the final sentence of the passage and thus indicates the author's main point: that classical education has value but also needs to include the study of science and technology that Dr. Bugliarello noted. Answer choice (B), therefore, is correct.

THE INCORRECT ANSWERS:

A Answer choice (A) definitely summarizes the details of the first and third paragraphs of the passage. But a summary alone is not enough to express the author's main point, which should essentially be a statement of argument. Answer choice (A) cannot be correct.

C Answer choice (C) summarizes only the details of the first paragraph and leaves out the author's suggestion for modernizing classical education at the end of the final paragraph. As a result, answer choice (C) cannot be correct, so it may be eliminated.

D The author certainly mentions history as an important feature of the classical curriculum, but this is simply a statement of fact. A statement of fact cannot function as a main point or main argument, so answer choice (D), which turns it into a statement of opinion ("most important") cannot be correct.

E At the end of the passage, the author suggests that the current approach to classical education *should* incorporate the modern studies of science and technology. But the author does not indicate that this has taken place or that it is widely embraced. Answer choice (E), therefore, cannot be correct.

QUESTION 22

Overview: In question 22, the student is asked to infer the details from Dr. George Bugliarello's statement about the need to provide more study of science and technology in the classical curriculum. More specifically, the question asks the student for what Dr. Bugliarello's statement implies about the traditional classical system. The author says, "Dr. George Bugliarello of Polytechnic University argues that the strict liberal arts focus of the classical trivium can no longer prepare the modern student adequately, because students also need a strong background in science and technology. As Dr. Bugliarello indicates, the modern world has a greater focus on science and technology than the medieval world, and any education limited in these areas will only handicap a student in the long run." In essence, Dr. Bugliarello's argument about the need for science and technology indicates that classical education—as it has been received from the medieval tradition—was more focused on the study of liberal arts subjects than on the study of science. This is hardly surprising, of course, given the fact that science had not developed very far during the Middle Ages. It is important to note, however, that the author *does not actually say* there was virtually no study of science and technology in the medieval curriculum; the student must simply infer this from the statements that are made, and the inference is a safe one. What is more, there is a good chance that the student will automatically infer this without realizing it. Question 22 is a good exercise in distinguishing between what is said and what is carefully and deliberately implied. The correct answer might almost seem *too* obvious, but the student should not be afraid to select it.

The Correct Answer:

E Clearly, the correct inference from Dr. Bugliarello's argument is that the medieval curriculum *did not* contain a strong focus on science and technology and *did* contain a strong focus on other subjects (namely, those of the liberal arts). **Answer choice (E)** is correct.

The Incorrect Answers:

A Question 22 ultimately asks for the immediate implication within Dr. Bugliarello's argument. Dr. Bugliarello might very well believe that classical education is no longer relevant and that educators should focus instead on reforming the current system of public education. But within the context of the passage, that statement cannot be derived. There is a hint of an inference that Dr. Bugliarello might not advise a classical curriculum, but there is no reason to believe—from the information in the passage alone—that he would not support a classical curriculum containing a strong study of science and technology. Answer choice (A) thus infers more than the passage implies, so it is incorrect.

B The passage is silent on Dr. Bugliarello's views concerning the current system of education. It is entirely possible that he supports it, just as it is possible that he does *not* support it. There is simply not enough information in the passage to indicate Dr. Bugliarello's views on this subject, so answer choice (B) cannot be correct.

C Clearly, answer choice (C) infers considerably more than might be derived from the passage. The author *does* indicate that the views of Dorothy Sayers and Dr. Bugliarello have merit and should somehow be combined for a stronger classical curriculum, but the author does not clearly link Dr. Bugliarello to the active updating of that curriculum, so it cannot be inferred that he is involved. Answer choice (C) cannot be correct.

D The author indicates strongly that the traditional medieval system of classical education was lacking in science and technology. There is no reason to believe, however, that some educators have not attempted to provide training in science and technology. The author definitely encourages a more widespread infusion of science and technology in the classical curriculum, but it is assuming too much, from the information in the passage alone, that *all* students who receive a classical education do not receive training in science and technology. Answer choice (D) infers too much, so it is incorrect.

Question 23

Overview: In question 23, the student is asked to select an answer choice that provides the best connotation for the word *classical* as it appears throughout the passage. The challenge in this question is distilling the author's use of *classical* alongside its traditional meaning. Historically, something that is considered to be *classical* has direct links to Ancient Greece. Over time, the word *classical* has come to take on a much wider range of meaning, from simple elegance within home design to the music of Ralph Vaughan Williams. Given this vast scope of possibility, the student needs to consider each answer choice in turn, because it will probably not be enough in this case to determine an accurate meaning without considering the options that are available. The student will just need to be very careful not to read meaning into the answer choices but to consider each answer choice individually and to compare each one to the passage in order to determine if that is really how the author is using it and, more importantly, *how it relates to the type of studies that the classical system embraces.*

THE CORRECT ANSWER:

C The word *humanistic* also has several possible connotations, but it is most closely associated with the study of the humanities and thus to the liberal arts. The author implies the importance of the liberal arts through Dr. George Bugliarello's arguments, so the student may infer that a classical education is strong in humanistic studies. As a result, **answer choice (C)** is correct.

THE INCORRECT ANSWERS:

A By indicating that the traditional mode of classical education could stand to be updated with a stronger focus on science and technology, the author indicates that it is *not* as thorough as it should be. Sayers's comments suggest that the classical system produces a "more rounded individual," but even she implied that there were and are limitations to the system. With the author's final remark, it may be inferred that the author would not describe the classical system as *thorough*, at least with a primary focus on humanities. What is more, *thorough* comes very close to being a judgment statement, and judgment statements are never correct when selecting synonyms for the Reading Comprehension section. Answer choice (A) cannot be correct.

B Apart from mentioning that classical education proved to be popular among the home-schooling community, the author does not discuss the societal demographics among those who currently employ a classical system, and there is no information about who received this form of education during the Middle Ages. It could be argued that anyone who received an education in the Middle Ages was among the elite, but that is not an argument to be derived from this passage, nor does this passage even hint of elitism in connection to classical education. Answer choice (B), therefore, cannot be correct.

D, E Answer choices (D) and (E) represents clear statements of judgment, so both should be eliminated at once. Whether or not the classical curriculum is *superior* or *ideal* is an individual opinion, and there is not enough information in the passage to define *classical* in either way. Answer choices (D) and (E) are incorrect.

QUESTION 24

Overview: Question 24 asks the student to identify the answer choice that best explains the reason that history is of such importance in the classical curriculum. The author says, "Furthermore, quadrivium subjects are all taught within the larger framework of history. In classical education, history is viewed as the subject that links the other studies together. As the study of history encompasses the study of all that has occurred, every other subject falls into its historical place, thus providing the scholar with an appreciation for the development of each field over time." The student does not need to dwell extensively on this question, but because the author does not expand any further on the significance of history, the student should infer the following: history is, of course, chronological, so the chronological study of subjects places them in the context of how ideas developed over time.

Ideas do not develop in isolation, so it is no mere coincidence that the political theories of John Locke and his views on man's ability to think for and rule himself developed out of the philosophical views of the Enlightenment, in which the traditions of the Middle Ages—man having been guided carefully by Church and state—were abandoned in favor of man as the empowered individual. As mentioned before, the student does not need to develop all of these thoughts clearly: it is enough that the student infers the reason that history is considered to be the tie that binds all other subjects of the classical curriculum together.

The Correct Answer:

C The correct answer accurately paraphrases and summarizes the reasons, as indicated in the passage, for why history is the central subject of the classical curriculum. **Answer choice (C)** is correct.

The Incorrect Answers:

A The author notes that history is important to the classical curriculum and offers an explanation for why this is the case, but the author does not mention other systems of education and the way that these systems rank the study of history. So, there is not enough information in the passage to assume that the classical system is the *only* system of education to place such a value on the study of history. Answer choice (A) cannot be correct.

B The discussion of history as central to the classical system is arguably interesting, and it *might* be unique to classical education (although as mentioned in the discussion for the previous answer choice this has no clear support in the passage). But the author does not seem to indicate that the study of history is *the most unique* factor, nor is there any way to determine this except by making a judgment statement. Answer choice (B) is incorrect.

D The author does not provide any clear detail about how instructors discuss the study of history, so there is no way to determine from the information in the passage alone that teachers *do* or *do not* mention history as a separate subject. Answer choice (D) cannot be correct.

E At no point does the author argue or even imply that the public education system has failed. The author mentions "recent concerns about the modern system of education in the United States." This alone does not indicate a failure, nor is there enough within the expression "modern system of education" to assume that a failure is entirely within the public education system. The comments from Dorothy Sayers indicate a much larger problem about the modern approach to education in general, and this is not necessarily limited to public education. Answer choice (E) may be eliminated as incorrect.

Question 25

Overview: Question 25 asks the student to identify the reason that the author includes the information about the quadrivium. The author's initial mention of the "recent concerns about the modern system of education" does not specify that the focus of the essay will be on primary and secondary education alone. That being said, the author also notes the following: "Dr. George Bugliarello of Polytechnic University argues that the strict liberal arts focus of the classical **trivium** can no longer prepare the modern student adequately…" Dr. Bugliarello's concerns relate directly to the trivium itself, so the author's final remarks seem to relate more to the trivium than to the quadrivium. As a result, the student needs to put the information about the quadrivium in the context of the passage as a whole. The author clearly chooses to mention the quadrivium first, discussing the subjects that are traditionally studied and noting the subjects that are often added to an updated quadrivium curriculum. When compared to the final statements in the passage, the early mention of the quadrivium seems to represent a kind of example of success, with post-secondary schools finding ways of embracing a classical approach to higher education but also adapting it to modern educational needs. As the author suggests, if colleges and universities can find a way to make the classical system relevant, there is reason to believe that primary and secondary schools can make it relevant as well through updating the trivium. The correct answer, therefore, will reflect the success of post-secondary schools with updating the quadrivium.

THE CORRECT ANSWER:

A **Answer choice (A)** most accurately expresses the author's purpose in discussing the quadrivium by identifying the relevance of the system through updating it. Answer choice (A) is thus correct.

THE INCORRECT ANSWERS:

B Far from indicating problems, the author seems to be indicating success with the quadrivium among some colleges and universities. If the author feels as though the application of quadrivium traditions in post-secondary schools has been problematic, there is no indication of it. Answer choice (B) cannot be correct.

C The author mentions the four traditional subjects of the quadrivium but also points out that most colleges and universities expand these subjects to include courses that the modern post-secondary student needs for a college education. This would indicate that the four subjects alone are *not* enough and that the author is not including the information about the quadrivium merely to point out that these subjects are valuable. Answer choice (C) cannot be correct.

D Answer choice (D) has no immediate relevance to the passage. The author never mentions the way that most colleges and universities organize the post-secondary education, and while the student will almost certainly know that colleges/universities require a "major" area of study, this alone does not mean that students do not study other subjects. What is more, this is simply not the point and has no connection to the point. Answer choice (D) is thus a red herring and should be eliminated as incorrect.

E Again, the author does not discuss the curriculum of non-classical colleges and universities, so there is no way to make a clear comparison between the subjects that are studied. Given the information provided in the passage, the author's real focus is not on the subjects themselves, which would probably all be studied anyway, but on the methods of study. The discussion of the importance of history within the classical education indicates that the approach to the subjects is not the same, even if the subjects themselves are. Because the author does not focus much on the methods of study, as is done in the second paragraph with the details about the trivium, there is no way to deduce any further information. Answer choice (E) cannot be correct.

QUESTION 26

<u>Overview</u>: Question 26 asks the student to select the answer choice that features the correct inference of Dorothy Sayers's comparison between modern education and medieval education. The author says, "In the essay, Sayers encourages educational reforms, arguing that medieval education

produced a stronger student and was far more successful than the educational systems that followed the Middle Ages: Sayers notes in particular that despite the high rates of literacy in Europe and elsewhere, people today are more vulnerable to media manipulation, have little ability to formulate serious arguments in a debate, and are no longer capable of distinguishing the good literature from the bad. Sayers posits that whatever its limitations, the classical system of the Middle Ages produced a stronger thinker and a more rounded individual." All of this suggests that despite the lower rate of literacy during the Middle Ages, those who were educated had stronger educations. And according to the author, Sayers reasons that the modern education does not teach students how to resist the reasoning manipulations of the media, or assemble a logical argument, or reject poor literature. In other words, Sayers believed that the modern system of education deprived students of valuable educational experience and left them unable to think clearly or effectively. The correct answer choice will express Sayers's concern of insufficiency in modern educational techniques.

The Correct Answer:

D **Answer choice (D)** most clearly identifies the implication in Sayers's comments about the problems of modern education when compared to medieval education, so answer choice (D) is correct.

The Incorrect Answers:

A Sayers clearly believed that the modern system of education was lacking in providing students with the ability to resist media manipulation. But this was just one of her concerns, and there is no indication that it was the primary or the most important concern. Answer choice (A), therefore, lacks necessary details and places too much significance on one element over others, so it cannot be correct.

B Although the author cites Sayers as recognizing lower literacy rates in the Middle Ages, there is no implication that modern schools focus excessively on literacy rates. The discussion of literacy rates is more intended to point out that fewer people in general were educated during the Middle Ages, but those who were educated had sound teaching that enabled them to reason clearly. The indication is that there are far higher rates of literacy in the modern world (because more people receive an education) but without equally high rates of people who are able to reason clearly. It *cannot* be assumed that modern schools *focus* on the literacy rates. Answer choice (B) thus infers too much, so it cannot be correct.

C Answer choice (C) offers a hypothetical statement, but it is one that does not actually have any support in the passage. As was mentioned before, the author does not fault the public educational system in particular but the modern approach to education in general, so answer choice (C) claims a specific reform that the author's statements do not support. Answer choice (C), therefore, is incorrect.

E The author does not discuss homeschooling in any detail, except to note that the classical approach to education has been popular among homeschooling parents. What is more, the author does not say anywhere that the classical system is particularly valuable for training individuals, so answer choice (E) assumes too much by combining unrelated ideas. Answer choice (E) is incorrect.

Question 27

Overview: Question 27 asks the student to select an answer choice that best describes the author's opinion in the final sentence regarding the potential for fusing classical techniques with the needs of the modern student. The sentence reads, "Perhaps there is a balance to be found in the perspectives of both Sayers and Bugliarello, and the classical education of the next few decades will find a way to fuse the strengths of the past with the needs of the future." Based on this statement, as well as the discussion of the quadrivium at the post-secondary level, it is clear that the author believes that updating the classical trivium to meet modern needs is valid and valuable. At the same time, the author is not demanding change, nor is there an indication of frustration about the lack of change. The author is simply making a suggestion on the positive note that such a course of action might be useful.

The Correct Answer:

B **Answer choice (B)** best describes the author's opinion as *optimistic*: the author sees the opportunity for change and believes that change will be valuable but is not necessarily insisting that it must happen. In this case, *optimistic* reflects the author's opinion of the benefits that will ensue from updating the classical trivium. Answer choice (B) is correct.

The Incorrect Answers:

A The word *vehement* suggests a strong opinion that is conveyed forcefully. This does not describe the author's opinion in the final sentence, or in any other part of the passage, so answer choice (A) cannot be correct.

C An attitude that is *diffident* is passive or lacking in interest. The author would not have written an entire passage about classical education if the attitude toward it was one of diffidence, nor does *diffident* describe the opinion itself. Obviously, the author is not insistent, but lack of insistence does not guarantee diffidence. Answer choice (C) is not correct.

D An *incredulous* opinion is one that doubts. Given the author's indication of the post-secondary success with the quadrivium, there is no reason to think that the author is doubtful of the success in updating the trivium. Answer choice (D) cannot be correct.

E The author does not express impatience at any point in the passage, nor can it be said that the author's tone is *impatient*. The author actually references "the classical education of the next few decades"; measuring time in decades does not generally indicate impatience, so it stands to reason that the author sees the recommended updating of the classical trivium as something to occur over time. Answer choice (E) is incorrect.

Logical Reasoning, Section IV

QUESTION 1

Overview: The first question in the fourth section of the test focuses on a situation in which a large charitable organization is preparing for a reduction in donations due to the weakness in the economy. The author of the passage explains that the head of the charitable organization reviews the receipts and has discovered that the amount received in donations has not dropped at all. The head of the organization knows that his donors tend to be faithful in sending in their donations, but he is surprised to find that they are still able to give the same amount of money.

The question then asks the student to determine the answer choice that best explains the anomaly between the anticipated slump in charitable donations and the fact that the charitable organization is receiving the same amount as before the time of economic weakness. To select the correct answer, the student needs to locate an answer choice that provides a *tangible and solid* reason for why people would continue giving money to charities in spite of the economic downturn. The correct answer will not offer an insubstantial explanation: feeling cannot come into the equation, however applicable it to real-life decision making, because the Logical Reasoning sections of the test, by their very definition, require logic and not emotion.

THE CORRECT ANSWER:

E **Answer choice (E)** provides the reason that is the clearest and most logical, if a bit forensic, for why people would continue to give the same amount to charitable organizations in spite of economic weakness: governments offer tax deductions for charitable donations, and people will continue to be motivated to receive tax deductions, especially during an economic downturn. Answer choice (E), therefore, is correct.

THE INCORRECT ANSWERS:

A Answer choice (A) is too tenuous to be correct. While it is true that the wealthiest members of society probably weather an economic downturn better than those who have less, it is assuming too much that this alone would motivate them to continue donating to charity. What is more, there is not enough information in the passage to suggest that this particular charitable organization receives most of its money from wealthier members of society, so answer choice (A) does not offer a solid explanation. Answer choice (A) is incorrect.

B Answer choice (B) seems like a good possibility, except that the passage makes no mention of the charitable organization lowering its expectations. In fact, the passage indicates that the organization did *not* lower its expectations, owing to the surprise on the part of the organization's head. Answer choice (B) contradicts important information in the passage, so it must be incorrect.

C It is certainly possible that the charitable organization has begun receiving government funding to continue to subsist. But the author of the passage indicates clearly that the receipt of the same amount of donations was unexpected, and the receipt of government funding would not be. Answer choice (C) cannot be correct.

D Answer choice (D) brings far too much feeling into the situation to be a solid explanation. In all reality, this might very well be a reason (and a poll might prove it to be true), but the student cannot deduce this from the information provided in the passage, nor can it function as a logical reason based on the requirements of the test. Answer choice (D) must be eliminated.

Question 2

Overview: In question 2, the student is provided with a statement made by a geophysicist about geomagnetic reversal, in which the magnetic fields of the earth literally switch—with the North Pole in the south, and the South Pole pointing in the north. The geophysicist notes that many of his colleagues are still unsure of the cause of this, and not much is known, but the geophysicist goes on to stress that if such a reversal occurred, it could have the potential for causing serious problems on the earth.

According to the geophysicist, a geomagnetic reversal would occur over very long periods of time and could leave the earth exposed to radiation from the sun. The question then asks for an answer choice that represents the geophysicist's primary argument. This is essentially a "main point" question, with the speaker of the passage identified to be a geophysicist. The student needs to peruse the passage carefully and define the main point that the geophysicist seems to be making. There are several important features: (1) scientists do not agree on what causes geomagnetic reversal, (2) scientists *do* agree that there are potentially important effects, (3) geomagnetic reversal would occur gradually and not quickly, and (4) this process has the potential for leaving the earth exposed to the sun's radiation. These four ideas indicate the primary foci of the paragraph, so the correct answer choice will combine them into a single coherent statement.

The Correct Answer:

C **Answer choice (C)** best combines the four ideas noted in the Overview above into a unified thought: scientists do not necessarily know the causes or even the results of geomagnetic reversal, but there is enough evidence to indicate that they should be paying close attention to it. Answer choice (C), therefore, is correct.

The Incorrect Answers:

A There is nothing in the passage to indicate that the geophysicist believes the information in answer choice (A). In fact, the geophysicist seems to believe that geomagnetic reversal could be a very serious issue with significant and dangerous effects. Answer choice (A) cannot be correct.

B The geophysicist makes no mention of previous geomagnetic reversals, and while the potential does exist for them to have occurred in the past, there is definitely not enough information in the passage to suggest that such a process did occur before or that it occurred while mankind lived on the earth. Answer choice (B) attempts to infer details that the passage does not provide, so it is incorrect.

D The geophysicist clearly believes that scientists should be paying attention to the potential for geomagnetic reversal, but there is no mention of government funding, nor does the geophysicist discuss anyone outside the scientific community. Answer choice (D) cannot be correct.

E The geophysicist does not clearly discuss the effects that the magnetic poles currently have on the natural functions of the earth, but given the concern that is expressed over geomagnetic reversal, it stands to reason that the geophysicist does not agree with answer choice (E). Therefore, answer choice (E) cannot be the geophysicist's main point, so it may be eliminated.

Question 3

Overview: Question 3 presents the student with information about white tea, noting specifically its similarities and differences to black and green tea. The author of the passage mentions that white tea is usually more "delicate" and "rare" than black or green tea and that it contains higher levels of certain chemicals—many of which have very positive health effects. The question then asks the student to identify the answer choice that can *not* be inferred from the passage. This is a fairly difficult question to answer correctly, because the student has to look closely to know for sure that the incorrect answers *actually can be* inferred. The correct answer, in this case, will be the answer choice that has absolutely no substance in the passage and cannot be inferred from any statements made.

The Correct Answer:

D The author of the passage mentions that white tea "contains considerably less fluoride than black or green tea." The author makes no comment anywhere else in the paragraph to indicate whether or not fluoride is a typical ingredient in tea, so it is impossible to determine from this alone if the lack of fluoride is viewed as a positive or a negative quality. Because the author of the passage is silent, **answer choice (D)** cannot be clearly inferred, so it is correct.

The Incorrect Answers:

A The author of the passage claims that white tea is "more delicate and rarer than black or green tea and has fewer producers." From this, the student may deduce that there are companies that process black tea but not white tea. Answer choice (A), therefore, may be inferred, so it is incorrect.

B In the middle of the passage, the student will read the following: "To produce white tea, basic tea leaves are picked when they are very young." This implies strongly that white tea is just a product of regular tea leaves being picked at a young age and is not necessarily a different variety than black or green tea. Answer choice (B) may be inferred, so it is incorrect.

C The passage notes several times the differences between white tea and black or green tea, in each case identifying the chemicals contained in white tea that may improve health. From this, the student may deduce that there are possible health benefits to drinking white tea, benefits that are not obtained from drinking black or green tea. The passage implies answer choice (C), so it is incorrect.

E Toward the end of the passage, the author claims that white tea has "much higher levels of theanine, which is known for its relaxing qualities." So it is possible that these relaxing qualities could be used in a therapeutic setting. Answer choice (E), then, can be inferred, so it is incorrect.

Question 4

Overview: Question 4 presents a conversation between Angelica and Luca, in which they are discussing the history of the "Roaring Twenties" and its connection to the advent of modernism. Angelica claims that the Roaring Twenties occurred as a "direct result of the social breakdown that occurred during World War I." The war left such strongly negative impressions that young people rejected the authority of their elders and the traditions that they represented. This, claims Angelica, was the start of modernism. Luca counters by arguing that the Roaring Twenties definitely suggests a more universal willingness to embrace modernism but that the Modern Age itself "had already begun in the mid-nineteenth century" with the philosophers and political scientists who were questioning authority and traditions long before World War I began. The question asks the student to identify the way that Luca responds to Angelica's argument. The student should recognize immediately that there is no polarization in Luca's answer: he does not outright agree or disagree with Angelica. Instead he partially agrees, but with conditions, the primary condition being the way that Angelica describes the origin of modernism. The correct answer choice will reflect this.

The Correct Answer:

A **Answer choice (A)** accurately notes that Luca acknowledges Angelica's point in part but suggests that she revise her starting point for modernism. Answer choice (A) is correct.

The Incorrect Answers:

B Luca does not necessarily criticize the substance of Angelica's argument. He agrees, in fact, that the Roaring Twenties *do* represent a rejection of authority and traditions. He disagrees, however, that this was unique to the post-war experience and indicates that it had begun previously. Answer choice (B) cannot be correct.

C At no point does Luca mention or criticize a logical fallacy that is embedded in Angelica's argument, so answer choice (C) should be eliminated immediately.

D Far from questioning the possibility of arriving at a conclusion, Luca merely disagrees with a part of Angelica's argument and seems to indicate that they *could* agree. Answer choice (D) cannot be correct.

E Luca does provide some alternate views, but his response is not necessarily a point-by-point disagreement. Instead, he offers a more general summary of why he disagrees. Answer choice (E) is incorrect.

Question 5

Overview: In question 5, the student is given information about the tiny island of Sark, one of four islands located in the English Channel and falling under the jurisdiction of the British Crown. For most of its history—and until 2008—Sark was considered a feudal state, and its ruler the Seigneur the head of a fiefdom. Today, Sark has about 600 residents, and most of them are past middle age (according to the passage). What is more, the island, which is only two square miles in landmass, has a horses-only policy and does not allow motor vehicles such as cars, nor are airplanes allowed to fly over the island. The question asks the student to determine the answer choice that best explains this horses-only policy.

From the information provided in the passage, the student should already begin to deduce that the reason might be primarily environmental: (1) the island is very small, (2) the landscape is fragile, and the climate is already heavily affected by the island's location in the English Channel, and (3) the residents are committed to retaining a sustainable quality on the island. The correct answer choice will combine these facts into a single coherent statement of explanation.

The Correct Answer:

D **Answer choice (D)** accurately expresses the environmental reasons for why an island such as Sark would refuse to allow motor vehicles. Answer choice (D), therefore, is correct.

The Incorrect Answers:

A Answer choice (A) is plausible from a purely practical position, but it does not take the other features of the passage into account, namely the focus on sustainable living and the problems that the island might already face by being located in the English Channel. What is more, the author of the passage notes that most of the residents are past middle age, so walking the entire island might be less possible as they grow older. Answer choice (A) is incorrect.

B Answer choice (B) cannot be correct, because the passage offers no explanation for how long the island of Sark has had a horses-only policy. Without knowing if the policy has been in place for long, it is impossible to know if the residents have become accustomed to it. Answer choice (B), therefore, may be eliminated.

C It is assuming too much about the lifestyle of residents on the island of Sark to argue that just because people live in small, self-contained villages they would not need to go elsewhere on the island. Answer choice (C) offers too vague and tenuous of a reason, so it is incorrect.

E Answer choice (E) is also an explanation that has no real connection to the information provided in the paragraph. And again, the passage does not clearly indicate how long the horses-only policy has been in effect, so it is impossible to claim with any certainty that this is an arbitrary or irrelevant policy dating from an earlier time when Sark was still a feudal state. What is more, answer choice (E) represents a judgment statement that cannot be inferred from the passage. As a result, answer choice (E) is incorrect.

QUESTION 6

Overview: Question 6 provides the student with information about the history of the name *Japan*, starting off by noting that the word is actually an exonym, or a name that is given to a country or people by those outside the country and is not the name by which the country identifies itself. The author of the passage points out that in Japan, the country is known as *Nippon* or *Nihon*, meaning "the sun's origin." The word *Japan* actually derives from the interaction between Portuguese sailors and the people of Malaysia, who referred to Japan as *Jepang* (a word that might have come from the Mandarin *Cipangu*). The author concludes by noting that the European name *Japan* has become common and that there are nine other languages that utilize it over the words *Nippon* or *Nihon*. The question then asks the student to select an answer choice that may be inferred, so as always with inference questions the student needs to take care to review each answer choice carefully and be able to link the correct answer directly back to a statement or more than one statement made in the passage.

THE CORRECT ANSWER:

B The passage states that *Japan* is an exonym and traces its origin back to the Mandarin language. This derivation is used in English and at least nine other languages, according to the passage, so at least ten languages use *Japan* and can thus trace this exonym back to its supposed Mandarin roots. **Answer choice (B)** is thus correct.

THE INCORRECT ANSWERS:

A At no point in the passage does the author make a judgment statement about the exonym *Japan*. The author's purpose is primarily information and not criticism. As a result, it is inferring too much on the part of the reader to claim that the author is offering an opinion on the reality of exonyms, and there is no clear statement in the passage that could be used strongly in support of a criticism. Answer choice (A) cannot be correct.

C The author makes no statement about how the Japanese value the names *Nippon* or *Nihon* with regard to non-Japanese usage, so the reader cannot infer from the information in the passage that it would be an insult to the Japanese people for those outside of Japan to use these names. Answer choice (C) cannot be correct.

D The author comments that the ultimate origin of the Malay *Jepang* is possibly Mandarin, but the author makes no immediate comment about whether or not the Mandarin word *Cipangu* meant the same as the Japanese words *Nippon* or *Nihon*. The student might know from personal study that this is, in fact, true; but the passage provides no indication of what *Cipangu* means, so the student cannot infer answer choice (D) from the information in the passage. Answer choice (D) is incorrect.

E The passage makes no reference to any exonyms other than *Japan*, so it is impossible to assume or argue from the passage that the name *Japan* represents a rarity. Answer choice (E) cannot be correct.

Question 7

Overview: In question 7, the student reads a statement made by a farmer in Norway regarding the rapid growth of the greylag goose population. At some point in the past, the greylag goose became an endangered species, and the Norwegian government stepped in to protect the geese. In consequence, the geese population grew so quickly that they became deleterious to farms by eating crops, but the farmers are unable to get rid of the geese due to the official protection under which the greylag goose falls. The farmer concludes that the government protection of the geese should be lifted and that the farmers should be allowed to remove the geese from their property in order to protect their crops.

The question asks the student to identify the flaw in the farmer's reasoning, and the student should recognize that the farmer's reasoning is guilty of an "all-or-nothing" conclusion: his solution to the problem of excess geese is to remove the endangered species protection for the geese. What the farmer fails to do, however, is also to consider that this could make the geese vulnerable to endangerment all over again. The farmer does not address this side of the concern and does not offer or suggest a compromise in this issue. As a result, his solution is not much of a solution at all, because it could create the same cycle of problems in the future.

This is a rather simple question, so the student should not worry about analyzing it too closely. The flaw in the farmer's reasoning should be easy to spot, and the answer choice that best reflects it is indeed the correct answer. This will not always be the case in the test, but it will *sometimes* be the case, so the student should watch for these kinds of questions.

The Correct Answer:

C **Answer choice (C)** best explains the flaw in the farmer's reasoning, as indicated in the Overview above: the farmer takes an "all-or-nothing" approach to the issue and assumes that the only way for farmers to protect their crops—since the greylag goose population has increased so much—is for the government to stop protecting the geese. The farmer makes no concession to the other side of the issue (that of the need for safeguarding the geese against population diminishment), and as a result his solution does little more than set the stage for repetition of the same problem scenario. Answer choice (C) is correct.

The Incorrect Answers:

A Answer choice (A) indicates a part of the problem with the farmer's reasoning: he *does* fail to offer an alternative solution to the problems that farmers are facing with the greylag geese, in the sense that his only suggestion is removing the restrictions. But the weakness in his reasoning is fairly specific, and answer choice (A) does not clearly explain the real problem with it. Answer choice (A) may be eliminated due to its unclear explanation.

B The farmer mentions no specific data, so it cannot be said that he relies on *questionable* data. Answer choice (B) is incorrect.

D While it is true that the farmer does not compare the situation with the greylag goose in Norway to similar situations in which an endangered species has grown its population and become a problem, there is nothing in his comments to suggest that he needs such information to complete his argument. Instead, the problem with his reasoning lies in too blunt of an approach and not in missing data.

E It is not surprising that the farmer sides with the other farmers. But the fault in his reasoning lies not in the side that he has taken but, in his refusal to see the other side of the issue. It could be said that he fails to demonstrate objectivity, but objectivity is a difficult quality to embrace, and the farmer who is struggling with the inundation of geese on his farm can hardly be expected to demonstrate full objectivity. In reality, the real problem with his reasoning is that he has proffered a solution that ultimately helps no one except in the immediate short term. If the official protection status is lifted, the farmers would be able to remove geese for a time, but it is likely that the goose population would decline all over again—ultimately leading to the same cycle of problems that the farmer is experiencing now and that other farmers would experience in the future. Answer choice (E) is too generic, so it cannot be correct.

Question 8

Overview: Question 8 presents the student with a more abstract line of reasoning, in which the author of the passage makes the distinction between theory and fact. Theory is represented as "an idea or hypothesis," while fact is shown to be "evidence or proof." The author goes on to indicate that theory *relies on* fact for support, while fact can stand on its own. As the passage progresses, the author provides context to this discussion by explaining the place of theory and fact in making a logical argument: theory is valid if it has fact to back it up, but without fact theory can only be "speculation." The question then asks the student to determine the answer choice that is implied by statements made in the passage. With this type of question, the student will definitely have to review the individual answer choices closely to locate the one that is correct. And as always with implication/inference questions, the student needs to be able to point back to the passage for the *clear statement(s) of implication* in order for the answer choice to be correct.

The Correct Answer:

E **Answer choice (E)** best expresses the implication made in the following statement: "Theory is not always unacceptable in a logical argument, but that theory must be based on comparable facts from similar situations or examples." In other words, the author is implying that a theory is perfectly valid when making a logical argument, but the theory requires fact from an analogous scenario for it to have a solid place within the argument's line of reasoning. Answer choice (E) is thus correct.

The Incorrect Answers:

A The author does imply that fact is valuable for supporting and developing theory in a logical argument, but the author does not imply a statement of opinion that fact is *always* more important and more valuable than theory. The author seems more focused on discussing the place of each in logical arguments and in considering the way that the two elements work together. From the author's comments, it is possible to infer that theory developed by fact could be a very effective technique for making a logical argument. Claiming that fact is always more significant than theory assumes more than the passage implies, so it cannot be correct. Answer choice (A) may be eliminated.

B The author makes no statement about *avoiding* theory. In reality, the author suggests that theory supported by fact could be very valuable in making a logical argument. Answer choice (B) assumes too much, so it cannot be correct.

C The author indicates that theory void of fact (within a logical argument) "usually ends in speculation." This means that theory without fact does not present a strong argument, but this does *not* mean that all theory in a logical argument (with or without fact) is the same as speculation. Answer choice (C) takes the author's words out of context, so it cannot be correct.

D The author does claim that "it is essential to distinguish between theory and fact." It *cannot* be inferred from this, however, that confusing theory with fact could lead to a logical argument that is *entirely false*. In reality, the author suggests that this could lead to a faulty or weak argument, but the author does not go to the extreme of the answer choice. As a result, answer choice (D) should be eliminated.

Question 9

Overview: In question 9, the student is given information about a large corporation that is in the process of turnover, with many older employees retiring simultaneously. At the same time, the economy is experiencing weakness, so the corporation has to make careful decisions about hiring new employees to replace the retiring employees. The corporation knows that there probably cannot be a simple one-to-one ratio of new employees taking over the jobs of retiring employees, because most of the retiring employees had knowledge and experience that a single employee would not have. In reality, the corporation would probably have to hire more than one new employee to take over the jobs of each of the retiring employees. But the passage goes on to say that this is apparently not the corporation's plan. In fact, the corporation expects to hire *fewer* new employees, with no change in work output but a reduction in salaries.

The question asks the student to select the answer choice that most clearly takes these various factors into account and explains the corporation's decision. To answer this question, the student needs to compile all of these elements into a single focus, asking what the details suggest: (1) older employees with many skills are retiring, (2) the corporation would need several employees to replace each retiree, (3) the corporation is planning to hire fewer employees, (4) the corporation expects to see the same amount of work output, and (5) the corporation plans to see reduced salaries. In short, the student should recognize that this all points in one direction. The corporation is planning on hiring very specialized workers who will do several jobs for lower salaries. The correct answer choice will reflect this.

The Correct Answer:

C **Answer choice (C)** provides information that the corporation is working with a headhunter to locate highly versatile workers who are willing to take on extra work but without the expected salary compensation. Answer choice (C), therefore, is correct.

The Incorrect Answers:

A The author of the passage notes that the corporation is *not* expecting to see a reduction in work output, so the fact that the corporation is moving to an overseas location is largely irrelevant as the corporation fully expects to see the same amount of work as before, regardless of location. What is more, answer choice (A) does not indicate that the move overseas would reduce the salary requirements, so it does not explain why the company would expect to pay less in salaries. Answer choice (A) may be eliminated.

B The passage indicates clearly that the outgoing employees will be retiring and that the company will need to replace them fully. As a result, answer choice (B) counters the statements made in the passage, so it cannot be correct.

D Answer choice (D) contradicts the statements made in the passage about the fact that the corporation "does not expect to see a reduction in the work output." Eliminating jobs without a clear indication that other jobs will pick up the slack would obviously eliminate immediate work output, so answer choice (D) cannot be correct.

E Answer choice (E) explains the expected reduction in salaries, but it does not explain the plan to retain the same work output with fewer paid employees. Answer choice (E) thus ignores an important part of the passage, so it cannot be correct.

Question 10

Overview: Question 10 presents the student with an editorial from a local art instructor, claiming that all local elementary schools should incorporate art lessons. The local art instructor argues that art encourages students to "pursue creativity without fear of restriction" while also boosting a student's performance in other subject areas. The local art instructor then cites studies from Japan, in which the student performance in math and science improved after the school added an art program for the students. The question asks the student to identify the statement that most clearly undermines the local art instructor's claims about the need for art lessons in local elementary schools. The student should review each answer choice quickly and carefully—and compare each to the statements made in the passage—to determine the one that suggests a weak point in the local art instructor's reasoning.

The Correct Answer:

D **Answer choice (D)** provides information that strongly questions the validity of the Japanese study that the local art instructor cites: the art instructor claims that the art lessons recently added to Japanese elementary schools were followed by an improvement of student performance in math and science. But if the Japanese schools also added a new math and science curriculum, the local art instructor's argument that art lessons boost student performance in other subjects becomes far less valid. Answer choice (D), therefore, most clearly undermines the local art instructor's claims.

The Incorrect Answers:

A Answer choice (A) is primarily a red herring. It redirects the student's focus to government funding for math and science programs—thus explaining why local elementary schools would focus on them more than on art programs—but it does not necessarily undermine the local art instructor's claims about the need for added art lessons in the classroom. Answer choice (A) may be eliminated as irrelevant.

B The local art instructor's association with a non-profit organization that is committed to encouraging art programs in schools is interesting, but it does nothing to undermine her arguments about the need for art lessons in local elementary schools. Answer choice (B) cannot be correct.

C Answer choice (C) has the potential for undermining the local art instructor's claims, except for the fact that it is too vague to do so. The local art instructor *does* claim that art lessons encourage student creativity and develop their creative skills. But the answer choice provides no clear evidence about the other unnamed subjects that allow for the development of creative skills, nor does it claim that the local elementary schools are currently teaching these subjects in particular or using programs that allow for creativity in these subjects. Answer choice (C) may be eliminated.

E The fact that local elementary schools once had art programs that were unpopular among students might explain why they have been hesitant to adopt them at present. But this in itself does not necessarily undermine the local art instructor's direct claims about art lessons encouraging creativity, benefiting the development of creative skills, and boosting student performance in other subjects. It may be argued that students who dislike an art program are unlikely to benefit from it, but the local art instructor does *not* argue that the schools should adopt the same program that they used in the past, and there is nothing in the answer choice to indicate that the schools would be required to adopt that program. Answer choice (E) is incorrect.

Questions 11 and 12

Overview: Questions 11 and 12 reference a passage about the early development of the camera and particularly the invention known as the *camera obscura*. According to the passage, the camera obscura is credited to Abu Ali Al-Hasan Ibn al-Haitham, an eleventh-century Arab scientist. The author of the passage goes on to note, however, that Ibn al-Haitham was not necessarily the first to invent a camera along the lines of the camera obscura and that there had been similar work in the fourth century BC from the Chinese philosopher Mozi and from Aristotle and Euclid in Greece. In the ninth century, Ibn al-Haitham's fellow Arab scientist Abu Yusuf Ya'qub Ibn Ishaq al-Kindi developed an early prototype of the camera obscura. The author concludes by noting that Ibn al-Haitham himself claimed that he was not the inventor of the camera obscura. In question 11, the student is asked to determine the answer choice that is best supported by statements made in the passage. This type of question is similar to an inference question, but it expands the inference into a full claim. An inference is simply something that the passage implies: A claim supported by statements in the passage goes beyond the inference to make an actual argument. In both cases, however, the student must focus on locating the sentences that support the initial inference. In question 12, the student must identify the answer choice that is *not* implied in the passage, so the student must pay attention to the selection of words in the answer choices, because individual words can determine whether the answer choice is correct or incorrect.

Question 11

The Correct Answer:

B **Answer choice (B)** offers a statement that has full support in the passage. The author of the passage claims, "Although Ibn al-Haitham is often credited with the creation of the camera obscura, he is also recorded as having said that he did not invent it." In addition, the author demonstrates that the eventual development of Ibn al-Haitham's camera obscura came after centuries of previous research on the subject, so it is perfectly correct to claim that it was the *result of discoveries in previous centuries that contributed to his research*. The author does not claim directly that Ibn al-Haitham was familiar with the work of the other scientists mentioned, but if he knew that he did not necessarily invent the camera obscura, it stands to reason that he knew of others who did work on such an object. Answer choice (B) is correct.

The Incorrect Answers:

A At no point does the author claim or suggest that Mozi by himself invented the camera obscura. Instead, the author indicates that Mozi did work on a pinhole camera that would ultimately contribute to the camera obscura. Answer choice (A) assumes too much, so it may be eliminated.

C The passage does claim that Aristotle and Euclid in Greece were doing work on pinhole cameras during the same century that Mozi in China was. But there is not enough information in the passage to forge a direct link between Aristotle's and Euclid's work and Mozi's work, so answer choice (C) infers more than the passage implies. Answer choice (C) cannot be correct.

D Answer choice (D) is tricky, because the passage suggests that Ibn Ishaq al-Kindi was utilizing a camera obscura in the ninth century before Ibn al-Haitham developed his own camera obscura in the eleventh century. The author does not, however, suggest that Ibn Ishaq al-Kindi is the real inventor of the camera obscura but that the work of previous centuries contributed to Ibn al-Haitham's work in the eleventh century. Answer choice (D) pushes the inference beyond what the passage allows, so it cannot be correct.

E At no point does the passage indicate that the camera is *usually considered a modern development*. The author of the passage references the "modern-day camera," but there are many modern-day objects known for being invented centuries (and even millennia) in the past, so the passage is not necessarily claiming the camera to be perceived solely as a current invention. Answer choice (E) infers what the passage does not clearly imply, so it cannot be correct.

Question 12

The Correct Answer:

A The passage suggests that Ibn al-Haitham utilized and benefited from the research of previous centuries on the camera obscura. But the passage does *not* imply at any point that he *stole* the research. In fact, Ibn al-Haitham recognized that he was not the real inventor of the camera obscura, so he clearly was not stealing research and claiming it as his own. **Answer choice (A)** is thus correct.

The Incorrect Answers:

B The author of the passage notes that "the Chinese philosopher Mozi had already begun developing a variety of a pinhole camera in the fourth century BC. Later in that same century, both Aristotle and Euclid remarked on the placement of light when projected through pinholes." And the author mentions Abu Yusuf Ya'qub Ibn Ishaq al-Kindi in the ninth century for more advanced work on light and pinholes. Clearly, the passage implies that before Ibn al-Haitham's recognized development of a full camera obscura in the eleventh century, there were scientists from earlier centuries who had begun the work on light and pinholes. Answer choice (B) cannot be correct.

C The passage does not state clearly that Mozi's work is the earliest on record, but given the fact that the passage is offering a history of the research leading up to Ibn al-Haitham's work, it may be inferred that the author mentions the earliest recorded work on this subject. Answer choice (C) is implied by default, so it is incorrect.

D, E Answer choices (D) and (E) reflect the inferences of the correct answer in question 11, so both are definitely implied in the passage. Answer choices (D) and (E) are incorrect.

Question 13

Overview: Question 13 records a statement made by a political activist in support of nationalized banks. The political activist argues that the influx of government money to the banks indicates a start of the nationalization process. Therefore, under international law, the government must compensate the banks "for the full value of the assets that are assumed" and that by providing federal funding to failing banks, the government has essentially done that already. As a result, the government should simply declare nationalization of the banks in order to offer the banks federal protection. The question then asks for the statement that most strongly undermines the political activist's argument about the need for official nationalization of the banks. The student should take care to read through the answer choices closely and compare each to the statements made by the political activist.

The Correct Answer:

D **Answer choice (D)** explains that the government itself is in debt to other nations. If the government nationalizes the banks, those banks become federal property that could conceivably be used to pay off that debt. As such, the federal protection would cease to exist, and the nationalization would have lost its purpose, as the political activist sees it. Answer choice (D) is correct.

The Incorrect Answers:

A The opinions of voters, while important at one level, do not necessarily undermine the political activist's argument directly. As the answer choice offers no clear indication about what the voters disagree with concerning nationalization, it is impossible to use this as a contrast for the political activist's statements. Answer choice (A) cannot be correct.

B The fact that a small percentage of U.S. banks do not need federal funding does not address the political activist's immediate statements, nor does this call into question the political activist's argument. There is nothing in the passage to indicate that the political activist is arguing for the nationalization of *all* banks (in fact, the political activist mentions the nationalization of "some" banks); it is just a statement about the benefit of nationalization for those that have already received federal funding. Answer choice (B) cannot be correct.

C Answer choice (C) offers a very tempting contradiction to the political activist's claims, until there is a closer comparison to the wording in the passage. The political activist claims that the government has "basically" compensated many banks. This suggests that there might still be a degree of compensation to be completed and that the governments would need to finish compensating the banks. The answer choice, however, suggests that the political activist claimed the compensation to be entirely complete, and this is untrue. Answer choice (C), therefore, cannot be correct.

E The lack of success among nationalized banks in the United Kingdom bears no immediate comparison to the potential for nationalized banks in the U.S. without further context. There is always the potential for variations in the two scenarios that could alter the success in the U.S. compared to the success in the United Kingdom. Without that information, answer choice (E) is irrelevant and may be eliminated.

Question 14

<u>Overview</u>: In question 14, the author of the passage provides the student with information about German composer Ludwig van Beethoven, who ultimately lost his hearing and yet continued to compose. The passage explains that the actual cause of Beethoven's deafness has never been determined clearly and that there are a variety of theories. The most significant theory is that Beethoven consumed or absorbed high quantities of lead, which is known for causing deafness. Beethoven also manifested several other examples of unusual behavior, all of which have been connected to lead poisoning as well. But, as the author of the passage concludes, there are some who remain unconvinced. The question then asks for the answer choice that best explains why some continue to question the validity of lead poisoning as a diagnosis for Beethoven's deafness. Selecting the correct answer choice requires the student to place each option against the context of the information in the passage, so the student needs to read carefully.

The Correct Answer:

C The fact that lead poisoning seldom leads to the variety of deafness that Beethoven developed—and the fact that Beethoven's other instances of unusual behavior are not necessarily unique to lead poisoning—most clearly suggests the reason that many still question lead poisoning as the reason for Beethoven's deafness. **Answer choice (C)** is correct.

The Incorrect Answers:

A The information about Beethoven's childhood typhus certainly calls into question the firm diagnosis of lead poisoning, but answer choice (A) does not provide any explanation of the other symptoms that have also been linked to lead poisoning. As such, it is an incomplete explanation, so it is incorrect.

B Answer choice (B) is far too hypothetical to be a clear explanation for Beethoven's deafness when compared to lead poisoning. As the answer choice does *not* argue that dunking the head in ice cold water has been known to cause hearing problems, but rather that it *could have* caused hearing problems, it is an insufficient explanation. Answer choice (B) is incorrect.

D As with answer choice (A), the information about tinnitus is useful and interesting. But without further information about the other symptoms that have been linked to lead poisoning, it is impossible for answer choice (D) to represent a satisfactory explanation. Answer choice (D) is incorrect.

E The fact that *some argue* in favor of a hereditary condition and an artistic temperament does not mean this constitutes a solid line of reasoning. It suggests instead the opinions of a few divorced from solid information to support those opinions. Answer choice (E) is interesting but weak as an explanation for the question, so it should be eliminated.

Question 15

<u>Overview</u>: Question 15 provides the student with information concerning the economic arguments about inflation and deflation. The author of the passage begins by noting that inflation is traditionally viewed in a negative light, with deflation traditionally seen as a period for the economy to find stable price levels. In recent years, however, economists have begun to argue in favor of inflation for economic growth, because inflation accompanies the growth of money supply. Prices might be higher than is considered normal or healthy for the economy, but higher prices usually signal higher incomes and more liquidity among consumers. The passage concludes with

the comment that economists believe inflation to be valuable during a period of economic recession. The question then asks the student to select an answer choice that may be inferred from statements made in the passage.

The Correct Answer:

E **Answer choice (E)** offers the unstated contrast to inflation by indicating why deflation would *not* help an economy: prices might be lower, but so are incomes, leaving consumers with less liquidity and less opportunity to return money into the economy through spending. Answer choice (E) is correct.

The Incorrect Answer:

A Far from recommending or valuing *severe inflation*, economists—according to the passage—recommend "low inflationary development." Answer choice (A) contradicts statements that are made in the passage, so it is clearly not inferred. Answer choice (A), therefore, is incorrect.

B The author of the passage suggests that inflation has "traditionally" been viewed as the exact reverse of how it is viewed today. As a result, it cannot be inferred from the passage that inflation has *historically* been viewed as healthy, with deflation viewed as unhealthy. Answer choice (B) cannot be correct.

C Answer choice (C) offers information that might be perfectly true, but there is nothing in the passage to suggest it. As a result, answer choice (C) must be eliminated as irrelevant.

D Answer choice (D) is tempting, because the author does specifically mention the value of "low inflationary levels." This would suggest that higher rates of inflation would not necessarily benefit an economy. At the same time, there is not enough information in the passage to suggest that higher rates of inflation can have *devastating effects on a healthy economy*. This assumes more than the passage implies, so answer choice (D) is incorrect.

Question 16

Overview: Question 16 presents a situation in which a popular electronics company has recently manufactured a new music-playing device, and they expect it to take off immediately with the public. According to the passage, the company is well known for its inventive new technology, and the product is being marketed for its easy portability as well as its technical superiority over competitor devices. As it turns out, though, the new device does not sell very well, and the electronics company realizes that the primary competitor's device is still selling much better, in spite of specific drawbacks. The question asks the student to identify an answer choice that best explains the reason for the new device to fail with the public, even though it is easier to use and more portable than the competitor's device. To answer this question correctly, the student must read through each answer choice and compare the information in the answer choice to the statements made in the passage.

The Correct Answer:

D **Answer choice (D)** offers the explanation that the new music-playing device, whatever its benefits of use and portability, does require owners to purchase music in a unique form that is not compatible with other forms. This means that anyone who has already purchased music will not be able to utilize the purchases and will have to spend even more money to acquire the same music in a different form. This would certainly create a hindrance to easy sales, so answer choice (D) best explains the disparity between the electronics company's expectations and the results. Answer choice (D) is correct.

The Incorrect Answers:

A It is interesting to find out that consumers have become accustomed to using the competitor's device and dislike the *style* of the new device, but this in itself does not provide a tangible enough reason for why the new device would be so unpopular. Given that the electronics company is said to be very popular and is "known for producing innovative technology," it is reasonable to assume that the new style plays into consumer preferences for this company. Answer choice (A) does not offer a satisfactory explanation for the public response, so it cannot be correct.

B The impending release of a new device from the competitor is useful information, but again this in itself does not offer a good explanation for why consumers would prefer the *old* competitor's device to the new device from the company discussed in the passage. Either way, consumers will have to purchase a new device, and since the answer choice does not mention that the competitor company is providing a refund for turning in an old device, there is no reason to assume that there is any immediate benefit to waiting for the upcoming competitor device. Answer choice (B) cannot be correct.

C Answer choice (C) directly contradicts the statements made in the passage: the company "recently began heavy marketing for a new music-playing device," and it is "excited about the new device, because it is much smaller than previous devices and is very light and highly portable." These statements suggest strongly that the electronics company took care to market the new music-playing device effectively. Answer choice (C) is clearly incorrect.

E The possibility of the president of the one electronics company leaving to work for the other electronics company is interesting but irrelevant to the immediate discussion of why the public would not be eager to purchase the new music-playing device. Without further information about the president deliberately sabotaging marketing attempts, there is no clear link between a staff change and a failed product. Answer choice (E) cannot be correct.

Question 17

Overview: Question 17 presents a statement from a psychiatrist concerning the use of behavioral training techniques for day traders. The psychiatrist notes that recovering from a loss and developing the self-discipline to trade again is one of the greatest challenges for day traders, and the psychiatrist claims that a specific behavioral training system (created by the psychiatrist) will be a great benefit to day traders who need to move past fear and trade with confidence. The question asks the student to select the answer choice that represents an assumption on which the psychiatrist's argument is founded. The correct answer is not necessarily obvious right away, but the student should pay attention to two different comments that the psychiatrist makes: (1) day trading requires "self-discipline and conscious discretion," and (2) the psychiatrist's behavioral training system utilizes "hypnosis and other subconscious techniques." In other words, the psychiatrist believes that it is possible to utilize subconscious techniques in a field requiring conscious self-discipline. The correct answer choice will reflect this.

The Correct Answer:

B **Answer choice (B)** correctly identifies the fact that the psychiatrist has developed a behavioral training system with subconscious techniques to use for traders, when their chosen field requires conscious self-discipline and activity. Answer choice (B) is correct.

The Incorrect Answers:

A The psychiatrist's recommendation of behavioral training specifically mentions "hypnosis and other subconscious techniques," but this does not in itself indicate that *all* behavioral training includes such techniques. Answer choice (A) infers too much, and it is certainly not the assumption on which the psychiatrist's argument is founded. Answer choice (A) is incorrect.

C The psychiatrist indicates that recovering from losses is a significant concern for many day traders, but answer choice (C) generalizes too much by claiming that *all* day traders develop fear after big losses and that *all* have a difficult time maintaining their trading plans. Answer choice (C) may be eliminated.

D The psychiatrist indicates that behavioral training techniques can positively affect some or even many day traders, but it is assuming too much to argue that the psychiatrist believes day trading is *impossible* without behavioral training techniques. Answer choice (D) cannot be correct.

E Answer choice (E) paraphrases statements in the passage incorrectly by arguing that successful trades should begin a certain way. What is more, the fact that this might be true does not necessarily mean that it represents the assumption on which the psychiatrist's argument is founded. Answer choice (E) indicates a side point rather than a main point, so it should be eliminated.

Question 18

Overview: Question 18 provides the student with information about the history of the word *diamond*. According to the passage, the stone itself originally came from India but passed through the Greek tradition as the word *adámas*, meaning "unbreakable" or "untamed." Before encountering physical diamonds, the Greeks had heard rumors of a very strong stone, and they developed a mythology around it, calling it *adamant* and giving the stone the quality of being unbreakable. The author notes that by the medieval era, the diamond was recognized as a real gem, but the adamant remained in the literary tradition for its mythical qualities. Contemporary writers continue to reference it as an allegory. The question asks the student to identify the answer choice that is best supported by the claims in the passage. This is primarily an inference question with the added quality of being a *claim* (see the discussion of question 11), so the student needs to approach it in a similar fashion to previous inference questions. The student should begin by considering whether the inference is correct and from there decide if the inference may be accurately converted into a claim. *Note*: A *claim* is a statement that is not necessarily a direct inference from the passage but is rather a statement that infers something from the passage and derives an argument from it. Another way to word this type of question is to ask whether or not the author of the passage would agree with the claim. If yes, the answer choice is probably correct. If no, the claim is assuming more than the author of the passage implies.

The Correct Answer:

B **Answer choice (B)** accurately provides an inference that has clear antecedent in the passage. The author of the passage claims, "By the Middle Ages, this came to be recognized as the diamond. Over time, the legendary adamant came to take on a mystical quality that passed into certain forms of medieval literature and, even today, has an allegorical place in some genres." This means that the inference and claim made in answer choice (B) are correct: the adamant *was* originally associated with mythical qualities, and as a result writers still utilize it in literature for its figurative (or allegorical) attributes. Answer choice (B) is correct.

The Incorrect Answers:

A At no point does the author indicate that it would have been better for the diamond to have remained a mystery in Western literature. In fact, the author makes virtually no judgment statements about the discovery of diamonds, focusing only on the facts about them. Answer choice (A) assumes far more than the passage suggests, so it is incorrect.

C Answer choice (C) is tricky, because the author does suggest that what was once known as the adamant was ultimately recognized to be the diamond. But the author also goes on to indicate that there are clear connotations in the use of each term, so the student cannot infer that the *terms themselves* may be interchanged without question. Answer choice (C) is incorrect.

D The author discusses the use of the Greek word *adámas* and its meaning, but the author does *not* clearly connect this word to a word of ancient India. The author says only that the gem itself was mined in India. Answer choice (D) assumes too much, so it cannot be correct.

E The author of the passage does not indicate whether or not the Greeks were correct in identifying the stone as unbreakable. In fact, the author suggests that the qualities now associated with the mythology of the adamant were just that—mythology. As a result, answer choice (E) assumes too much, so it cannot be correct.

Questions 19 and 20

Overview: Questions 19 and 20 reference a passage that discusses the early research about the possibility of life on Mars. The passage begins by explaining that scientists have been considering this topic "in earnest" since the middle of the nineteenth century. The English scientist William Whewell claimed that Mars might have a similar landscape to Earth. Additionally, scientists discovered that Mars has days approximately 24 hours long, although the seasons are twice as long as seasons on Earth, given the axial tilt in combination with the elongation of the orbit of Mars. Late nineteenth-century scientists observed that there appeared to be canals on the planet, and there was argument about previous civilizations. But the later work of scientists with more powerful telescopes showed that Mars has no water or oxygen in its atmosphere.

Question 19 asks the student to select the answer choice that is *strictly implied* within the statements about canals on Mars, so the student needs to review each answer choice carefully and compare each one to the statements in the passage. The correct answer choice will be an inference, but this inference will only utilize the information provided in the passage and will not assume more than the passage can explain.

Question 20 asks for a simple inference, so the student must read closely to determine which answer choice has clear implication in the passage.

Question 19

The Correct Answer:

E **Answer choice (E)** offers a clear link between the fourth and fifth sentences of the passage. The author of the passage notes that some scientists claimed to see canals on the surface of Mars and argued for the presence of intelligent life, while later scientists discovered that there was no water or oxygen in the atmosphere of Mars. From this, the student may deduce that the discovery of the lacking elements in Mars's atmosphere made it impossible for earlier civilizations to exist there. Therefore, the "canals" must have been confused with some other feature on the landscape of Mars, and answer choice (E) is correct. (*Note*: This is also historically true. Stronger telescopes revealed that what were assumed to be canals did not actually exist on the surface of Mars.)

The Incorrect Answers:

A The passage is not entirely clear about who was believed to have been the "earlier civilizations" rumored to have lived on Mars, but the author *does* imply that the earlier civilizations would have required water and oxygen, and the belief about the life was related to "intelligent life forms." From this, the student may infer that earlier civilizations with intelligent beings (similar to humans, if not actually humans) were likely believed to have been on Mars, and the author is proving this theory incorrect with the discovery of the lacking elements in Mars's atmosphere. The student cannot infer from the information in this passage alone, however, that *all* life forms require water and oxygen. Answer choice (A) infers more than the passage is focused on implying, so it is incorrect.

B As indicated in answer choice (A), the author of the passage seems to be implying that the previous inhabitants on the surface of Mars were believed to be human or similar to human beings in their intelligent ability to develop civilizations (that included canals). Answer choice (B), therefore, is also incorrect.

C The author of the passage implies strongly that the canals—as they were observed—did not even exist and were confused with another feature on the landscape of Mars. The passage notes that William Wallace and others were able to "debunk the canal theory"; as such, it cannot be inferred that there were canals at all. Answer choice (C) cannot be correct.

D The passage indicates clearly that William Wallace was just one scientist whose research indicated the canal theory to be impossible, so he alone cannot be credited with debunking it. Answer choice (D) assumes too much, so it is also incorrect.

Question 20

The Correct Answer:

C By showing the gradual development of an understanding of Mars, its atmosphere, and landscape since the middle of the nineteenth century, the author of the passage hints strongly that early scientists argued for and relied on incorrect information due to equipment that was not strong enough to be fully accurate. As a result, the student may definitely infer the statement made in **answer choice (C)**, so it is correct.

The Incorrect Answers:

A Answer choice (A) might very well be true: there are probably scientists who continue to hold out for the possibility of life forms being discovered on Mars. But that information in itself cannot necessarily be derived from the information in the passage. Answer choice (A) infers too much, so it is incorrect.

B The author of the passage focuses only on the canal-theory and the research that debunked belief in intelligent (human or human-like) life forms developing earlier civilizations on Mars. The author does *not* argue, however, that this research *showed conclusively* that life had never existed on Mars. Answer choice (B) also infers too much, so it cannot be correct.

D Far from implying the information in answer choice (D), the author implies something entirely different. The passage notes, "Mars experienced days that spanned virtually the same length of hours as on Earth but with seasons that were approximately double the length due to Mars's axial tilt in combination with its highly elongated orbit." If the seasons are twice the length of those on Earth, then it stands to reason that the years are as well. In other words, one year on Mars is equivalent to two years on Earth. Answer choice (D) cannot be correct.

E The author of the passage mentions water and oxygen as missing in the atmosphere of Mars. It is impossible to say that *many other essential elements* are lacking in the atmosphere of Mars. Answer choice (E) assumes far more than the passage implies, so it must be incorrect.

Question 21

Overview: In question 21, the student is given a statement from a medical sales agent who is advertising the benefits of a new surgical device that is intended to assist in making a specific procedure faster and less invasive for the patient. The medical sales agent relies on the reasoning that the new device has received positive feedback from the audience that has tested it, so it will be "universally useful to all surgeons and patients." The question then asks the student to identify the logical fallacy and to select an answer choice that contains a similar logical fallacy. Students who are familiar with logical fallacies will recognize what is known as the converse fallacy of argument, in which a special case (i.e., the test audience at the area hospitals) becomes a rule (i.e., it helped some people, so it will help everyone). In this case, the medical sales agent relies on tests done only on a small group and with no further details about the group itself and the types of tests that were done. There are many different variables that could affect this outcome and limit the value of the device to a larger audience; without the information about these variables, the conclusion is too broad. Even if the student does not recognize the logical fallacy by name, the student should be able to recognize the problem in the reasoning: the medical sales agent claims that the few who valued the new device represent the population at large. The correct answer choice will argue from a similar position of *special situation = rule.*

The Correct Answer:

E Although the similarities do not appear to be exact, **answer choice (E)** does offer a similar logical fallacy to that of the medical sales agent. The argument is made that 80% of the voters in the western district of a state dislike a piece of proposed legislation (*special situation*), and the conclusion is derived that it must be a poor piece of legislation that offers no benefits to anyone (*rule*). As in the statement from the medical sales agent, no further details are provided about this audience and their reasoning; a conclusion is drawn simply by the statistics of one group. Answer choice (E) is correct.

The Incorrect Answers:

A The fallacy contained within answer choice (A) is one of *affirming the consequent*: it draws the conclusion from something that does not necessarily support the conclusion. Not parking a car in the garage might make it rusty, but a rusty car does not necessarily mean the owner failed to park it in the garage. Answer choice (A) is definitely a logical fallacy, but it is not similar to the fallacy of special situation = rule.

B, D Answer choices (B) and (D) provide examples of the *argumentum ad baculum*, or the argument based on fear: if something is done (or not done), something bad will happen, which no one wants, so a certain action must (or must not) be taken. Both answer choices

(B) and (D) represent logical fallacies, but these fallacies are not that of special situation = rule.

C Answer choice (C) represents the *argumentum ad hominem*, or the argument that makes its point by attacking someone else. In some cases (and specifically in this case), the attack might be unrelated to the argument at hand (i.e., the connection between using animals for medical research and purchasing an SUV). This is definitely a logical fallacy, but it is not the fallacy of special situation = rule. Answer choice (C) cannot be correct.

Question 22

Overview: Question 22 references a passage discussing the recent scientific focus on the dangers of ground-level ozone. According to the author of the passage, ground-level ozone "occurs when strong sunlight combines with nitrous oxide and volatile organic compounds." This has been known to scientists in Los Angeles for some time, and they believed that the specific geophysical situation of that city in a basin-like setting has made it vulnerable to ground-level ozone. But scientists in Chicago have recently discovered that Chicago experiences high levels of ground-level ozone as well, although that city has a geophysical setting totally unlike Los Angeles.

The author of the passage concludes by noting that the scientists in Chicago now believe that advective heating—occurring when a strong wind pulls in heat but does not circulate it effectively—is the real cause of large amounts of ground-level ozone. The author finishes with a comment that Los Angeles receives a great deal of wind off the Pacific Ocean, and the question asks the student to determine which answer choice is implied within the passage. This is an inference/implication question, so the student must read carefully, particularly since the implication is not connected to a certain section of the passage but may come from any part of it.

The Correct Answer:

A The author of the passage does not directly explain the reason for mentioning advective heating in the fourth sentence and then mentioning that Los Angeles receives strong ocean winds in the final sentence, but the student may deduce from this that the author is pointing to advective heating as the source of ground-level ozone in Los Angeles and not the city's location "sitting in a natural basin with little circulation." **Answer choice (A)** is correct.

The Incorrect Answers:

B The author does reference Chicago as the Windy City, but this alone does not necessarily guarantee that Chicago receives the same amount of wind as Los Angeles (or vice versa). This expression is simply a common colloquial usage in referring to Chicago, and the author utilizes it while discussing wind in that city. It might be true that Chicago and Los Angeles receive comparable amounts of wind, but the passage does not clearly imply this, so the student cannot infer it. Answer choice (B) is incorrect.

C The author of the passage focuses only on ground-level ozone and makes no comment on ozone in the upper levels of the atmosphere. The student might know from prior knowledge that the statement in answer choice (C) is, in fact, true: ozone in the upper regions of the atmosphere is both safe and essential. But the passage itself does not imply this, and there is no sentence that clearly points to such a comment. Answer choice (C) infers too much, so it cannot be correct.

D While the author of the passage does mention that ground-level ozone can have "dangerous effects," the author does not specify what these effects might be. Although *respiratory problems* seems like a logical explanation for the problems that might occur, there is nothing in the passage to suggest this directly, so the student cannot infer answer choice (D). As a result, answer choice (D) is incorrect.

E Far from suggesting the statement made in answer choice (E), the passage seems to contradict it implicitly. The author does say that Chicago sits on a "flat, open plain," but this is only to contrast the location of Chicago with the location of Los Angeles. The author also indicates that Chicago experiences advective heating, with winds that are *not* circulating well, so answer choice (E) cannot be correct. It may be eliminated immediately.

Question 23

Overview: Question 23 presents a statement from a psychologist concerning the issue of news and the psychological response among Americans at watching the news. The psychologist argues that "Americans feel more stress after watching a news program than before it," largely because the news programs focus on the negative stories over the positive stories. In addition, the psychologist goes on to indicate that the graphic images in the news stories contribute to higher levels of stress. As a result, the psychologist concludes that the media should provide a balance to negative stories by showing positive stories as well, since studies show that stress levels are reduced after people view positive stories. The question then asks the student to select an answer choice that best describes the flaw in the psychologist's reasoning.

In order to answer this question correctly, the student needs to sort through the psychologist's flow of thought, because the passage might not seem to hold a clear example of flawed reasoning at first. But there is a problem embedded in this argument that can be identified. The psychologist argues: (1) the American media is expected to report news objectively whether it is positive or negative, (2) the media is clearly *not* objective in selecting its stories due to the obvious rate of negative stories that are covered, (3) Americans experience more stress after watching negative news stories, particularly negative news stories that contain graphic images, and (4) the media should select news stories to provide a better balance between the negative stories and the positive stories.

From this, it becomes clear that the psychologist begins by criticizing news programs for denying objectivity in the way that stories are selected, but concludes by suggesting that news programs subjectively select a balance of positive and negative. In other words, the psychologist demands objectivity but then suggests subjectivity. The correct answer choice will reflect this.

The Correct Answer:

B **Answer choice (B)** accurately explains that the psychologist accuses the media of subjectivity but then goes on to suggest that subjectivity is necessary as long as it is a different kind of subjectivity. Answer choice (B) is correct.

The Incorrect Answers:

A The psychologist attacks the media for the selection of negative stories, but there is no clear attack on the reporting within the stories, nor does the psychologist claim that the media reports negative stories in a subjective way. Instead, the psychologist is focused on the subjectivity of selection, so answer choice (A) cannot be correct.

C The psychologist does not have two separate arguments that are combined. Instead, the psychologist has a single argument: the news media is too subjective in selecting negative stories and needs to find a balance between positive and negative. That is one complete argument, so answer choice (C) cannot be correct.

D The psychologist does claim, "When the news program presents a positive story, however, the stress level goes down." This is a sufficient counter to the previous statement, "A recent report in a major psychological journal has indicated that Americans feel more stress after watching a news program than before it. When graphic images accompany a negative story, the stress level gets even higher." Because answer choice (D) does not indicate *why* this would not be a good indication of the benefits of positive stories, it is too vague to be correct. Answer choice (D) may be eliminated.

E Answer choice (E) is difficult, because there is nothing in the passage to counter it, and yet there is nothing in the passage to suggest that it is clearly true. The latter is the key to the problem with the answer choice. Because there is no context for *why* the psychologist would need to distinguish among negative stories, there is no reason, based on the information provided in the psychologist's statement, to believe that this is necessary. Had the psychologist referenced different types of negative stories, answer choice (E) might be valid. With no mention of this element, however, answer choice (E) is largely irrelevant and may be eliminated.

Question 24

Overview: In question 24, the author of the passage focuses on the way that unborn babies are able to hear and even develop preferences for music. The passage claims that an unborn baby's hearing organs begin development at four weeks, and the baby can hear by four months. The passage goes on to claim that unborn infants can "hear clearly" in the womb at six months, and "some biologists believe that they are already developing a partiality for certain kinds of music" by that point. The author notes that there are companies who are currently developing prenatal listening devices to feed classical music to their children (due to the perceived benefits of listening to classical music), yet the passage concludes by noting that there is research suggesting that unborn babies respond best to the type of music the mother enjoys most. The question then asks the student to determine the answer choice that is implied regarding the issue of unborn babies and listening to music. The student should approach this as an inference/implication question and review each of the answer choices carefully to locate an antecedent statement (or statements) in the passage.

The Correct Answer:

C The author claims that "research has indicated that classical music has very positive effects on the mind development of unborn babies. Some research suggests, however, that the baby is most likely to respond positively to the mother's musical preference, because her favorite music is most likely to relax her." In other words, classical music is possibly beneficial, but the unborn baby is best served by listening to music that the mother likes. **Answer choice (C)** accurately states this, so it is correct.

The Incorrect Answers:

A Answer choice (A) makes a statement of argument that utilizes language not clearly used in the passage. The author of the passage notes that playing music for the unborn baby might very well be beneficial, but the author does not suggest the judgment statement that *astute parents* should introduce music to their unborn child. This infers more from the author's tone than is clearly present, so answer choice (A) cannot be correct.

B Answer choice (B) is incorrect due to the strength of the word choice. The passage notes that "research has indicated that classical music has very positive effects on the mind development of unborn babies." This means that classical music *might* be of benefit for the developing minds of unborn babies. It does not mean unequivocally that it is the *best music* with the *most positive effects*. Answer choice (B) may be eliminated.

D The author indicates that unborn babies are often most comfortable with the mother's preference, but the passage does not necessarily claim that babies *will definitely* develop similar preferences. The passage seems to indicate that the baby is responding positively to the mother's preference, and while this means that the baby ultimately develops a similar preference, the word "definitely" is too strong to be inferred from the passage. Answer choice (D) cannot be correct.

E The author of the passage indicates that babies can develop partiality. But the author makes no mention of the baby indicating a dislike for the music, and while it is possible that the unborn child can express a certain sense of discomfort, there is nothing in the passage to indicate that the infant will *make its dislike for music very clear*. This assumes just a little too much, so it cannot be correct.

Question 25

Overview: The final question in the fourth section of the test references the history of the Cyrillic alphabet, beginning in the ninth century AD with the work of the missionary brothers Cyril and Methodius. The author of the passage claims that the Cyrillic alphabet is a combination of the Greek alphabet and the now-obsolete Glagolitic alphabet. There are currently six Slavic languages and five or more non-Slavic languages that use Cyrillic, and during the time of the Soviet Union, there were upwards of fifty languages utilizing Cyrillic script. In 2007, Cyrillic became the third official alphabet of the European Union. The question asks the student to determine which answer choice is *not* implied in the passage, so the student needs to read through each answer choice carefully and decide if there is a sentence (or sentences) in the passage that *clearly implies* the statement made in the answer choice.

The Correct Answer:

B **Answer choice (B)** claims that the Slavic peoples were not literate and had no alphabet, but the passage does not imply this anywhere clearly. In fact, the passage notes that Glagolitic was "an obsolete Slavic form," or an obsolete Slavic alphabet. This would indicate that the Slavic peoples *did* have an alphabet of some kind (just perhaps not a comprehensive one—hence the value of Methodius and Cyril's work) and were literate. Answer choice (B) assumes more than the passage implies, so it is correct.

The Incorrect Answers:

A The passage indicates that "the Cyrillic alphabet is credited to the brothers Cyril and Methodius, natives of Thessalonika who became missionaries to the Slavic peoples." This statement implies that Cyril and Methodius developed the Cyrillic alphabet in conjunction with their missionary work, so answer choice (A) is implied and cannot be correct.

C The author of the passages notes that "many languages have rejected the use of the Cyrillic alphabet since the USSR's collapse." The word "rejected" suggests a deliberate change on the part of the nations, and it may be inferred that the change was due to a negative association with the USSR. Answer choice (C) may be inferred, so it is incorrect.

D The author of the passage states, "Today the Cyrillic alphabet is used for six Slavic languages and at least five non-Slavic languages in nations that stretch from Eastern Europe to Mongolia." While it is clear that not all of the nations utilizing Cyrillic are in Europe, it stands to reason that several of them are. With the decision by the European Union to make

Cyrillic an official alphabet, it may also be inferred that Cyrillic has enough of a presence to warrant this recognition. Answer choice (D) may thus be inferred and so is incorrect.

E The second sentence of the passage notes that Cyril and Methodius "utilized a type of Greek script in combination with the Glagolitic alphabet, an obsolete Slavic form, in order to create a writing system for sounds not existing in Greek." This implies that the Greek alphabet alone was not enough for recording the language system of the Slavic peoples, so answer choice (E) may be inferred. Answer choice (E) is thus incorrect.

Writing Sample Topic

How to Approach the Sample Essay

There is no right or wrong answer for the writing sample, and LSAC does not actually give the essay a score. But the law schools to which the students apply will receive a copy of the essay, so students need to shape a response that indicates their writing skills to these schools. There are several important considerations to keep in mind when developing the essay:

1. Schools want to know that students have strong communication skills, so the essay should be clear and concise and provide a solid response to the topic, with a strong development of each paragraph.
2. The essay should stay entirely on topic: students should not veer off the point by including unnecessary examples or by failing to address the primary focus of the topic. The key is to remain relevant and answer the topic question with clear exposition.
3. Essay writing establishes that a student is able to develop persuasive ideas and organize them effectively. Schools look for these skills, so the essay provides students with the opportunity to indicate an ability to make a credible and well-developed argument in written form.

How to Overcome Test Anxiety

Just the thought of taking a test is enough to make most people a little nervous. A test is an important event that can have a long-term impact on your future, so it's important to take it seriously and it's natural to feel anxious about performing well. But just because anxiety is normal, that doesn't mean that it's helpful in test taking, or that you should simply accept it as part of your life. Anxiety can have a variety of effects. These effects can be mild, like making you feel slightly nervous, or severe, like blocking your ability to focus or remember even a simple detail.

If you experience test anxiety—whether severe or mild—it's important to know how to beat it. To discover this, first you need to understand what causes test anxiety.

Causes of Test Anxiety

While we often think of anxiety as an uncontrollable emotional state, it can actually be caused by simple, practical things. One of the most common causes of test anxiety is that a person does not feel adequately prepared for their test. This feeling can be the result of many different issues such as poor study habits or lack of organization, but the most common culprit is time management. Starting to study too late, failing to organize your study time to cover all of the material, or being distracted while you study will mean that you're not well prepared for the test. This may lead to cramming the night before, which will cause you to be physically and mentally exhausted for the test. Poor time management also contributes to feelings of stress, fear, and hopelessness as you realize you are not well prepared but don't know what to do about it.

Other times, test anxiety is not related to your preparation for the test but comes from unresolved fear. This may be a past failure on a test, or poor performance on tests in general. It may come from comparing yourself to others who seem to be performing better or from the stress of living up to expectations. Anxiety may be driven by fears of the future—how failure on this test would affect your educational and career goals. These fears are often completely irrational, but they can still negatively impact your test performance.

Review Video: 3 Reasons You Have Test Anxiety
Visit mometrix.com/academy and enter code: 428468

Elements of Test Anxiety

As mentioned earlier, test anxiety is considered to be an emotional state, but it has physical and mental components as well. Sometimes you may not even realize that you are suffering from test anxiety until you notice the physical symptoms. These can include trembling hands, rapid heartbeat, sweating, nausea, and tense muscles. Extreme anxiety may lead to fainting or vomiting. Obviously, any of these symptoms can have a negative impact on testing. It is important to recognize them as soon as they begin to occur so that you can address the problem before it damages your performance.

Review Video: 3 Ways to Tell You Have Test Anxiety
Visit mometrix.com/academy and enter code: 927847

The mental components of test anxiety include trouble focusing and inability to remember learned information. During a test, your mind is on high alert, which can help you recall information and stay focused for an extended period of time. However, anxiety interferes with your mind's natural processes, causing you to blank out, even on the questions you know well. The strain of testing during anxiety makes it difficult to stay focused, especially on a test that may take several hours. Extreme anxiety can take a huge mental toll, making it difficult not only to recall test information but even to understand the test questions or pull your thoughts together.

Review Video: How Test Anxiety Affects Memory
Visit mometrix.com/academy and enter code: 609003

Effects of Test Anxiety

Test anxiety is like a disease—if left untreated, it will get progressively worse. Anxiety leads to poor performance, and this reinforces the feelings of fear and failure, which in turn lead to poor performances on subsequent tests. It can grow from a mild nervousness to a crippling condition. If allowed to progress, test anxiety can have a big impact on your schooling, and consequently on your future.

Test anxiety can spread to other parts of your life. Anxiety on tests can become anxiety in any stressful situation, and blanking on a test can turn into panicking in a job situation. But fortunately, you don't have to let anxiety rule your testing and determine your grades. There are a number of relatively simple steps you can take to move past anxiety and function normally on a test and in the rest of life.

Review Video: How Test Anxiety Impacts Your Grades
Visit mometrix.com/academy and enter code: 939819

Physical Steps for Beating Test Anxiety

While test anxiety is a serious problem, the good news is that it can be overcome. It doesn't have to control your ability to think and remember information. While it may take time, you can begin taking steps today to beat anxiety.

Just as your first hint that you may be struggling with anxiety comes from the physical symptoms, the first step to treating it is also physical. Rest is crucial for having a clear, strong mind. If you are tired, it is much easier to give in to anxiety. But if you establish good sleep habits, your body and mind will be ready to perform optimally, without the strain of exhaustion. Additionally, sleeping well helps you to retain information better, so you're more likely to recall the answers when you see the test questions.

Getting good sleep means more than going to bed on time. It's important to allow your brain time to relax. Take study breaks from time to time so it doesn't get overworked, and don't study right before bed. Take time to rest your mind before trying to rest your body, or you may find it difficult to fall asleep.

Review Video: The Importance of Sleep for Your Brain
Visit mometrix.com/academy and enter code: 319338

Along with sleep, other aspects of physical health are important in preparing for a test. Good nutrition is vital for good brain function. Sugary foods and drinks may give a burst of energy but this burst is followed by a crash, both physically and emotionally. Instead, fuel your body with protein and vitamin-rich foods.

Also, drink plenty of water. Dehydration can lead to headaches and exhaustion, especially if your brain is already under stress from the rigors of the test. Particularly if your test is a long one, drink water during the breaks. And if possible, take an energy-boosting snack to eat between sections.

Review Video: How Diet Can Affect your Mood
Visit mometrix.com/academy and enter code: 624317

Along with sleep and diet, a third important part of physical health is exercise. Maintaining a steady workout schedule is helpful, but even taking 5-minute study breaks to walk can help get your blood pumping faster and clear your head. Exercise also releases endorphins, which contribute to a positive feeling and can help combat test anxiety.

When you nurture your physical health, you are also contributing to your mental health. If your body is healthy, your mind is much more likely to be healthy as well. So take time to rest, nourish your body with healthy food and water, and get moving as much as possible. Taking these physical steps will make you stronger and more able to take the mental steps necessary to overcome test anxiety.

Review Video: How to Stay Healthy and Prevent Test Anxiety
Visit mometrix.com/academy and enter code: 877894

Mental Steps for Beating Test Anxiety

Working on the mental side of test anxiety can be more challenging, but as with the physical side, there are clear steps you can take to overcome it. As mentioned earlier, test anxiety often stems from lack of preparation, so the obvious solution is to prepare for the test. Effective studying may be the most important weapon you have for beating test anxiety, but you can and should employ several other mental tools to combat fear.

First, boost your confidence by reminding yourself of past success—tests or projects that you aced. If you're putting as much effort into preparing for this test as you did for those, there's no reason you should expect to fail here. Work hard to prepare; then trust your preparation.

Second, surround yourself with encouraging people. It can be helpful to find a study group, but be sure that the people you're around will encourage a positive attitude. If you spend time with others who are anxious or cynical, this will only contribute to your own anxiety. Look for others who are motivated to study hard from a desire to succeed, not from a fear of failure.

Third, reward yourself. A test is physically and mentally tiring, even without anxiety, and it can be helpful to have something to look forward to. Plan an activity following the test, regardless of the outcome, such as going to a movie or getting ice cream.

When you are taking the test, if you find yourself beginning to feel anxious, remind yourself that you know the material. Visualize successfully completing the test. Then take a few deep, relaxing breaths and return to it. Work through the questions carefully but with confidence, knowing that you are capable of succeeding.

Developing a healthy mental approach to test taking will also aid in other areas of life. Test anxiety affects more than just the actual test—it can be damaging to your mental health and even contribute to depression. It's important to beat test anxiety before it becomes a problem for more than testing.

Review Video: Test Anxiety and Depression
Visit mometrix.com/academy and enter code: 904704

Study Strategy

Being prepared for the test is necessary to combat anxiety, but what does being prepared look like? You may study for hours on end and still not feel prepared. What you need is a strategy for test prep. The next few pages outline our recommended steps to help you plan out and conquer the challenge of preparation.

Step 1: Scope Out the Test

Learn everything you can about the format (multiple choice, essay, etc.) and what will be on the test. Gather any study materials, course outlines, or sample exams that may be available. Not only will this help you to prepare, but knowing what to expect can help to alleviate test anxiety.

Step 2: Map Out the Material

Look through the textbook or study guide and make note of how many chapters or sections it has. Then divide these over the time you have. For example, if a book has 15 chapters and you have five days to study, you need to cover three chapters each day. Even better, if you have the time, leave an extra day at the end for overall review after you have gone through the material in depth.

If time is limited, you may need to prioritize the material. Look through it and make note of which sections you think you already have a good grasp on, and which need review. While you are studying, skim quickly through the familiar sections and take more time on the challenging parts. Write out your plan so you don't get lost as you go. Having a written plan also helps you feel more in control of the study, so anxiety is less likely to arise from feeling overwhelmed at the amount to cover.

Step 3: Gather Your Tools

Decide what study method works best for you. Do you prefer to highlight in the book as you study and then go back over the highlighted portions? Or do you type out notes of the important information? Or is it helpful to make flashcards that you can carry with you? Assemble the pens, index cards, highlighters, post-it notes, and any other materials you may need so you won't be distracted by getting up to find things while you study.

If you're having a hard time retaining the information or organizing your notes, experiment with different methods. For example, try color-coding by subject with colored pens, highlighters, or post-it notes. If you learn better by hearing, try recording yourself reading your notes so you can listen while in the car, working out, or simply sitting at your desk. Ask a friend to quiz you from your flashcards, or try teaching someone the material to solidify it in your mind.

Step 4: Create Your Environment

It's important to avoid distractions while you study. This includes both the obvious distractions like visitors and the subtle distractions like an uncomfortable chair (or a too-comfortable couch that makes you want to fall asleep). Set up the best study environment possible: good lighting and a comfortable work area. If background music helps you focus, you may want to turn it on, but otherwise keep the room quiet. If you are using a computer to take notes, be sure you don't have any other windows open, especially applications like social media, games, or anything else that could distract you. Silence your phone and turn off notifications. Be sure to keep water close by so you stay hydrated while you study (but avoid unhealthy drinks and snacks).

Also, take into account the best time of day to study. Are you freshest first thing in the morning? Try to set aside some time then to work through the material. Is your mind clearer in the afternoon or evening? Schedule your study session then. Another method is to study at the same time of day that you will take the test, so that your brain gets used to working on the material at that time and will be ready to focus at test time.

Step 5: Study!

Once you have done all the study preparation, it's time to settle into the actual studying. Sit down, take a few moments to settle your mind so you can focus, and begin to follow your study plan. Don't give in to distractions or let yourself procrastinate. This is your time to prepare so you'll be ready to fearlessly approach the test. Make the most of the time and stay focused.

Of course, you don't want to burn out. If you study too long you may find that you're not retaining the information very well. Take regular study breaks. For example, taking five minutes out of every hour to walk briskly, breathing deeply and swinging your arms, can help your mind stay fresh.

As you get to the end of each chapter or section, it's a good idea to do a quick review. Remind yourself of what you learned and work on any difficult parts. When you feel that you've mastered the material, move on to the next part. At the end of your study session, briefly skim through your notes again.

But while review is helpful, cramming last minute is NOT. If at all possible, work ahead so that you won't need to fit all your study into the last day. Cramming overloads your brain with more information than it can process and retain, and your tired mind may struggle to recall even previously learned information when it is overwhelmed with last-minute study. Also, the urgent nature of cramming and the stress placed on your brain contribute to anxiety. You'll be more likely to go to the test feeling unprepared and having trouble thinking clearly.

So don't cram, and don't stay up late before the test, even just to review your notes at a leisurely pace. Your brain needs rest more than it needs to go over the information again. In fact, plan to finish your studies by noon or early afternoon the day before the test. Give your brain the rest of the day to relax or focus on other things, and get a good night's sleep. Then you will be fresh for the test and better able to recall what you've studied.

Step 6: Take a practice test

Many courses offer sample tests, either online or in the study materials. This is an excellent resource to check whether you have mastered the material, as well as to prepare for the test format and environment.

Check the test format ahead of time: the number of questions, the type (multiple choice, free response, etc.), and the time limit. Then create a plan for working through them. For example, if you have 30 minutes to take a 60-question test, your limit is 30 seconds per question. Spend less time on the questions you know well so that you can take more time on the difficult ones.

If you have time to take several practice tests, take the first one open book, with no time limit. Work through the questions at your own pace and make sure you fully understand them. Gradually work up to taking a test under test conditions: sit at a desk with all study materials put away and set a timer. Pace yourself to make sure you finish the test with time to spare and go back to check your answers if you have time.

After each test, check your answers. On the questions you missed, be sure you understand why you missed them. Did you misread the question (tests can use tricky wording)? Did you forget the information? Or was it something you hadn't learned? Go back and study any shaky areas that the practice tests reveal.

Taking these tests not only helps with your grade, but also aids in combating test anxiety. If you're already used to the test conditions, you're less likely to worry about it, and working through tests until you're scoring well gives you a confidence boost. Go through the practice tests until you feel comfortable, and then you can go into the test knowing that you're ready for it.

Test Tips

On test day, you should be confident, knowing that you've prepared well and are ready to answer the questions. But aside from preparation, there are several test day strategies you can employ to maximize your performance.

First, as stated before, get a good night's sleep the night before the test (and for several nights before that, if possible). Go into the test with a fresh, alert mind rather than staying up late to study.

Try not to change too much about your normal routine on the day of the test. It's important to eat a nutritious breakfast, but if you normally don't eat breakfast at all, consider eating just a protein bar. If you're a coffee drinker, go ahead and have your normal coffee. Just make sure you time it so that the caffeine doesn't wear off right in the middle of your test. Avoid sugary beverages, and drink enough water to stay hydrated but not so much that you need a restroom break 10 minutes into the test. If your test isn't first thing in the morning, consider going for a walk or doing a light workout before the test to get your blood flowing.

Allow yourself enough time to get ready, and leave for the test with plenty of time to spare so you won't have the anxiety of scrambling to arrive in time. Another reason to be early is to select a good seat. It's helpful to sit away from doors and windows, which can be distracting. Find a good seat, get out your supplies, and settle your mind before the test begins.

When the test begins, start by going over the instructions carefully, even if you already know what to expect. Make sure you avoid any careless mistakes by following the directions.

Then begin working through the questions, pacing yourself as you've practiced. If you're not sure on an answer, don't spend too much time on it, and don't let it shake your confidence. Either skip it and come back later, or eliminate as many wrong answers as possible and guess among the remaining ones. Don't dwell on these questions as you continue—put them out of your mind and focus on what lies ahead.

Be sure to read all of the answer choices, even if you're sure the first one is the right answer. Sometimes you'll find a better one if you keep reading. But don't second-guess yourself if you do immediately know the answer. Your gut instinct is usually right. Don't let test anxiety rob you of the information you know.

If you have time at the end of the test (and if the test format allows), go back and review your answers. Be cautious about changing any, since your first instinct tends to be correct, but make sure you didn't misread any of the questions or accidentally mark the wrong answer choice. Look over any you skipped and make an educated guess.

At the end, leave the test feeling confident. You've done your best, so don't waste time worrying about your performance or wishing you could change anything. Instead, celebrate the successful completion of this test. And finally, use this test to learn how to deal with anxiety even better next time.

Review Video: 5 Tips to Beat Test Anxiety
Visit mometrix.com/academy and enter code: 570656

Important Qualification

Not all anxiety is created equal. If your test anxiety is causing major issues in your life beyond the classroom or testing center, or if you are experiencing troubling physical symptoms related to your anxiety, it may be a sign of a serious physiological or psychological condition. If this sounds like your situation, we strongly encourage you to seek professional help.

Thank You

We at Mometrix would like to extend our heartfelt thanks to you, our friend and patron, for allowing us to play a part in your journey. It is a privilege to serve people from all walks of life who are unified in their commitment to building the best future they can for themselves.

The preparation you devote to these important testing milestones may be the most valuable educational opportunity you have for making a real difference in your life. We encourage you to put your heart into it—that feeling of succeeding, overcoming, and yes, conquering will be well worth the hours you've invested.

We want to hear your story, your struggles and your successes, and if you see any opportunities for us to improve our materials so we can help others even more effectively in the future, please share that with us as well. **The team at Mometrix would be absolutely thrilled to hear from you!** So please, send us an email (support@mometrix.com) and let's stay in touch.

If you'd like some additional help, check out these other resources we offer for your exam:
https://MometrixFlashcards.com/LSAT

Additional Bonus Material

Due to our efforts to try to keep this book to a manageable length, we've created a link that will give you access to all of your additional bonus material.

Please visit https://www.mometrix.com/bonus948/lsat to access the information.

Made in the USA
San Bernardino, CA
05 February 2020

64023294R00208